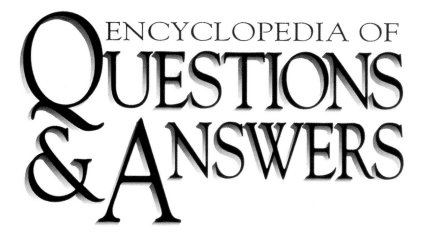

ENCYCLOPEDIA OF
Questions & Answers

Brian Williams

ENCYCLOPEDIA OF

QUESTIONS
&ANSWERS

KINGFISHER

NEW YORK

KINGFISHER
Larousse Kingfisher Chambers Inc.
95 Madison Avenue
New York, New York 10016

First edition 1997

LIBRARY OF CONGRESS CATALOGING-IN-PUBLICATION DATA
William, Brian.
The Kingfisher encyclopedia of questions and answers / Brian
Williams.—1st ed.
p. cm.
Includes index.
Summary: Questions and answers provide information on such topics
as general science, earth and space, the human body, and plants and
animals.
1. Science—Encyclopedias, Juvenile. 2. Science—Miscellanea—
Juvenile literature. [1. Science—Miscellanea. 2. Questions and
answers.] I. Title.
Q121.W55 1997 503—DC21 97-12668 CIP AC

ISBN 0-7534-5099-2

Produced by Miles Kelly Publishing Ltd.
Designer: Smiljka Surla
Editors: Rosie Alexander, Kate Miles,
Angela Royston
Assistant Editors: Susanne Bull, Lynne French
Picture Research: Yannick Yago

ACKNOWLEDGMENTS

The publishers wish to thank the artists who have contributed toward this book. These include the following:

Susanna Addario; Hemesh Alles; Marion Appleton; Hayward Art Group; Craig Austin; David Barnett; Peter Bull; Vanessa Card; Tony Chance; Kuo Kang Chen; Harry Clow; Stephen Conlin; Peter Dennis; Richard Draper; Eugene Fleury; Chris Forsey; Mark Franklin; Terry Gabbey; Sheila Galbraith; Mark George; Jeremy Gower; Ruby Green; Ray Grinaway; Nick Harris; Nicholas Hewetson; Adam Hook; Christian Hook; Christina Hook; Richard Hook; Tony Kenyon; Mike Lacey; Claire Littlejohn; Mick Loates; Bernard Long; Alan Male; Shane Marsh; Jamie Medlin; Nicki Palin; Alex Pang; Roger Payne; Mel Pickering; Maurice Pledger; Bryan Poole; Sebastian Quigley; Claudia Saraceni; Guy Smith; Tony Smith; Michael Steward; Simon Tegg; Ian Thompson; Ross Watton; Steve Weston; Linda Worrall; David Wright;

Photographs

The publishers wish to thank the following for supplying photographs for this book:

Page 14 (BC) Corbis; 20 (TR) Corbis; 21 (BC) Rich Kirchner/ NHPA; 25 (BR) Corbis; 26 (TR) Corbis; 29 (B) ZEFA; 33 (BC) ZEFA; 34 (BR) David Frazier/ Science Photo Library; 45 (TR) ZEFA; 49 (TR) NHPA; 50 (TR) Corbis; 62 (C) Mehau Kulyk/ Science Photo Library; 65 (CL) Firework Ltd; 68 (T) ZEFA; 71 (TL) Jerome Yeats/ Science Photo Library; 73 (TR) Geoff Tompkinson/ Science Photo Library; 75 (BC) Corbis; 78 (TL) Yves Baulieu/ Publiphoto Diffusion/ Science Photo Library; 81 (TL) Corbis; 96 (CR) Ford; 111 (T) Henry Ausloos/ NHPA; 116 (TL) Bill Coster/ NHPA; 122 (BC) Kevin Cullimore/ Tony Stone Images; 123 (TL) David B. Fleetham/ Oxford Scientific Films; 126 (BR) G.I. Bernard/ Oxford Scientific Films; 131 (B) Hans Reinhard/ Bruce Coleman Ltd.; 136 (C) Georgette/ Douwma/ Planet Earth Pictures; 139 (BL) Stan Osolinski/ Oxford Scientific Films; 142 (BR) Eric Soder/ NHPA; 145 (CR) Alain Compost/ Bruce Coleman Ltd.; 146 (TC) Linda Burgess/ The Garden Picture Library; 146 (C) John Glover/ The Garden Picture Library; 147 (R) Tim Ridley/ Larousse Archives; 149 (TL) E.A. Janes/ NHPA; 149 (CR) Jerry Pavia/ The Garden Picture Library; 150 (TR) Michael Tweddie/ NHPA; 150 (B) David Middleton/ NHPA; 151 (TR) Jerry Pavia/ The Garden Picture Library; 163 (BR) Science Photo Library; 167 (TR) Simon Fraser/ Science Photo Library; 167 (BR) Jeremy Mason/ Science Photo Library; 179 (TL) Will & Deni McIntyre/ Science Photo Library; 182 (BL) Ian West/ Bubbles; 183 (TL) Jeremy Bright/Robert Harding Picture Library; 183 (BL) Robert Harding; 188 (BL) David Hanson/ Tony Stone Worldwide; 189 (TR) Simon Potter/Telegraph Colour Library; 189 (BL) Andy Cox/ Tony Stone Images; 191 (TR) AKG Photo; 193 (BL) Donna Day/ Tony Stone Images; 194 (BR) Tony Stone Images; 195 (BR) David Joel/ Tony Stone Worldwide; 198 (BR) F. Rombout/ Bubbles; 199 (TL) St. Bartholomews Hospital/Science Photo Library; 199 (R) Dave Bartruff/Corbis; 202 (TL) Peter Lambert/ Tony Stone Worldwide; 202 (BR) The Hutchison Library; 203 (TR) c 1996 Corel Corp.; 204 (TL) c 1996 Corel Corp.; 204 (TR) Christine Osborne Pictures; 206 (BR) Jean-Leo Dugust/ Panos Pictures; 207 (BL) Carla Signorini Jones/ Images of Africa Photobank; 207 (BR) Jeremy A. Horner/The Hutchison Library; 209 (TL) Hugh Sitton/ Tony Stone Images; 209 (BR) Spectrum Colour Library; 210 (TL) Oldrich Karasck/ Tony Stone Images; 212 (CL) Paul Harris/ Tony Stone Images; 212 (BR) c 1996 Corel Corp.; 213 (TL) Alain le Garsmeur/ Panos Pictures; 214 (BC) Paul Chesley/ Tony Stone Worldwide; 215 (TR) c 1996 Corel Corp.; 216/7 (CR) Spectrum Colour Library; 218 (TL) ZEFA; 218 (BL) Spectrum Colour Library; 219 (CR) Spectrum Colour Library; 222 (BL) Rohan/ Tony Stone Images; 223 (TL) ZEFA; 225 (TR) ZEFA; 225 (BR) D. Saunders/ Trip; 228 (CR) c 1996 Corel Corp.; 231 (TR) ZEFA; 231 (BL) Jaemsen/ ZEFA; 232 (BR) Spectrum Colour Library; 235 (C) ZEFA; 237 (CR) Spectrum Colour Library; 238 (BR) The Hutchison Library; 238 (BL) ZEFA; 239 (BR) Paul Chesley/Tony Stone Worldwide; 239 (BL) Jeff Britnell/Tony Stone; 241 (TR) Luc Delahaye/ Sipa Press/ Rex Features; 242 (TC) Sipa Press/ Rex Features; 242 (BR) John Lamb/ Tony Stone Images; 242 (BL) Persuy/ Sipa Press/ Rex Features; 243 (TL) Spectrum Colour Library; 245 (BL) Images Colour Library; 245 (CR) Marian Morrison/ South American Pictures; 246 (CL) Eric Lawne/ The Hutchison Library; 247 (TL) Robert Harding Picture Library; 247 (BR) Jon Burbank/The Hutchison Library; 254 (CR) Andrew Hill/ The Hutchison Library; 260 (C) Palais de Versailles, Musee Historique AKG Photo; 260 (BR) Peter Newark's Historical Pictures; 261 (TL) Peter Newark's American Pictures; 261 (C) Popperfoto; 261 (BC) Popperfoto; 266 (TR) The Hulton Getty Picture Collection Ltd.; 268 (CR) Corbis; 271 (BR) Simon Krectmem/Reuter Popperfoto; 275 (BL) AKG Photo; 278 (CT) E.T. Archive; 278 (B) AKG Photo; 279 (CT) AKG Photo; 279 (BL) E.T. Archive; 279 (BR) Popperfoto; 281 (TL) The Hulton Getty Picture Collection Ltd.; 281 (BL) Mary Evans Picture Library; 281 (BR) AKG Photo; 282 (BR) Mary Evans Picture Library; 282 (CL) Disney Video; 283 (TC) The Bettman Archive/ Corbis; 284 (BR) Ancient Art & Architecture Collection Ltd.; 285 (BR) Leipzig Museum/ AKG Photo; 286 (CT) Peter Newark's American Pictures; 286 (BR) Corbis; 286 (CL) Peter Newark's American Pictures; 288 (CL) Steve Etherington/ EMPICS; 288 (BR) Mike Blake/ Reuters Popperfoto; 289 (TL) The Times/ Rex Features; 289 (BR) Popperfoto; 293 (TL) Nelson Museum, Monmouth; E.T Archive 293 (R) AKG Photo London; 294 (BL) BFI Stills, Posters & Designs; 295 (TL) Peter Newark's American Pictures; 295 (BC) Peter Newark's American Pictures.

CONTENTS

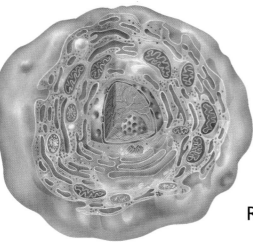

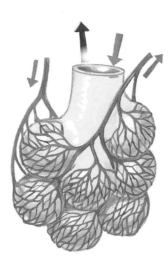

INTRODUCTION

Question: What's the best way to find out about something? *Answer:* Ask questions about the subject. *Question:* What's the next best way to find out about something? *Answer:* Look up the subject in a book. *Question:* What's the best book to look up these subjects in? *Answer:* The *Encyclopedia of Questions and Answers.*

In the *Encyclopedia of Questions and Answers* you have the best of both worlds for curious minds—lots of questions you would like to ask on hundreds of different topics and a highly informed expert ready to supply the answers. You will find these answers not simply beneath the questions, but in the captions to the pictures, in labels on the illustrations, and in the many fact boxes throughout the encyclopedia. You will also discover challenging quizzes at the end of each section to test your memory and general knowledge.

Words alone cannot always explain complex ideas. That is why the *Encyclopedia of Questions and Answers* has hundreds of illustrations. There are photographs, diagrams, charts, and maps, to show you what things look like and to help you understand how things work and where places are. And look out for the small cartoon boxes—they are informative and fun, too.

You will find sections here on Earth and Space, Science, Human Body, Animals and Plants, Peoples and Countries, and History. While this encyclopedia cannot cover every question you would like to ask on these areas, it will give you a wonderful start.

Enjoy this book, pick up thousands of facts, and keep asking questions!

EARTH FACTS

How big is the Earth?

The Earth's circumference (the distance around the world) at the Equator is 24,901 miles (40,091 km). Its diameter (the distance across the center) at the Equator is 7,922 miles (12,756 km). The Earth is slightly smaller when measured between the Poles (7,907 miles [12,730 km]), so it is not an exact sphere. If you could put the world on scales, it would weigh over 6 sextillion tons.

▼ **This cutaway of the Earth shows the upper rocky layer, the lithosphere. The crust beneath the oceans is much thinner than the crust beneath the continents.**

What is the Earth made of?

The Earth is a huge ball of rock. The top layer is the crust of the Earth. It is as little as 3¾ miles (6 km) thick beneath the oceans. Then comes a thick layer of rock called the mantle, which goes almost halfway down to the Earth's center. As it gets deeper, it gets hotter, and beneath the mantle is a layer of hot, liquid rock called the outer core. Finally, at the center of the Earth is the inner core—a huge ball of hot but solid rock. It begins 3,000 miles (5,000 km) beneath our feet. At the center, its temperature is thought to reach 8,100°F (4,500°C). Scientists know about the Earth by studying earthquakes, by comparing the Earth with meteorites, and by looking at its size and shape.

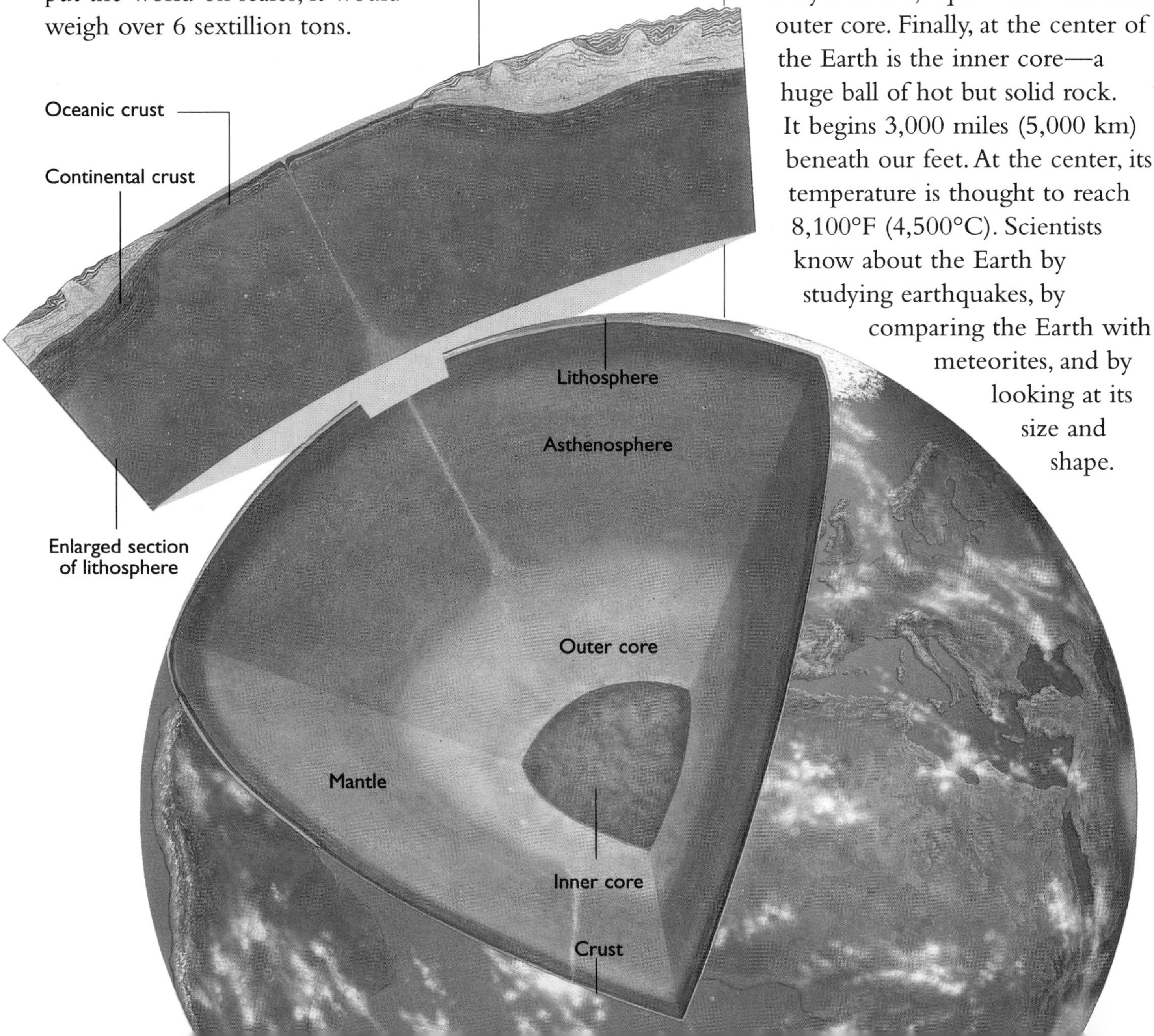

Oceanic crust

Continental crust

Enlarged section of lithosphere

Lithosphere

Asthenosphere

Outer core

Mantle

Inner core

Crust

Sun being formed

Earth

▲ **The Earth was formed at the same time as the Sun. Material around the Sun cooled and collided to build up bodies that in time became planets.**

How old is the Earth?

Many scientists believe that the universe began to form over 15 billion years ago. The Earth is much younger. It is about 4.6 billion years old. They have worked this out by studying rocks in meteorites which have landed on Earth from outer space. Meteorites are lumps of rock which were formed at the same time as the Earth. Scientists have also calculated the Earth's age from the rate at which elements of the radioactive metal uranium decay (break down) into lead.

Why is the Earth round?

The world is round for the same reason that a raindrop and a bubble are round. If possible, a liquid naturally shapes itself into a ball. When the Earth formed, it was hot and liquid. Because it was floating in space, it became round. When the liquid rock cooled and hardened into solid rock, the Earth stayed round.

Actually, the Earth is not perfectly round, but is slightly flattened at the Poles. This flattening is caused by the speed of its spin.

The Earth is the only planet known to have enough oxygen for living things. In sunlight, plants give off oxygen, keeping the planet alive.

Is the Earth solid?

The crust is solid, but the rocks of the mantle are so hot that they are partly molten, somewhat like hot toffee. The outer core is even hotter—between 4,000°F (2,200°C) and 9,000°F (5,000°C)—and is completely molten and liquid. At the very center is a ball of hot rock, squashed so tightly that it is solid. The core is far too hot and solid to drill through.

What are rocks made of?

The Earth's crust is made up of rock. Rocks are solid clusters of minerals (chemical substances composed of crystals). The minerals quartz, feldspar, and mica are found in granite rocks, for example.

Is the Earth a unique planet?

No other planet orbiting the Sun is like the Earth. Only the Earth has the necessary conditions for life (as we know it) to exist.

What is the biosphere?

The biosphere is the Earth's "skin" of soil, water, and air. Within it live all the planet's plants and animals. No other planet in the Solar System has such a biosphere.

Why does the Earth orbit the Sun?

Like other planets, the Earth is held in a path, or orbit, around the Sun. The Sun's gravity is the force that holds it in place. The Earth travels 595 million miles (958 million km) around the Sun in 365 days 6 hours and 9 minutes. This is called a year.

How much land is there?

Less than one-third of the Earth is covered by land. The land is older than the oceans. The rocks of the largest landmasses—the continents—are up to 3.8 billion years old. The oldest rocks in the ocean are less than 200 million years old. The Earth's surface is about 71 percent water. This water includes the oceans, ice, and water vapor in the atmosphere.

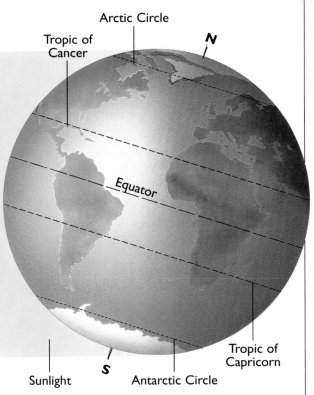

Where is the Equator?

The Equator is an imaginary line around the middle of the Earth. It is the line of 0 degrees latitude. The fattest part of the Earth is just below the Equator where the planet bulges.

Where is the North Pole?

The North Pole is near the middle of the Arctic Ocean. It is the point where all the lines of longitude meet on the map. The South Pole is in the Antarctic continent.

EARTH FACTS

- Diameter: 7,907 miles between the Poles, 7,922 miles at the Equator.
- Distance around: 24,901 miles (40,091 km).
- Surface area: 197 million sq. mi.
- Area covered by water: 71 percent.
- Age: 4.6 billion years.
- Oldest rocks: 3.8 billion years.
- Thickness of crust: 12½ mi. (20 km) (average).
- Temperature at center: 8,100°F (4,500°C).
- Distance from Sun: 93 million mi. (average).
- Distance from Moon: 235,000 mi. (minimum).

◀ **This picture of the Earth shows the tropics, the polar circles, and the Equator. The Earth turns on its axis (an imaginary line between the North and South Poles). More sunlight reaches the Equator than the Poles.**

▶ **The Northern Hemisphere includes Asia, North America, and Europe. The Southern includes Australia, southern Africa, and most of South America.**

Where are the tropics?

The tropics are regions of the Earth that lie north and south of the Equator. Each of the tropics is about 1,600 miles (2,600 km) wide. The Tropic of Cancer is 23°27′ north of the Equator. The Tropic of Capricorn is 23°27′ south of the Equator. These two lines of latitude (imaginary lines on the Earth's surface) mark the boundaries of a region where the Sun shines directly overhead.

What are hemispheres?

A hemisphere is half of a globe. On maps and globes, the Equator (0 degrees latitude) divides the planet into two halves—the Northern and Southern Hemispheres. An imaginary line around the Earth from the North Pole to the South Pole (the line of 0 degrees longitude) divides the Eastern and Western Hemispheres.

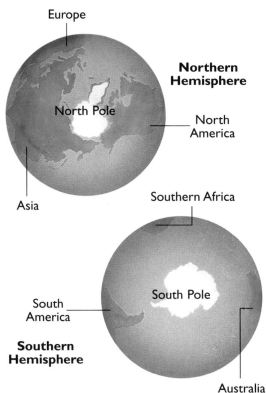

What is the Earth's axis?

Take an orange and push a stick through its middle. The stick marks the axis of the orange. There is, of course, no stick through the Earth—its axis is an imaginary line between the Poles. The Earth's axis is tilted about 23.5° from the vertical.

Why do we have day and night?

The Earth turns on its axis as it orbits the Sun, so part of the Earth is sunlit (day) while part is in shadow (night). Since the Earth spins all the time, day and night follow each other continually. Sunrise marks the start of day, and sunset the coming of night.

In midsummer in the Arctic (facing the Sun), it is always daylight and northern Europe and North America have long summer days. In Antarctica at this time, it is always night. In midwinter it is the other way around. Antarctica has permanent daylight, while the Arctic is in darkness, and northern Europe and North America have short days.

Axis

▲ **We have seasons because of the way the Earth orbits the Sun. The Earth is tilted and so first one Pole, then the other, leans toward the Sun.**

The Ancient Greeks believed that the Sun was a god called Helios. He rode across the sky in a chariot of flames. This explained sunset and sunrise.

Why do we have seasons?

The seasons (spring, summer, fall, winter) occur because the Earth is tilted on its axis. As the Earth moves around the Sun, the hemisphere that is tilted toward the Sun gets more of the Sun's rays and so is warmer and has summer. The people in that hemisphere see the Sun passing higher across the sky, and the day length is longer. Meanwhile the part tilted away from the Sun has winter because it is less warm. There the day length is shorter. At the Equator, day length varies very little.

◀ **The Moon moves in orbit around the Earth (green arrow). The Earth travels in orbit around the Sun (blue arrow). All three are spinning like tops at the same time.**

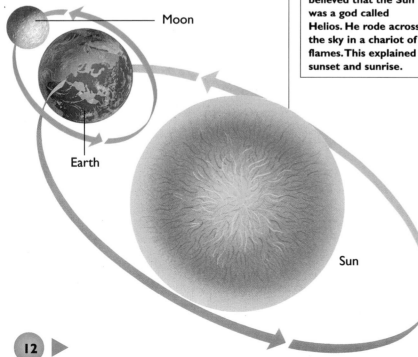

Moon

Earth

Sun

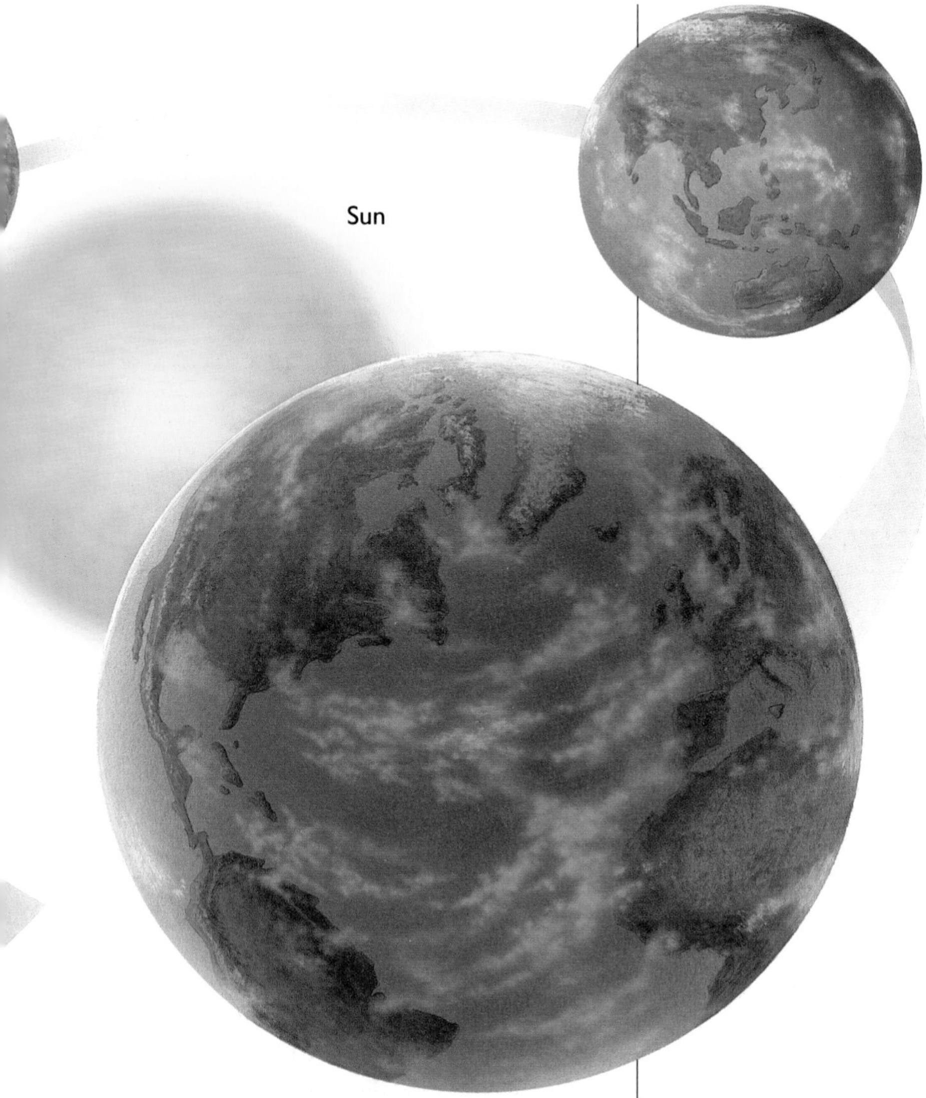

Sun

Does a compass needle point to the North Pole?

No. The magnetized needle of a compass always turns to point in the direction of the Earth's north magnetic pole. The north magnetic pole is not the same as the geographic North Pole.

Changes in the Earth's magnetic field make the magnetic poles change positions, following circular paths with diameters of about 100 miles (160 km), but they never stray far from the geographical North and South Poles. The north magnetic pole is in northern Canada. The south magnetic pole is in Antarctica. About 450 million years ago the south magnetic pole was in what is now the Sahara Desert.

Every 200,000 to 300,000 years the poles reverse. North becomes south and south becomes north.

▼ The Earth's magnetic field stretches far into space. Like all magnets, the Earth has north and south magnetic poles.

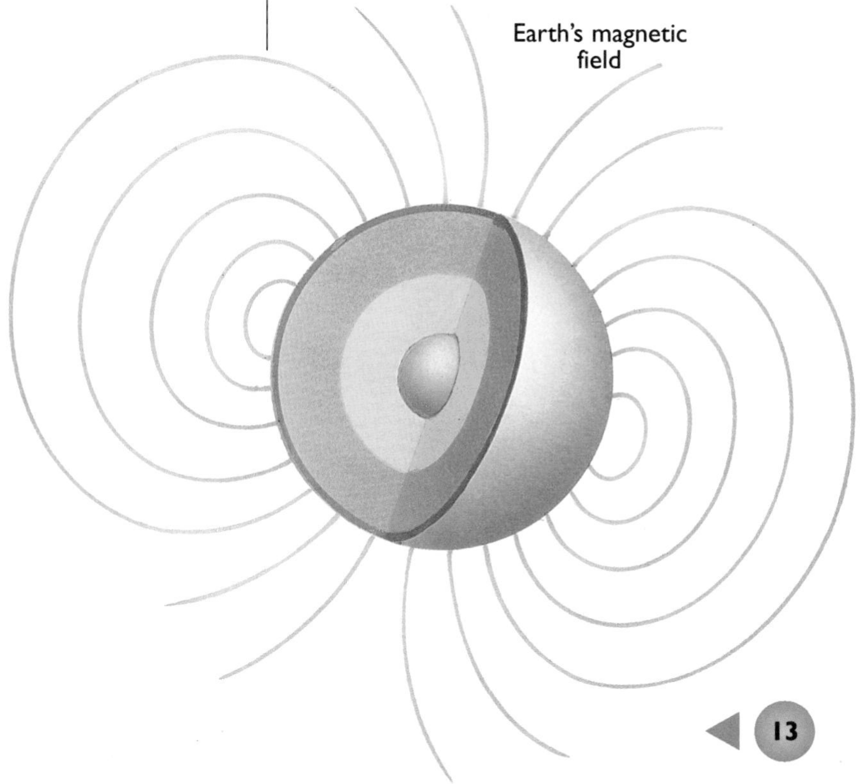

▲ Since the Earth's axis is tilted, the hemispheres are at different angles to the Sun. In the hemisphere tilted toward the Sun, day length is longer. This is why days are longer in summer.

How is the Earth like a magnet?

The Earth acts like a giant dynamo. Movements inside it create electrical currents that make a magnetic field with north and south poles, somewhat like a bar magnet. The Earth's magnetic field stretches far into space for about 37 million miles (60 billion km). The Sun and the other planets also have magnetic fields.

Earth's magnetic field

GEOGRAPHY

What do geographers do?

Geographers study the Earth, its features, and its living things. They look at the Earth's landscapes: where people, animals, and plants live. They study such features as rivers and deserts. They study where cities are built, what industries produce, how humans and nature alter the landscape. Using survey equipment, they make precise measurements of the Earth's features. From these measurements, accurate maps of various kinds are made. Geographers help plan the cities and countryside in which we live.

When was the Earth first measured?

About 200 B.C. the Greek scientist Eratosthenes measured the distance around the Earth. He found the angle of the Sun's rays at different places that were a known distance apart. Using geometry, he worked out the Earth's circumference as 252,000 stadia (about 28,500 miles [46,000 km]). His measurements were a little inaccurate: in fact the modern figure for the Earth's greatest circumference is 24,901 miles (40,091 km).

When were the first maps made?

People probably drew rough maps of their own lands over 5,000 years ago. A clay tablet made about 2500 B.C. in Babylonia (now part of Iraq) appears to show what looks like a river valley with mountains on either side.

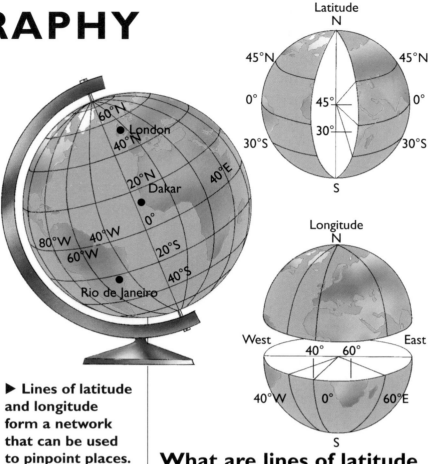

► Lines of latitude and longitude form a network that can be used to pinpoint places. The lines are measured in degrees. Greenwich, in London, England, is at 0° longitude, the Equator is at 0° latitude.

What are lines of latitude and longitude?

A map has a network of lines across it. The lines running east–west are lines of latitude, or parallels. The north–south lines are lines of longitude, or meridians. The lines make it easier to find a place on the map. The Ancient Greek geographer, Ptolemy, was the first mapmaker to draw such lines.

◄ The first reasonably accurate maps of the world were drawn in the 1500s. Most were based on the tales of seamen and travelers in distant lands.

When did the Americas first appear on maps?

Before 1500, maps made in Europe did not show the Americas. It was unknown to Europeans until Christopher Columbus sailed across the Atlantic Ocean in 1492. Soon mapmakers began to show the coast of the eastern Americas. The name "America" was first used on a German map in 1507.

When did sailors first use maps?

The first charts (sea maps) were made in Europe in the 1300s. They were called portolan charts and showed the Mediterranean coast in some detail. Sailors could recognize bays and headlands. A web of lines joined the various ports shown on the map, to help sailors find the right direction.

How is height shown on a map?

Height is difficult to show on a flat map. Color shading shows areas that are the same height above sea level. Contour lines on a map also show height. The closer together contour lines are, the steeper the slope.

What is a map projection?

No flat map can be entirely accurate because the Earth's surface is curved. A map projection is a means of transferring the curved surface onto a flat map. One map projection can be imagined by wrapping a sheet of paper around a globe. It was made popular (though not invented) by the Flemish mapmaker Gerardus Mercator (1512–1594).

▶ Taking aerial photographs is one way to make maps. The photos are taken with an overlap, as shown in this picture. Viewing pairs of photos together gives a 3-D image, so contours can be plotted.

▼ Two common map projections are Mercator's and the zenithal or azimuthal. In the zenithal projection, the paper is flat and touches the globe at one point.

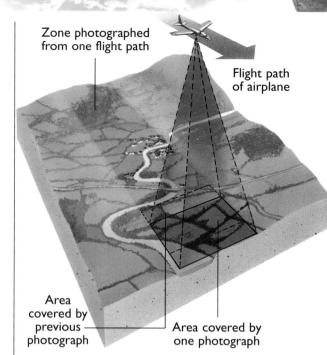

Zone photographed from one flight path

Flight path of airplane

Area covered by previous photograph

Area covered by one photograph

How are modern maps made?

Most maps are made from photographs taken from airplanes or from satellites orbiting the Earth. They show the land and sea in great detail.

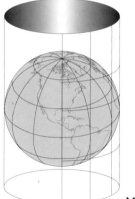

Mercator's projection (cylindrical)

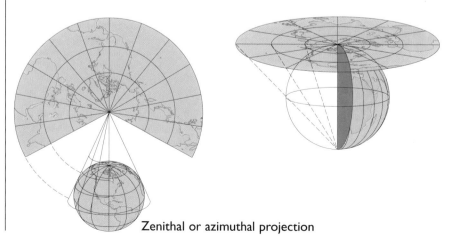

Zenithal or azimuthal projection

EVER-CHANGING EARTH

How is the Earth always changing?

Since the Earth was formed over 4.6 billion years ago, it has changed in many ways. Some changes happen so slowly that they are not noticeable in a person's lifetime. Earthquakes and volcanoes, however, can alter landscapes in hours. Glaciers, rivers, and the oceans also alter the face of the Earth, but they may take thousands of years.

How can continents move?

The Earth's crust is formed of a number of separate curved plates. The plates float like giant rafts on a thick sticky mass of molten rock. Heat from within the Earth sends currents moving through the molten mass, and these cause the plates to move. As the plates move, so do the continents resting on them.

All seven continents on the Earth today—Africa, Asia, Antarctica, Australia, Europe, and North and South America—were once part of one gigantic super-continent called Pangaea, which later broke up.

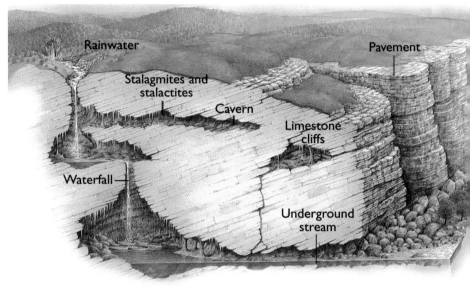

Rainwater

Stalagmites and stalactites

Cavern

Pavement

Limestone cliffs

Waterfall

Underground stream

▲ Caves, caverns and potholes are formed by water wearing away soft limestone rocks. Drips of calcite-bearing water form stalactites and stalagmites.

▼ Pangaea began to break up about 200 million years ago, to form the continents we know today.

How are caves made?

Most caves are hollowed out of rock by underground water. The water trickles down from the Earth's surface, dissolving some of the rock to form small passages and openings. Carbon dioxide in the air can make the water slightly acidic, and this acid eats away at the rock. Streams may also flow into and through the cave, making it bigger.

What makes a landslide?

Landslides are falls of rock and mud sent cascading down a mountain or hillside. The cause is often an earthquake or volcanic eruption. The movement of the surface causes loose or wet surface material to break away and slide downhill. A big landslide can bury a whole valley. Heavy rains can send mud slipping down a hillside. The risk of this kind of landslide is greater when trees on mountain slopes are felled—a major problem in some developing countries.

100 million years ago

Today

200 million years ago

How can we tell stalactites from stalagmites?

Stalactites and stalagmites form inside limestone caves. The water that drips steadily from the roof contains a mineral called calcite. The water dries, but the calcite remains and slowly builds into a column. Stalactites grow downward, from the cave roof. Stalagmites grow upward, from the cave floor. Sometimes the two columns meet to form a pillar.

Why are high mountain tops covered in snow?

High mountain tops are surrounded by very cold air. For every 3,300 feet (1,000 m) in height, the temperature falls by 41°F (5°C). The highest mountains are snow-covered all year round. The highest mountains in the

▶ Stalactites and stalagmites look like long icicles of rock. Stalactites grow down from the cave roof, stalagmites grow up from the floor.

ICE AND CAVE FACTS

■ In eastern Italy there is a cave known as the Room of Candles. Its white stalagmites look like candles.

■ Don't sit and watch a stalactite grow. It can take 1,000 years to get ½ inch (1 cm) longer!

■ During the last Ice Age, 28 percent of the Earth was ice-covered. Today, about 10 percent is covered by ice.

■ The world's longest glacier is the Lambert Glacier in Antarctica, which is over 240 miles (400 km) in length.

■ The world's deepest cave is at Rousseau Jean Bernard in France. It is 5,034 feet (1,535 m) deep.

■ The longest cave system is beneath Mammoth Cave in Kentucky. It is at least 329 miles (530 km) long.

■ Sarawak Chamber in Indonesia is the world's biggest cavern. It is 2,300 feet (700 m) long, 980 feet (300 m) wide, and 230 feet (70 m) high.

world are found in long ranges such as the Himalayas (Asia), the Andes (South America), the Rockies (North America), and the Alps (Europe).

What is a glacier?

A glacier is a moving "river" of ice. Glaciers are found in polar regions and in high mountains, wherever more snow falls in winter than is lost through melting and evaporation in summer. The icy mass creeps slowly downhill. Glaciers shape landscapes, flattening hills and carving out valleys. When a glacier reaches the sea in very cold regions, huge blocks of ice break off to form floating icebergs. The largest icebergs in the world are found in the ocean around Antarctica.

Pyramidal peak

Cirque

Crevasses

Movement of glacier

▶ A glacier wears away a valley. The head of the valley weathers into an armchair-shape known as a cirque. Crevasses or cracks often appear in glaciers. Rocks pushed along by the ice pile up as a moraine.

Snout

Terminal moraine

What is an avalanche?

An avalanche is a sudden fall of snow and ice down a mountainside. Avalanches are very dangerous because they can bury and kill people. They happen when so much snow falls that the layers of snow on the mountainside become too heavy and suddenly give way and slide or fall down. Avalanches also happen in spring when the warm weather begins to melt the snow so that it slides more easily. Earthquakes, and even sudden loud sounds, can also cause avalanches.

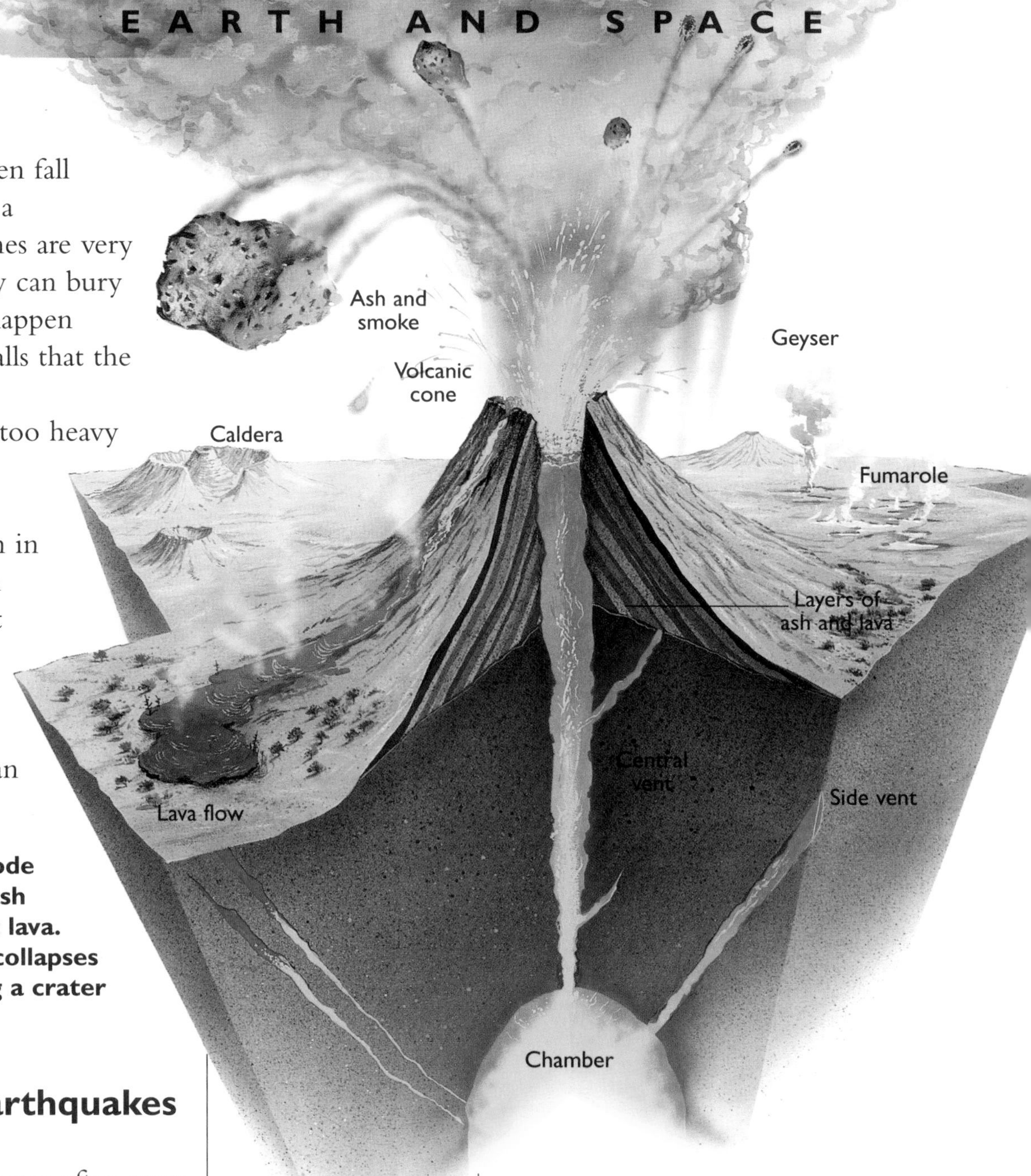

▶ **A volcano may explode violently, blowing out ash and steam and red-hot lava. Sometimes a volcano collapses around its vent, leaving a crater called a caldera.**

Ash and smoke

Volcanic cone

Caldera

Geyser

Fumarole

Layers of ash and lava

Central vent

Side vent

Lava flow

Chamber

What causes earthquakes and volcanoes?

Earthquakes and volcanoes often seem to occur together. They happen most often in parts of the Earth where two of the plates making up the crust meet. Rocks either are pushed up to form mountains or ridges, or sink down into the Earth's mantle to create trenches. This movement makes the Earth's surface unstable, and earthquakes and volcanoes are likely to occur. Scientists can tell where earthquakes and volcanoes are likely to happen, but they cannot predict exactly when.

The people of Ancient China believed that the Earth was balanced on the shoulders of a giant ox. Earthquakes happened when the ox shifted the Earth from one shoulder to the other.

Why do geysers spout hot water?

A geyser is a gushing fountain of hot water and steam. Geysers are found in areas of volcanic activity, such as Iceland. Hot volcanic rocks heat underground water, which bubbles up as a hot spring. If water deeper down is heated further, it turns to steam and pushes up the cooler water above it to form a geyser. "Old Faithful" geyser in Wyoming has spouted every 76 minutes for the last 80 years.

Why do some volcanoes explode?

When a volcano erupts, magma (molten rock) from deep inside the Earth is pushed up toward the surface. Red-hot lava (the name given to magma when it pours out above ground) flows out of the volcano. Smoke and ash belch upward, darkening the sky.

An explosive volcano contains very thick lava. The lava is pushed upward very slowly and may form a plug, sealing the volcano. Pressure builds up inside until gas and ash burst through, blowing the top off the volcano in a huge explosion.

What happens in an earthquake?

In an earthquake, the ground begins to shake. This shaking may last for

VIOLENT EARTH FACTS

■ The largest volcano is Mauna Loa in the Hawaiian Islands. It measures 74 mi. (119 km) across its base.

■ When Krakatoa volcano exploded in 1883, it was heard in Australia, 3,100 mi. (5,000 km) away.

■ There are more than 500 active volcanoes.

■ In 1201 there was a terrible earthquake in the eastern Mediterranean. It is possible that over a million people were killed.

■ In 1906 the San Francisco earthquake started fires that destroyed much of the city.

■ In 1995, an earthquake struck Kobe, Japan. Over 5,000 people died, and a third of the city buildings were destroyed.

■ Every year there are 1,000 earthquakes strong enough to cause some damage.

only a few seconds or for minutes. Buildings may shake, crack, and collapse. Surface cracks open up across fields and rocks, and whole chunks of land may sink suddenly.

Earthquakes happen in places where there are great cracks, or faults, in the rocks below ground. These places are at the edges of the huge plates, or sections, in the Earth's crust. The plates slowly move past or toward each other. Where two plates meet, the rocks on either side of the gap slide past each other, which can make the ground shake.

Where do the worst earthquakes happen?

Some of the worst earthquakes have happened in China. In 1556, an earthquake at Shensi killed over 800,000 people. Then in 1976, history repeated itself. An earthquake at Tangshan killed about 750,000 people. This is the worst earthquake disaster of modern times.

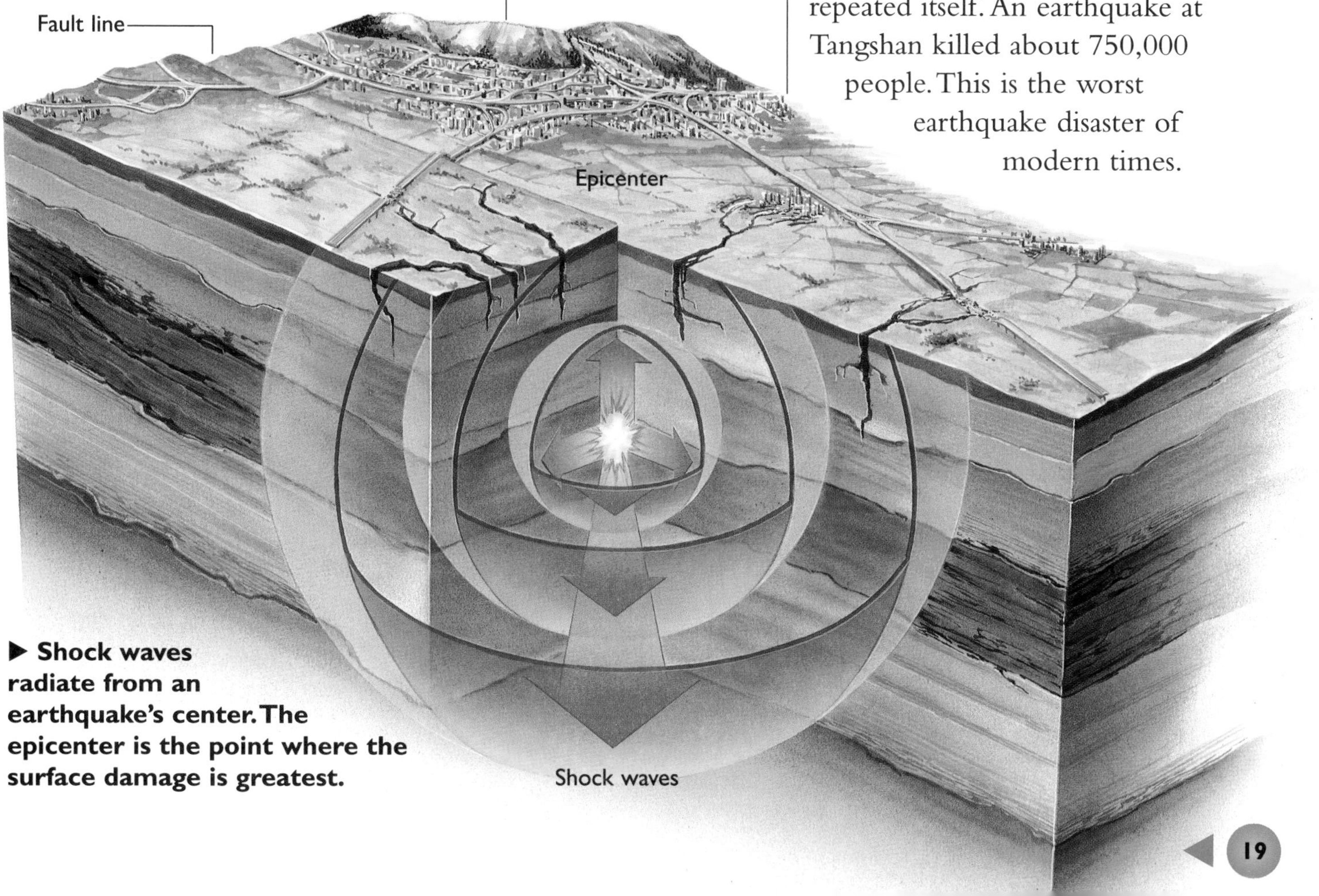

Fault line

Epicenter

▶ **Shock waves radiate from an earthquake's center. The epicenter is the point where the surface damage is greatest.**

Shock waves

LANDSCAPES

What is a desert?

A desert is a region that has less than 10 inches (25 cm) of rain a year. Deserts cover between one-eighth and one-seventh of the Earth's land. Hot deserts lie between 20 and 30 degrees to either side of the Equator. There are cold deserts too, which are always covered by snow and ice. Cold deserts cover one-sixth of the world's surface.

What is an oasis?

An oasis is a patch of green in the desert. Plants grow there because there is water from a well or an underground spring. The water is trapped deep down in the rocks beneath the desert. Palm trees and vegetables can be grown in an oasis. Some oases support fairly large towns.

Which is the biggest desert?

The Sahara in northern Africa is easily the biggest desert in the world. Look at a map of Africa and you will see how much of northern Africa is covered by the Sahara. It fills a vast area of 5½ million square miles (9.1 million sq km), which is bigger than the whole of Australia.

Where are seas of sand?

In some hot deserts, an erg or "sand sea" may form. The biggest is the Grand Erg Oriental in Algeria and Tunisia, covering 121,740 square miles (196,000 sq km) with dunes 980 feet (300 m) high.

DESERT FACTS

■ Death Valley, in the Mojave Desert of California, is the hottest spot in North America. A high of 134°F (56.7°C) has been recorded there.

■ The Sahara was not always dry. Prehistoric paintings show it as a fertile land with grass and rivers.

■ The Sun is a cheap source of power in the desert. In Saudi Arabia, there are solar-powered payphones for desert travelers.

■ Desert ostriches eat sand. It probably helps them digest their food.

■ Desert nights are cold. In winter, temperatures often fall below freezing.

■ Australia has large areas of desert. The two largest are the Gibson and Great Victoria deserts.

■ Only about 20 percent of the world's hot deserts are sandy.

▲ In sandy deserts, winds blow the sand into wavelike shapes known as dunes. The dunes move and form different shapes.

What is sand?

Sand is made up of tiny mineral grains, the biggest of which are only about 1/16 inch (2 mm) across. Sand is rock broken apart and crumbled by weathering. The most common mineral in sand is quartz. However, not all deserts are sandy. Only about one-fifth of hot deserts are covered with sand. Other deserts are rocky, stony, or scrubby.

Are all deserts hot?

Most deserts are found in hot countries, but not all. One of the world's largest deserts, the stony Gobi Desert in central Asia, has short, hot summers but cold winters. Antarctica is a frozen desert.

How are islands made?

Some islands are chunks of land that became separated from continents. The British Isles, for example, were once joined to Europe. Others are volcanoes that have risen up above the sea. The islands of Japan are volcanic islands.

How are coral reefs formed?

The tiny coral animals of warm seas create some of the oceans' most spectacular sights—coral reefs. The limestone remains of the animals build up into walls and ridges of coral. Plants and animals move in to colonize the coral reef. Coral reefs are found only in tropical oceans; coral animals cannot live in cold water.

The Great Barrier Reef off the coast of northeastern Australia is the world's longest reef. It is over 1,240 miles (2,000 km) long.

What is an atoll?

An atoll is a doughnut-shaped coral island. First, a fringing reef of coral forms on the outer rim of a volcanic island that is slowly sinking into the ocean floor. In time, mud and sand pile up on top of the reef, and plants begin to grow. The central volcanic island has by now sunk completely under the water. Only the circular reef remains. There are many coral atolls in the Pacific Ocean.

What is it like at the South Pole?

The polar regions of the Arctic and the Antarctic are vast frozen deserts. At the South Pole there is no life of

▲ **Coral reefs form when a volcanic island rises from the sea. A fringing reef of coral grows, forming a ring or atoll which remains after the island has sunk.**

any kind. Snow and ice lie thousands of feet thick. For half the year there is permanent darkness.

How thick is the Antarctic ice?

The thickest ice in the Antarctic is 15,740 feet (4,800 m) deep. That is more than ten times the height of the world's tallest skyscraper. The Antarctic covers about 5½ million square miles (14 million sq km)—bigger than either Europe or Australia. However, the land of Antarctica is actually smaller than Australia. Its huge size is due to the enormous mass of ice covering it. Antarctica contains almost nine-tenths of all the ice on Earth.

How big was the biggest iceberg?

The biggest icebergs are the great, flat bergs that break away from the Antarctic ice sheet. Along the edge of the Ross Ice Shelf in the Antarctic the rise and fall of the tide cracks the ice. Icebergs break loose. The largest iceberg ever seen was over 11,970 square miles (31,000 sq km), bigger than the country of Belgium.

◄ **The South Pole is one of the coldest and bleakest places on Earth. There is now a permanent scientific base there, where modern polar explorers can find a warm welcome.**

How much of the Earth is forested?

In prehistoric times, people had not begun to clear forests to make room for cities, farms, and factories. About 60 percent of the Earth's land area was forested then. Today only about 30 percent is covered by forest.

Which forests have the most trees?

The richest forests on Earth are the tropical rain forests. In North America or Europe a small area of typical forest might contain about ten kinds of trees. The same area in a Brazilian or Indonesian rain forest might have over 100 different kinds of trees.

Where is the canopy in a rain forest?

The tops of the tall trees in a rain forest make up the canopy. The canopy receives the most sunlight and it grows thickly. It can form a dense roof, shadowing plants lower down. The tallest trees grow up through the lower layers, toward the sunlight. In the canopy live many animals such as monkeys, birds, and insects.

What is tundra?

The tundra is a zone near the Arctic where the climate is mostly too cold and dry for trees. Most of the tundra is snow-covered much of the year. Mosses, lichens, and tough grasses grow on the tundra, seen briefly during summer when the snow melts.

▶ The roots of tundra plants grow only to about 12 in. (30 cm) before meeting frozen ground. Many plants flower during the brief summer.

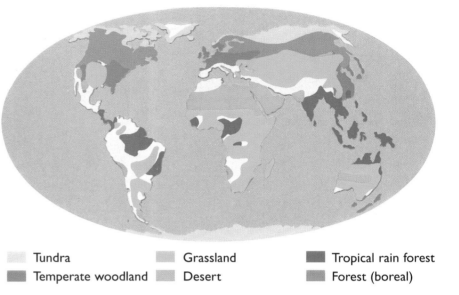

Tundra Grassland Tropical rain forest
Temperate woodland Desert Forest (boreal)

▲ The world's main vegetation zones.

It rains almost every day in a rain forest. It gets hotter and stickier, until in the afternoon there's a thunderstorm. Then it's dry again.

Where was the world's largest prairie?

The Great Plains of the Midwest once stretched from southern Texas up into Canada. It was the biggest on Earth, and in places the grass was as tall as a person. Today little remains of the original prairie. Since the 1800s, people have plowed it and planted it with crops such as wheat. This means there are fewer prairie animals too.

Lichen

Where is the Grand Canyon?

The Grand Canyon is in Arizona. It is as much as 18 miles (29 km) wide and 5,600 feet (1,700 m) deep in places. It is the longest gorge in the world, 217 miles (349 km) in length. The Grand Canyon was formed by the Colorado River cutting deep into the rock.

Which mountain range has the highest peaks?

The world's 20 highest mountains are all in the Himalaya-Karakoram range in Asia. All these mountains are over 26,000 ft. (8,000 m) high.

The highest mountain above sea level is Mount Everest in the Himalayas. Working out the exact height of such great mountains in remote regions is difficult. In 1860 surveyors calculated that Everest was 28,995 ft. (8,840 m) high. In 1973 this was corrected to 29,021 ft. (8,848 m). In 1987 satellite measurements gave its height as 29,070 ft. (8,863 m).

▲ The Grand Canyon is one of the natural wonders of the world.

▼ These are the highest mountains on the seven continents, ranged in order of size.

Why are there fjords in Scandinavia?

During the Ice Age, glaciers and ice sheets covered Scandinavia. Glaciers and ice sheets grind and cut into the landscape across which they move. Glaciers seek out the easiest paths down a mountain, such as river valleys. The ice deepens the valleys, and after it melts, water flows in from the sea. These deep, narrow inlets are called fjords. There are also fjords in Chile, Alaska, and New Zealand.

Everest, Asia
29,028 ft. (8,863 m)

Aconcagua, South America
22,831 ft. (6,959 m)

McKinley, North America
20,320 ft. (6,194 m)

Kilimanjaro, Africa
19,340 ft. (5,895 m)

Vinson Massif, Antarctica
16,859 ft. (5,140 m)

Kosciusko, Australia
7,310 ft. (2,228 m)

Elbrus, Europe
18,508 ft. (5,642 m)

ATMOSPHERE AND WEATHER

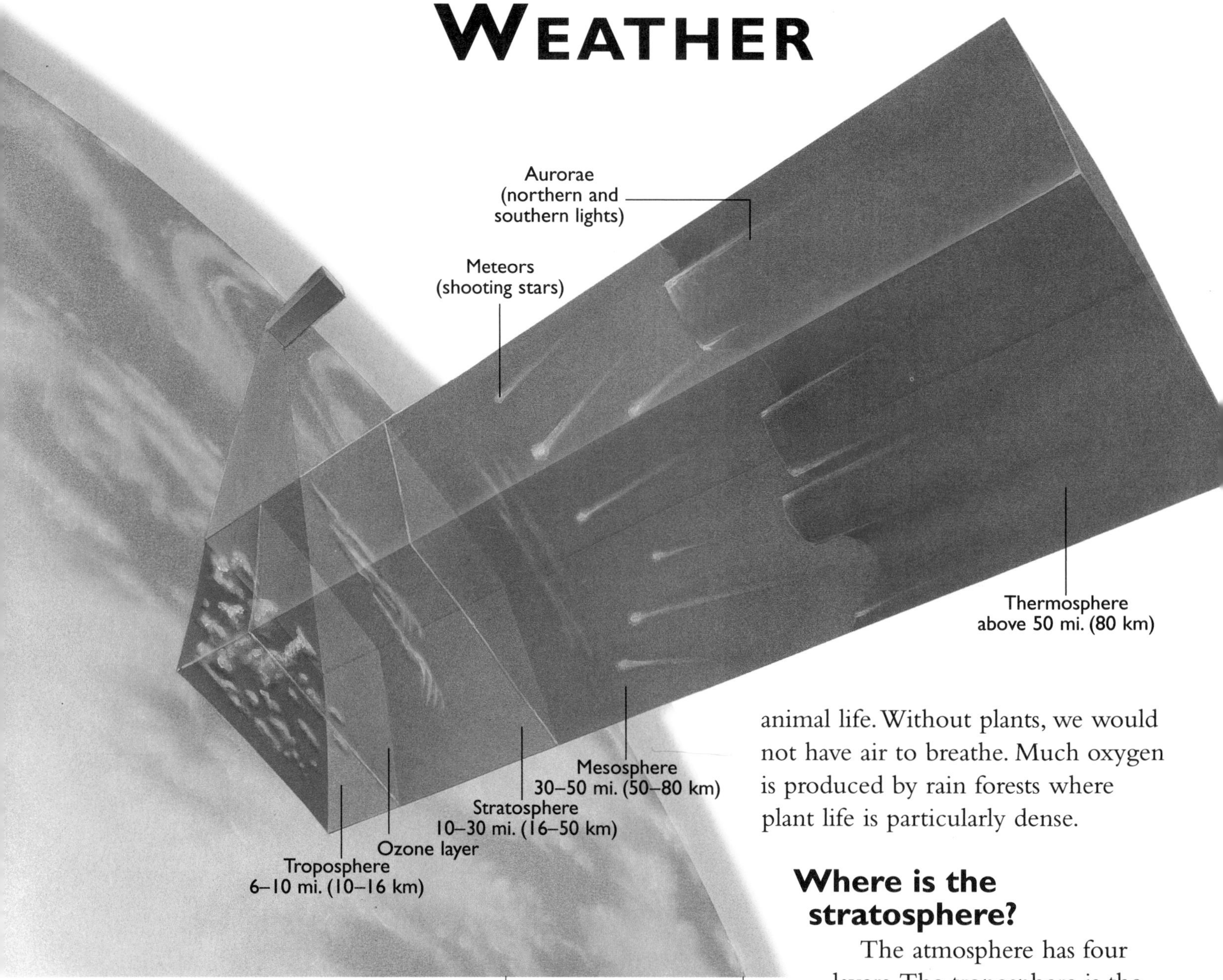

Aurorae
(northern and
southern lights)

Meteors
(shooting stars)

Thermosphere
above 50 mi. (80 km)

Mesosphere
30–50 mi. (50–80 km)

Stratosphere
10–30 mi. (16–50 km)

Ozone layer

Troposphere
6–10 mi. (10–16 km)

What is the atmosphere?

The atmosphere is the layer of gas surrounding the Earth. The layer is surprisingly thin, yet without it there would be no life on Earth. When the Earth was young, the atmosphere consisted mainly of poisonous gases. Plants (which give off oxygen during photosynthesis) have made the atmosphere capable of supporting

▲ Air surrounds
the Earth like a
transparent shell.
The layers of the
atmosphere shield
us from most of
the Sun's
dangerous rays.

animal life. Without plants, we would not have air to breathe. Much oxygen is produced by rain forests where plant life is particularly dense.

Where is the stratosphere?

The atmosphere has four layers. The troposphere is the lowest layer. It is between 6 and 10 miles (10–16 km) thick. Above it is the stratosphere, about 30 miles (50 km) deep. Higher still is the mesophere, to about 50 miles (80 km). The upper layer is called the thermosphere. The thermosphere has two parts, the ionosphere and the exosphere. Temperature differences mark the boundaries between the layers.

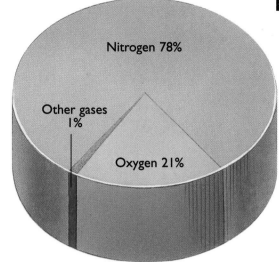

Nitrogen 78%

Other gases 1%

Oxygen 21%

What is air?

Air is a mixture of gases. The most plentiful gases in air are nitrogen (78 percent) and oxygen (21 percent). The remaining 1 percent is made up of water vapor and very small amounts of ozone, carbon dioxide, argon, and helium.

Why is the sky blue?

Light reaches the Earth from the Sun. Sunlight looks white, but is actually a mixture of all the colors in the rainbow. When light rays from the Sun pass through the atmosphere, some are scattered by the tiny bits of dust and water in the air. Blue rays are scattered most and reach our eyes from all angles. We see more blue than any other color and this makes the sky look blue.

Why are sunsets red?

At sunset the Sun is low in the sky and farther away from us as we look toward it. The light rays from the Sun have to pass through more layers of air to reach our eyes. This extra air scatters out all the colors in the sunlight except red. Only the red rays come straight to our eyes, and so we see a red sunset.

◄ Our air is mostly nitrogen gas, which makes up nearly four-fifths of the air. About one-fifth of the air is oxygen, the gas we need to breathe. Other gases and water vapor make up the rest.

ATMOSPHERE FACTS

■ The lowest layer of atmosphere is where weather happens.

■ Planes fly above the clouds. Here the skies are clear and the air is thin.

■ Air is heavier than you think. The average roomful of air weighs more than 100 lbs (45 kg)—as much as 20 bags of potatoes!

■ The ozone layer is in the stratosphere.

■ In the mesosphere, 30–50 mi. (50–80 km) above our heads, it is freezing cold.

■ The outer layer of the thermosphere is called the exosphere. It extends as far as 5,000 mi. (8,000 km). Here it is very hot, above 3,900°F (2,200°C).

▶ "Red sky at night, shepherd's delight." This old rhyme suggests that a brilliant red sunset (with few clouds) means a fine day tomorrow.

Where is the ozone layer?

Ozone is a form of oxygen. In the atmosphere, ozone forms when oxygen reacts under the influence of sunlight. Most ozone forms near the Equator and is shifted by the winds around the Earth. The ozone layer is an invisible screen. The ozone filters out harmful ultraviolet rays from the Sun. Scientists have discovered holes in the ozone layer, over Antarctica and Arctic. These holes are believed to be caused by harmful gases given off by aerosol sprays, refrigerators, and factories.

Who went up in a balloon to study air?

No one had explored the atmosphere before balloons were invented. The French chemist Joseph Louis Gay-Lussac (1778–1850) made balloon flights over Paris to study the air. He found that air is the same mixture at different heights, although its pressure, temperature, and moistness change the higher you go.

What are the northern and southern lights?

The northern lights, or aurora borealis, are marvelous displays of colored lights in the sky, like an enormous laser show. You can see them in or near the Arctic. The southern lights, or aurora australis, are seen in or near Antarctica. The lights are caused by electrical particles from the Sun hitting the atmosphere and giving off bursts of light.

Why does sunlight tan the skin?

Sunlight contains ultraviolet rays. We cannot see them, but they are vital to health. They enable skin cells to make vitamin D. However, ultraviolet rays damage the outer layer of skin. The body reacts by making more of a brown pigment called melanin. This darkens the skin. The ozone layer acts as a sunblock, shielding us from most of the ultraviolet rays.

What do we mean by climate?

Climate is the usual weather of a place over a long time. Weather can change from day to day, but climate stays the same. The Earth has five major climatic zones. They are polar (cold); cold forest (cold winters); temperate (mild winters); desert (dry); and tropical rainy (warm and moist).

What makes rain?

Water from the oceans, lakes, rivers, and plants is evaporated by the Sun's heat to form water vapor. This vapor, or gas, is held in the air. Air rises when warm, or when forced to

▶ **The northern lights produce a brilliant light show in the sky, as energized particles hit the atmosphere.**

The melanin pigment that gives us a tan is missing in some people. They are albinos and can be of any race. Their skin and hair are very pale, and because the iris of the eye is colorless, blood vessels show through. Albinos cannot develop a protective suntan, so they have to avoid the sun if they can.

WEATHER FACTS

■ Dust and smoke from volcanoes or forest fires can make the Sun and Moon appear green or blue.

■ Every snowflake is a unique six-sided crystal of frozen water molecules.

■ Even in summer, clouds contain ice. Most of the ice melts as it falls, except during occasional summer hailstorms.

■ One of the world's wettest places is Cherrapunji, India, which has nearly 43 in. (11,000 mm) of rain a year.

■ The South Pole is the driest: only 3 in. (40 mm) a year. Chicago has 33 in. (840 mm) and London 24 in. (600 mm).

rise over mountains, or when heavier cold air pushes underneath it. As the warm, moisture-laden air rises, it cools. The water vapor condenses back into water droplets, which mass together to form clouds. As the air rises, more vapor turns to water. The clouds grow bigger. When the water droplets are too big for the air to carry, they fall as rain and the cycle begins again.

Temperature

Drizzle

What are the highest clouds in the sky?

High clouds include cirrus, cirrostratus, and cirrocumulus. These clouds are formed mainly of ice crystals. Cirrus clouds are wispy clouds and can form at heights up to 32,800 feet (10,000 m). The rare nacreous or mother-of-pearl clouds can be over 65,600 feet (20,000 m) high.

Why do some lands have monsoons?

A monsoon is a wind that blows from sea to land in summer and from land to sea in winter. In hot lands near the Equator the air heats up in summer and rises. Cool air, carrying moisture from the ocean, is drawn

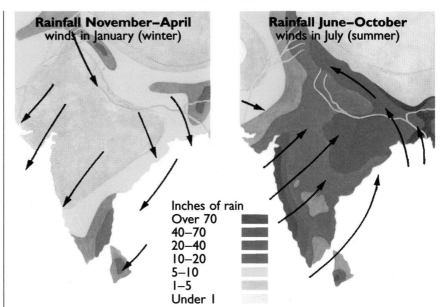

Rainfall November–April winds in January (winter)

Rainfall June–October winds in July (summer)

Inches of rain
Over 70
40–70
20–40
10–20
5–10
1–5
Under 1

▲ **The Indian sub-continent receives rain-carrying winds from the Indian Ocean during the monsoon season. In winter, the winds blow in the other direction.**

inland to take the place of the rising warm air. The cool winds bring rain which is often torrential. In India the monsoon lasts for three to four months, bringing rain in summer. In winter, there is much less rainfall.

What makes a rainbow?

Sunlight is a mixture of colors. When the Sun's rays pass through falling raindrops, the raindrops act like tiny mirrors or glass prisms. They bend and scatter the light into all its colors. We see a rainbow when the Sun is behind us and the rain in front of us. You can make your own rainbow with a water sprinkler or hose on a bright, sunny day.

It may not rain cats and dogs, but it can rain frogs and fish! The animals are sometimes sucked up from ponds by extra-strong winds and fall with the rain.

Wet snow

Dry snow

Sleet

Rain

◀ **Whether water falls as drizzle, rain, sleet (a mixture of snow and rain) or snow, depends on the temperature of the air and the ground.**

▶ **A rainbow is caused by sunlight shining on a screen of water droplets. Light rays are bent (refracted), reflected, and then refracted again as they strike each droplet.**

Rainbow

Raindrop

Light rays

Reflected and refracted light

Where is the hottest place on Earth?

The hottest places are near the Equator, which receives the Sun's strongest rays. In 1922 a temperature of 136°F (58°C) in the shade was recorded in the Libyan Desert in north Africa. Another very hot place is Death Valley in California, where a temperature of 134°F (56.7°C) was measured in 1913.

Which is colder: the North or South Pole?

The South Pole gets colder than the North Pole ever does. The coldest spot on Earth is at the Vostok base in Antarctica, near the South Pole. In July 1983 the temperature there fell to −128.6°F (−89.2°C).

What is frost?

The layer of white frost that covers the ground on cold mornings is made by moisture in the air. On cold nights the water vapor in the air freezes when it meets the cold ground. A thin layer of ice crystals forms frost.

What causes lightning?

Lightning is a huge electric spark. During a thunderstorm, very large electric charges build up inside clouds and on the ground. The charges build up until a flash of lightning shoots through the air between them. Lightning can flash from the cloud to the ground or between two clouds.

Lightning is a sequence of flashes. First a leader stroke zigzags to the ground. The main flash then surges upward. Other flashes may follow in quick succession.

WEATHER FACTS

■ The biggest thunderclouds tower 10 mi. high, nearly twice the height of Mt. Everest.

■ Weather forecasting is not easy. A small change in the air over the Arctic can cause a hurricane in the tropics!

■ Wind force is measured on the Beaufort Scale, invented in 1806 by an English admiral. On this scale, calm is 0 and a hurricane is force 12.

■ Warm, dry air flowing down the side of a mountain range can raise temperatures suddenly. Such winds are called fohns or chinooks.

Never shelter under a tree in a thunderstorm. It could be struck by lightning. You are safest inside.

What is thunder?

Thunder is the sound air makes as it expands when it is warmed by the heat of a flash of lightning. We see the lightning flash almost as it happens. The sound of the thunderclap travels much more slowly, and we hear it a few seconds later.

The nearer you are to a thunderstorm, the closer together are the lightning flash and the thunderclap. Count the seconds between them, then divide the number by three and you have an estimate of how many miles away the thunderstorm is.

Why do winds blow?

As the Sun heats the air it causes winds. Warm air expands, making it lighter than cold air. Because it is lighter it rises, and cool air flows in to take its place. The Sun's heat is greatest at the Equator. The warm air here therefore rises, cools as it does so, and moves outward. Cooler air moves in underneath it, to create the winds of the world. Winds move at different speeds. A slow wind is a breeze. A fast wind is a gale, strong enough to damage houses.

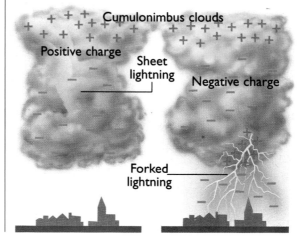

Cumulonimbus clouds
Positive charge
Sheet lightning
Negative charge
Forked lightning

◄ **Positive electrical charges collect at the top of clouds, negative charges at the bottom. Sheet lightning flashes inside or between clouds. Forked lightning flashes to the ground.**

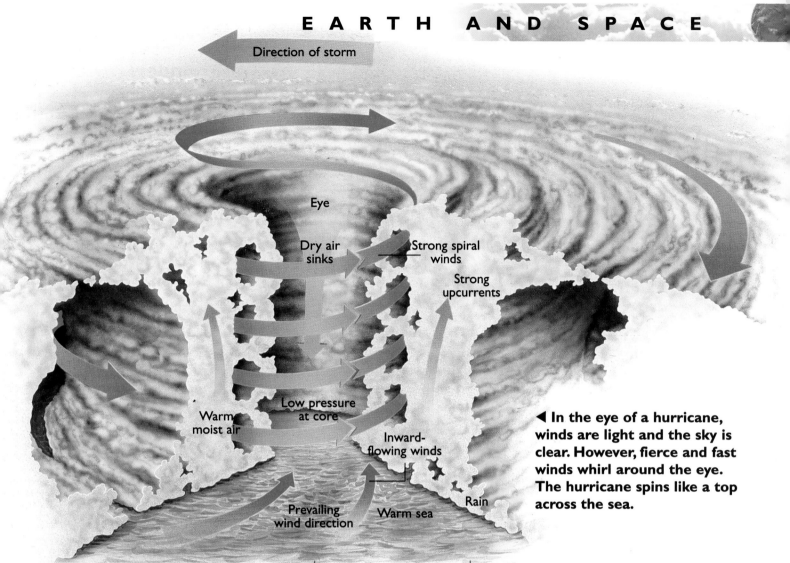

Direction of storm

Eye

Dry air sinks

Strong spiral winds

Strong upcurrents

Warm moist air

Low pressure at core

Inward-flowing winds

Rain

Prevailing wind direction

Warm sea

◄ In the eye of a hurricane, winds are light and the sky is clear. However, fierce and fast winds whirl around the eye. The hurricane spins like a top across the sea.

Why do hurricanes begin over the ocean?

A hurricane is a violent tropical storm. In a hurricane winds spiral around very rapidly. Hurricanes form over the ocean near the Equator, where the air is very warm and moist. The warm air rises rapidly, and cooler air rushes in beneath it. The air begins to move like a giant whirling top. Hurricanes form in the Atlantic Ocean. Similar storms in the Pacific Ocean are called typhoons, in the Indian Ocean cyclones. Hurricanes are usually about 400 miles (650 km) across. The winds in these storms travel at up to 125 miles (200 km) per hour. The most likely time for hurricanes is late summer and fall.

▼ Tornadoes can cause terrible damage as they twist across the countryside.

What is a tornado?

A tornado is a storm wind similar to a hurricane. It forms over the land when huge masses of clouds meet. The clouds whirl around each other. Then they join to create an enormous funnel. The tip of the funnel spins down to the ground, where it sucks up everything in its path. Tornadoes in the Midwest rip across country at 30 miles (50 km) per hour and can be heard 25 miles (40 km) away.

OCEANS, RIVERS, AND LAKES

What is a current?

A current is a stream of water moving through the ocean. There are surface currents and deep water currents. Great surface currents carry warm water from the Equator. The water cools and mixes with colder water as it moves away from the heat of the Equator. When the current turns toward the Equator again, its waters are cold. Offshore currents are caused by tide movement. Winds cause the much larger currents circling in the oceans in regular patterns. The Gulf Stream is a warm water current which begins in the Gulf of Mexico, then runs northeast toward Europe.

▼ Ocean currents are moved in regular patterns by the winds. Near the Equator, the main currents are blown westward. Near the poles they are blown eastward.

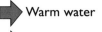

Warm water

Cold water

How big can waves be?

Each wave in the ocean is made up of water droplets moving in a circle. The wind pushes the wave upward, forming a crest. Then gravity pulls it down again, into a trough. This up- and down-movement of water in waves has been used to drive generators. Storm waves, driven by high winds, often rise 40 feet (12 m) or more in an open sea. The highest sea wave seen from a ship and officially recorded in 1933 was 112 feet (34 m) high. The biggest wave measured by instruments was 86 feet (26.2 m) high in 1872 in the North Atlantic. Such waves are rare.

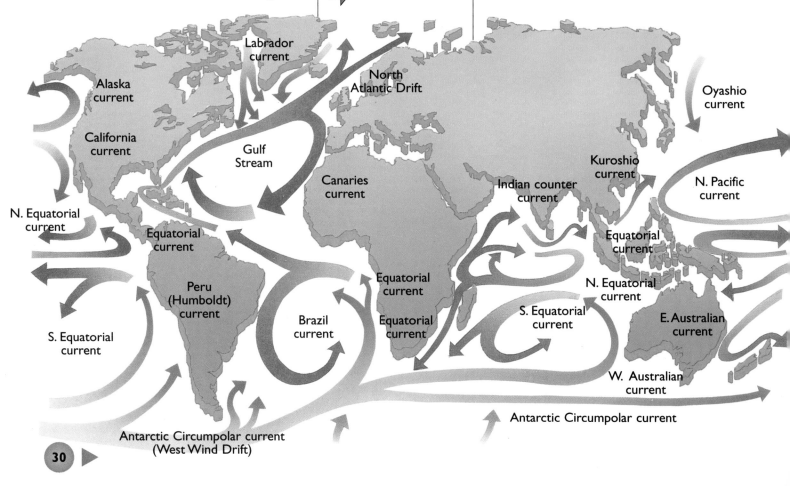

Why is seawater salty?

The saltiness of the sea comes from minerals. Minerals are washed into the sea from the land by rivers, which dissolve minerals from the rocks over which they flow. The most plentiful mineral in seawater is sodium chloride, or common salt.

Why do the tides rise and fall?

Ocean tides rise (flood) and fall (ebb) about twice every 24 hours. Tides are caused by the gravitational pull of the Sun and Moon on the Earth. They pull the oceans toward them. The land is pulled too, but water moves more easily, making a giant wave. As the Earth spins, the wave travels around the Earth, causing the tides.

Away from the shore, the ocean plunges to a depth of about 2.5 miles in most places. It's like going down a high mountain!

▼ The seabed is cut through with valleys (trenches) and also has mountains (guyots) and volcanoes. The continental shelf slopes down gradually.

Where is the deepest point in the oceans?

The deepest point in the oceans is the bottom of the Mariana Trench in the Pacific. Measurements of the trench have varied from 35,804 feet (10,916 m) to 36,192 feet (11,034 m) below the surface.

Where is the continental shelf?

In most places, land does not stop suddenly at the coast. It slopes gently away beneath the sea to a depth of about 577 feet (180 m). This undersea land is called the continental shelf. At the outer edge of the shelf the steeper continental slope begins, leading down to the deep ocean floor, known as the abyss.

Coral reef Volcanic islands Guyot Deep ocean trench Continental slope Continental rise Continental shelf

Continental crust Oceanic crust

Which is the biggest ocean?

The three great oceans are the Pacific, the Atlantic, and the Indian. The Pacific is by far the biggest ocean on Earth. It covers over 64 million sq. mi. (166 million sq km).

▼ The five world oceans compared: the Pacific is by far the largest.

Atlantic Ocean 41,000,000 sq. mi.
Antarctic Ocean 12,450,965 sq. mi.
Arctic Ocean 5,540,540 sq. mi.
Pacific Ocean 64,186,300 sq. mi.
Indian Ocean 28,378,378 sq. mi.

What is the ocean bottom like?

The deep basins of the ocean floor are formed from heavy rock called basalt. Layers of mud overlie the deep oceanic trenches and level parts of the ocean floor. Some of the mud is filled with the remains of dead plants and animals and is called ooze. It is hundreds of feet deep in places. There are great mountain ranges, too, beneath the oceans. Many undersea mountains are volcanoes, the tops of which form islands on the surface.

How can seawater be made drinkable?

Seawater is about seven times more salty than water that is safe to drink. Anybody who drinks only seawater will die. Their body would dry out as it tried to rid itself of all the salt. Many ways to remove the salt from seawater (desalinate it) have been tried. The simplest way is to distil it. This can be done by boiling seawater in a container and diverting the steam into a cold bottle. The steam leaves the salt behind in the container so that fresh water condenses in the bottle. Large desalination plants do produce drinking water from the ocean, but they are expensive to operate and produce relatively small amounts of fresh water.

WATER FACTS

■ In 1960 the bathyscaphe *Trieste* dived into the deepest part of the Pacific: the Mariana Trench, about 36,000 ft. (11,000 m) down.

■ The longest river is the Nile in Africa, which is 4,143 mi. (6,670 km) long.

■ Next longest is the Amazon in South America, at 4,005 mi. (6,448 km).

■ The world's largest delta is formed by the Ganges and Brahmaputra rivers. It is 300 mi. (480 km) long and 100 mi. (160 km) wide.

■ The Amazon pushes out so much water that fresh water from it is found up to 112 mi. (180 km) out at sea.

What is a delta?

A delta forms where a river meets the sea. The river flows more slowly, and deposits mud, sand, and even boulders. This material piles up, forming new land. The delta is shaped like a triangle. It derives its name from the letter Δ (delta) in the Greek alphabet.

How are canyons made?

A canyon is a deep valley cut by a river. A narrow canyon with steep rocky walls is a ravine or gorge. The biggest canyon in the world is the Grand Canyon in Arizona.

Which is the longest river?

The Nile in Africa and the Amazon in South America are close rivals for the title of the world's longest river. Most measurements make the Nile the longest (see box).

◀ A river's course can take it through various stages, from its source to its mouth.

Glacier
Meltwater
Waterfall
Rapids
Stream
River
Oxbow
Tributary stream
Meander
Flood plain
Estuary
River mouth

Where does a river begin?

River water comes from rain, from lakes and springs, and from melting ice and snow. A river begins as a trickling stream. Its starting point is called the source and is often on a mountain. All rivers start on high ground and flow downhill, under the pull of the Earth's gravity.

How are swamps formed?

When a slow-moving river moves through lowlands, it may form a swamp—an area of wetland. A swamp has more woody plants (trees and shrubs) than a marsh. Close to the sea, salt water and fresh water often mingle and mix in a swamp. A swamp is always waterlogged. A marsh is only water-covered part of the time (by the incoming ocean tide).

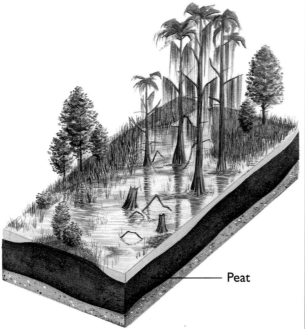

Peat

Where is the highest waterfall?

Waterfalls are found in the upper part of a river's course. They are made in places where the river crosses a layer of hard rock. The hard rock is worn away more slowly than the softer rock downstream, forming a "step" which gets gradually deeper. Water plunges over the step, creating a waterfall. At the Angel Falls, or Cherunmeri, in Venezuela, the water falls 2,647 feet (807 m) in a single drop. This is the world's highest waterfall. Its other sections make the total drop of this waterfall 3,211 feet (979 m).

LAKE FACTS

■ The Great Lakes were formed by glaciers moving over the Earth's crust.

■ Lake Baikal in Russia is the deepest lake. At its deepest point it is almost 1¼ mi. (2 km) deep.

■ Lake Victoria is the largest lake in Africa and the third largest in the world.

■ The world's largest underground lake was discovered in a cave in Namibia, Africa, in 1986. Its surface covers 10,077 sq. mi. (26,100 sq km).

■ Britain's largest lake is Loch Lomond in Scotland. It has a surface area of over 27 sq. mi. (70 sq km) and it is more than 18½ mi. (30 km) long.

◀ **Leaves falling into a shallow lake form a peat ooze at the bottom. This ooze gets thicker, forming a bog or swamp.**

◀ **Angel Falls were spotted by an American pilot named Jimmy Angel in 1935.**

How are lakes formed?

Most lakes are in areas once covered by glaciers. A glacier cuts deep valleys as it moves. Earth and boulders carried along by the glacier are deposited when it melts, making a dam. Melting ice from the glacier fills the valley to make a lake. Other lakes are formed in the craters of extinct volcanoes or sometimes when a river changes its course.

Where are the Great Lakes?

The Great Lakes of North America are the largest group of freshwater lakes in the world. The biggest is Lake Superior, with an area of 31,660 square miles (82,000 sq. km). There are four other Great Lakes: Huron, Michigan, Erie, and Ontario.

What is the world's largest lake?

The Caspian Sea on the borders of Russia, Azerbaijan, Turkmenistan, Kazakhstan, and Iran is the biggest body of inland water in the world. The sea's area is about 144,000 square miles (372,000 sq. km) and it is 745 miles (1200 km) long. Its waters are salty, so it is thought of as a sea rather than a lake. A canal links the Caspian with the Black Sea.

ENVIRONMENT AND RESOURCES

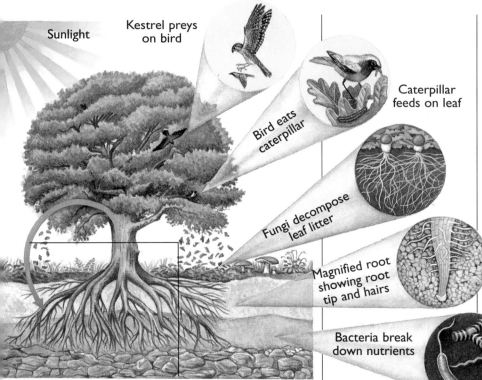

Sunlight

Kestrel preys on bird

Bird eats caterpillar

Caterpillar feeds on leaf

Fungi decompose leaf litter

Magnified root showing root tip and hairs

Bacteria break down nutrients

Falling leaves decompose (break down) and the nutrients pass into the soil

◀ The Sun's energy is harnessed by plants and passed on to animals when they feed. Bacteria and plants absorb energy from animals' dead bodies.

Why are animal and plant species valuable?

It is a tragedy to lose one species of animal or plant. Once it has gone there is no way that it can be reintroduced. Scientists fear that by the year 2050 as many as half the Earth's animal and plant species could be extinct. Yet each species is a storehouse of genetic resources. For example, drugs made from the rosy periwinkle, a plant of the Madagascar forest, are now used to help treat children suffering from leukemia (a form of cancer). If this plant had died out, its value would never have been known.

Is there a balance of nature?

Plants and animals depend on one another in various ways. All living things depend on their environment. This is the "balance of nature." The balance is very delicate since so many living things are involved. Upsetting one part of the structure—by people overhunting an animal, for instance, or by introducing another animal— can upset the whole. A group of living things (plants and animals) that live together in a particular place is known as an ecosystem.

▼ These are all species in danger of dying out. The thylacine, a Tasmanian marsupial, may already be extinct.

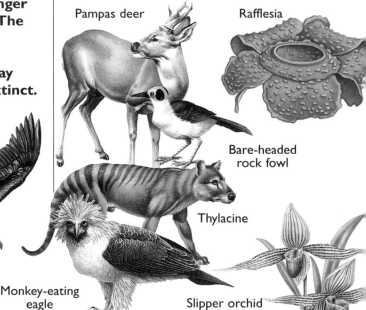

Pampas deer

Rafflesia

California condor

Bare-headed rock fowl

Thylacine

Mississippi alligator

Monkey-eating eagle

Slipper orchid

Scree   Wind

Rain

Wind

Dust bowl

Lake

Rain

River

Caves

Sea

Glacier

Which environments are richest?

Some environments are very rich in living things. Tropical rain forests have the greatest mix of species. A 6-mile (10 km) patch of forest may be home to more than 2,000 plant species, 400 kinds of birds, 150 butterflies, 100 reptiles, and 60 amphibians. There are so many insects that no one can count them!

Which was the first national park?

Hunting parks and forests reserved for kings were an ancient form of nature reserve. Animals were protected (except from the royal hunters) and people were kept out. The first true national park set up to protect nature and wildlife for everyone to enjoy was Yellowstone National Park in Wyoming, founded in 1872.

Could life exist without soil?

Much of the Earth's surface is covered with soil. Soil is a mixture of mineral and organic (living) particles, dead plant and animal matter, air, and water. Life as we know it depends on soil. Most plants grow in soil, taking food from it. Animals in turn eat plants.

▲ **Wind and water are powerful forces of erosion. Rocks and soil are moved from higher levels by glaciers and rivers and then deposited lower down.**

NATIONAL PARKS FACTS

■ In 1576 a wooded nature reserve was set aside by the Dutch government. This was one of the world's first nature parks.

■ Large national parks in Africa include Tsavo (Kenya), Serengeti (Tanzania), and Kruger (South Africa).

■ India's first national park was the Corbett National Park, where tigers are now protected.

■ Sweden set up Europe's first true national parks in 1909.

National parks could be becoming too popular. If too many people visit them, the wildlife they protect are put under pressure.

What is erosion?

Natural forces affect rock and soil, through erosion and weathering. Rain can wash away fertile topsoil, and winds can blow away thin soils, leaving bare rocks on which plants cannot grow. This is erosion in action. Erosion can cause new deserts to be formed. Alternate heating and cooling of rock can crack them into smaller pieces, to be washed away by rain and rivers. Even mountains, over millions of years, are worn away. Rainwater can also react with minerals to dissolve rock. Wearing away of rocks is called weathering.

What keeps soil fertile?

A fertile soil is rich in humus. Humus is a fine organic matter made by microbes, or soil bacteria, as they break down dead plants and animal waste. Soil microbes work best in warm, airy soil, where there is plenty of leaf mold or grass. A fertile soil needs the right amounts of minerals and water. Plants help to keep land fertile. If large plowed fields are left unplanted in dry weather, the soil becomes dusty. Winds can then blow away the topsoil. Trees and hedges are important in protecting fields from wind erosion.

Why is pollution a problem?

Human beings have always polluted their surroundings, with rubbish or smoke for example. The problem now is that so many more people pollute and spoil our world in many ways. We release gases and smoke into the air. We pour poisons into water. We damage the soil with chemicals. We drop litter, cover fields with concrete, and make a lot of noise. Pollution can make people ill and kills wildlife.

What is smog?

Smog is a mixture of pollutants that causes a foglike haze over a city. It is worst in places with lots of cars or factories close to the center of town. These give off chemical fumes and smoke. Cities with bad smog include Mexico City, Los Angeles, Athens, Beijing, Tehran, and Lagos. Breathing smoggy air is said to be as harmful as smoking forty cigarettes a day.

What started warming the Earth?

In the past, the Earth's climate warmed and cooled over millions of years. Since the 1700s, however, people have caused a far more rapid climate change. The Industrial Revolution which began in the 1700s brought factories, railroads, fast-growing cities, and automobiles. Carbon dioxide and other gases have been poured into the atmosphere from burning fuels such as coal and oil in factories, homes, and vehicles. This change, brought about by the Industrial Revolution, is warming the Earth and affecting its climate.

▶ Factories and power stations give off waste gases. Chemicals in these gases cause acid rain.

Gases react with clouds

Acid rain

Waste gases produced by industry

Waste gases and steam

Forests and lakes damaged by acid rain

If the Earth gets too hot, some ice at the Poles could melt. The seas would rise and drown many cities along low-lying coasts.

What causes acid rain?

All rain is slightly acid. But air pollution from factories and fuel-burning power plants can increase the amount of chemicals in the air, making rain more acid. This acid rain may fall far away from its source and damage the environment. Trees may die, lakes may become unfit for fish to live in, and buildings may be eroded by the chemical action of the acids in the rain.

▶ Los Angeles seen on a day when its smog is severe. Smog is a dark, sulfurous fog containing dust and soot particles. It pollutes the atmosphere of many cities.

What happens to our garbage?

Most of the garbage we throw away is dumped into holes in the ground or tipped into the sea. In some countries it is burned in incinerators. Only a small amount of it is recycled, or treated so that the materials in it (paper, glass, metal, and plastics, for example) can be reused.

What is recycling?

Recycling means reusing materials such as paper, metal cans, and glass jars. It makes good sense. Although saving your old newspapers does not save endangered trees, it does save energy. The paper industry grows trees for papermaking, just as a grain farmer grows wheat. Recycled paper production uses half as much energy as making paper from new wood and only a third as much water. In addition, the paper we throw away into dumps rots slowly and gives off methane gas, which contributes to global warming.

Burned in an incinerator

Methane gas used to make electricity

Buried in landfill

Used as compost

Recycled to make new products

▲ **How we get rid of garbage. Rotting garbage gives off methane gas which can be burned to make electricity. Kitchen and garden waste can be made into compost. Other materials can be recycled.**

What causes an oil slick?

Oil tankers regularly wash out their tanks before they reload. A tanker accident at sea can form a huge patch or slick. If this slick washes ashore, it fouls beaches and kills seabirds, fish, and other animals. Detergents and other chemicals used to clean up oiled beaches may do as much damage as the oil itself.

Can volcanoes affect climate?

The smoke and ash from a volcano pours out into the atmosphere to form clouds. The clouds can blot out the Sun and so cool the Earth. This happened when Mount Pinatubo erupted in the Philippines in 1991.

Crushing glass

Glass for recycling

Melting glass in furnace

Hot glass

Bottle bank

Bottle mold

Supermarket

Filling and capping bottles

◄ **Glass is easy to recycle. Used glass is collected, cleaned, broken into small pieces, and melted. Then it is molded into new bottles, which are filled for use again.**

THE UNIVERSE

Gravity cannot st[...]
the expansion of [...]
universe

An ever-expanding universe

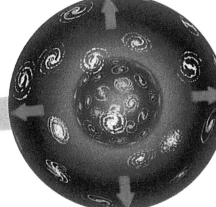

Big Bang

Galaxies fly apart
after the Big Bang

A finite universe

Big Bang

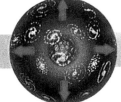

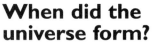

Gravity stops
expansion of the
universe

What is space?

Space is nothing—or almost nothing. It is the space that lies between the Earth and the Moon, between the planets of the Solar System, and between the stars. Space is almost empty. It does not contain any air. A piece of space the size of a house would contain a few atoms of gases and perhaps some specks of dust.

What holds the universe together?

The same force that keeps your feet on the ground holds the whole universe together. This is the force of gravity. Gravity extends through space between planets, between stars and between galaxies (groups of stars). It keeps the planets together in the Solar System and holds the stars together in huge galaxies.

▲ The universe may keep on expanding, galaxies flying apart for-evermore. Or it may all rush together in a "Big Crunch" and start a new universe.

To see how the universe is getting bigger, paint some spots on a balloon (for galaxies) and watch them get bigger as you blow it up.

When did the universe form?

A long time ago, all the galaxies in the universe would have been squeezed into a small space. Perhaps a great explosion happened, causing the galaxies to spread out. This explosion, or Big Bang, would have happened about 15 billion years ago.

How big is the universe?

No one knows for sure how big the universe is. There may be parts of the universe beyond the reach of our telescopes. Also, astronomers are not sure that light comes from the most distant objects in the universe in straight lines. The lines could be curved, making the objects closer than they appear to be. However, they could be as much as 15 billion light-years away.

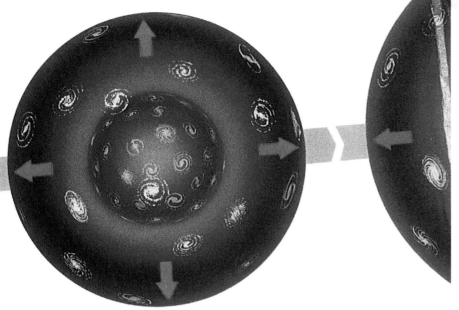

A series of universes
A completely new universe begins

Big Crunch   Big Bang

How do we know the universe is getting bigger?

Astronomers can measure the speed with which stars and galaxies are moving. Most of them are moving away from us. The farther away a galaxy is, the faster it appears to be moving away. This means that the universe is getting bigger. No one knows for certain if the universe will ever stop growing.

Where are we in the universe?

The universe is everything that exists —all the planets, moons, stars, and galaxies put together. The universe stretches out in all directions. There may be parts of the universe that we cannot see through our telescopes, and so we cannot tell where exactly we are in the universe.

UNIVERSE FACTS

■ In 1965, scientists found a very feeble warmth in space. This is all that's left of the fantastic heat given off by the Big Bang.

■ Imagine the edge of the universe (as far as we can see it) is a hollow ball the size of the Earth. On this scale, the Milky Way galaxy would be 130 feet (40 m) across. The Earth would be too small to see without a microscope!

■ Cosmologists study how the universe began.

■ Scientists think they have found at least one Earth-sized planet orbiting a distant star. The planet is 30,000 light-years away.

What is the difference between a planet and a star?

A star is a huge ball of hot glowing gas, like the Sun. A planet is a world like the Earth. The Sun and stars produce their own light. The planets are lit by light from the Sun. In the night sky, you cannot tell the planets from the stars. They all look like tiny points of light, because they are far away. However, the planets are nearer than the stars. Through a powerful telescope, you can see that the planets are other worlds. The stars are so very distant that they still look like points of light, even through the most powerful telescope. Astronomers think that some stars have planets orbiting around them, just like the Sun.

Which star is nearest to the Earth?

The star Proxima Centauri is the nearest to us, at a distance of 4.2 light-years. Next closest are Alpha Centauri (4.3 light-years) and Barnard's Star (6 light-years).

How do astronomers gaze into the past?

Light reaching us from even the closest stars has taken several years to cross the vast distances of space. The light from the star nearest the Earth takes four years to reach us. This means we see the star as it looked four years ago, and so we say it is four light-years away. Therefore, when astronomers study light from these stars, they are seeing them as they were many years ago.

THE SUN

How big is the Sun?

The Sun is 864,906 miles (1,392,500 km) across, 109 times the diameter of the Earth. It weighs 333,000 times as much as the Earth, and its volume is so huge that it could swallow up 1,300,000 Earths. If the Earth were the size of a tennis ball, the Sun would be as big as a house.

What is the Sun made of?

The Sun is a huge, self-luminous ball of intensely hot gas. Its temperature is so high that it glows white hot, giving out light and heat rays. Most of the gas in the Sun is hydrogen. This is slowly turning into another gas, helium, inside the Sun. As it does so, it produces tremendous amounts of heat. The bright surface of the Sun is called the photosphere.

When did the Sun begin to shine?

The Sun began to shine about 5 billion years ago. It formed from a cloud of gas and dust floating in space. The cloud gradually got smaller and became thicker. As the cloud shrank, the center heated up. Eventually, it became so hot that it began to glow and the Sun was born. The rest of the cloud formed the Solar System, including planets, moons, asteroids, and comets.

▼ If we could cut a slice out of the Sun, we would see layers of hydrogen below the surface. There are sunspots and huge streamers of glowing gas called prominences forming arches of fire.

Does the Sun move?

The Sun appears to move across the sky from dawn to dusk. However, this motion is caused by the Earth spinning. The Sun only seems to be moving; it is we who are moving and not the Sun. Nevertheless, the Sun moves in other ways. It spins as the Earth does, though slowly, but because it is made of gas, different parts spin at different rates—the equator spins fastest, the Poles are

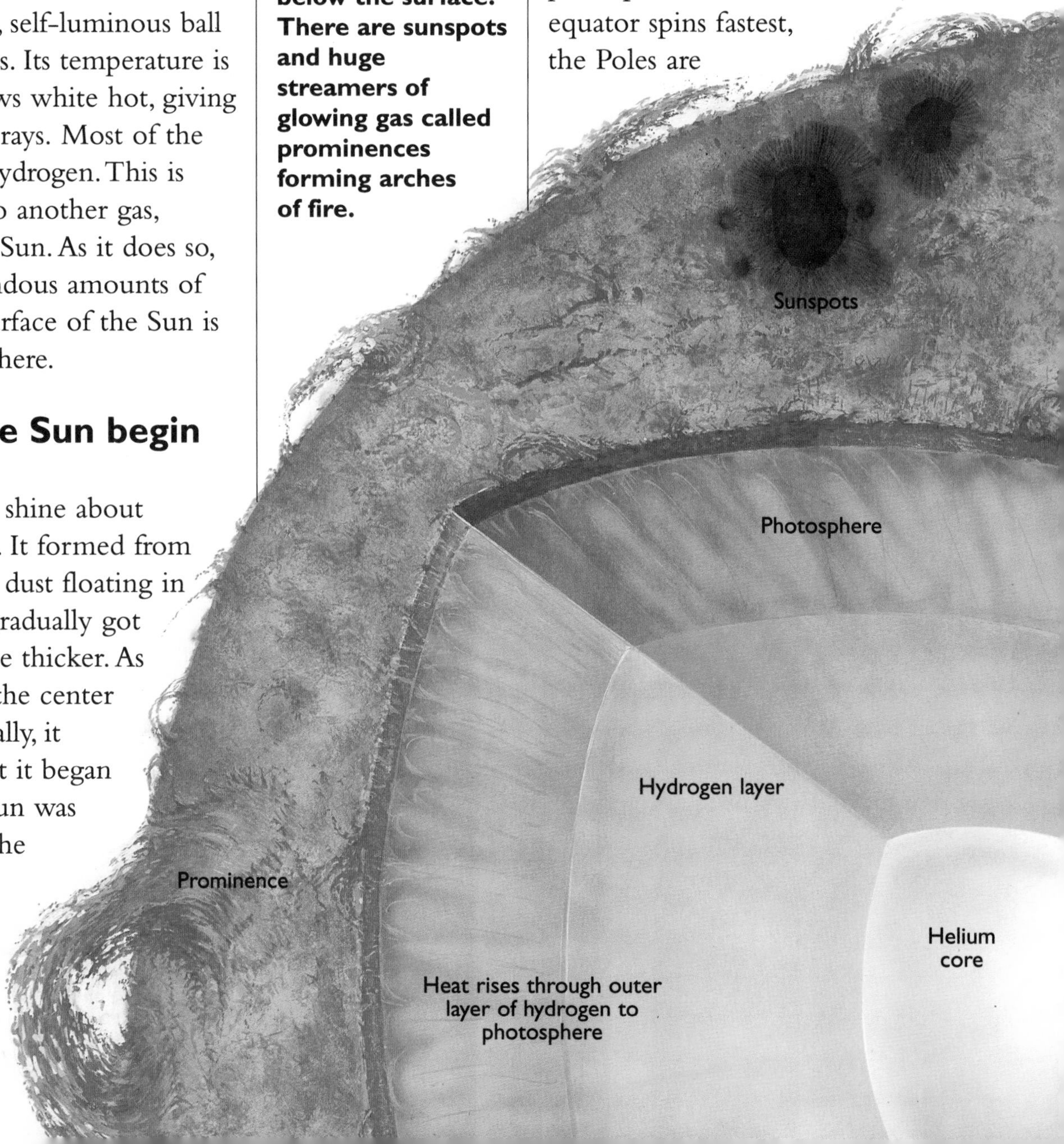

Sunspots

Photosphere

Hydrogen layer

Prominence

Helium core

Heat rises through outer layer of hydrogen to photosphere

slowest. Also, as the Earth moves around the Sun with the Moon, so the Sun moves around the center of the Galaxy, taking the Earth and the rest of the Solar System with it.

What happens during an eclipse of the Sun?

The Moon moves in front of the Sun during an eclipse of the Sun. It gets dim outside, and the Sun appears to get smaller, like a new moon. In a total eclipse, the Sun disappears for a short time and it becomes dark and cold outside. During an eclipse of the Moon, the Moon seems to get smaller and may disappear. This is because the Earth moves in front of the Sun, and its shadow falls on the Moon.

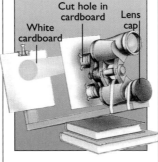

WARNING

■ It is very dangerous to look directly at the Sun.

■ A person who looks directly at the Sun through binoculars or a telescope can be blinded for life.

■ NEVER look at the Sun in this way. Use binoculars to project an image of the Sun onto some cardboard.

Cut hole in cardboard
White cardboard
Lens cap

What are sunspots?

Sunspots, looking like darker patches, appear and disappear on the surface of the Sun. Chinese astronomers studied them as early as 300 B.C. European astronomers were puzzled by sunspots. Because they believed the Sun was a "perfect sphere" in the heavens, they denied that there were any "imperfections" on its surface.

Where is the Sun hottest?

At the center. Here, where the nuclear reactions that keep the Sun shining are going on, the temperature is 27 million degrees F (15 million degrees C). The surface temperature is only 10,000°F (5,600°C)—56 times the temperature of boiling water!

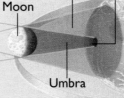

Total eclipse seen here
Penumbra
Moon
Sun
Sunlight
Umbra
Earth
Moon's orbit

Will the Sun grow hotter or colder?

The surface temperature of the Sun is about 10,000°F (5,600°C). The Sun is an "average" star, in terms of its size and brightness. Billions of years from now, it will swell up to become a "red giant" perhaps a hundred times its present size. The Earth itself may even be engulfed by the gigantic Sun. In time, the red giant Sun will shrink and become a tiny, very dense star called a "white dwarf." As its life ends, it will gradually cool and become invisible.

▲ When the Moon passes between the Earth and the Sun, it casts a shadow and causes an eclipse. Within the central shadow, or umbra, the Sun is completely hidden.

Who first said the Earth travels around the Sun?

The Polish astronomer Nicolaus Copernicus published a book in 1543 that upset many people's ideas about the universe. Copernicus declared that the old theory that the Earth was the center of the universe was wrong. In his book he showed a drawing of the Solar System, with the Sun at its center and the six known planets circling it. Many people were alarmed by these new ideas, but modern astronomy was built on the foundations of Copernicus's theory.

THE MOON

How big is the Moon?

The Moon is 2,159 miles (3,476 km) across—about the same width as Australia. Its total area is less than four times the size of Europe.

Where does the Moon come from?

Scientists believe that the Moon formed when the Solar System was formed, at the same time as the Earth. This was about 4.6 billion years ago.

Why is the Moon covered in craters?

There are craters on Earth. They are made by meteorites crashing from space, and also by volcanoes. The same kinds of craters occur on the Moon. The action of the weather smoothes out most of the craters on Earth. However, there is no weather on the Moon, so its craters have never changed and never will.

How does the Moon stay up in the sky?

The Moon is pulled by the Earth's gravity, just like anything that falls to the ground. It moves around the Earth in a path, or orbit, that is almost circular. In this way, it keeps about the same distance from the Earth. It is an average of 239,000 miles (385,000 km) away, or thirty times the diameter of the Earth. If the Earth were an orange, the Moon would be about the size of a cherry and 6 feet (2 m) away.

I
2
3
4

▲ The Moon may have been made by a space collision, when a planet-sized body smashed into the Earth (1). Debris formed a cloud orbiting the Earth (2 and 3) which finally formed the solid Moon (4).

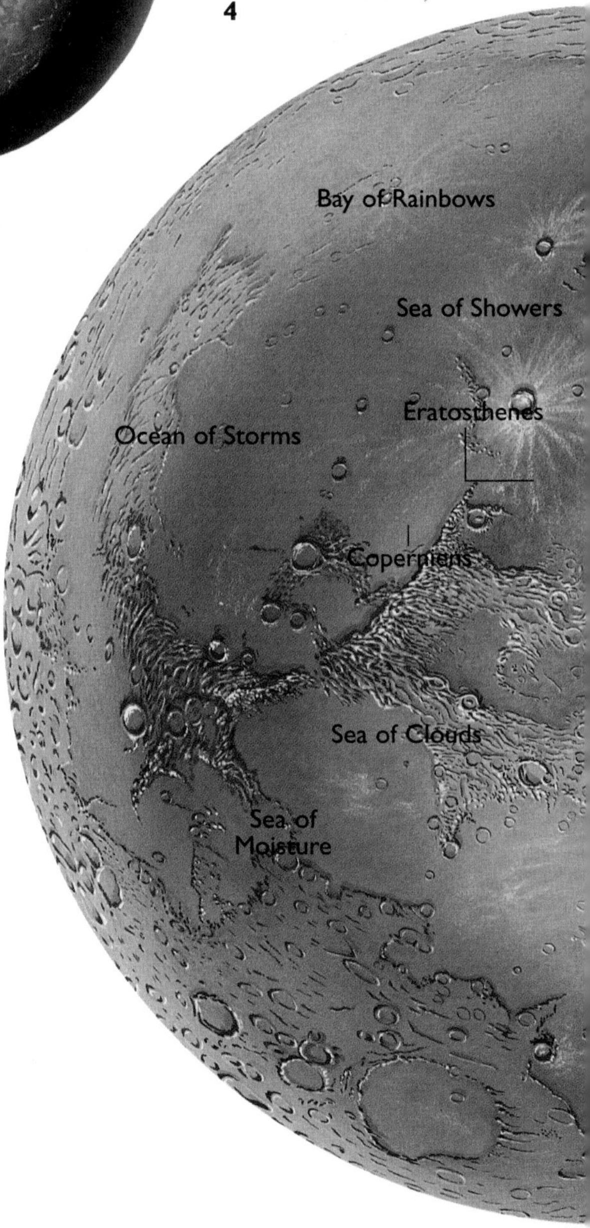

▶ The near side of the Moon, the side we see from Earth, has huge plains, called maria ("seas" in Latin). These plains were formed by floods of volcanic lava. There are also huge craters.

Bay of Rainbows

Sea of Showers

Ocean of Storms

Eratosthenes

Copernicus

Sea of Clouds

Sea of Moisture

Why does the shape of the Moon change in the sky?

Every four weeks, the Moon goes from a crescent-shaped new moon to a round full moon and back again. These changes are called phases. The Moon does not actually change shape. As it moves around the Earth, different parts become lit up by the Sun. We see only the lit-up parts.

How high could you jump on the Moon?

You could jump higher on the Moon than on Earth because your body would weigh six times less there. This is because the Moon's

The Moon's gravity isn't as strong as Earth's. You would be about six times lighter on the Moon. So you could jump six times higher—but only without a space suit.

gravity is one-sixth of the gravity on Earth. However, this doesn't mean that you could jump six times as high as you can on Earth, because you would have to wear a heavy and bulky spacesuit to stay alive.

Why is the Moon lifeless?

The Moon is only 2,159 miles (3,476 km) across. Its gravity is too weak to hold down the gases left in its atmosphere after it formed. They floated away into space, leaving the Moon a dead, airless world.

How fast does the Moon spin?

The Moon spins once each time it goes around the Earth. That means it spins once every 29.25 days—the same time it takes to complete one orbit around the Earth.

Can we see all of the Moon?

One side of the Moon is always turned away from the Earth—the dark side of the Moon. As the newly formed Moon cooled, the Earth's gravity pulled at it. This slowed the Moon's spin and raised a bulge on the side nearer the Earth. Because the Moon spins once as it orbits, this same side always faces Earth.

How does the Moon affect the Earth?

The pull of the Moon causes the rise and fall of the ocean tides. The Moon can also black out the Sun's light during an eclipse. When this happens, a black shadow covers part of the Earth, which darkens.

Sea of Serenity

Sea of Crises

Sea of Tranquility

Sea of Fertility

Sea of Nectar

Southern Sea

MOON FACTS

■ Before spacecraft flew around the Moon, no human had ever seen the far side.

■ Because the Moon has no wind or weather, footprints left by astronauts will remain undisturbed forever.

■ Craters on the Moon were formed by smaller bodies hitting the surface. The far side of the Moon has far more craters than the near side.

■ Moon rock is older than any rock yet found on Earth. The oldest Moon rock found is 300 million years older than any rock found on Earth.

■ The Moon is pretty small. It is only 2,159 mi. (3,476 km) across, less than the width of the U.S.

THE PLANETS

How were the planets formed?

The Sun and its planets were formed at about the same time. A whirling cloud of gas and dust collected in space. It grew denser and denser as gravity squeezed the gas and dust together. Most of the cloud formed the Sun. What was left over became the planets.

Who are the planets named after?

All the planets, except for one, are named after gods and goddesses in Greek or Roman legends. For example, the biggest planet, Jupiter, is named after the Roman king of the gods. The exception is our planet, which we call Earth. This is because the other planets were thought to be in heaven, like the gods, and our planet lay beneath, like the earth. Five of the planets can be seen with the unaided eye and were named thousands of years ago. They are Jupiter, Saturn, Mars, Venus, and Mercury. Uranus was found in 1781, Neptune in 1846, and Pluto in 1930.

If the Earth were the size of an orange, the Moon would be the size of a cherry.

▼ The nine planets of the Solar System move in orbits at different distances from the Sun. By far the biggest are the giant planets Jupiter and Saturn. Four planets have rings.

What is the difference between a planet and a moon?

A planet is a world that goes around the Sun. A moon is a smaller world that goes around a planet. All except two of the planets have moons. The Earth and Pluto have only one, whereas Jupiter has sixteen. Mercury and Venus have none.

What is the Solar System?

The Solar System is made up of the Sun and all the bodies that go around the Sun. These are the planets and their moons, the asteroids or minor planets, meteoroids, and comets. Each

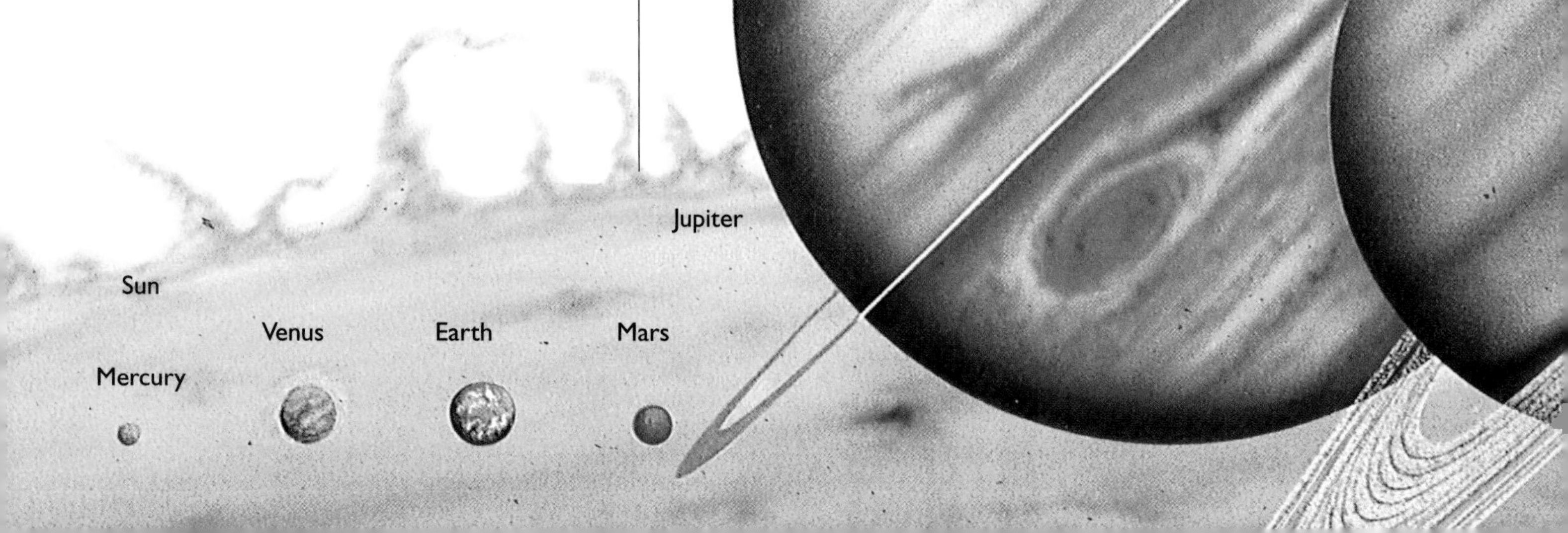

Sun

Mercury

Venus

Earth

Mars

Jupiter

moves in a particular path or orbit around the Sun. The Sun's force of gravity holds all these bodies together in the Solar System because it is bigger than they are.

How many planets are there?

The Sun has nine planets. They are Mercury, which is closest to the Sun, followed by Venus, Earth, Mars, Jupiter, Saturn, Uranus, Neptune, and finally Pluto. Pluto is usually the most distant planet, but at the moment it is closer to the Sun than Neptune and will be until 1999.

Which is the smallest planet?

Pluto is the smallest planet. Its diameter is 1,398 miles (2,250 km). This is about two-thirds the size of our Moon and only twice the size of the largest asteroid.

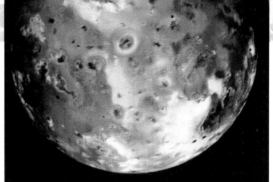

▶ Io is a small moon of Jupiter. It has active volcanoes. Jupiter has 15 other known moons.

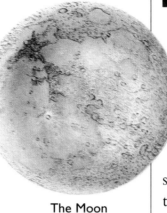

The Moon

Pluto

Which is the biggest planet?

The biggest planet is Jupiter. Its diameter is 88,695 miles (142,800 km), more than eleven times the diameter of the Earth. In volume, Jupiter is more than 1,300 times the size of the Earth! Jupiter is so massive that it weighs 2½ times as much as the other eight planets put together.

Which planet has the most moons?

Saturn has at least 18 moons. A moon is a small world going around a planet. It is held in orbit by the planet's gravity.

FACTS ABOUT THE PLANETS			
PLANET	Distance from the Sun in mi.	Diameter at equator in mi.	Time taken for 1 orbit
■ Mercury	36 million	3,030	88 days
■ Venus	67 million	7,518	224 days
■ Earth	93 million	7,922	365.25 days
■ Mars	142 million	4,220	687 days
■ Jupiter	483 million	88,695	11.9 years
■ Saturn	886 million	74,534	29.5 years
■ Uranus	1.78 billion	32,298	84 years
■ Neptune	2.79 billion	30,062	164.8 years
■ Pluto	3.66 billion	1,398	247.7 years

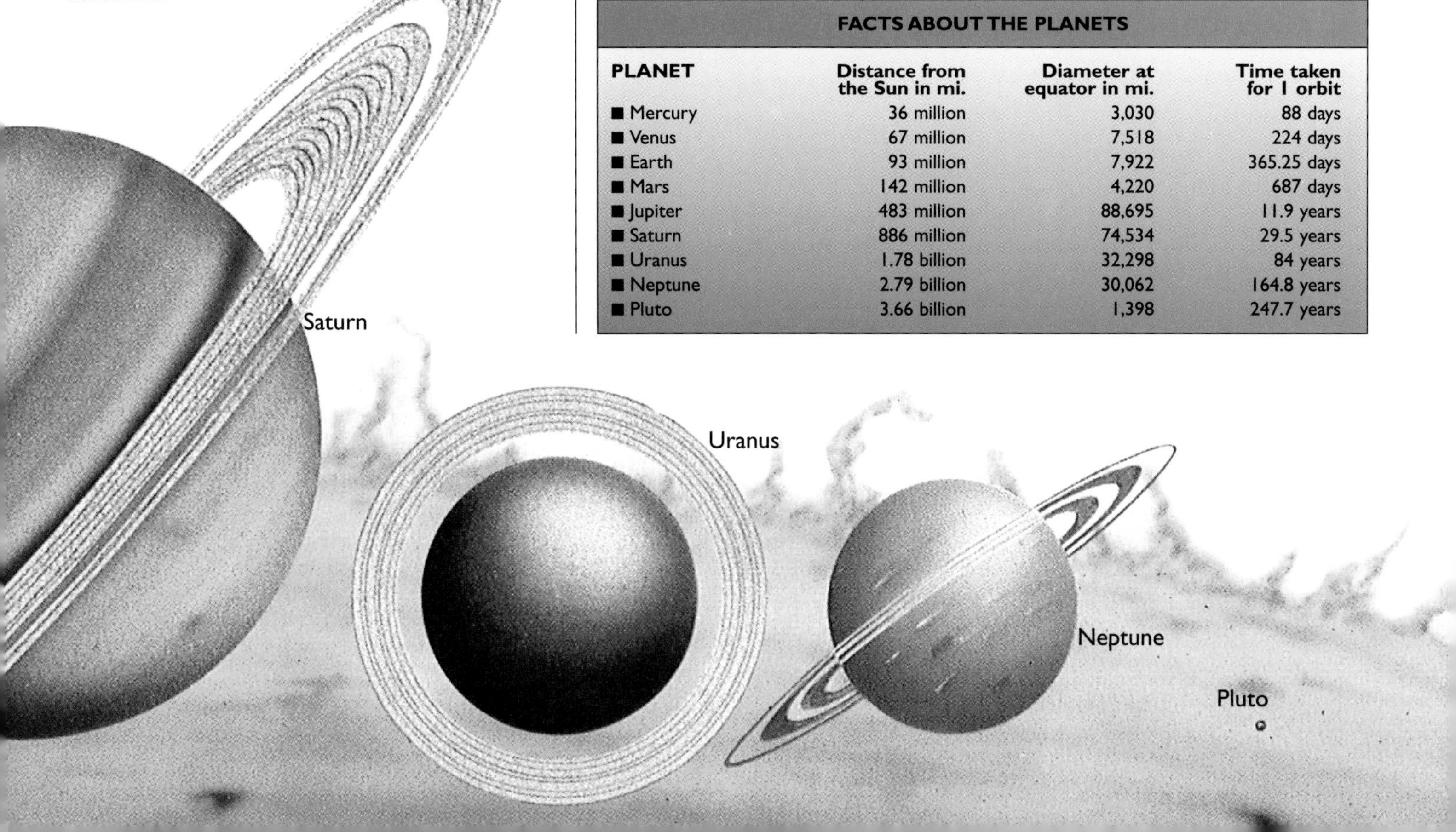

Saturn

Uranus

Neptune

Pluto

Where does the Solar System end?

The most distant planet, Pluto, is often thought to be at the edge of the Solar System. Its orbit takes it an average distance of 3.7 billion miles (5.9 billion km) from the Sun. However, some comets are thought to travel halfway to the nearest star—a distance of about two light-years. This would make the Solar System about four light-years across, which is nearly 27 trillion miles (40 trillion km).

The word "planet" comes from the Greek word *planetes*, which means "wanderer." The Greeks saw "wandering" stars in the night sky.

Where are the inner and outer planets?

The inner planets are the four planets nearest to the Sun. They are Mercury, Venus, Earth, and Mars, all made of rock and metal. The five other planets —Jupiter, Saturn, Uranus, Neptune, and Pluto—are farther away from the Sun and are called the outer planets. These, except Pluto, are gaseous.

▼ The planets and asteroids go around the Sun in flattened circles, or ellipses.

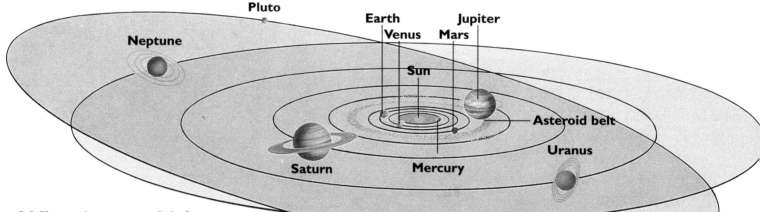

Pluto
Neptune
Earth
Venus
Jupiter
Mars
Sun
Asteroid belt
Saturn
Mercury
Uranus

What is an orbit?

An orbit is the circular or oval path that something follows as it moves through space. The planets move in orbits around the Sun, and moons travel in orbits around planets. Satellites orbit the Earth. To get into orbit around the Earth, a spacecraft has to fly out into space beyond the atmosphere, where it is partly free from the Earth's gravity.

Which planets have rings around them?

Four planets have rings around them —Jupiter, Saturn, Uranus, and Neptune. The rings are thin belts of rocks orbiting the planets. Saturn's rings make it the most beautiful planet in the sky.

▼ The four giant planets all have rings. Saturn has the biggest ring system.

Jupiter

Saturn

Uranus

Neptune

Which planet is so hot that lead would melt there?

The hottest planet is not Mercury, the planet nearest the Sun. It is Venus, the second nearest. It is very hot on Venus because, unlike Mercury, Venus has an atmosphere. The atmosphere acts somewhat like the windows in a greenhouse and helps to heat the surface of the planet. The temperature there is about 890°F (475°C), which is hot enough to melt several metals, including tin, lead, and zinc. No plants or animals could live on the scorching, rocky surface.

Which planet turns so slowly that one day lasts two years?

Mercury is so near the Sun that the Sun has slowed its rotation. It spins so slowly that one complete day on Mercury—from one sunrise to the next—takes 176 Earth days. This is equal to two of Mercury's years, which are 88 Earth days long. On Mercury, you would have two birthdays every day!

Does a planet have to be bigger than a moon?

A moon is always smaller than the planet around which it moves. A smaller body always orbits around a larger body, because the larger body has a greater force of gravity. However, not all moons are smaller than all planets. Our Moon and six other moons of the outer planets are all bigger than the tiny planet Pluto. But Pluto may once have been a moon of Neptune.

PLANET FACTS

■ Mercury holds two records: it is the planet with the longest day and the shortest year.

■ Mars has two small rocky moons, Deimos and Phobos.

■ There are valleys on Mars that look like dried-up riverbeds.

▶ **Mars is a rocky planet and seems to be without life. It has an ice cap, mountains, and craters.**

▲ **Mercury is the planet closest to the Sun. It is heavily scarred with craters, probably formed many millions of years ago.**

What is the Red Planet?

The Red Planet is the fourth planet from the Sun, Mars. When it nears the Earth, it looks like a bright red star in the sky. Mars looks red because its surface is made of red soil and rock. Even its sky is red, because red dust floats in the atmosphere.

Which planet spins faster than any other?

The planet that spins the fastest is also the largest planet— Jupiter. It spins once around every 9 hours 50 minutes, 2½ times as fast as the Earth. A point on Jupiter's equator is moving around the planet's center at a speed of about 28,000 miles (45,000 km) per hour. This is so fast that it makes Jupiter bulge in the middle.

Where is the highest mountain in the Solar System?

There were once volcanoes on Mars. A volcanic mountain, Olympus Mons, rises 14 miles (23 km) above the surface. This is the highest mountain in the Solar System.

Which planet could float on water?

If you could take the planets and place them in a vast ocean of water, most of them would sink immediately. However, one would float. This planet is Saturn, which is the second largest planet in the Solar System. Because it is made mostly of gas and liquid, it is less dense, or lighter than water and would float. All the other planets are more dense.

Are there any living things on other planets?

The Moon, and the planets and their moons, do not have air like our world. They are also very hot or very cold. People could not live there, neither could the animals and plants that live on Earth. Astronauts that went to the Moon did not find life there, nor did the *Viking* space probes that landed on Mars. In 1996 some scientists became excited when they discovered what they thought might be fossil bacteria on Mars. But other scientists were more doubtful.

It is very unlikely that there are living things anywhere else in the Solar System.

Are there any more planets beyond Pluto?

Astronomers believe that there may be an unknown planet beyond Pluto. They have searched for it with telescopes, but the mystery planet has not been found. If the planet does exist, it could disturb the paths of space probes moving among and beyond the outer planets. In this way, astronomers may discover the planet.

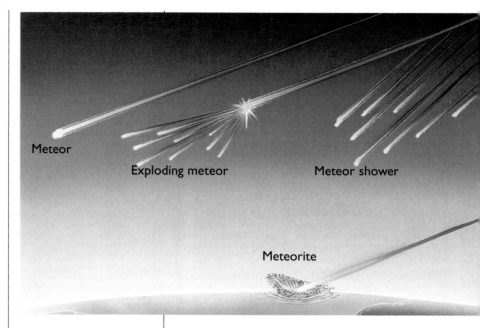

▲ A meteor shower is seen when the Earth passes through a swarm of meteoroids—particles thrown out from the crumbly heart of a comet.

COMET FACTS

■ Some comets take thousands of years to go around the Sun once.

■ Comet Encke, first seen in 1786, hurries around the Sun in just over three years!

■ The most famous comet is named after Edmund Halley (1656–1742), an English scientist.

■ Halley believed that comets seen in 1531, 1607, and 1682 were in fact the same one. He predicted it would return in 1758. And Halley's Comet did, on Christmas Day!

What are shooting stars and meteorites?

A shooting star looks like a star that suddenly shoots across the night sky. It lasts only a second or two before disappearing. It is in fact not a star at all but a small particle of rock that strikes the Earth's atmosphere from space. It moves so fast that it heats up as it moves through the air, becoming white hot before burning away. A particle or piece of rock that moves through space is called a meteoroid. If it burns up in the atmosphere, it is called a shooting star or meteor. Some meteoroids are big enough to survive their fiery descent and strike the ground. These are called meteorites.

What is a comet?

A comet is thought to be composed of small rocks and dust particles cemented together by frozen gas and ice. It orbits around the Sun and appears to hang in the sky like the Moon. It is actually moving through space at about the same speed as a planet moves around the Sun.

Are comets dangerous?

We have little reason to fear comets. The Earth has even passed through the tail of Halley's Comet with no apparent damage.

Where are asteroids found?

Asteroids are small worlds that orbit the Sun as planets do. They are also called minor planets. There are thousands of asteroids, most only a few miles across. They lie in a huge belt around the Sun between Mars and Jupiter.

Could an asteroid hit the Earth?

Some asteroids move in orbits that can bring them close to the Earth, so collisions are possible. Some scientists believe that an asteroid hitting the Earth led to the climate changes that caused the the extinction of the dinosaurs about 65 million years ago.

▶ **The asteroid belt between Mars and Jupiter contains about 100,000 bodies bigger than ½ mile (1 km) across. The orbits of some unusual asteroids are shown here.**

▶ **Halley's Comet crosses the orbit of the Earth once every 76–77 years. It was last close to us in 1986.**

Saturn's orbit

Jupiter's orbit

Hidalgo

Apollo

The Trojans

Icarus

Mars' orbit

Earth's orbit

Asteroid belt

Juno

Hektor

Ceres

Our Moon (to scale)

Psyche

Eunomia

Vesta

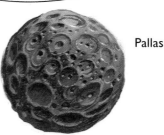
Pallas

Davida

STARS AND GALAXIES

Where do stars form?

Stars form in clouds of gas and dust, as the Sun did. Far away in space, there are huge clouds of gas and dust called nebulae. Some nebulae are luminous and shine with light, and it is there that stars are forming. This process is going on right now.

How far away is the nearest star?

The nearest star to the Earth is the Sun. It is 93 million miles (152 million km) away, or nearly 12,000 times the diameter of the Earth.

How far away is the most distant star?

Our Sun is one of about 100,000 million stars that make up the galaxy. The most distant stars on the other side of the galaxy to the Sun are about 80,000 light-years away. However, there are millions of other galaxies much farther away, each containing millions of stars.

Which is the brightest star?

The brightest star in the sky is the Sun. It outshines all the other stars because it is so near to us. The brightest star in the night sky is Sirius. It actually produces 25 times as much light as the Sun. Other stars are even brighter, and may be as much as a million times more luminous than the Sun. They look fainter than Sirius because they are much farther away.

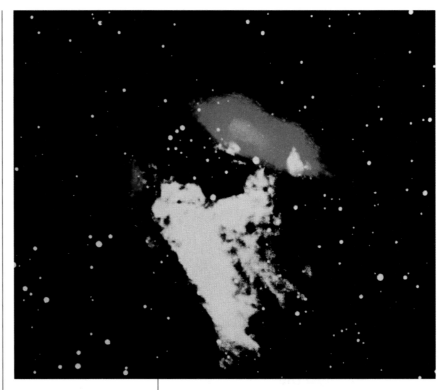

▲ An infrared photograph of the Swan Nebula, a cloud of young stars and gas in the constellation Sagittarius.

Did you know that stars are being born all the time? Young stars begin their lives in star-nurseries called clusters.

How many stars are there in the sky?

On a very clear night, far from a town, you could count about 2,000 stars in the sky. From all points on the Earth, about 6,000 stars can be seen in all. With a telescope, many fainter stars reveal themselves. There are millions upon millions of stars in the universe.

Is the Sun an unusual kind of star?

To us on Earth, the Sun looks enormous and very bright. But this is only because we live so close to the Sun. Compared with most stars, it is of average size and brightness and it is not in any way unusual. There are millions of other "suns," many bigger and much brighter.

What is a supernova?

A supernova is a star that suddenly flares up, becoming millions of times brighter. It gets so bright that it may be seen during the day, but it soon fades. A supernova is a very rare sight, because it is the explosion that marks the end of a large star. The last supernova observed in our galaxy was seen by Johannes Kepler (1571–1630) in 1604.

Why do the stars twinkle?

The light from a star has to get through the atmosphere before it reaches our eyes. The atmosphere contains moving layers of air. The layers bend the path of the starlight a little, and make the star appear to twinkle. In fact, stars shine steadily.

▼ **Star maps show the constellations of the Northern and Southern Hemispheres. Each major constellation has a name. Some of these are listed in the box (right).**

Some Northern Hemisphere constellations

CONSTELLATION FACTS

Northern Hemisphere
1 *Pegasus*, Flying Horse
2 *Pisces*, Fish
3 *Aries*, Ram
4 *Cygnus*, Swan
5 *Aquila*, Eagle
6 *Cassiopeia*, Lady in Chair
7 *Perseus*, Champion
8 *Taurus*, Bull
9 *Orion*, Hunter
10 *Draco*, Dragon
11 *Polaris*, Pole Star
12 *Ursa Minor*, Little Bear
13 *Hercules*, Hercules
14 *Corona Borealis*, Crown
15 *Bootes*, Herdsman
16 *Ursa Major*, Great Bear
17 *Lynx*, Lynx
18 *Gemini*, Twins
19 *Cancer*, Crab
20 *Canes Venatici*, Hunting Dogs
21 *Leo*, Lion

Southern Hemisphere
1 *Aquarius*, Water-Bearer
2 *Phoenix*, Phoenix
3 *Grus*, Crane
4 *Orion*, Hunter
5 *Lepus*, Hare
6 *Columba*, Dove
7 *Tucana*, Tucan
8 *Sagittarius*, Archer
9 *Volans*, Flying Fish
10 *Triangulum Australe*, Southern Triangle
11 *Ara*, Altar
12 *Scorpius*, Scorpion
13 *Crux*, Cross
14 *Lupus*, Wolf
15 *Hydra*, Water Snake
16 *Corvus*, Crow
17 *Libra*, Scales
18 *Crater*, Cup
19 *Virgo*, Virgin

▲ **Very few star patterns look like the things they are named after. Leo, the Lion, is one that does.**

What are constellations?

The stars form patterns in the night sky that never change. These patterns are called constellations. Long ago, people gave them names like the Swan, the Scorpion, the Big Dipper, and Orion the Hunter because the patterns resembled animals, familiar objects, people, or gods. We still use their names for the constellations. Sometimes the names are in Latin. The Swan, for example, is Cygnus.

Some Southern Hemisphere constellations

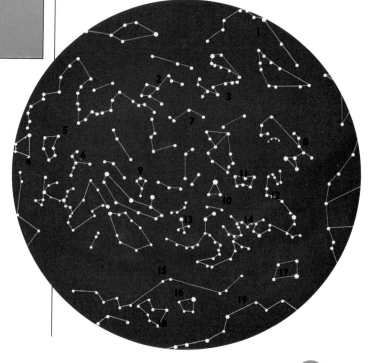

What is the Milky Way?

The Milky Way is the name of the great band of stars that stretches across the night sky. When we look at the Milky Way, we are looking into the vast group of millions of stars that make up our galaxy.

What is a galaxy?

A galaxy is a great group of millions of stars. Our galaxy, the Milky Way, is shaped like a flat disk with spiral arms of stars. It is about 100,000 light-years across. There are millions of other galaxies in the universe. They form groups and even larger superclusters.

Why can stars be seen only at night?

Stars cannot be seen during the day because the Sun is so bright. Its light spreads out over the sky, making it appear blue. The stars are still there in the sky, but our eyes adjust to the bright blue of the sky and cannot make out the fainter stars. At dawn and dusk, when the sunlight is pale, the brightest stars and planets can be seen quite clearly.

▲ The Milky Way stretches across the sky like a milky cloud, spinning in space.

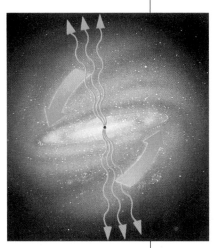

▲ Quasars are incredibly bright. Perhaps a black hole at the center of these mysterious distant galaxies is sucking in stars, sending matter spinning around, and giving off enormous energy.

What is a quasar?

Quasars are mysterious galaxies that astronomers discovered in 1960. They are sources of light or radio waves and are the most distant objects known.

What is the most distant object we can see without a telescope?

The great spiral galaxy of Andromeda can be seen as a faint cloud in space. It is a spiral galaxy, like our own Milky Way, made up of millions of stars. Andromeda is 2.2 million light-years away and is the farthest object visible from Earth with the naked eye.

Where are we in our own galaxy?

The Milky Way is made up of many millions of stars, of which our own Sun is just one. If you imagine the galaxy as a wheel lying on its side, with the hub as its center, the Sun lies roughly two-thirds of the way out toward the rim.

SPACE EXPLORATION

Who first used a telescope to study the heavens?

The Italian scientist Galileo learned of the invention of the telescope and built one for himself in about 1610. With his telescope, Galileo discovered a universe far larger than anyone had imagined. He could see "ten times as many stars." He discovered four of the moons of Jupiter. Turning his telescope on our own Moon, he saw that it had a rough surface, pitted with craters.

▲ **Galileo Galilei (1564–1642) was one of the great scientists of his day. He built his own telescopes to study the night sky.**

Which was the first planet to be discovered?

The five nearest planets to us— Mercury, Venus, Mars, Jupiter, and Saturn—have been known since prehistoric times. In 1781, the British astronomer Sir William Herschel accidentally discovered a new planet while searching the stars with his telescope. It was later named Uranus. In fact, Uranus can be seen with the naked eye, but no one had realized that it was a planet.

▲ **Yuri Gagarin, the world's first cosmonaut.**

◀ **William Herschel (1738–1822) discovered the planet Uranus through a home-made telescope.**

Who took the first photographs of the Moon?

John Draper of the United States took the first astronomical photographs of the Moon in 1840, not long after the invention of photography. Now, astronomers view distant stars with powerful computers and cameras.

A photographic plate exposed for several hours can collect the very faint light from a star too distant to be seen through the largest optical telescope.

Who was the first man in space?

A Russian cosmonaut (astronaut) named Yuri Gagarin (1934–1968) made the first manned spaceflight. He was launched into space aboard the spacecraft *Vostok 1* on April 12, 1961, and made one orbit of the Earth before landing 1 hour 48 minutes later.

Who first stepped on the Moon?

The American astronaut Neil Armstrong (born 1930) became the first person to set foot on the Moon on July 21, 1969. He was commander of *Apollo 11*. As he descended from the lunar module of the spacecraft and stepped onto the Moon, he said these now famous words: "That's one small step for man, one giant leap for mankind." Armstrong was followed a little later by Edwin Aldrin (born 1930), his fellow astronaut.

When did the first spacecraft go into space?

The first rocket to go beyond the atmosphere into space was an American rocket in 1949. But the first true spacecraft was the first satellite to go into orbit around the Earth. This was the Russian satellite *Sputnik 1*, which was launched into space on October 4, 1957. It had no person or animal aboard. Instead it sent information back to Earth by radio. The second satellite, *Sputnik 2*, carried a dog into space.

How fast does a spacecraft travel?

To reach the Moon or any of the planets, a spacecraft has to be launched away from the Earth at a speed called the escape velocity. This is 6.8 miles (11 km) per second or 24,845 miles (40,000 km) per hour—fast enough to go once around the world in an hour. This speed is reached high above the Earth, and the spacecraft then coasts on through space to its destination. If it does not reach escape velocity, it will either fall back to Earth or go into orbit.

What do satellites do?

A satellite is any body or object that moves around another. However, most people use the word "satellite" to mean an artificial object that orbits the Earth. These satellites make scientific observations of space and of the Earth below, sending back pictures that help us to forecast the weather, for example. Satellites also send television programs and telephone calls from one continent to another.

SPACE FACTS

- *Luna 2* (USSR 1959) crashed into the Moon.
- *Luna 9* (USSR 1966) was the first spacecraft to soft-land on the Moon.
- *Venera 4* (USSR 1967) landed on Venus.
- *Salyut 1* (USSR 1971) was the world's first space station.
- *Vikings 1* and 2 (USA 1976) made the first landings on Mars.
- *Voyager 1* (USA) flew past Jupiter in 1979 and Saturn in 1980.
- *Voyager 2* (USA) flew past Uranus in 1986 and Neptune in 1989.
- *Galileo* probe (USA) entered Jupiter's atmosphere in 1995.

▼ Shown here are three satellites: *Meteosat*, a weather satellite; *IRAS*, which studied comets; and *Solar Max*, which looked at the Sun.

Meteosat

IRAS

▼ The Space Shuttle can launch satellites from its large cargo bay. It can also carry sections of a space station to be assembled by astronauts in orbit.

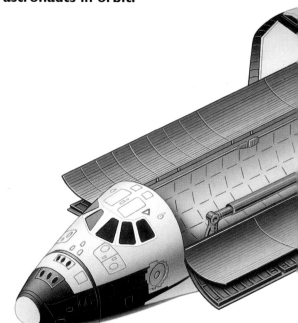

What does the Space Shuttle do?

The Space Shuttle is a reusable spacecraft. Unlike all earlier spacecraft, it can be used again and again. It takes off from Earth like a rocket, but lands like an airplane. The Space Shuttle cannot fly to the Moon or planets. It goes into orbit around the Earth. There, the crew can do scientific work, place satellites in orbit, and visit satellites and space stations in orbit. The first Space Shuttle was launched in 1981.

Solar Max

Astronauts using the toilet in space wear seatbelts. Space toilets don't flush. Everything is sucked away.

▼ **A space suit is made of layers of plastic. It provides oxygen for the person inside to breathe. It allows the astronaut to work comfortably outside the spacecraft.**

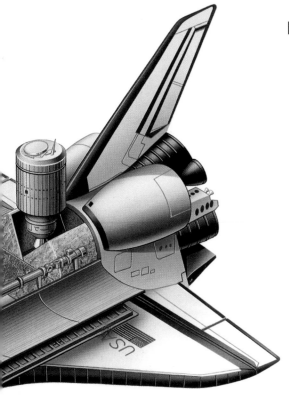

How much would you weigh in space?

If you were to travel in space, you would weigh nothing at all for most of your flight! Only when the engines were firing at the beginning and end of the flight would you have any weight. In between you would float in midair in the cabin of the spacecraft. This is because without gravity there is nothing to pull the astronaut to the floor of the cabin.

How can people live in space?

There is nothing in space to keep people alive—no air, no water, and no food. Without protection, a person would die in seconds. A spacecraft provides air, water, and food for the astronauts. Outside, they must wear space suits, which have an air or oxygen supply, drink, camera, and computers. The space suit also has cooling and heating systems, for it can be very hot or very cold in space.

15 layers of plastic

What is a space station?

A space station is a laboratory orbiting the Earth. Parts of the station are brought up by rockets and assembled in space. Teams of astronauts and scientists can live in a space station for up to a year.

How many people have stood on the Moon?

In 1969 *Apollo 11* made the historic first manned landing on the Moon. From 1969 to 1972 the United States sent seven Apollo missions to the Moon. One mission, *Apollo 13*, failed to make a landing but returned safely after an explosion on board the spacecraft. The other six missions all succeeded. In all, 12 astronauts have stood on the Moon.

What was the first real space rocket?

The first rocket that could fly fast enough and high enough to enter space was the German *V2* missile. It was first fired in October 1942, flying a distance of 125 miles (200 km) and landing within 2½ miles (4 km) of its target. After World War II the United States and the U.S.S.R. used captured *V2*s to help start their spaceflight and missile programs.

What happens to people in space?

Astronauts have stayed in space for about a year. When they return to Earth, they are a little taller. Because there is less gravity in space, their bones are less squashed together.

EARTH AND SPACE QUIZ

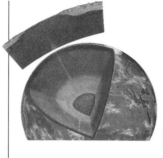

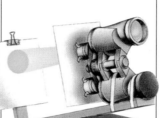

ATOMS

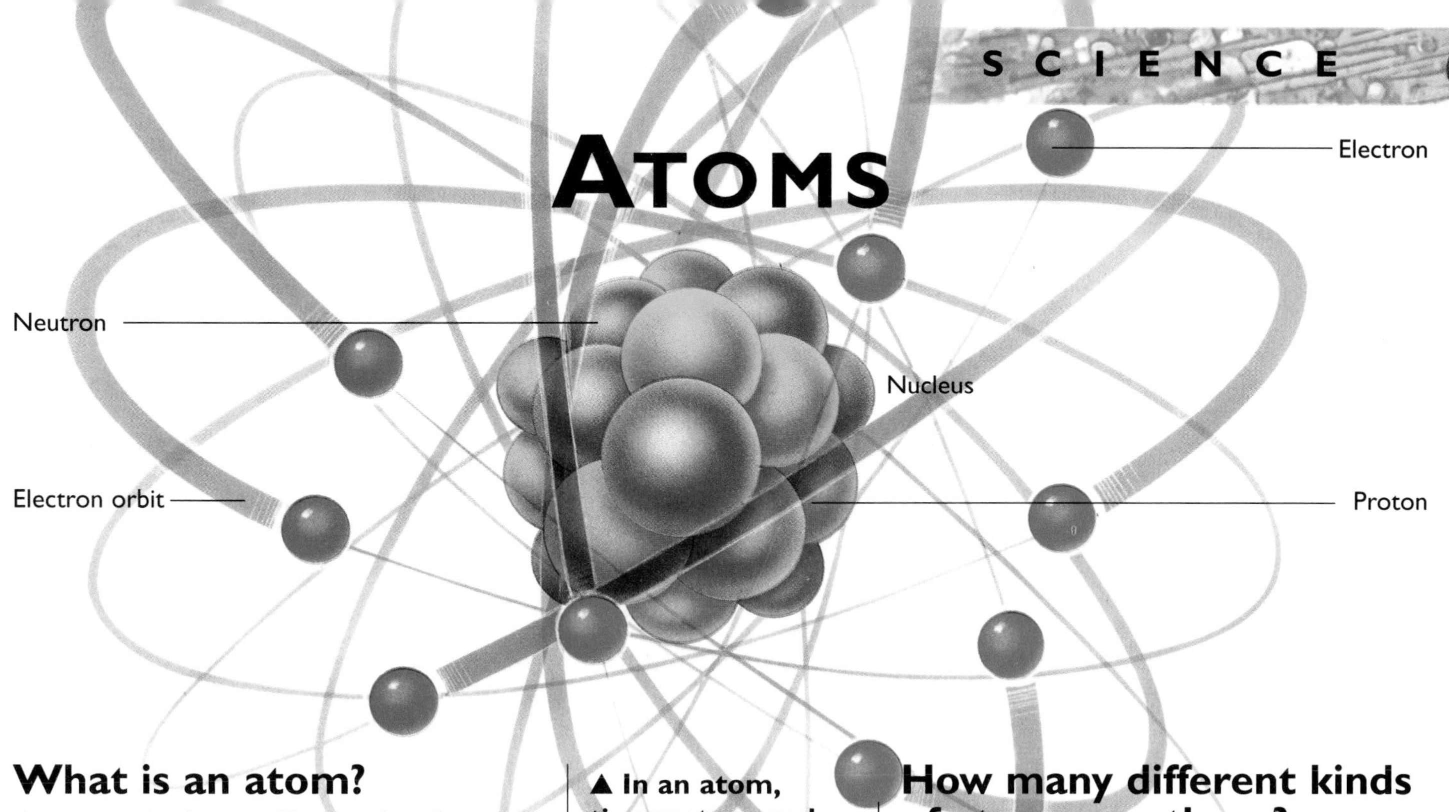

Neutron

Electron

Electron orbit

Nucleus

Proton

What is an atom?

An atom is the smallest unit of a chemical element—iron or copper, for example—to have its own recognizable identity. Scientists can tell the atoms of one element from those of another by their structure. Atoms are the building blocks of the elements, which make up all matter in the universe.

At the center of an atom is its nucleus, which is made up of tiny particles called protons and neutrons. Orbiting the nucleus are other particles called electrons, held in place by electrical charges. The arrangement of protons, neutrons, and electrons is different for each kind of atom.

How big is an atom?

Atoms are too small to be seen with the naked eye. But scientists using high-powered electron microscopes have photographed atoms. They look like fuzzy white dots.

The nucleus is ten thousand times smaller than the atom itself. Electrons are smaller still.

▲ In an atom, tiny protons and neutrons make up the center or nucleus. The particles orbiting the nucleus are called electrons.

▼ Atoms are very small. If an atom were as big as your fingernail, your hand could pick up the Earth!

How many different kinds of atoms are there?

There are 92 different chemical elements found in nature. Therefore there are 92 different kinds of atoms forming these separate elements. A few other elements and atoms have been made by scientists in the laboratory. An atom of uranium is two hundred times heavier than an atom of hydrogen, but in fact all atoms are roughly the same size. There are about two million atoms in the thickness of this page.

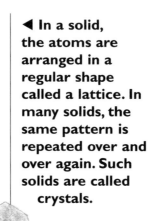

◀ In a solid, the atoms are arranged in a regular shape called a lattice. In many solids, the same pattern is repeated over and over again. Such solids are called crystals.

What are molecules?

A molecule is the smallest part of a substance that retains the nature of the substance. Take paper, for example. The thickness of each page of this book is roughly 100,000 paper molecules. If each paper molecule were broken up, it would no longer be paper, just a random group of atoms. Every molecule of a substance is made of exactly the same number of atoms linked together in exactly the same pattern.

Molecules are tiny. There are at least as many molecules in a teaspoon of water as there are teaspoonfuls of water in the Atlantic Ocean.

Who first tried to weigh atoms?

The British chemist John Dalton (1766–1844) worked out that a molecule of water always contains the same proportions of oxygen and hydrogen. He thought oxygen atoms must be heavier than hydrogen atoms. In fact an oxygen atom weighs 16 times more than an hydrogen atom.

ATOM FACTS

■ In the 400s B.C., the Greek scientist Democritus gave the name "atom" to what he thought was the smallest particle of matter.

■ In 1818 Jons Berzelius, a Swedish chemist, classified 45 different substances by their atomic weights.

■ Berzelius also suggested referring to elements by the first letter or letters of their names—for example O = oxygen.

■ Atoms are incredibly light. There are trillions of hydrogen atoms in an ounce.

■ Electrons whizz around at amazing speed. They constantly change positions as they orbit the nucleus, making billions of trips in just one millionth of a second.

Who discovered electrons?

Electrons were discovered in 1895 by Sir Joseph John Thomson (1856–1940), a British scientist. He worked at Cambridge University and was investigating the rays produced when an electric current passed through a vacuum. For this discovery he received the Nobel Prize for Physics in 1906.

Sir Joseph John Thomson

Who first split the atom?

Until the early 1900s, nobody knew how the atom was arranged. Sir J. J. Thomson thought that the atom looked something like a round fruit cake, with electrons scattered around like raisins. Ernest Rutherford, in 1911, and Niels Bohr, in 1913, put forward different ideas.

Rutherford (1871–1937), a New Zealander, discovered the nucleus of the atom and proved that the electrons were very light. Bohr (1885–1962), a Dane, devised the "sun and planets" model of particles orbiting the nucleus of the atom. Most scientists today accept this theory.

Rutherford did what the Ancient Greeks thought impossible. He split the atom, and in so doing changed one substance into another. He bombarded atoms of nitrogen gas with alpha particles. This changed them into oxygen and hydrogen atoms. Rutherford first split the atom in 1919, while working at Cambridge University in Britain.

Why does splitting the atom release so much energy?

The great scientist Albert Einstein (1879–1955) devised a formula to explain why, when an atom is split by a neutron, the mass of all the pieces is actually less than the mass of the original atom plus the neutron. Einstein's formula was $E = mc^2$. It can be explained as follows: E = energy released; m = mass lost; c^2 = the speed of light squared. The energy released in a nuclear reaction is equal to the mass lost multiplied by c^2. And c^2 is huge, for light travels at 186,000 miles (300,000 km) a second! Even if the mass m is tiny, the energy E will be very great. The value of c^2 is 300,000 multiplied by 300,000!

What is radioactivity?

A few of the heaviest atoms, being unstable by nature, can break down and change into other atoms. As this breakdown, or decay, takes place, radiation is given off. The French scientist Henri Becquerel (1852–1908) discovered radioactivity in uranium in 1896. Radioactivity occurs in nature. It also happens when the atom is split by scientists. Radioactive rays are dangerous to health because they can affect the way cells work in the body. This causes radiation sickness and can lead to serious illnesses.

▼ In 1919 the scientist Ernest Rutherford managed to split the atom. He changed nitrogen into oxygen by bombarding it with alpha particles. This important advance led the way to nuclear power.

Proton

Nitrogen-14

Alpha particle

Oxygen-17

▶ In nuclear fission, a neutron splits an atom, starting a chain reaction. In nuclear fusion, light nuclei join together, forming an atom and a neutron.

Why is nuclear energy so named?

The word "nuclear" comes from "nucleus," the core of the atom. When there is a change in the nucleus of an atom, energy is released. This is called nuclear energy. It is found naturally in the Sun and stars as well as on Earth. Scientists can also produce this energy in a nuclear power plant or a nuclear weapon.

What is the difference between nuclear fission and nuclear fusion?

Both of these are kinds of nuclear reactions. In fission a heavy nucleus (usually uranium) splits. In fusion, light nuclei fuse, or come together. Fusion produces a thermonuclear reaction and is the most powerful source of energy known. Nuclear fission is used in nuclear power plants and in atomic bombs. Fusion is used in hydrogen bombs and may one day be harnessed to provide unlimited power, using a hydrogen-like fuel called deuterium found in seawater.

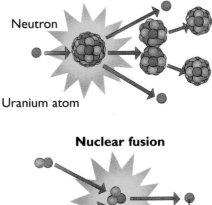

Nuclear fission

Neutron

Uranium atom

Nuclear fusion

Helium atom

Neutron

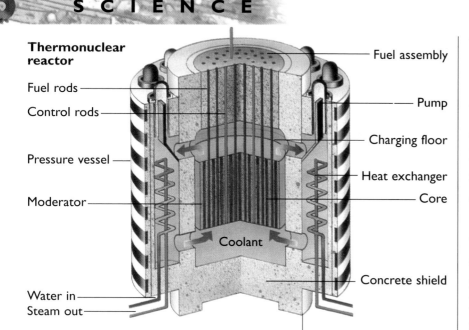

Thermonuclear reactor

Fuel rods

Control rods

Pressure vessel

Moderator

Water in

Steam out

Fuel assembly

Pump

Charging floor

Heat exchanger

Core

Coolant

Concrete shield

How does a reactor make electricity?

A nuclear power plant works in the same way as an ordinary coal- or oil-burning power plant, by heating water to make steam to drive turbines. The heat to make the steam comes from the enormous energy released by a chain reaction inside the plant's reactor.

What happened at Chernobyl?

In April 1986 there was a serious accident at the Chernobyl nuclear power plant in the Ukraine (then part of the U.S.S.R.). A reactor exploded and radioactivity poisoned plants and animals. Some people died. Many others were moved to new homes away from the area. The reactor was sealed in concrete forever.

▶ The reactor of a nuclear submarine heats water to make the steam that drives the submarine's turbine engines.

▲ The core of a thermonuclear reactor contains the uranium fuel rods. Heat from fission of the fuel converts water into steam for driving turbine generators to make electricity.

A recent kind of X-ray device is called a body scanner or C.A.T. scanner. It rotates around the patient's body, sending out a pencil-thin beam of X-rays. A computer screen shows the result—a whole slice of the body.

What is an isotope?

Nearly all elements have atoms of two or more different weights. Atoms that belong to the same element, yet have different weights, are called isotopes. For example, hydrogen has three isotopes which are called protium, deuterium, and tritium.

Some radioactive isotopes are useful in industry and medicine. For example, the radiation from the isotope cobalt 60 is used instead of X-rays to take photographs through metals and so detect cracks and other faults. Radioactive isotope scanning is used by doctors to study the workings of people's organs.

Why can nuclear submarines stay at sea for such a long time?

A nuclear submarine is driven by turbine engines which use steam heated by a nuclear reactor. The reactor uses so little fuel the submarine seldom has to return to port to refuel. The world's first nuclear-powered submarine was the U.S. Navy's *Nautilus* (1955). A lump of uranium fuel the size of an electric lightbulb provided enough energy to drive the submarine 62,100 miles (100,000 km). In 1960 *USS Triton* circled the world under water in three months without refueling.

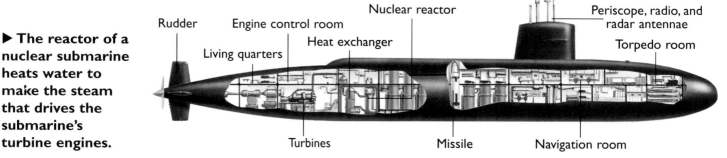

Nuclear reactor

Periscope, radio, and radar antennae

Torpedo room

Engine control room

Heat exchanger

Rudder

Living quarters

Turbines

Missile

Navigation room

ELEMENTS AND MATTER

What is an element?

An element is a substance made up of only one kind of atom. All the atoms in an element have the same atomic number, and it is impossible to break up an element into parts that have different chemical properties.

There are 92 elements found in nature. Others can be made only in the laboratory during atomic reactions. In all, 109 elements have been officially found, though scientists claim to have discovered two more.

The most common element in the Earth's crust is oxygen (about 50 percent by weight). Next comes silicon (about 28 percent by weight). Each element has a symbol that stands for its name; for example, He (helium), Cu (copper), Zn (zinc), Fe (iron). This makes it easier to write out long chemical formulas.

▶ Flame tests can identify chemical elements. Platinum wires dipped in a compound of these elements make different colors when heated by a Bunsen burner.

▼ The periodic table shows all the elements in order of atomic number. Elements of atoms with similar structures and properties are logically grouped together. The main groups are non-metals, alkali metals, transition metals, and the inner transition series metals.

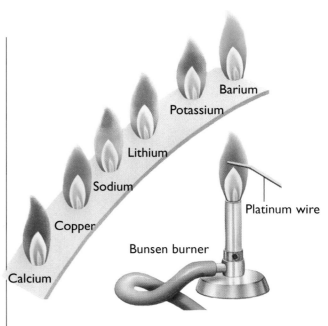

Barium
Potassium
Lithium
Sodium
Copper
Calcium
Platinum wire
Bunsen burner

What is a mineral?

Gold, silver, and mercury are examples of pure elements, but most chemical elements react with other elements so readily that they are not found alone on Earth. Instead, they combine (join) with one another as minerals. Some 3,000 minerals are known.

Alkali metals	**Transition metals**			**2** Helium **He**

Legend:
- Alkali metals
- Non-metals
- Transition metals
- Inner transition series
- **1** Hydrogen **H**

3 Lithium Li	4 Beryllium Be										5 Boron B	6 Carbon C	7 Nitrogen N	8 Oxygen O	9 Fluorine F	10 Neon Ne
11 Sodium Na	12 Magnesium Mg										13 Aluminum Al	14 Silicon Si	15 Phosphorus P	16 Sulfur S	17 Chlorine Cl	18 Argon Ar
19 Potassium K	20 Calcium Ca	21 Scandium Sc	22 Titanium Ti	23 Vanadium V	24 Chromium Cr	25 Manganese Mn	26 Iron Fe	27 Cobalt Co	28 Nickel Ni	29 Copper Cu	30 Zinc Zn	31 Gallium Ga	32 Germanium Ge	33 Arsenic As	34 Selenium Se	35 Bromine Br	36 Krypton Kr
37 Rubidium Rb	38 Strontium Sr	39 Yttrium Y	40 Zirconium Zr	41 Niobium Nb	42 Molybdenum Mo	43 Technetium Tc	44 Ruthenium Ru	45 Rhodium Rh	46 Palladium Pd	47 Silver Ag	48 Cadmium Cd	49 Indium In	50 Tin Sn	51 Antimony Sb	52 Tellurium Te	53 Iodine I	54 Xenon Xe
55 Cesium Cs	56 Barium Ba	57-71 Lanthanide series	72 Hafnium Hf	73 Tantalum Ta	74 Tungsten W	75 Rhenium Re	76 Osmium Os	77 Iridium Ir	78 Platinum Pt	79 Gold Au	80 Mercury Hg	81 Thallium Tl	82 Lead Pb	83 Bismuth Bi	84 Polonium Po	85 Astatine At	86 Radon Rn
87 Francium Fc	88 Radium Ra	89-103 Actinide series	104 Rutherfordium Rf	105 Element 105	106 Element 106	107 Element 107	108 Element 108	109 Element 109									

57 Lanthanum La	58 Cerium Ce	59 Praseodymium Pm	60 Neodymium Nd	61 Promethium Pm	62 Samarium Sm	63 Europium Eu	64 Gadolinium Gd	65 Terbium Tb	66 Dysprosium Dy	67 Holmium Ho	68 Erbium Er	69 Thulium Tm	70 Ytterbium Yb	71 Lutetium Lu
89 Actinium Ac	90 Thorium Th	91 Protactinium Pa	92 Uranium U	93 Neptunium Np	94 Plutonium Pu	95 Americium Am	96 Curium Cm	97 Berkelium Bk	98 Californium Cf	99 Einsteinium Es	100 Fermium Fm	101 Mendelevium Md	102 Nobelium No	103 Lawrencium Lr

What are the three states of matter?

The three states in which matter exists are solid, liquid, and gas. Solids have both shape and volume; their molecules are held together tightly. Liquids have volume too, but no shape; their molecules are held together less tightly, so that a liquid will flow into a container. Gases have neither volume nor shape; their molecules are free to move around and a gas will fill any container that encloses it.

When you dry your hair, warm air blown from the dryer turns the water on your hair to water vapor, which is absorbed by the air. Washing on a line dries this way too.

Can matter change its state?

Many substances change state quite easily, when heated or cooled. Water is a liquid at normal temperature but changes to a gas (water vapor) when heated. When water is cooled, it becomes a solid (ice). When ice is heated, it changes first to water and then to water vapor (steam).

What is evaporation?

When a liquid is heated, it will change to a vapor. The steam coming from a boiling kettle is water vapor: a gas. The same thing happens when hot sun shines on a wet road: water vapor can be seen rising. This is evaporation. Evaporation can be used to extract salt from salty water. Boiling causes the water to evaporate as vapor, and solid salt crystals are left behind.

▲ If you pour hot water (liquid) onto ice (solid), you see water vapor (gas) rising. Water is the only compound that is liquid in its natural form.

► These long colored streamers are crystals growing in a solution of sodium silicate (water glass).

Why does a balloon burst when you squeeze it?

If you blow up a balloon and then squeeze it, the volume of air inside is reduced, and its pressure increases. Eventually the pressure of air inside becomes so great that the balloon bursts. This is a practical demonstration of one aspect of gases' behavior discovered in 1662 by the scientist Robert Boyle (1627–1691).

How are crystals formed?

Crystals are solids found in nature in an almost endless variety of sizes and shapes. Most solid matter, including nearly all minerals and metals, are crystalline. You can watch crystals form in a sugar solution. If you add sugar to water, the sugar dissolves to make a sugar and water solution. If you heat the solution to boiling point, the water will begin to evaporate. The remaining solution will contain more and more sugar. Eventually, the water that is left will be "saturated" with sugar and the sugar will begin to form crystals.

What is a chemical reaction?

When two or more substances are put together, they may mix, as when you mix sand and water in a bucket, but remain separate substances. However, if a chemical reaction takes place, they may undergo a chemical change and become a different kind of substance. For example, when zinc is added to hydrochloric acid, a reaction occurs. The products are hydrogen gas and zinc chloride.

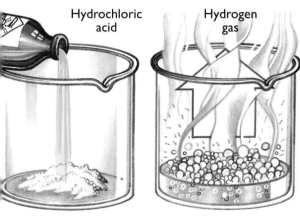

Hydrochloric acid

Hydrogen gas

Zinc

Zinc chloride

What is a compound?

A compound is a substance made up of two or more elements which cannot be separated by physical means. For example, water is a compound of hydrogen and oxygen. Each water molecule is made up of two hydrogen atoms joined to one oxygen atom by invisible forces called bonds.

Why does iron go rusty?

When a piece of unpainted iron or steel is left outside in the damp air, it soon goes rusty. Rust can eat into the surface of metal objects, such as car bodies. Rust is an example of a chemical reaction, or combination, between the iron in the car body and

► **An iron chain will rust in air or water. Air and water contain oxygen. Oxygen is very effective at taking electrons from iron atoms to form a compound called iron oxide, seen as brownish-red rust.**

◄ **Zinc is a metal. Hydrochloric acid is a liquid. When zinc and hydrochloric acid are mixed, the acid reacts with the metal to form a salt, zinc chloride.**

Salt speeds up rusting. You can test this by putting pieces of steel wool in two tubes. Fill one tube with plain tap water. Mix salt and water in the other. See which piece of steel wool rusts first. Try the same experiment with boiled water. Boiling removes air from the water. What happens to the steel wool?

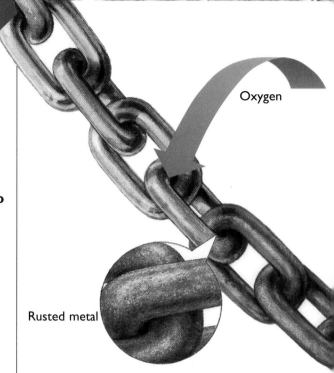

Water

Oxygen

Rusted metal

the oxygen in the air. This reaction is called oxidation and produces iron oxide, or rust. A coating of paint, or of a nonrusting metal such as chrome, prevents rust by keeping oxygen from reaching the iron.

What did Lavoisier discover?

Antoine Lavoisier, who lived from 1743 to 1794, was a French scientist and one of the founders of modern chemistry. His most important discovery was that matter cannot be destroyed during a chemical reaction, even though it may change its appearance. This is one of the basic laws of science: the law of conservation of mass. It means that the amount of matter produced by a chemical reaction must always be the same as the amount that took part in the reaction. Lavoisier was executed on the guillotine during the French Revolution.

Why are there so many carbon compounds?

Carbon is the only element whose atoms are able to join together to form chains, rings, and other more complicated bonds. This means that there is a huge number of organic (carbon) compounds; nearly four million are known.

What are diamonds made of?

Diamond is a form of carbon. It is the hardest substance known. Natural, uncut diamonds look dull and have little luster. The brilliant gems that are so valuable are made by careful cutting and polishing.

What is an acid?

An acid is a chemical compound containing hydrogen and at least one other element. For example, sulfuric acid (formula H_2SO_4) is made up of hydrogen (H), sulfur (S), and oxygen (O). Acids are normally found as liquids.

Certain acids, known as organic acids, are found in food plants. For example, citric acids are found in lemons and oranges, and malic acid is found in apples, plums, and rhubarb.

Why are some acids dangerous?

In concentrated form, some acids are so strong that they burn skin and even dissolve metals. When diluted with water, they are less harmful.

▼ Carbon occurs in three forms. In diamond, the carbon atoms are arranged in a regular framework called a lattice. In graphite, the atoms are in layers. Amorphous carbon has no regular structure.

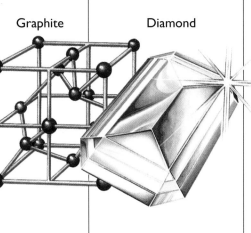

Graphite   Diamond

ACID FACTS

■ Some acids can eat through glass, and so must be kept in special containers.

■ The human body produces weak hydrochloric acid to aid the breakdown of foods during digestion.

■ Sulfuric acid is probably the most important chemical compound. It has dozens of uses, including making fertilizers and drugs.

■ When World War I began in 1914, lots of nitric acid was needed to make explosives such as nitroglycerine. German chemist Fritz Haber invented a new way to make nitric acid by heating ammonia and air.

How can you test for acid?

A simple test for an acid is to dip a piece of blue litmus paper into the liquid. Litmus paper is stained with a blue dye from a fungus which turns red in acid. If acid is present, the litmus paper will turn red.

What is a base?

A base is a substance that reacts with an acid to form a salt plus water. Most bases are the oxides or hydroxides of metals: in other words they are the products of reactions with oxygen or hydrogen. One of the most easily remembered chemical rules concerns acids and bases. It is this: Acid + Base = Salt + Water. When this happens, the acid and base are said to neutralize one another.

What is a metal?

Elements can be divided into two basic groups: metals and non-metals. Metals can be made to shine or have a luster, they conduct heat and electricity easily and they are "malleable"—they can be beaten into shape or pulled out into wire. More than 70 of the known elements are metals.

What is an alloy?

An alloy is a mixture of metals or of metal and another substance. Copper, for example, is a pure metal. When copper and tin (another pure metal) are mixed together by being heated until they melt, they make an alloy called bronze—the earliest known alloy. Copper and zinc together make brass. Steel is an alloy of iron and carbon.

Which metal most easily conducts heat and electricity?

Silver has the highest conductivity of all known metals. It is also valued for its beautiful appearance. Because it is easily worked, and has a bright, light-reflecting finish, it has been used since ancient times for making jewelry, coins, and ornaments.

Which is the most abundant metal on Earth?

The metal found most plentifully in the Earth's crust is aluminum, which makes up about 8 percent of the crust. It is found not as a pure metal but as an ore called bauxite.

Which metals give color to fireworks?

Strontium burns with a red light; copper, green; sodium, yellow; barium, green; and magnesium, a brilliant white light.

What is the air around us mostly made of?

About 78 percent (by volume) is nitrogen, about 21 percent is oxygen. Carbon dioxide, water vapor, helium, and other gases make up the rest.

Heat never stays still. It is always moving. When you stir a hot drink, heat energy moves from the drink into the spoon. That's why the spoon gets hot.

▶ A fire extinguisher smothers a fire with carbon dioxide gas. Without oxygen, the fire dies.

◀ People who make fireworks know that certain metals will give off different colors when the fireworks are burned.

▲ A modern airship is filled with helium gas. Helium is not as light as hydrogen, but it is safer because it does not burn.

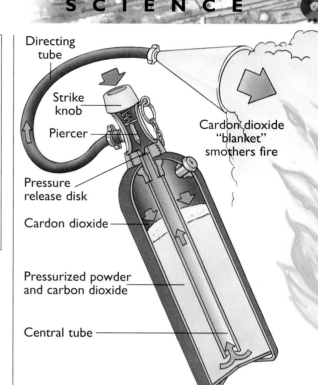

Directing tube

Strike knob

Piercer

Pressure release disk

Cardon dioxide

Pressurized powder and carbon dioxide

Central tube

Cardon dioxide "blanket" smothers fire

Why will carbon dioxide put out fires?

Carbon dioxide gas will not support combustion. Pure carbon dioxide is also heavier than air. If sprayed on a fire from a fire extinguisher it forms a blanket, cutting off the oxygen which would otherwise feed the flames.

Which gas is most suited for use in balloons and airships?

Hydrogen is the lightest gas and was used in early balloons and airships. But it has the great disadvantage of being highly flammable, and several large airships have exploded with great loss of life. Helium is second to hydrogen in lightness. Because helium does not catch fire, it is much safer and is used in modern lighter-than-air craft. The two gases helium and hydrogen make up most of the matter in the Sun and other stars.

ELECTRICITY, MAGNETISM, AND ELECTRONICS

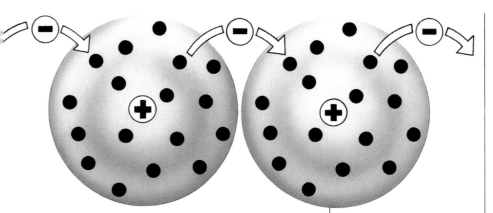

What is electricity?

Electricity is a form of energy. It is produced when electrons, tiny atomic particles, move from one atom to another. Although scientists had known that this mysterious energy existed, its workings were not understood until the secrets of the atom began to be revealed about a century ago.

Without electricity, our lives would be very different. We would have no radios or television sets, no telephones, no computers. Our streets and homes would be lit by oil or gas lamps, and we would have none of the gadgets that we take for granted today.

Who proved that lightning was electric?

In 1752, Benjamin Franklin (1706–1790) determined to find out if electricity and lightning were connected. He carried out a very dangerous experiment. He took a kite and attached to it a metal rod. Then he tied the end of the kite string to a

▲ The positively-charged (+) protons of an atom attract negatively-charged (–) electrons. Electricity flows when electrons are free to move from one atom to another.

▼ In Franklin's experiment, lightning sent an electric charge down the kite string to a key, producing a spark.

door key and went out into a thunderstorm. When he flew the kite into a thundercloud, he saw sparks flash and felt a shock as electricity from the cloud passed from the kite down the string to the key. Never try this experiment yourself!

After this, Franklin made and tested the first lightning rod. Today, all tall buildings are fitted with lightning rods, which attract lightning more readily than the buildings. The connecting cable safely carries the electricity to the ground, preventing damage to the building.

How can objects be electrically charged?

All matter is made up of atoms. Normally, each atom has the same number of electrons and protons (see page 57). The positive charge of the protons and the negative charge of the electrons cancel each other out. But if this balance is upset, the object becomes electrically charged. For example, if a balloon is rubbed with cloth, electrons pass from the cloth to the balloon. The balloon becomes negatively charged, and the cloth, having lost electrons, becomes positively charged. Unlike charges always attract each other, so the cloth clings to the balloon.

What is a conductor?

A conductor is a material through which electricity can pass. Electricity travels more easily through some materials than others. Metals are good conductors of electricity. Lightning rods are made of copper, which conducts electricity easily.

◀ **Rub a balloon against a wool or nylon sweater. This makes static electricity build up on the balloon's skin. Hold the balloon against a wall, and it should cling there.**

About 100 years ago, few people had electricity in their homes. The first electrical gadgets were dangerous, and people sometimes risked their lives using them.

▶ **Rubber is a good insulator. It has few free electrons and so does not conduct electricity well. Plastic, ceramics, and glass, also poor conductors, are used as insulators in electrical equipment.**

What are superconductors?

When made very cold, certain substances have almost no resistance to electricity; they become superconductors. This was first observed in 1911 using mercury. More than 25 other metals, including copper and various alloys, behave in the same way. Superconducting coils that allow current to flow practically nonstop are used in particle accelerators. New materials that superconduct at room temperature are being developed.

What is an insulator?

An insulator is a material that will not conduct electricity. Good insulators are diamond, glass, paper, plastic, rubber, and many gases. That is why the wires inside an electrical cable are enclosed in a rubber or plastic sheath. The plug on the end of the wire is also made of rubber or plastic. The insulating material protects us from getting a shock when we touch the cable or the plug because it does not conduct electricity easily.

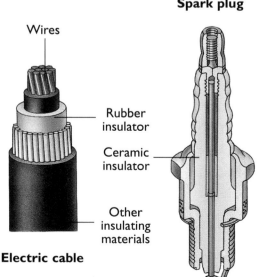

Spark plug

Wires

Rubber insulator

Ceramic insulator

Other insulating materials

Electric cable

How does electricity travel?

If you put six dominoes in a line, flat and end to end, you can do an experiment to see how electricity moves along a wire. Each domino must touch the next one. Draw back the lead domino and tap it sharply against the next in line. Watch what happens. Each domino moves just a little, except for the end one, which shoots away. The electrons in a wire move in the same way. When one end is "pushed" by an electrical force, each electron in the wire moves just a little, but together they send a fast and powerful signal along the wire.

What is an electrical circuit?

In order to flow, a current must be able to find its way around a circuit. For example, if you connect a wire from one terminal of a bell to a battery, you must also connect another wire from the second terminal back to the battery. The circuit is now complete, and the bell will work.

Who made the first battery?

Alessandro Volta (1745–1827) was an Italian scientist interested in electricity. In 1799, Volta used zinc and copper disks separated by damp paper to make a "cell" that produced an electrical current. By standing

▲ Electricity is carried from power plants through cables.

Lens

Bulb

Reflector

▲ In a flashlight, the chemistry that goes on inside the dry battery produces enough electricity to light up a small bulb. The reflector and lens spread the light given by the bulb.

several cells in a pile, he discovered that he could produce a stronger current. Volta improved his "voltaic pile" by using acid or salt solution instead of water to moisten the paper. He had made the first battery.

What is a dry battery?

A dry battery is the kind you use in a flashlight. It has a zinc case (negative), and inside is a chemical paste surrounding a carbon rod (positive). So it is not really dry at all; the paste has enough moisture to allow the cell to work. Nickel-cadmium batteries, used in razors, are dry batteries that can be recharged.

Switch

Carbon rod

Zinc container

Ammonium chloride paste

Manganese dioxide in bag

What is a magnet?

A magnet is a piece of metal with the power to attract other substances. Iron and steel make good magnets. A magnet has two poles, north and south, near its ends. Unlike poles (north and south) attract each other, just as opposite (+) and (−) electrodes do. Like poles (north and north, south and south) repel each other. Try putting two bar magnets together and watch what happens. Can you tell which are the magnets' like poles?

How did a lodestone point the way?

In ancient times people discovered that the lodestone (an ore now known as magnetite) could attract small pieces of iron. If a bar made from lodestone was spun, it always swung to face north. This strange behavior made the lodestone valuable as a direction finder—the first magnetic compass. The Chinese are said to have used lodestone compasses as early as 2000 B.C.

Who discovered electromagnetism?

In 1820 a Dane, Hans Christian Oersted (1779–1851), discovered the magnetic effect. He was working with a battery and an electrical circuit, when he noticed that every time he brought a wire through which current was flowing near a magnetic compass, the compass needle jumped. When he disconnected the wire from the battery, the compass needle jumped again. Oersted's discovery that magnetism and electricity were closely connected, and that one could produce the other, was of immense scientific importance.

What does a magnetic field look like?

To see a magnetic field, you need some iron filings, a piece of thin cardboard, and a magnet. Sprinkle the filings on the cardboard. Place the magnet underneath and tap the cardboard gently. The filings will form a pattern. The field is strongest around the poles of the magnets.

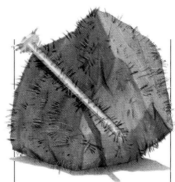

▲ A lodestone is a lump of naturally magnetic rock. Its scientific name is magnetite. In ancient times lodestones were thought to be magical because they could pick up iron nails and other iron objects.

▼ Iron filings sprinkled on paper over a magnet, show the pattern of the magnetic field.

How does a simple dynamo work?

A dynamo is a generator that turns mechanical energy into electrical energy. It has an armature (a coil able to spin on its axis) positioned between the poles of a magnet. When the armature turns, a current flows in the coil each time it crosses the force field of the magnet.

An electric motor works in the opposite way to a dynamo. It turns electrical energy into mechanical energy. When current is passed through the coil, the armature rotates and keeps moving for as long as the current continues to flow.

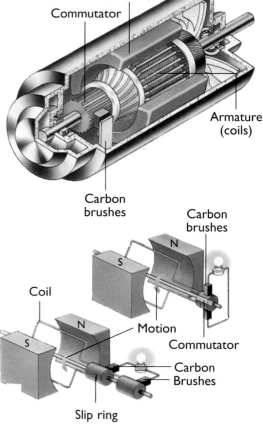

Field structure (magnet)

Commutator

Armature (coils)

Carbon brushes

Coil

Carbon brushes

Motion

Commutator

Carbon Brushes

Slip ring

▲ Dynamos (top) are generators tha turn mechanical motion into electric current. Both alternating current (bottom left), and direct current (bottom right) can be produced.

Where does our electricity come from?

The electricity that we use is made by giant generators, or dynamos, in power plants. A thermal power plant converts heat into electricity by burning fuel to boil water to produce steam. The steam drives turbine generators. The fuel may be oil, coal, or nuclear fuel (uranium). Another kind of power plant uses the energy of moving water to drive the generators and is called a hydroelectric power plant.

▶ In a lightbulb, current flows through the filament. The filament has a high electrical resistance and gets so hot that it glows brightly.

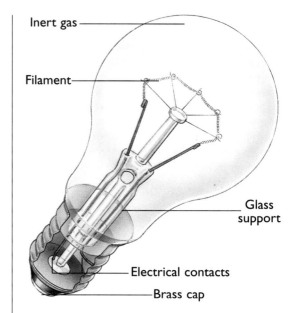

Inert gas

Filament

Glass support

Electrical contacts

Brass cap

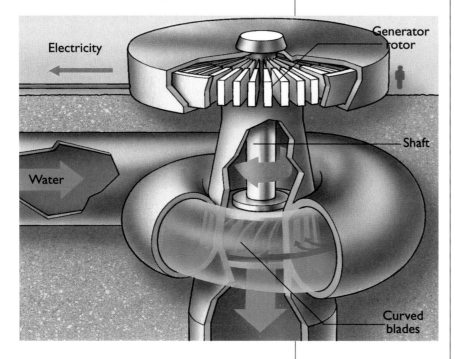

Electricity

Water

Generator rotor

Shaft

Curved blades

How does a fuse act as a safety device?

A fuse cuts off the electricity supply in a circuit when something goes wrong. Inside the fuse is a thin wire, able to carry a safe amount of current but no more. If an electrical appliance overheats it will start to use more electricity. The thin wire in the fuse (usually in the plug) heats up and melts. This breaks the circuit and cuts off the electricity.

▲ A hydroelectric turbogenerator converts the energy of flowing water into electrical energy. The water drives turbines which turn the shaft of a generator rotor.

What makes a lightbulb glow?

The thin wire, or filament, inside a lightbulb resists the flow of current through it. When electricity is passed through the bulb, the filament becomes hot and glows brightly. To prevent the filament from burning away completely, the glass bulb is filled with a mixture of inert gases (usually argon and nitrogen). The filament in most lightbulbs is made of tungsten.

How do "electronic eyes" work?

When light strikes certain substances, an electrical effect is produced. This electricity is called photoelectricity. The "magic eye" that automatically opens a door as you approach, or operates a burglar alarm, is worked by photoelectricity. A beam of light shines on a photoelectric cell. When the beam is interrupted (by someone walking through it) the cell activates an electrical circuit. The circuit may start a motor to open a door or (in a burglar alarm) set off a bell.

What is an integrated circuit?

An integrated circuit is a complicated arrangement of transistors and other components on a single piece, or chip, of semiconductor material. The first one was made in 1958. Making circuits smaller and smaller allows an incredible amount of electronic power to be contained in a tiny space. Hundreds of electronic components can be fitted into an integrated circuit the size of a letter in this sentence.

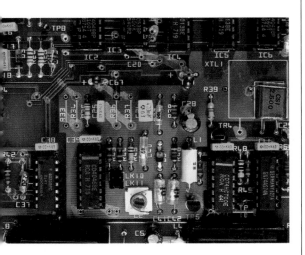

Why do microchips work so quickly?

Inside a microchip, the components are crammed together into a very tiny space. Electrical charges can move between them in almost no time at all, so the chip does its work at amazing speed.

What was the first electronic computer?

A huge machine called E.N.I.A.C., completed in 1946 in the United States, was the world's first electronic computer that could do many mathematical tasks. The name E.N.I.A.C. is short for Electronic Numerical Integrator And Calculator.

USEFUL TERMS

Bit: Binary digit; a numeral in binary notation (0 or 1).

Byte: Space in a computer's memory occupied by one letter or numeral.

Data: Information processed by a computer.

Hardware: Physical parts of a computer system.

Network: Several computers connected, e.g. by a modem (telephone).

Software: Programs for a computer.

◀ **Printed circuit boards are found in all sorts of things including computers, cars, and washing machines. The circuit board links components such as microchips, diodes, capacitors, and transistors.**

How does a computer use its memory?

A computer has four main parts. It has a central processing unit or "brain." It has an input unit that feeds in data (usually linked to a keyboard), and an output unit that produces finished work (for example, as a printout on paper). The fourth and vital part is the memory unit, where the computer stores the information it needs to carry out its work. The computer stores this data as electrical charges on magnetic disks.

How do bar codes work?

In a supermarket, the checkout assistant "reads" each item in your cart electronically by scanning the pattern of black and white stripes marked on the package. This pattern is the bar code, containing information which is passed automatically to a main computer, recording each item sold.

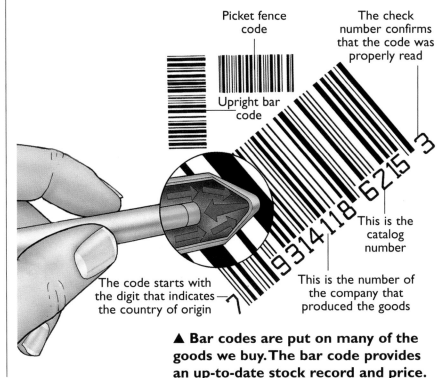

Picket fence code

The check number confirms that the code was properly read

Upright bar code

This is the catalog number

The code starts with the digit that indicates the country of origin

This is the number of the company that produced the goods

▲ **Bar codes are put on many of the goods we buy. The bar code provides an up-to-date stock record and price.**

LIGHT AND SOUND

What is light?

No one really knows what light is made of. In the 1600s Sir Isaac Newton thought light was made up of bulletlike particles which he called corpuscles. The Dutch scientist Christiaan Huygens (1629–1693) thought light was made up of pulses, or waves, traveling through space. Modern science has found some truth in both theories. Light certainly does travel in waves, but it also behaves as if it were made of particles. Scientists now call these light particles photons.

Light is a form of energy, similar to heat. It is the only type of energy we can see. Light comes from a star, such as the Sun, and travels through space. Stars shine as a result of their immense nuclear energy.

The shortest light waves that we can see are blue or violet. The longest light waves we can see are red. There are other waves, shorter and longer, that we cannot see but some animals can. A bee sees colors beyond violet, but it sees red objects as black.

▶ **Light is a kind of electromagnetic radiation. It travels as a wave made up of an electric field and a magnetic field at right angles to each other and to the direction of the wave's travel.**

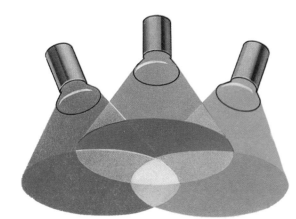

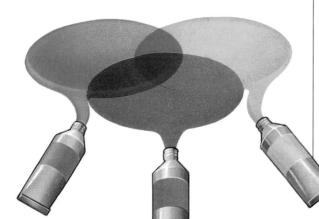

◀ **The three primary colors when mixing light are red, green, and blue. Added together, they make white. Paint pigments mix differently. Their primary colors are yellow, blue, and red. Mixed together, they make brown.**

How fast does light travel?

Light travels at enormous speed, at roughly 186,000 miles (300,000 km) a second. At this speed, the light from the Sun still takes more than eight minutes to reach the Earth. The speed of light was first measured accurately in 1676, by Olaf Roemer (1644–1710) of Denmark. Nothing travels faster than light.

Light wave

What are light waves?

If you throw a pebble into a pool, it sends out ripples of waves. Light also travels in waves. In 1873 the British scientist James Clerk-Maxwell (1831–1879) discovered the wave structure of light after 20 years' research. He showed that light is made up of vibrating waves of electrical and magnetic fields. The vibrations take place at right angles to the direction of the wave's motion, and to each other. Maxwell was the first to suggest that light was a form of electromagnetic radiation. He went on to state that other kinds of rays must also exist, invisible to the eye.

What makes light bend?

Light is bent when it is bounced back from a surface such as a mirror. This bending is called reflection. Light is also bent when it travels from one transparent surface to another. This bending is called refraction. It explains why a pencil standing half in and half out of water looks broken.

What makes the colors of the rainbow?

The rainbow is nature's spectrum. Falling drops of rain behave like tiny prisms. They break up white sunlight into the colors of the spectrum.

The first person to show that white light is a mixture of colors was Sir Isaac Newton. Between 1665 and 1666, he carried out experiments in a darkened room. He put a glass prism in a beam of sunlight streaming through a small hole in the wall, and saw it split into the colors of the rainbow: red, orange, yellow, green, blue, indigo, and violet. When he placed a second prism in the colored beam, he saw the light rays bend back and become white again.

▼ **When light passes through a glass prism, it splits into the colors of the rainbow: red, orange, yellow, green, blue, indigo, and violet. This is known as the spectrum.**

▶ **When you look in a mirror, your left side looks to be on your left. If you were looking at another person, their left side would be to your right. Light always travels in straight lines. So the mirror reflects light rays from your left side straight back to you on the left.**

LENSES AND MIRRORS FACTS

- The first mirrors were made of highly polished metal, such as bronze.

- Making glass mirrors, by coating one side of the glass with silver to make it reflect light, was not perfected until the 1600s.

- A lens that is thinner in the middle than at the edges is said to be concave.

- A lens that is thicker in the middle than at the edges is convex.

- A concave lens spreads light passing through it and makes objects looks smaller. A convex lens narrows the light and makes things look bigger.

- The Arabs knew of the magnifying glass about the year 1000. The first spectacles were made soon after this.

Why do mirrors reflect our images?

Everything reflects light, even the pages of this book. But most surfaces are rough, so the light is diffused, or spread in all directions. We can see the pages of this book from wherever we stand in the room. A mirror's smooth, shiny surface reflects light much more accurately as parallel rays, so giving a clear image.

Who invented the telescope?

Lenses are glass or plastic disks that bend light to make objects look larger or smaller. In about 1600 a Dutch spectaclemaker named Hans Lippershey put two lenses together and looked through them at the weather vane on a distant church. He was startled to see how large the weather vane appeared. He had made the first telescope. Soon telescopes were being made all over Europe.

Spectrum

Glass prism

How does a periscope work?

A simple periscope can be made with two flat mirrors, set at an angle of 45°. Light is reflected from the top mirror down to the lower one. In this way, it is possible to see an object over a wall, or above water, even when you are in a submerged submarine.

Who invented the microscope?

The microscope was invented in the early 1600s, and there are several claimants for its invention, among them Zacharias Janssen of Holland. What is surprising is that lenses had been known and made in Europe for more than 300 years before this invention, but no one had thought of combining them to make either a microscope or a telescope.

What are the most powerful microscopes?

The best optical microscope cannot magnify an object more than two thousand times. An electron microscope can magnify more than a million times. Electromagnetic fields are the microscope's "lenses." A hot wire filament sends a stream of electrons in a beam to hit the object to be examined. The denser areas of the object stop some electrons passing through. The rest travel on and hit a television screen or a photographic plate. The result is a "shadow picture" of the object.

▶ In the late 1800s, it took so long to take a photo that people needed a backrest to help them sit still. Eyes looked blurred if the sitter blinked.

Submarines have periscopes so people inside can see what is going on above water while the submarine stays hidden. Submarines often cruise with just the periscope showing. But the world's longest periscope is on land. It is 88½ feet (27 m) long and is used at a U.S. laboratory. Scientists there can study nuclear reactors without being exposed to dangerous radiation.

When was the first photograph taken?

The earliest photograph was taken by the French scientist J.N. Niépce (1765–1833) in 1826. It was made on an asphalt-coated pewter plate, and shows a view from a window. The exposure took eight hours.

In the 1830s and 1840s two new photographic processes were developed. They were the daguerreotype of the Frenchman L.J.M. Daguerre (1789–1851) and the calotype of the Englishman W.H. Fox Talbot (1800–1877). Daguerre's process used a silver-copper plate; the calotype used sensitive paper. In 1888 the American George Eastman (1854–1932) invented the Kodak camera, which used roll film.

Television waves		Microwaves			Visible light		X-rays			Cosmic rays	
Radio waves		Radar waves		Infrared rays		Ultraviolet rays			Gamma rays		

Long wavelength

Short wavelength

10^3 10^2 10^1 1 10^{-1} 10^{-2} 10^{-3} 10^{-4} 10^{-5} 10^{-6} 10^{-7} 10^{-8} 10^{-9} 10^{-10} 10^{-11} 10^{-12} 10^{-13} Meters

Are there rays that we cannot see?

In the 1870s James Clerk-Maxwell (1831–1879) predicted other forms of radiation beyond the visible spectrum —in other words, ones we cannot see. The electromagnetic spectrum is a band of radiation of which light is just one part. The rays travel through space in waves of varying lengths. We can see light rays, but other parts of the spectrum are invisible to the eye. At the red end of the visible light spectrum are infrared, microwaves, radar, television, and radio waves. At the other (violet) end of the spectrum are ultraviolet, X-rays, gamma rays, and cosmic rays.

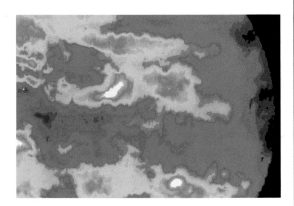

What can infrared photography show up?

We feel infrared rays when we sit in front of an electric heater and feel the "radiant" heat from its bars. More than half of the Sun's energy comes to us in the form of infrared rays. Infrared photography from space can detect tiny temperature changes on Earth.

▲ **The electromagnetic spectrum ranges from long wavelength radio waves through light waves to short wavelength gamma rays. All electromagnetic waves travel at the speed of light.**

Because dense cloud covers Venus, radar had to be used to map the planet's surface. In 1990 the *Magellan* spacecraft sent back a radar picture of Venus, revealing its active volcanoes and craters.

◄ **A near infrared map of the cloud cover over Venus, taken by the *Magellan* space probe in 1990. Infrared photos of the Earth can reveal diseased crops in fields, and track warm and cold water currents in the oceans.**

Who discovered X-rays?

The German scientist Wilhelm Roentgen (1845–1923) discovered X-rays by accident in 1895. He was experimenting with a cathode ray tube and noticed that crystals in the same room glowed when the tube was switched on. Even when he moved the crystals to the next room, they still glowed. Roentgen realized that invisible rays were causing the glow. The rays could even penetrate solid walls. He called them X-rays (X = unknown).

How was radar invented?

Radar was invented in the 1930s. It worked by transmitting a radio beam from the ground. Any object crossing the beam (such as an airplane) produced an "echo," and this could be received on the ground and used to work out the height and position of the airplane.

How did the laser get its name?

The first laser was made in 1960 by an American scientist named Theodore H. Maiman. Its name comes from a set of initials that stand for Light Amplification by Stimulated Emission of Radiation. A laser produces a beam of light so powerful it can burn a hole through metal. Unlike the light from a flashlight, a laser beam spreads hardly at all.

What is a hologram?

The Greek word *holos* means "whole." A hologram is a "whole picture," or a three-dimensional picture. A hologram is made by illuminating an object with laser light. The three-dimensional picture is viewed by shining a laser of the same color or wavelength through the hologram. The principle of the hologram was worked out by the Hungarian-born physicist Dennis Gabor (1900–1979) in 1948, but making a hologram was not possible before the invention of the laser.

How can light be used to send telephone calls?

In a telephone, sounds are changed into electrical signals and sent through wires. In 1966 scientists succeeded in using lasers to carry telephone calls by changing the electrical signals into light-pulses. Instead of wires, they used optical fibers—very long, thin glass rods. The light-pulses travel inside the rods, kept in by the mirrorlike sheath. At the end of the cable the pulses are changed back into sounds.

▼ **An optical fiber carries sound as pulses moving along strands of glass.**

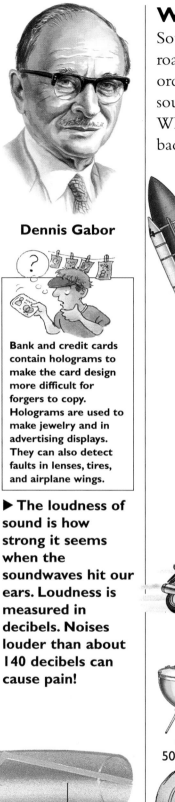

Glass strands

Glass sheath

Dennis Gabor

Bank and credit cards contain holograms to make the card design more difficult for forgers to copy. Holograms are used to make jewelry and in advertising displays. They can also detect faults in lenses, tires, and airplane wings.

▶ **The loudness of sound is how strong it seems when the soundwaves hit our ears. Loudness is measured in decibels. Noises louder than about 140 decibels can cause pain!**

What causes sound?

Sounds can be very different—the roar of a jet engine, the music of an orchestra, the song of a bird—but all sounds are made in a similar way. When an object vibrates (moves backward and forward), it produces sound.

Sound is a form of energy. Like light, it travels in waves. But sound needs something to travel through. Sound cannot travel in a vacuum such as space.

Rocket liftoff
150–190 decibels

Jet liftoff
120–140 decibels

Thunder
95–115 decibels

Motorcycle
70–90 decibels

Vacuum cleaner
60–80 decibels

Orchestra
50–70 decibels

Talking
30–60 decibels

Whispering
20–30 decibels

Falling leaves
20 decibels

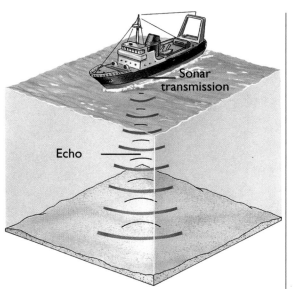

Sonar transmission

Echo

What causes an echo?

Have you ever stood inside a big gymnasium and heard your voice echoing from the thick concrete walls? The same thing happens inside a cave, or where there are cliffs or high walls. The echo is caused by the sound waves bouncing off the hard wall. The sound is reflected back to your ear, and you hear an echo of your voice.

Ships use echo sounders, devices that send out pulses of sound, to tell how deep the water is. This technique is known as sonar, which is short for SOund Navigation And Ranging.

Why is the Moon a silent world?

You can hear sounds under water. In fact, sound travels faster through water than through air. Sound can also travel through metal, such as steel. But no sound can travel across the airless surface of the Moon. The astronauts who explored the Moon talked to one another by radio. There were no other sounds, not even when they hit a rock with a hammer. It is impossible for sound to travel through the

◄ **Ships use sonar to tell how deep the seabed is. The echoes bounce back from the bottom. Using this method, a survey ship can chart the seabed.**

▼ **A sound's frequency is the number of vibrations per second, and is measured in Hertz (Hz). We can hear sounds between about 16 Hz and 20,000 Hz. Some animals emit and receive frequencies far beyond those we can hear.**

Is there really a sound barrier?

Before the late 1940s no airplane had flown faster than sound. People wondered if there was a mysterious "sound barrier," but the invention of jet planes proved it could be broken. Jets flew faster than sound without being shaken apart and without harm to their pilots. Today the supersonic airliner *Concorde* regularly carries passengers across the Atlantic at twice the speed of sound.

Are there sounds we cannot hear?

Human ears are most sensitive to sounds at around 2,000 Hertz (Hz). The lowest sound we can hear is about 16 Hz and the highest is about 20,000 Hz. Dogs can hear higher-pitched sounds. Some dog owners use whistles that make a sound too high for them to hear, but which is heard perfectly well by their pet.

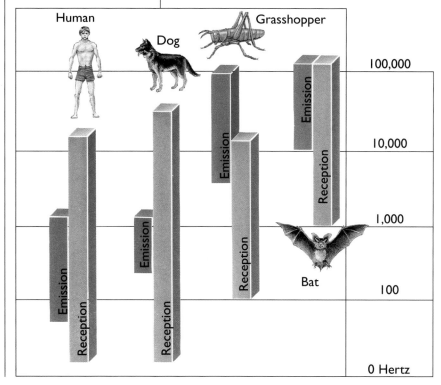

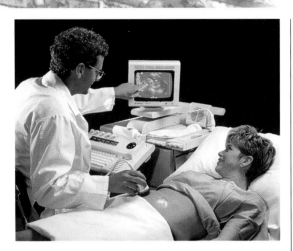

How do doctors examine unborn babies with the help of sound waves?

Ultrasonic waves penetrate flesh and other soft body parts, just like X-rays, and they can be used to produce pictures of the inside of the body. Because the sound waves have no harmful effects, doctors use ultrasonic scanners to examine pregnant women. The scan shows if the unborn baby in the womb is healthy and growing properly.

When were sounds first recorded?

The first sound recording was made by Thomas Alva Edison (1837–1931) in 1877 on a machine he called the "phonograph." Sounds were picked up by a vibrating membrane, and the vibrations made a needle cut spiral grooves on a cylinder covered with tinfoil. When a second needle was moved along the grooves, the sounds were reproduced by means of another vibrating membrane and amplified through a horn.

◄ The "tape recorder" invented by Valdemar Poulsen did not look much like a modern portable stereo. The sound was stored on metal wire, not on plastic tape.

◄ An ultrasound scanner shows how an unborn baby is developing inside the womb of a pregnant woman.

▼ Edison's phonograph of 1877 recorded sounds as grooves cut into a foil-covered cylinder. Flat records were invented in 1887.

► In digital recording the signals are changed into off-on electrical pulses. Analog recording builds up a continuous sound "image."

When was recording tape first used?

The first experiments with sound recording on tape were made in 1898 by a Dane, Valdemar Poulsen (1869–1942), using magnetized metal wire. In the 1930s paper tapes were developed, and reel-to-reel tape recorders appeared in the 1940s. Today's cassette players use plastic tape coated with magnetic material.

What is digital recording?

In older recording systems, the electrical signals are stored as a continuous wave pattern. These build up a replica or analog of the original sounds. In digital recording, as used on music CDs, the sound waves are converted into electrical pulses which are coded as a series of numbers (digits) in binary form. Digital recordings give more accurate reproduction, because they store much more information about the sounds being recorded.

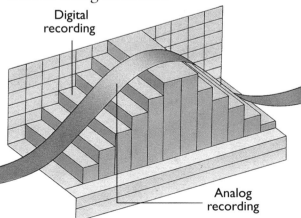

Digital recording

Analog recording

ENERGY AND MOTION

What is energy?

Energy is the ability to do work. When you walk upstairs, or even when you are resting, your body is working, and uses energy. The spring inside a clockwork motor provides the energy to drive the mechanism. A flashlight battery provides the energy needed to light up the bulb. The Sun's energy enables plants to grow. In fact, all living things depend on the Sun for their energy. Energy can neither be created nor destroyed.

Where does energy come from?

Energy comes from matter. Everything in the universe is made up of matter, so in some form energy is found everywhere. Even the tiniest atomic particles can be changed into energy. Matter can be changed into energy and energy can be changed into matter.

Are there different kinds of energy?

Energy that is stored up is called potential energy. Water stored behind a dam, an archer's bow drawn and ready to fire—both of these are examples of potential energy. Falling water and an arrow shot from a bow each have kinetic energy. Potential and kinetic energy are both forms of mechanical energy. There are other kinds of energy too: thermal or heat energy, chemical energy, nuclear energy, and radiant energy.

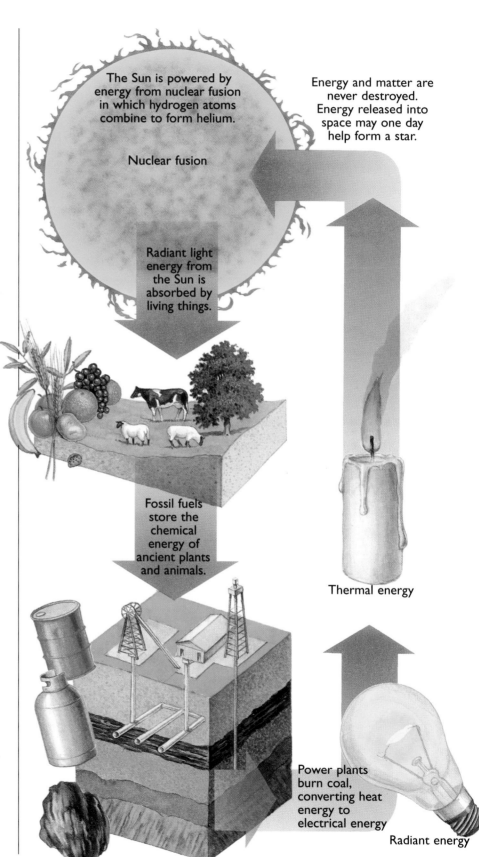

The Sun is powered by energy from nuclear fusion in which hydrogen atoms combine to form helium.

Nuclear fusion

Energy and matter are never destroyed. Energy released into space may one day help form a star.

Radiant light energy from the Sun is absorbed by living things.

Fossil fuels store the chemical energy of ancient plants and animals.

Thermal energy

Power plants burn coal, converting heat energy to electrical energy

Radiant energy

What are fossil fuels?

Much of the energy we use at home and at work comes from the burning of so-called fossil fuels such as coal, oil, and gas. These fuels were formed millions of years ago from the remains of plants and animals.

Why do things become hot?

Heat is the transfer of energy from one substance to another. If you rub a piece of cloth with your hand, the cloth will begin to feel warmer. The rubbing has produced heat, as a result of friction.

How can heat travel?

Heat travels in several ways. The heat you feel when you hold a saucepan handle is carried by conduction. The heat energy inside a kettle is carried by convection. A campfire keeps you warm because it sends out heat waves by radiation. Substances that carry heat well are called good conductors of heat. Metals are the best conductors—that is why we use metal cooking pots.

In the Fahrenheit scale the boiling point of water is 212°. In the Celsius or Centigrade scale it is 100°. Scientists use the Kelvin scale, in which the boiling point of water is 373°. On this scale, water freezes at 273°.

▼ The air above a warm radiator (left) rises and cool air moves in creating a convection current. Heat from a match (center) sets molecules of air moving, causing heat rays. As a metal spoon gets hot (right), molecules at the heated end move faster and collide with their neighbors, setting them moving.

Who invented the Fahrenheit scale for measuring temperature?

The earliest scale for measuring temperature was invented by a Dutchman named Gabriel Fahrenheit (1686–1736) in the early 1700s. This scale, named after him, has the freezing point of water at 32 degrees. In 1742 a Swede named Anders Celsius (1701–1744) suggested a scale in which the freezing point of water would be fixed at 0 degrees.

What is the coldest anything can be?

When a substance is warmed, its molecules move around faster. When it is cooled, they move more slowly. The coldest that anything can get is when its molecules stop moving. This is at a temperature of −460°F (−273°C), or "absolute zero." Scientists have not yet achieved zero, but they have managed temperatures close to it.

Conduction

Convection

Radiation

◄ **The ice in an iceberg is less dense than the surrounding water, so it floats. Water expands (and so becomes less dense) when it becomes colder than 39°F (4°C).**

Why does an iceberg float?

Unlike most liquids, water expands (gets bigger) when it freezes and becomes less dense as a result. An ice cube will therefore float in a glass of water and not sink. This fact explains why huge icebergs float and also why rivers do not freeze solid in winter. Ice forms as a floating layer on top, and this layer stops further freezing beneath. If the ice sank to the bottom, the river would quickly freeze solid.

What are the oldest known machines?

A machine is a device for doing work, and the oldest known machines are the simplest: such as the wedge, the lever, and the inclined plane. These were used by Stone Age people 100,000 years ago. Their inventors are unknown. The wheel was a later discovery, and was not in common use until about 5,000 years ago.

ICE FACTS

■ Salt water freezes at a lower temperature than freshwater.

■ The thickest ice in the world covers the Antarctic continent to a depth of 15,744 feet (4,800 m).

■ Only the tip of an iceberg shows above water. About 80 percent of an iceberg (or even more) is hidden beneath the water's surface.

■ The largest icebergs come from the Antarctic ice cap. The biggest was 200 mi. (320 km) long and 60 mi. (97 km) wide.

How does a lever work?

The lever is a simple machine that moves objects. The commonest kind is called a first-class lever. The object to be moved is known as the load, and the force needed to move it is call the effort. The lever needs a pivot, or fulcrum. Using a branch as a lever and resting it on a small rock (the fulcrum), it is possible to lift a much heavier weight. When Stone Age people discovered this, they had invented one of the basic machines: the lever.

▼ **Three simple machines are seen on building sites. The crowbar is a lever. So is the wheelbarrow. The hammer acts as a lever too. The fulcrum is the worker's shoulder joints, and the load is the hammer head.**

Hammer

Load

Fulcrum

Crowbar

Wheelbarrow

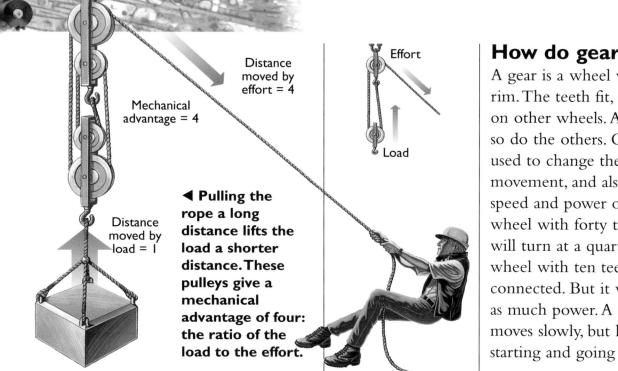

Distance moved by effort = 4

Mechanical advantage = 4

Distance moved by load = 1

Effort

Load

◀ **Pulling the rope a long distance lifts the load a shorter distance. These pulleys give a mechanical advantage of four: the ratio of the load to the effort.**

How do more pulleys make less work?

A pulley is a useful machine for changing the direction of a force. For example, by pulling downward on a rope running over a pulley wheel, you can lift a load upward. The more pulleys there are, with one continuous rope running through them, the greater the mechanical advantage and so the greater the load that can be lifted with the same effort.

When were building cranes first used?

The Romans introduced the crane, a machine for lifting loads using the principle of the pulley. Their cranes were worked by treadmills. Slaves trudging inside the treadmill produced the effort needed to lift the load of building stone.

More than 2,000 years ago King Hieron of Syracuse challenged Archimedes (c.287–212 B.C.) to show what simple machines could do. The Greek scientist built a system of pulleys. Unaided, he lifted a ship out of the water onto the land!

▼ **Inertia in action. A car stays still or moves steadily in a straight line unless it is stopped by another force — such as the brick wall in this picture.**

How do gears work?

A gear is a wheel with teeth along its rim. The teeth fit, or mesh, with teeth on other wheels. As one wheel turns, so do the others. Gear wheels can be used to change the direction of a movement, and also to increase the speed and power of a machine. A big wheel with forty teeth, for example, will turn at a quarter the speed of a wheel with ten teeth, if they are connected. But it will have four times as much power. A car in low gear moves slowly, but has more power for starting and going uphill.

What is inertia?

To start an object moving, a force is needed. When you kick a ball, the ball begins to move. It keeps moving until some other force stops it. The ball has inertia. It rolls on until stopped by another force (your foot perhaps, or a wall, or the friction of the ground). All moving objects have inertia: they try to keep moving until a force opposes them. Have you ever been standing on a bus when it stopped suddenly? People are thrown forward, because of the inertia affecting their bodies.

Why does a pendulum swing?

You can make a simple pendulum by fastening a weight to the end of a length of cord. Hold the cord so that the weight hangs vertically. When you give the pendulum a push, it swings away from you. The force of your push gives it motion. When it reaches the lowest point of its swing, the pendulum does not stop but swings on, this time upward. Inertia keeps it going until a stronger force (gravity) halts it and the pendulum swings back down toward the vertical again.

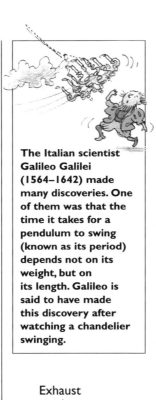

The Italian scientist Galileo Galilei (1564–1642) made many discoveries. One of them was that the time it takes for a pendulum to swing (known as its period) depends not on its weight, but on its length. Galileo is said to have made this discovery after watching a chandelier swinging.

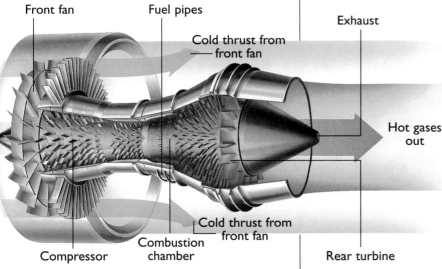

Front fan   Fuel pipes

Cold thrust from front fan

Exhaust

Hot gases out

Cold thrust from front fan

Compressor   Combustion chamber   Rear turbine

How does a jet engine work?

A jet engine is an action–reaction engine. It shoots out a mass of hot gas, and the force of this gas pushing in one direction produces another equally strong force in the opposite direction. For every action (here, the hot gas shooting out backward), there is an equal and opposite reaction (the jet plane flying forward). Sir Isaac Newton (1642–1727) knew this, long before jet planes. This was his Third Law of Motion.

▲ A jet engine sucks in air with a fan. The air is compressed and forced into the combustion chamber, where fuel is sprayed in and burns. Hot, expanding gases spin a rear turbine that drives the compressor and the fan. Finally, gases shoot out of the exhaust, producing thrust.

How can an iron ship float?

A hollow object has low density because it is mostly filled with air. Even an iron ship will float in water because of the air inside. However, if the vessel is holed, water pours in and pushes the air out. The overall density of the ship becomes greater than that of water, and the ship sinks.

How can objects float in air?

Air is fluid, like water, but it has such a low density that few objects will float in it. Hydrogen gas is lighter than air, so a balloon filled with hydrogen is less dense than air and will rise upward. Eventually, it will reach a height where the air is so thin that the hydrogen no longer has a lower density, and can rise no higher.

Why do things fall to Earth?

Gravity is a force which pulls us, and everything else, toward the Earth. Gravity is what makes rain fall downward and not upward. Gravity explains why, if you throw a ball into the air, it will fall back to Earth again.

Gravity is one of many forces that act on objects on Earth. A plane flying through the atmosphere is thrust forward by its engines, but held in place above the ground by air pressure under its wings acting against the pull of gravity.

The planet Earth exerts a gravitational force on everything. But much smaller bodies also produce a similar effect. Between any two objects there is a gravitational force.

Why do the planets keep moving in their orbits?

The planets have been moving ever since the formation of the Solar System. They were given their starting "push" then, millions of years ago, and have kept moving around the Sun ever since. The Sun's massive gravitational force holds the planets in orbit around it. They keep moving because there is no force in the Solar System powerful enough to stop them and no friction force opposing them.

How much would you weigh on the Moon?

The weight of an object is the force of gravity acting upon it. Weight is really measured in newtons (the newton is a unit for measuring force). Mass is measured in pounds (or kilograms). The mass of an object never changes, but if you traveled to the Moon, you would weigh less than on Earth, because the Moon has only one-sixth of the Earth's gravity.

What is it like to be weightless?

People inside a spacecraft orbiting the Earth float around inside, as if swimming in air. There is no gravity from Earth to pull them down. If an astronaut lets go of a tool, it drifts around instead of falling to the floor. Imagine trying to eat off a plate!

▲ A toy gyroscope will balance so long as it keeps spinning fast enough. The wheel's axle points continuously in the direction it is first set at.

▲ As they escape Earth's gravity, astronauts become weightless. On the Moon, there is very little gravity, so an astronaut can bounce around. In space, an astronaut floats.

How can a gyroscope balance on a pencil point?

A gyroscope looks like a spinning-top inside a wheel-like frame. Once set spinning, it will not alter its direction. If balanced on a pencil point, it will not fall off so long as it keeps spinning. The pull of gravity (which tries to upset the gyroscope) is countered by another force called precession, found in spinning bodies. This makes the gyroscope move around the point of the pencil as if it were in orbit.

What causes friction?

Friction is produced when two surfaces rub against one another. Even a smooth-looking surface is actually covered with tiny holes and bumps, as can be seen by looking through a microscope. The rubbing together produces heat. This is why a match struck on a matchbox bursts into flame. There is friction between even the most insubstantial surfaces such as air and water.

Why don't trains have rubber tires like cars and trucks?

Running a vehicle on rails is actually more efficient than running it on a road. This is because a solid wheel, like that of a train, creates less friction than an air-filled tire (as on a car), since a solid wheel does not flatten out under pressure. So it is easier to pull a heavy load along a train track than along a road. But without some friction to "stick" the wheels to the rails, a train's wheels would spin helplessly and not grip at all.

SPACE AND TIME

The width of a digit (finger) became the inch.

Inch

Palm

From thumb to little finger (stretched) was a span.

The yard was the length of a man's arm from nose to fingertip.

Two palms = one span
Four palms = one cubit.

The cubit was the length from fingers to elbow.

A fathom was a man's armspan

▲ In the ancient world, parts of the body were used as measuring units including the digit, span, and cubit. According to the Bible, Goliath was six cubits and one span high, so he was 10 ft., 8 in. (3.2 m) tall.

A pace = one yard

One foot

When was zero first used in sums?

We could not count without a figure for nothing, or zero. One way is to leave a blank, but early mathematicians soon found they needed a special symbol: 0. The zero was in use by the 7th century in India and Southeast Asia, and may have been used in China even earlier.

Who invented the decimal system?

We have ten fingers and ten toes, so counting in tens (the decimal system) seems sensible. But counting can be done in lots of other ways. As early as 1400 B.C. the Chinese used decimals. They wrote the number 365 as "three hundred plus six decades (tens) plus five days." Decimals did not reach Europe until the 10th century.

How was the human body used in measurement?

Ancient civilizations relied on "body-measurement." The smallest unit of length was the "finger" or "thumb." A cubit (the distance from a person's elbow to their fingertips) was equal to 30 fingers (roughly 20 inches [50 cm] in modern terms). A hand's width, normally taken as 4 inches (10 cm), is still the unit used to measure the height of horses.

Where was the metric system first made official?

The metric (decimal) system of weights and measures was adopted in France after the French Revolution of 1789. Before then, people in Europe had used various old measures. The metric system is now used in many parts of the world, especially by scientists.

What is geometry?

Geometry is the branch of mathematics that has to do with the study of shapes and sizes. The name comes from Greek words meaning "Earth measurement," and it was by using geometry that Greek mathematicians first calculated the size of the Earth. Every advance in science has been aided by geometry, for without it we could not make entirely accurate measurements. In about 300 B.C. the Greek mathematician Euclid wrote a book called *Elements* in which he brought together many Greek geometrical discoveries. Euclid's textbook still inspires mathematicians.

How often can you expect to throw a six when playing dice?

Mathematicians have long sought ways of solving problems involving unpredictable factors, such as the fall of dice. The Frenchman Blaise Pascal worked out the basic "laws of probability" in 1642, using dice. The simplest problem is this: a die has six sides, each with a different value. When you throw it, each side has an equal chance of falling uppermost. The probability that one side will do so is therefore 1 in 6.

MATHS FACTS

- As long ago as 3000 B.C., the Egyptians used geometry for land surveys and for building.

- Arabs invented algebra in the 9th century.

- Negative numbers, such as -1, -2, -3 and so on, were unknown in Europe until the 1500s, though the Chinese used them long before.

- The acre is still used as a field measurement by many farmers. In the Middle Ages, an English acre was the area of land an ox could plow in a day —22 furrows (lengths) or "furlongs."

- The 17th-century French mathematician Pierre de Fermat (1601–1665) had a secret test for finding prime numbers. He could give almost instant answers.

- There is an endless number of prime numbers. There are more than 660,000 between 1 and 10 million.

Euclid thought 6 was a "perfect" number. 1, 2, and 3 divide exactly into 6. Added together, they make 6. Euclid knew of three more perfect numbers: 28, 496, and 8,128. After that, perfect numbers get very big!

Where did Arabic numerals come from?

The Arabic numerals we use today were first used in India and reached Europe about the year A.D. 1000. A book written in 1202 by an Italian mathematician named Leonardo Fibonacci (1170?–1250?) did much to persuade Europe's scientists that they must use Arabic numerals in order for mathematics to progress.

Who first proved that the angles of a triangle always add up to 180 degrees?

The Ancient Greeks were fascinated by geometry. They knew that a circle is made up of 360 degrees, a number probably chosen by the Babylonians. No matter what its shape, a triangle has angles that always add up to 180 degrees. This was first proved by Euclid about 300 B.C.

Why do mathematicians hunt for prime numbers?

A prime number is one that can be divided only by itself and 1. For example, 12 is not a prime number because it can be divided by 1, 2, 3, 4, and 6. On the other hand, 11 is: it can be divided only by 1 and 11. What mystifies mathematicians about prime numbers is that they follow no pattern. A Greek named Eratosthenes (*c.*276–194 B.C.) worked out a slow, but effective, method of finding prime numbers, over 2,000 years ago.

◀ If you roll a die, what is the chance of rolling a number higher than 2? Four of the six possible numbers are greater than 2, so the probability of rolling one of them is 4/6 or 2/3.

The probability of throwing a number greater than two

Possible outcomes

Successful outcomes

Probability of throwing greater than two is therefore four out of six

Who counted in suns and nights?

People have measured time in a number of ways. Early people counted the days (from sunrise to sunset). But not all used the "day" as their unit. The Comanche tribe of Native Americans counted in "suns," Greenlanders counted in "nights."

Who first worked out how long a year is?

More than 3,000 years ago, the priests of Babylon were skilled in astronomy and kept accurate records of the passing of the seasons. They calculated how long it took the Earth to complete one year's cycle around the Sun, and worked this out as 365 days 5 hours 42 minutes and 14 seconds. The modern calculation is only 26 minutes and 55 seconds longer.

▲ Hundreds of years ago, the Aztec people of Mexico made a calendar. It was a huge stone shaped like the Sun. Signs for the days were carved around the edge.

People born in a leap year on February 29 have to wait four years for their next "special" birthday. A leap year can always be divided by four with nothing left over. The years 1996, 2000, and 2004 are all leap years.

Why were leap years found necessary?

The Romans based their calendar on the Moon's monthly phases. The Roman calendar started off with 360 days, but was then reduced to only 355. It became clear that the calendar was gradually getting out of step with the seasons. So Julius Caesar ordered a new calendar of 365.25 days. Every fourth year an extra day was added, to use up the quarter-days. This became a leap year. Before the new calendar could begin, an extra-long year was needed to put things straight. The year 46 B.C. had 445 days and, not surprisingly, was known as "the year of confusion."

When did people protest at having 11 days stolen?

Julius Caesar's calendar, named the Julian calendar, was used until the 1500s. By then, it too was out of step. Easter was falling in summer instead of spring. Pope Gregory XIII, head of the Roman Catholic Church, ruled that there should be a new calendar from 1582. Britain kept to the old calendar until 1752. That year, September 2 was followed by September 14. People took to the streets protesting that they had had 11 days stolen from their lives!

Who had two calendars?

People of the Maya civilization in Central America (from about A.D. 250 to 1500). One calendar had 365 days, divided into 18 months of 20 days, with five "unlucky" days at the end of the year. Maya fortune-tellers used a sacred calendar with 260 days.

Water clock

Sundial

When were sundials and water clocks used?

Sundials were used as "shadow clocks" more than 3,000 years ago in Babylonia. An upright stick casts a shadow as the Sun's rays alter position during the day. (Remember, this is because the Earth is moving, not the Sun.) Around the stick is a dial marked out with the hours.

The Ancient Egyptians and Greeks used water clocks. There were various types, but they all worked on the same principle. Water dripped slowly out of a container. As the water level fell, so did a float on the surface. To the float was attached a pointer which marked the passing of the hours on a scale.

When were mechanical clocks invented?

Medieval monks needed to know the times for prayers during the day. They wanted a clock that would ring a bell at regular intervals. The machinery that made this possible was invented in the 1300s. Falling weights provided the force needed to ring a bell, and the fall of the weights was regulated by a mechanism known as an "escapement." The movement of the escapement gave the clockwork its familiar "tick-tock" sound.

▲ **In an Egyptian water clock, water poured slowly from one pot to another. The Egyptians also had sundials. In Babylonia, people marked the face of the sundial into 12 hours. The dial shown here has Roman numerals.**

▲ **John Harrison (1693–1776) made the first reliable chronometer, or ship's clock, in the 1700s. It had a slowly unwinding spring inside, so it kept time accurately.**

▶ **The cross-staff and backstaff: early navigational instruments.**

Were there hands on the first clocks?

Early clocks were intended only to "strike" the hours, with a bell. They were very inaccurate, losing perhaps 15 minutes a day. But people were not worried about minutes; they needed to know only what hour it was. Clocks struck every quarter-hour, and that was precise enough. After all, there were no trains or buses to catch. Not until the 1600s were clocks with minute hands and faces marked into 12 hours common.

How did the early sailors find their way?

Few seamen in ancient times ventured out of sight of land. The Greeks invented a sundial-like device, the astrolabe, for finding longitude (east-west position) and calculating the time of day. The astrolabe did not reach northern Europe until much later, in the 14th century. Later, sailors made use of instruments called the simple cross-staff and the improved backstaff (1595) to discover their latitude (north-south position) by measuring the precise angle of the Sun above the horizon.

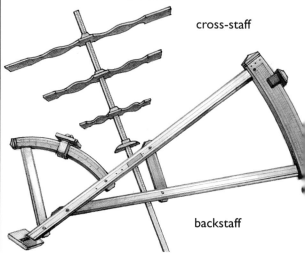

cross-staff

backstaff

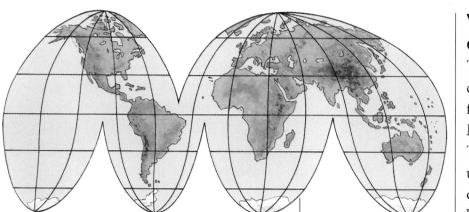

Why is a flat map never really accurate?

A map in a book is flat. But the Earth is round, and its features cannot be drawn accurately on a flat surface. Try peeling an orange, and you will find you cannot lay the skin out flat on a table without it breaking. Every map is drawn in a way that makes some feature (such as area) accurate, but other features (such as shape) less so. This is called a projection.

Why do air travelers have to alter their watches?

The world is divided into 24 time zones. The time in each zone differs by one hour from the time in the next. East of Greenwich in England (where it is Greenwich Mean Time, or GMT), the time is later. West of Greenwich, the time is earlier. Noon in Greenwich is 7 A.M. (5 hours earlier) in New York and 3 P.M. (3 hours later) in Moscow. The United States (apart from Alaska and Hawaii) covers four time zones: Eastern, Central, Mountain, and Pacific. Travelers flying west must put their watches back. Flying east, they must put them forward. So if a flight from New York to San Francisco takes five hours, you land at the same time as you set off.

▲ To make a map on a flat surface, a section of the world's surface has to be shown as if it were flat. It is as if the peel of an orange is cut off and then laid out flat on the table.

▼ Since 1884, the world has had standard time zones. These are based on Greenwich Mean Time. In each time zone, time differs by one hour. Travelers crossing the International Date Line gain or lose a day.

When was B.C. and A.D. dating introduced?

There are many different systems for dating. Muslims begin their calendar from the Hegira, the flight of Muhammad from Mecca in A.D. 622. The Christian calendar, now widely used worldwide, begins with the birth of Jesus. Dates before then are followed by the letters "B.C." ("Before Christ"). Dates after then are prefixed by the letters A.D. (Latin "Anno Domini" or "Year of Our Lord"). A.D. dating was suggested by a monk-mathematician named Dionysius Exiguus (died 556) in 525. It was much later that B.C. was adopted, in the 1600s.

How do archaeologists measure time?

Archaeologists uncover the past, layer by layer. Objects can be dated by measuring the amount of radioactive carbon-14 left in charcoal, wood, or animal bones. Tree growth-rings, especially those of the bristlecone pine of California, which can live as long as 4,600 years, can be used to help to correct errors in radiocarbon dates.

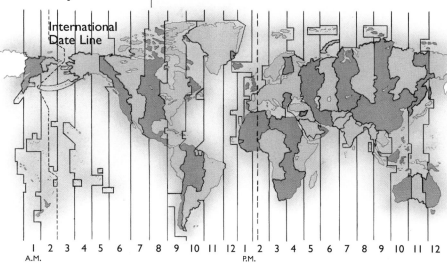

International Date Line

| 1 | 2 | 3 | 4 | 5 | 6 | 7 | 8 | 9 | 10 | 11 | 12 | 1 | 2 | 3 | 4 | 5 | 6 | 7 | 8 | 9 | 10 | 11 | 12 |

A.M.   P.M.

Which clocks are the most accurate?

Atomic clocks keep the most accurate time. These are based on the vibration rate of certain atoms. Most atomic clocks use the vibrations of a cesium atom to regulate quartz crystals. Some scientific clocks, incredibly, are accurate to one second in a million years.

Can time slow down?

Albert Einstein (1879–1955) published his *Special Theory of Relativity* in 1905. He believed that length, mass, and time were all affected by motion; and he thought that nothing could travel faster than the speed of light. Near the speed of light, mass would be infinite, length would be zero and time would slow down almost to a stop.

What are light-years and parsecs?

Space is so vast that ordinary units of measurement such as the mile or kilometer are of little use. Scientists measure the universe in light-years and parsecs. A light-year is the distance light travels in a year: about 6 trillion miles (9.5 trillion km). A light-year is roughly 3.25 parsecs (one parsec equals 1.9×10^{13} miles [3×10^{13} km]).

Could we send spacecraft to the stars?

The stars are so far away that travel to them is out of the question—at least for the foreseeable future. The fastest spacecraft yet built would take more than 150,000 years to arrive at even the closest star.

▲ This atomic clock counts the vibrations of light given off by atoms. It should lose less than one second in a million years!

On a 24-hour clock, 9 o'clock in the morning is shown as 0900 and 9 o'clock in the evening is shown as 2100. Train and bus timetables use this system to avoid confusion between morning and evening.

Could we travel through time?

Storytellers and filmmakers have made exciting stories about people traveling backward or forward through time. Such adventures remain in the world of science fiction. No one has yet built a time machine, and most scientists do not believe time travel is possible.

What is a time capsule?

People sometimes bury containers to preserve various items, as a record of their time. The capsule might contain clothes, photos, tapes, toys, books, even food. The idea is that one day in the future, historians will dig up the capsule and study the contents. There is one extra-large time capsule in the United States which has a car and a motorcycle inside!

What is biological time?

Plants and animals follow natural rhythms or cycles (wake-sleep, night-day). Some sea animals even time their activities to the changing tides. A fish called the grunion, for example, swims ashore to breed at regular 14-day intervals. This rhythm matches the peak tides.

Another kind of time is called geological time. This is measured in millions of years, from the origin of the Solar System through the aging of the Earth.

How old is the universe?

The universe is about 15 billion years old. Scientists work out the age by measuring the rate at which distant stars have cooled down since the universe began. Some scientists have suggested that stars may cool down more slowly than was thought, so the universe may be even older.

When did people first decide the universe was changing?

Only in the 20th century have scientists shown that the universe is changing all the time. Before then, it was thought that the universe had always been exactly the same. In 1948 a group of scientists put forward the idea of a "steady-state" universe, which has always existed and will always exist. Now this idea has little support.

SPACE FACTS

Time and distance in space are just mind-boggling.

■ The Solar System (the Sun and its planets) is about a million times wider than the diameter of the Earth.

■ Our galaxy, the Milky Way, is about 100 million times wider than the Solar System.

■ The Andromeda galaxy is the most distant star cluster that we can see without a telescope.

■ Andromeda is two million light-years away. This means that the light from this galaxy began its journey to Earth over two million years ago.

■ Astronomers use a measure of time called the cosmic year. This is the time it takes the Sun and its planets to rotate once around the center of the Milky Way— 225 million years.

How did the universe begin?

Most scientists now think that the universe came into being with a huge explosion, known as the "Big Bang." The explosion sent matter flying apart, and the universe has continued to expand ever since. Radio astronomers have picked up radiation that does not seem to come from any single source, but is spread throughout space. They believe this radiation may be the result of the Big Bang.

Who thought of Venus as a lion?

Ancient peoples made the universe the setting for fabulous stories. To the people of Babylon, Venus was a bright shining lion roaming the universe. Every dawn, the great god El killed the lion, only for it to return at night.

▶ **Most scientists believe a gigantic explosion called the Big Bang started the universe expanding. The galaxies are speeding apart from one another, and the universe is getting bigger all the time.**

DISCOVERIES AND INVENTIONS

When were the first tools made?

The first tools may have been made by apelike creatures that scientists have named *Australopithecus*, whose remains have been found in southern and eastern Africa. They used sticks and stones as weapons. Scientists have discovered some simple pebble-tools these primitive creatures made more than two million years ago.

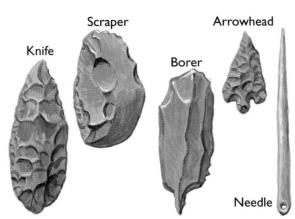

Scraper

Knife

Borer

Arrowhead

Needle

How did people discover fire?

Primitive people feared fire, as animals do. A forest fire, started by lightning, sent them fleeing. But someone, somewhere, must have plucked up courage to seize a burning branch and used it to start a small fire for warmth and protection from fierce animals. These first fires were kept burning constantly, for no one yet knew how to make fire using simple tools.

▲ Before the wheel was invented, people used logs as rollers to move heavy stones for building, so perhaps it is not surprising that the first wheels were wooden.

◀ Early people used flint for making tools such as knives, scrapers, borers, and arrowheads. They made needles from animal bones.

Who invented the wheel?

No one knows when or where the wheel was first used, but it was one of the most important of all human inventions. The wheel seems to have been invented before 3000 B.C., probably in several different places. It may be that wheels were first used by potters to turn clay pots, before they were fixed to carts and revolutionized transportation. The first carts had two solid wheels, made from pieces of wood fastened together. Spoked wheels, as used on chariots, were much lighter and a great improvement.

◀ People made fire using a bow drill. As the point of the drill turned rapidly, friction produced enough heat to start wool or dry moss smoldering.

When did the first farmers harvest crops?

Archaeologists in Israel have found flint sickles (tools used for cutting grain) thought to be 13,000 years old. Microscopic examination of the sickle blades shows they were probably used to harvest cultivated, not wild, cereals. If this is so, farming began much earlier than was previously thought. Until recently the earliest evidence of cereal planting, found in Syria, was 11,000 years old.

How is iron smelted?

Iron was first made by heating iron ore in a furnace with charcoal and limestone. As the charcoal burned, the molten iron ran down and cooled into a solid mass. This "bloom" was then hammered and reheated to purify the iron. The process of melting down iron ore is called smelting. The "Iron Age" began about 1500 B.C., in the Near East.

One of the most important inventions of all time was the eyeglass. The first recorded statement came from Roger Bacon in 1268 when he wrote about the use of lenses in glasses.

▶ Tipping out a furnace of molten steel. All metals come from ores dug up from the ground. The ore is heated until the metal melts. It is poured into molds to cool and harden.

When was steel first made?

The Romans knew how to make steel of a kind, and metal smiths in China and elsewhere probably also made steel by accident. During the Middle Ages, Toledo, Spain, was famous for its steel swords. Large-scale steel production was not possible until the invention of an industrial steelmaking process. This was done by Sir Henry Bessemer (1813–1898), who invented his "converter" to make steel in 1856.

When were candles first used?

Candles have been in use for at least 3,000 years, and probably longer. They are mentioned in the Old Testament of the Bible. The Romans burned candles made from flax coated with wax and pitch. Beeswax and tallow (animal fat) were also often used.

◀ More than half the world's steel is made by the basic oxygen process, illustrated here. The electric arc and open hearth are two other common steelmaking processes.

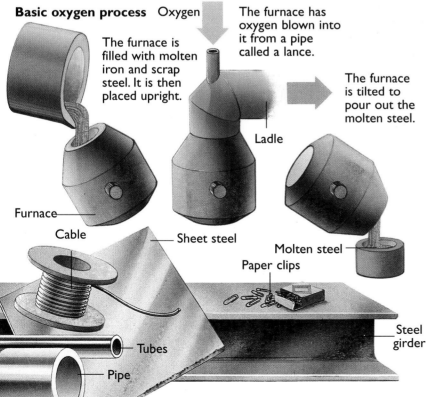

Basic oxygen process Oxygen

The furnace is filled with molten iron and scrap steel. It is then placed upright.

The furnace has oxygen blown into it from a pipe called a lance.

The furnace is tilted to pour out the molten steel.

Ladle

Furnace

Cable

Sheet steel

Molten steel

Paper clips

Steel girder

Tubes

Pipe

Who enjoyed central heating 2,000 years ago?

Wealthy Romans lived in large houses with under-floor heating, known as a hypocaust. Slaves fed fuel onto a fire which sent hot air circulating beneath the raised floor of the house. Hot air also made its way through flues in the walls, which allowed smoke to escape. Romans living in parts of their empire far from sunny Italy (such as Britain) must have been grateful for this luxury. The fire also heated water for the bathroom.

How long have people used weighing machines?

Accurate scales or weighing machines are vital for science, and also for trade and business. The Ancient Egyptians had equal arm balances, much the same as are still used today. Such balances have been in use for some 7,000 years!

COMMUNICATING

■ Prehistoric people sent messages by using drumbeats, fires, and smoke signals.

■ The first writing was picture-writing, so people drew pictures to tell a story.

■ The people of Sumer in Mesopotamia invented a form of picture-writing about 3500 B.C.

■ Long scrolls were awkward to carry. So for sending messages, people used wax tablets. They wrote on the soft wax with a pointed stick.

■ People in Ancient Rome were able to read the news. A handwritten news sheet of 59 B.C. was a forerunner of the newspaper.

In Ancient Egypt, few people went to school. Some boys trained as scribes. A scribe's job was writing. He had to learn more than 700 hieroglyphs. Spelling tests were a nightmare!

▼ **Egyptians making papyrus into paper. Papyrus is made from a kind of reed. The stages of the process turned the reeds into a smooth paperlike writing material.**

I Papermakers cut and peeled the reeds.

Who were the first people to use paper?

Paper was first made in China about 2,000 years ago. Before the invention of papermaking machines in the 1800s, each sheet of paper was made separately by hand. The only machines involved were trip hammers, driven by waterwheels. These ground rags mixed with water into a pulp. The pulp was then put in a vat, and a wire screen was dipped into it. The screen picked up a thin coating of pulp. It was lifted out, shaken, and laid on felt, and was put in a screwpress to press out the moisture. Each sheet was then peeled off the felt and hung up to dry.

2 They cut the reed stems into thin slices and laid them in rows, one on top of the other.

3 They hammered them until the sticky plant juices glued them together.

5 Finally, all the pieces of papyrus paper were glued into a long strip and rolled into a scroll.

4 Next they used a smooth stone or a special tool to rub the surface of the papyrus paper smooth.

When were cannon first used in battle?

The Chinese invented gunpowder rockets, but cannon were not used for battle in Europe until the 1300s. The early guns were clumsy and fired solid cannon balls. Often their metal barrels exploded under the force of the gunpowder, doing more damage to their own side than to the enemy.

▲ This early cannon of the 1400s fired solid stone balls. It could not shoot far, but it could knock down castle walls.

Why did Leonardo's flying machine never fly?

The Italian artist and engineer Leonardo da Vinci (1452–1519), dreamed up inventions that were centuries ahead of their time. He drew plans for a submarine, a parachute, an armored vehicle something like a tank, a helicopter, and a flying machine. His flying machine was never built, for no engine existed to power it. The age of light, powerful motors was still several hundred years away.

In 1482 Leonardo da Vinci told the Duke of Milan that he could build portable bridges, cannons and ships, as well as armored vehicles and catapults!

What was the first steam engine used for?

In 1698 an English engineer named Thomas Savery (1650–1715) devised "an engine for the raising of water and occasioning motion to all sorts of mill works." His engine pumped water from the shafts of tin mines in Cornwall, England. It worked by cooling steam so that it condensed, creating a partial vacuum which "sucked up" water through a pipe.

▶ James Watt improved Newcomen's steampumping engine, making it more powerful. This is his 1775 version, which was soon at work in factories throughout Britain.

Who was called "Father of the Steam Age?"

The Scottish engineer James Watt (1736–1819) is said to have been inspired to improve the steam engine by watching a kettle boil. In 1764 he was trying to repair a model steam engine of the kind invented by Thomas Newcomen (1663–1729). Realizing how inefficient this kind of steam engine was, Watt added a separate condenser to make it more powerful. He also worked out how to change the up and down motion of the beam engine into rotary motion, suitable for driving machinery. These improvements earned James Watt fame as the "Father of the Steam Age."

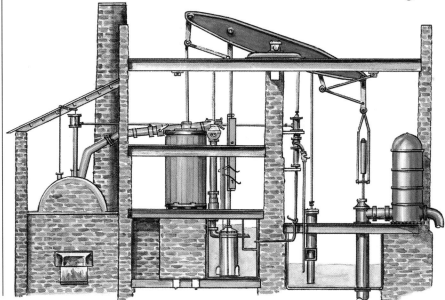

Who built the first reaping machine?

In the 1830s the American Cyrus Hall McCormick (1809–1884) invented a horse-drawn machine to cut grain. The mechanical reaper was followed in the 1850s by the combine harvester.

When were fertilizers first used?

Farmers have always used animal manure to restore the goodness in the soil. It was not until the 1800s that they began applying chemical fertilizers. In 1842 John Bennet Lawes (1814–1900) of Britain found out how to produce super-phosphate from rock. This was the beginning of the chemical fertilizer industry.

How deep was the first oil well?

The Chinese were able to extract oil from below the ground 2,000 years ago, but the first modern oil well was drilled in Pennsylvania in 1859. The pioneer driller was Edwin L. Drake, who bored through 23 yards (21 m) of rock to strike oil. This was 30 years before the first car. The oil was burned in oil lamps.

Who was the most inventive inventor of all time?

This title probably belongs to the inventor Thomas Alva Edison (1847–1931), who had more than a thousand inventions to his credit. Among them were the electric lightbulb, the phonograph, and the kinetoscope, which was an early form of the movie camera.

The best-attended single-day sports event in the world is a car race — the Indianapolis 500. It is called 500 because the cars must cover 500 miles (800 km). The oval track was made from 3.2 million bricks, which earned it the name the Brickyard, as it is still called.

▼ Cars rolling off one of the first assembly lines in the United States.

When were cars first built on an assembly line?

Until 1914 cars were built one by one, as wagons had always been. A group of workers finished one car before starting on the next. The industrialist Henry Ford (1863–1947) changed all this by introducing the first assembly line into his factory. Cars moved along an automated conveyor system. Each part (seats, engine, wheels, and so on) was put on in turn as the conveyor moved along carrying the car bodies. Instead of taking 13 hours to build a Ford Model T car, it took only one and a half hours using the new assembly line. So the cars cost less.

▶ The Model T Ford first appeared in 1908. It became America's most popular car.

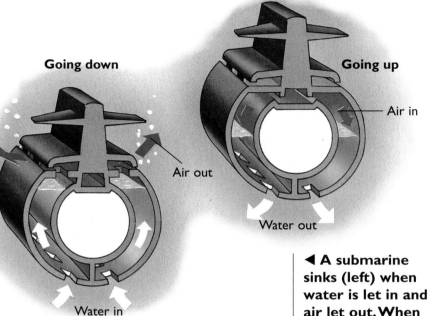

Going down

Air out

Water in

Going up

Air in

Water out

How does a submarine dive?

A submarine dives by flooding ballast tanks with water. The tanks are hollow spaces between the craft's inner and outer hulls. When the submarine is about to dive, valves are opened to let seawater flood the tanks. The submarine loses buoyancy and dives. To surface, water is expelled from the tanks by blowing in compressed air. This makes the submarine more buoyant, and it rises.

What is an aqualung?

Skindivers have ventured below the sea since ancient times, but they could stay below only for as long as their breath allowed. A diver in heavy diving gear relies on air pumped down through a hose. In the 1930s self-contained diving gear was invented. Divers carry air in bottles on their backs, and breathe through valves in their face-masks. This aqualung equipment was developed by Jacques Cousteau (1910–1997) of France.

◄ **A submarine sinks (left) when water is let in and air let out. When air blows water out, the submarine rises (right).**

Without the elevator the modern skyscraper would never have been built. The World Trade Center in New York City has 244 elevators. These travel at up to 1,600 feet (485 m) per minute—about 20 miles (32 km) per hour.

Why were there no skyscrapers before the 1880s?

The taller a stone building is, the thicker must be the walls at its base, to support its enormous weight. This fact limited the height of buildings until the 1880s, when steel frameworks were tried for the first time. In 1885 the Home Insurance Building in Chicago was the first building to have walls that were not load-bearing. It was held up by a metal skeleton of girders and, though only ten stories high, was the forerunner of the skyscrapers for which American cities became famous. By the 1930s, buildings of 100 stories, such as the Empire State Building in New York, were possible.

Flippers

Aqualung (air-tank)

Air hose

Diving suit

Weighted belt

Pressure gauge

Flotation vest

Face mask

◄ **A diver wears a rubber wetsuit, flippers, and face-mask. A thin layer of water trapped between the suit and the body helps keep the diver warm.**

How does a refrigerator stay cold?

When a liquid evaporates (becomes a vapor, or gas) it takes heat from its surroundings. Inside the coils of pipe in a refrigerator is a gas, such as ammonia. This gas is heated and then cooled. Cooling turns the gas into a liquid. As the liquid passes around the refrigerator pipes, it absorbs heat and becomes a gas again. Each time this cycle is repeated, the refrigerator becomes colder inside.

Food spoils because of the activities of tiny bacteria. Such bacteria multiply rapidly when the temperature is higher than about 50°F (10°C). At lower temperatures the bacteria reproduce less rapidly, and food keeps fresh longer.

When were frozen foods first sold?

Long ago, people realized that snow and ice kept food fresh. But until the 1800s there was no way of making ice. Before then, winter ice was cut into blocks and stored in ice houses, but by the summer it had all melted. In 1834 Joseph Perkins discovered how to make ice artificially.

◀ Modern plastics are light yet strong, ideal for children's toys. Millions of copies can be made from a single mold.

What was the first plastic?

In 1862 a British chemist named Alexander Parkes (1813–1890) showed a new discovery at an exhibition in London. The new substance he had made was cellulose nitrate, which he called "Parkesine." It was the first plastic, a tough material. Parkesine was later renamed celluloid and developed by an American, John Wesley Hyatt (1873–1920).

When were aerosol sprays first used?

The aerosol spray can was invented in 1941 by an American, Lyle D. Goodhue. The container (containing paint or hairspray, for instance) also contains a propellant—a gas under pressure. The gas, mixed with the contents, sprays out when the button on the can is pressed. It is important that aerosols contain only gases that do not damage the atmosphere.

Alexander Graham Bell invented the telephone, but he also produced a kite that could carry a person; in 1917 he built a hydrofoil boat which reached 70 mph.

▼ The iceman delivering ice blocks was a familiar sight before people had refrigerators and freezers at home.

TRANSPORTATION AND COMMUNICATION

What was the earliest vehicle?

The most ancient of all vehicles is perhaps the sled. This was used in Stone Age times, and not just in snow. Putting a load (such as an animal killed for food) on a sled made it easier to drag, because the smooth wood produced less friction as it rubbed against the rough ground. Putting runners on the sled made it even easier to drag. One day someone added wheels—and made the first cart.

Who built the first steam-driven vehicle?

A French soldier named Nicolas Cugnot (1725–1804) built a carriage driven by a steam engine in 1763. It had three wheels, and Cugnot thought it would be useful for hauling cannon. Unfortunately, it was very slow, and after a few test runs, it went out of control and overturned. His superiors decided to stick with horse-drawn artillery, and Cugnot's ill-fated machine was locked up for safety.

How did the Rocket outstrip its rivals?

Steam locomotives that could run under their own power on road or rails were developed in the early 1800s. In 1829, British pioneers gathered to race their steam locomotives at the Rainhill trials.

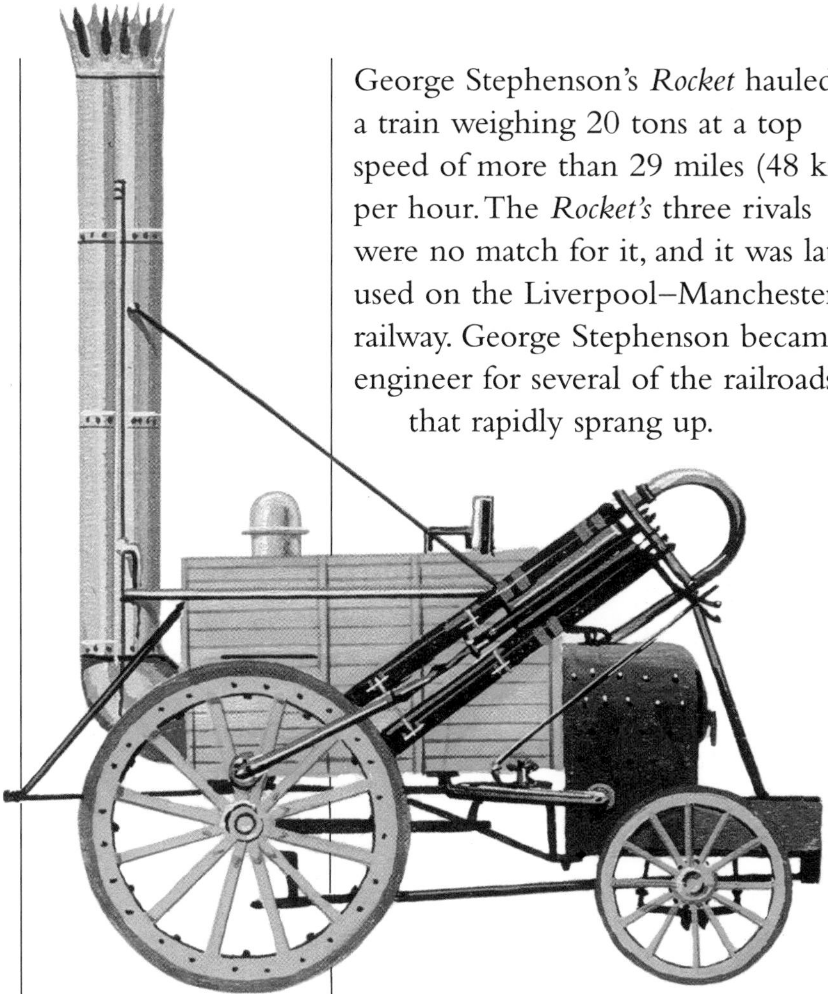

▲ Stephenson's *Rocket* was the fastest steam locomotive of its day. Inside its boiler were five tubes, so more water was heated. This meant more steam drove the *Rocket's* pistons.

George Stephenson's *Rocket* hauled a train weighing 20 tons at a top speed of more than 29 miles (48 km) per hour. The *Rocket's* three rivals were no match for it, and it was later used on the Liverpool–Manchester railway. George Stephenson became engineer for several of the railroads that rapidly sprang up.

When was the first electric railroad opened?

In 1879 a 300-yard (274 m) stretch of electric tramway was opened in Berlin, Germany. It was the brainchild of Werner von Siemens (1816–1892). Four years later, his brother Wilhelm (1823–1883) opened an electric railway in Northern Ireland. By the 1920s electric lines were operating throughout the world. Electric trains are now so advanced that the French TGV train has exceeded 310 miles (500 km) per hour.

When did the modern bicycle appear?

Several improvements in bicycle design in the 1800s brought about the shape we know today. The pedals were moved from the front wheels to a position between the wheels, and a chain drive was added. Wire-spoke wheels, sprung saddles, gears, ball bearings, and a free-wheel device were other important changes made by the 1880s. Last to be added was the pneumatic (air-filled) tire.

Who built the first internal combustion engine?

In 1863 a Frenchman named Etienne Lenoir (1822–1900) designed an engine that burned coal gas. He used it to drive a cart. In 1864 the Austrian Siegfried Marckus built a similar engine which used gasoline vapor, and designed an electrical ignition system.

When did the first motor vehicle take to the road?

The first motor vehicle powered by a gasoline engine was a three-wheeler built in 1885 by Karl Benz (1844–1929), a young German engineer. His first trial run in his "horseless carriage" ended in an accident, when he drove it into a wall. That same year, Gottlieb Daimler (1834–1900) built a motorcycle. By 1886 Daimler had produced his first car. It had a single cylinder engine and a top speed of 18 miles (29 km) per hour.

▶ **Karl Benz built his first car in 1885. It had three cart-style wheels and was steered by moving the front wheel.**

Induction	Compression	Power	Exhaust
Fuel and air mixture in	Mix squeezed; spark causes ignition	Combustion (explosion)	Waste gases out through valve

▲ **Inside a four-stroke gasoline engine. The up-and-down piston movement is changed to an around-and-around movement of the drive shaft linked to the wheels.**

In 1865, just after the first steam coaches appeared the "Red Flag Act" ruled that any car should have someone walking in front of it carrying a red flag!

What makes a car engine go?

The power of the car engine comes from an explosion. If gasoline is mixed with air and then ignited by a spark, it explodes. In the internal combustion engine, the explosions are controlled inside cylinders. Each explosion pushes a piston downward. The pistons are connected to a series of shafts which in turn are connected to the wheels of the car.

▶ A cutaway of the 1983 record-breaking jet car *Thrust 2*. It was really an engine on wheels, with a small space for the driver.

How fast can a car travel?

Cars fitted with rocket and jet engines can travel much faster than those with ordinary gas engines. In 1997 Andy Green set a new record in the jet-engined *Thrust SSC* with an average speed of 714 miles (1,149 km) per hour.

What were the first boats like?

The earliest boat was probably a floating log. Then people learned how to build rafts by lashing together logs or bundles of reeds. They hollowed out tree trunks to make canoes. The first boats were driven by paddles. Sails came later.

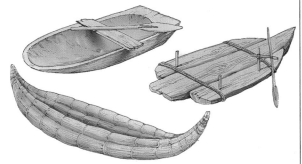

▲ The first boats were dugout canoes made by hollowing out tree trunks, reed boats, and rafts made from planks of wood.

The very first car to go faster than 62 mph (100 km/h) did not run on oil but was battery-powered. It was called *La Jamais Contente*. Amazingly, it did this about 100 years ago in 1899.

Surface-piercing hydrofoil

Fully submerged hydrofoil

▲ Hydrofoils can skim over water at more than 68 mph. There are two types of hydrofoil, each having a different foil shape.

When did ships first have rudders?

Early ships were steered by a large oar hung over the stern. Chinese vessels were probably the first to be fitted with a rudder, and by the 1200s ships with rudders had appeared in Europe.

Who built the first steamboat?

By the late 1700s inventors in several countries were experimenting with the new power of steam to drive ships. In 1783 a French nobleman, the Marquis de Jouffroy d'Abbans (1751–1832), built a boat with paddles worked by a steam engine. He called it the *Pyroscaphe* (meaning "fire-craft"). It was the first steamboat.

Who invented the steam turbine?

The high-speed steam engine was made possible by Sir Charles Parsons (1854–1931), a British engineer who invented the turbine in 1884. Steam was passed through the blades of a series of spinning rotors, which converted the steam's energy into fast circular motion. Parsons built a steam turbine-powered launch, *Turbinia*, that startled naval experts in 1884.

Why can a hydrofoil travel faster than an ordinary speedboat?

A hydrofoil has special legs, or foils, beneath its hull. When motionless, the hydrofoil floats low in the water like a normal craft. But at speed it lifts up on its foils. This reduces the friction between the hull and the water.

Who were the first people to fly?

Over the centuries, many brave but misguided experimenters have tried to fly. We know of nobody who succeeded before November 21, 1783, when two men, Pilatre de Rozier and the Marquis d'Arlandes, flew in a Montgolfier hot-air balloon above Paris. Their flight lasted 25 minutes.

Why did Orville Wright lie on his stomach during the first airplane flight?

The Wright brothers, Wilbur (1867–1912) and Orville (1871–1948), made the first sustained flight in a powered craft when their *Flyer 1* took to the air on December 17, 1903. It had a homemade gas engine set on the right-hand wing. To keep the plane stable, the pilot (Orville, on the first historic flight) had to lie on the left-hand wing.

Can aircraft fly without engines?

A glider is an airplane without an engine. It stays aloft by diving at a very flat angle, or by soaring on rising currents of warm air.

▲ Two brothers, Joseph (1745–1799) and Etienne (1740–1810) Montgolfier, built the world's first hot-air balloon to carry people into the air.

The parachute may have been used as long ago as the 1400s. Drawings made then show cone-shaped canopies, with people dangling underneath.

When did jets first fly?

Piston engines were found not to work well at high altitude, where the air is thin, or at very high speeds. A new type of engine was needed. As early as 1930 a British engineer named Frank Whittle (born 1907) had patented a jet engine design, but the first jet plane to fly was German. This was the *Heinkel He 178,* tested in 1939. British and American jets flew soon afterwards, during World War II.

How does a helicopter fly backward?

A helicopter's rotor blades act as both wings and propellers. To hover, or to fly upward, the blades are kept flat. To fly forward, the blades are tilted forward so that they "bite" into the air. To move backward, the rotor blades are tilted toward the tail.

How does a jump-jet hover in midair?

The *Harrier* is an example of a vertical takeoff or "jump-jet." It has four swiveling nozzles which direct exhaust gases from the jet engines.

Exhaust nozzle

Turbofan jet engine

◄ The *Harrier* takes off and hovers with its jet nozzles pointing downward. To fly forward, the pilot simply swivels the nozzles to direct the jet thrust backward.

Who first sent a radio message across the Atlantic Ocean?

Guglielmo Marconi (1874–1937), an Italian engineer, developed the idea of wireless telegraphy—sending messages in Morse code by radio. The Morse signals were produced by a series of electromagnetic shock waves. The first message sent across the Atlantic Ocean by Marconi consisted of a single letter—S—in Morse code.

Who invented the telephone?

As early as the 1600s people knew that it was possible to send speech along a wire. Two cans linked by a length of string will show you how. But the modern telephone was first demonstrated by Alexander Graham Bell (1847–1922) in 1876. His equipment used two electromagnets which picked up vibrations in a thin sheet of iron (the diaphragm). The vibrations were caused by the sound waves from a person speaking. This principle—the changing of sound waves into electrical signals—explains how the telephone works.

Who took the first moving pictures?

The first cameras needed a very long exposure of the photographic plate— as long as 15 minutes for one picture. To make moving pictures, film must be exposed much faster, at around 16 frames (or exposures) a second. In 1877 Eadweard Muybridge (1830–1904) set up 12 cameras alongside a racetrack to settle a bet. A horse's owner wanted to know if his

IMPORTANT DATES

Communication Firsts

- 1826 Invention of photography, Joseph Niépce (France).
- 1837 Electric telegraph, Samuel Morse (U.S.).
- 1876 Telephone, Alexander Graham Bell (Scotland/U.S.).
- 1878 Microphone, David Edward Hughes (England/U.S.).
- 1888 Kodak camera, George Eastman (U.S.).
- 1895 Radio, Guglielmo Marconi (Italy).
- 1927 First talking picture, *The Jazz Singer* (U.S.).
- 1929 Electronic television system, Vladimir Zworykin (U.S.).
- 1956 Videotape recording, A. Poniatoff (U.S.).
- 1962 First TV pictures across the Atlantic, Telstar (U.S.).
- 1979 Compact disc, Sony (Japan) and Philips (Netherlands).

▲ An early model of the telephone. The inventor, Alexander Graham Bell, first used the device to call his assistant in another room.

horse lifted all four legs at once while galloping. Muybridge's cameras proved that it did. He fixed the still photos on a moving wheel and then projected them with a lantern to make it appear that the horse was galloping.

Who took movie cameras out of the studio?

In France, the Lumière brothers, Auguste (1862–1954) and Louis (1864–1948), pioneered outdoor filming in the 1890s. Their cameras (in which the film reel was turned by a handle) were light enough to carry. They also reduced the speed at which film was exposed to 16 frames a second rather than the 48 used by earlier pioneers. This saved film and reduced flickering. Moving picture shows became popular with the public.

How were television pictures first sent across the Atlantic?

In 1962 the Telstar communications satellite relayed TV pictures between North America and Europe for the first time. A network of communications satellites now orbits the Earth to provide worldwide live television coverage.

When were video recordings first made?

Copies of TV programs had to be kept on film until the invention of videotape recording in the 1950s. The tape stores the image as a sequence of magnetic signals. Videotape made possible the "action replay" of sports events. Video cassette recorders became popular from the 1970s.

SCIENCE QUIZ

THE ANIMAL KINGDOM

How do scientists think life on Earth began?

There are many theories about how life arose. One popular scientific theory states that the Earth had existed for at least 1 billion years before the first signs of life appeared. As the planet cooled, its atmosphere formed. Rains filled the seas, where life began, perhaps because lightning sparked chemical reactions in the primeval "soup" of elements on the young planet. Minerals from rocks formed and reformed new chemical combinations innumerable times, until an unusual chemical combination appeared: a living cell that could feed and reproduce itself. Over millions of years these cells slowly evolved into plants and animals. This is not the only theory of how life began on Earth. Many other people believe that God created the Earth and all living things.

All animals move, even the limpet, which moves about one inch (2.5cm) in its lifetime. Animals take advantage of their ability to move by eating plants.

▼ **The evolution of species is thought to have shaped the "family tree" of life. The prehistory of the Earth is marked into eras, each one of many millions of years.**

What is the difference between an animal and a plant?

The main difference is that animals eat other animals or plants for food, but most plants make their own food. Another difference is that an animal can move and a plant stays in the same place all the time.

What is a family of animals?

When animal experts talk about a family of animals, they do not just mean parents and young. Different animals with similar bodies are said to be in the same family. Wild cats, such as lions, tigers, and leopards, and pet cats all belong to the cat family. The bear family includes polar bears, brown bears, honey bears, and so on.

Mammals
Birds
Reptiles
Amphibians
Bony fish
Sharks and rays
Jawless fish
Echinoderms
Brachiopods
Insects (arthropods)
Crustacea (arthropods)
Molluscs
Worms
Single celled organisms
Single-celled
Bacteria
Fungi
Algae
Mosses
Horsetails
Ferns
Cycads
Conifers
Flowering plants

ozoic ra	Mesozoic Era	Paleozoic Era	Precambrian Era	Paleozoic Era	Mesozoic Era	Cenozoic Era
0	100 200 300 400 500	600	Millions of years 600	500 400 300	200 100	0

What are fossils?

Fossils are found in rock, such as sandstone, that was once soft sand or mud. Fossils are the hardened remains of plants and animals that once lived on Earth. The most common fossils are the shells, teeth, or bones of animals or the tough outer skins of plants. Soft parts of living things are not often preserved.

What were the first land animals?

The early animals were invertebrates —animals with no backbones. They were either soft (jellyfish) or shelled (trilobites). The first animals with backbones (vertebrates) were fishes. The first creatures to move to the land were the ancestors of today's insects and spiders. They fed on the first land plants and on one another. Amphibians —animals that can live on land and in water—appeared about 900 million years ago. They probably developed from fish that crawled out of water onto land and breathed air. Their bony fins evolved into legs and feet.

▶ **Early fish were covered in bony armor. Dunkleosteus was a giant flesh-eater with large teeth to grab its prey.**

▲ **Extinct sea animals such as ammonites are found as fossils. The hard shell was buried by mud and sand that hardened into rock. Millions of years later, the fossil is exposed.**

Dinosaurs ruled the Earth for a very long time. The first ones appeared about 225 million years ago and the last ones we know about died out some 160 million years later.

When did dinosaurs rule the Earth?

For about 160 million years (from 225 million years ago to 65 million years ago) a group of reptiles called dinosaurs were the most successful animals on Earth. Some were small, but others were giants.

Which were the most fearsome dinosaurs?

The most terrible of the meat-eating dinosaurs were creatures such as *Allosaurus*, which lived in Jurassic times (180 to 130 million years ago) and *Tyrannosaurus*, of the Cretaceous Period (130 to 65 million years ago). These animals were nearly 40 feet (12 m) long, and their jaws were lined with razor-sharp teeth. Some other hunting dinosaurs had huge, knifelike claws.

What happened to the dinosaurs?

There are no living dinosaurs today. They seem to have died out at the end of the Cretaceous Period (65 million years ago). Maybe the plants the plant-eating dinosaurs ate died out. Another answer may be that a comet or meteorite hit the Earth, causing an explosion that threw clouds of dust into the atmosphere. The dust blotted out the Sun, plants died—and so did the dinosaurs.

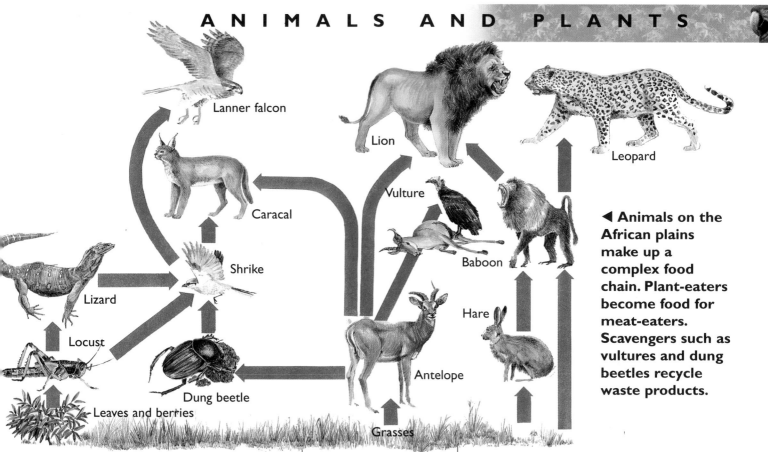

Lanner falcon

Caracal

Lion

Leopard

Vulture

Shrike

Baboon

Lizard

Hare

Locust

Dung beetle

Antelope

Leaves and berries

Grasses

◀ **Animals on the African plains make up a complex food chain. Plant-eaters become food for meat-eaters. Scavengers such as vultures and dung beetles recycle waste products.**

What is a species?

A species is the smallest group of animals that are able to breed among themselves and not with members of another species. Their offspring must also be able to breed successfully. Members of the same species usually look very similar. Human beings are all members of the species *Homo sapiens*.

What is a food chain?

A food chain is a simple way to describe how energy passes from one living thing to another. Here is one example: the grass on the North American prairie grows using energy from the Sun. Grazing animals, such as rabbits and field voles, eat the grass. Coyotes and hawks then eat the rabbits and voles.

▶ **A giraffe can reach higher than other leaf-eating animals. It can also spot danger a long way off.**

ANIMAL FACTS

■ There are about 1.3 million species of animals on Earth today.

■ About 96 percent are invertebrates (animals without backbones).

■ Some experts think there are up to 30 million more species.

■ There are about 4,000 mammals. Compare this to more than 50,000 species of spiders and their relatives!

■ There are about 8,600 species of birds.

■ There are about 6,000 species of reptiles.

■ There are about 2,300 species of amphibians and around 21,000 fish.

■ The longest-lived animal may well be the quahog clam, a shellfish that can live 220 years.

Which is the biggest animal in the world?

The biggest animal that has ever lived is the blue whale. It may grow to more than 98 feet (30 m) in length, and weighs about 157 tons (160 tonnes) when fully grown. Blue whales have been hunted by whalers and are now rare.

Which is the tallest animal?

The tallest animal in the world is the giraffe. A giraffe may reach a height of as much as 20 feet (6 m)—as high as a two-story house.

Giraffe

How many different kinds of animal can fly?

Three: birds, bats, and flying insects. There was one other group of flying animals in the past, the pterosaurs or pterodactyls. They were reptiles, but they are all extinct now. There are also animals that glide rather than fly. They can travel a long way like this, but they don't flap their wings as true fliers do. Gliding animals include the flying squirrels, the flying lemurs, a flying lizard, and even a flying frog. They all have large flaps of skin that help them to glide slowly down.

What is a predator?

A predator is an animal that lives by killing and feeding on other animals. The animals it hunts are its prey. An animal that eats other animals is also called a carnivore. Animals that eat plants are called herbivores. Those that eat all sorts of different food, as people do, are called omnivores.

Which animals give birth to live young?

Mammals—animals such as dogs, cats, monkeys, and kangaroos—are the main groups of animals to do this. But some other animals also give birth to live young, including some fish, snakes, insects, and starfish. These species are all exceptions to the rule.

Mice

Humans

The pitcher plant digests insects. It produces a honeylike substance which attracts insects. They slip and fall into the plant. The plant then digests them.

▼ Molluscs are animals with soft bodies, often protected by hard shells. The octopus is a mollusc without a shell.

Scallop

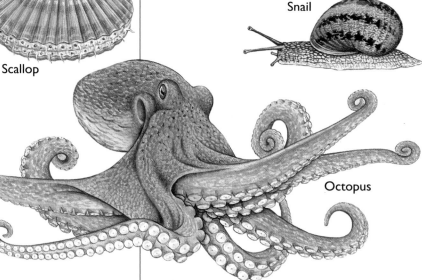

Snail

Octopus

◄ Humans and mice are mammals. The young are fed with milk from their mother. Only mammals feed their offspring in this way.

What is the simplest kind of animal?

A protozoan—it is made up of just one cell. One drop of pond water, when viewed through a microscope, can contain hundreds of these tiny creatures. More than 50,000 different kinds of protozoans are known to exist, and there are probably more!

What is a mollusc?

A mollusc is an animal whose soft body is covered by a thick skin called a mantle. The mantle often secretes a shell, which may lie outside the body, as in snails, or inside, as in cuttlefish. As the mollusc grows, it secretes more shell accordingly.

Which are the most numerous animals in the world?

Of the animals large enough to be seen without a microscope, insects are by far the most numerous. Some estimates have put the number of insects at around one billion billion. For every human being alive in the world, there are about 200 million insects!

MAMMALS

How many mammals are there?

There are about 4,000 species of mammal in the world. A mammal is a warm-blooded animal, which means that it uses some of its food to keep itself warm. Its body is either wholly or partially covered in hair. Female mammals give birth to live young, and feed them on milk produced in glands called mammary glands (from which mammals get their name).

Why do some mammals sleep through winter?

During the winter, many animals in cold countries hide away and sleep. This sleep is called hibernation. Frogs, toads, lizards, snakes, and insects, such as butterflies, all hibernate. So do some mammals, including bats, mice, ground squirrels, chipmunks, and even bears. They do so because food is so hard to find in winter that they would starve. In their deep sleep, their bodies cool down and their heartbeat slows down. They use little energy and live off fat they stored in their bodies before they went to sleep.

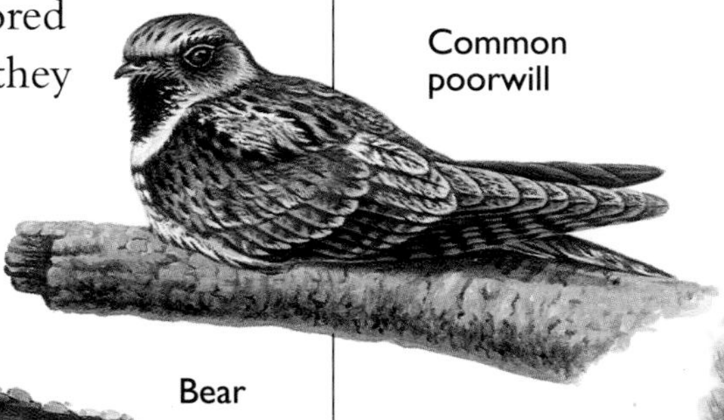

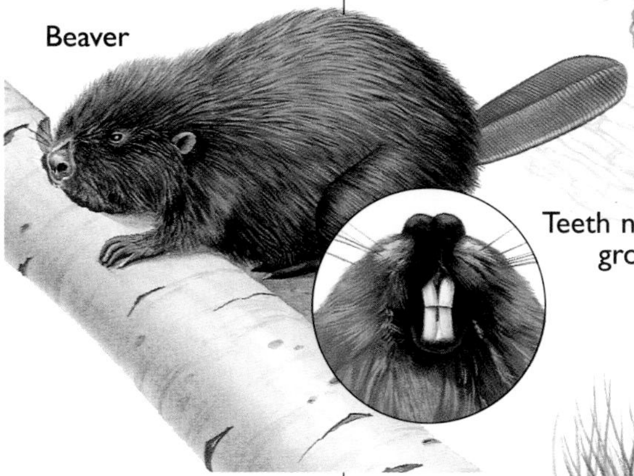

Beaver

Squirrel

Teeth never stop growing

Porcupine

▶ Rodents are animals with large teeth which they use for gnawing. They can crack nuts (squirrel) or chop down small trees (beaver). Their teeth keep growing and are worn away with use.

Common poorwill

Bear

Bats

Dormouse

What is a rodent?

Rodents are the most common group of mammals alive in the world. They include rats, mice, voles, squirrels, beavers, and porcupines. They are small to medium-sized animals with chisel-shaped front teeth which are good for gnawing. Their success may partly be due to the fact that they breed quickly and have large families. Many have several litters a year.

◀ Animals that hibernate eat enough before hibernation to last through winter. The poorwill of North America is the only bird known to hibernate.

109

Why do mammals have hair?

Mammals have hair primarily to keep them warm. But the hair on some mammals has also been modified to serve other functions. Hedgehogs have specially stiffened hair to provide them with protection, while other animals' hair may be colored to provide an effective camouflage. Some stiffened hairs, such as cats' whiskers, are extremely sensitive to touch.

What is a marsupial?

A pouched mammal such as a kangaroo or koala. A marsupial gives birth to its young when they are very small, like tiny pink worms. The young climb through the mother's fur into a pouch, where they feed on milk until they are large enough to leave. Although most marsupials live in Australia, some are found in New Guinea and the Americas.

▲ A bat builds up a "sound picture" in its brain based on the echoes it hears. It hunts by sound, chasing flying insects, such as moths, at night.

Kangaroos use their strong, muscular tails to balance as they hop. Otherwise, a kangaroo would probably fall on its nose!

◄ The wombat, kangaroo, and opossum are marsupials that live in Australia. They carry their young in pouches.

Wombat

Kangaroo

Opossum

How do bats find their way in the dark?

Bats use sound to find their way in the dark and to catch insects. They send out high-pitched squeaks, then listen for the echoes as the sounds bounce off objects in their path.

Why do antelopes graze in large herds?

The open plains where antelopes graze provide little protection from predators, and so antelopes seek safety in large numbers. With so many pairs of eyes, ears, and nostrils on the alert, it is virtually impossible for a predator to spring a surprise attack. Also, large numbers of animals fleeing in all directions can confuse a predator, giving the prey a chance to escape.

What is the difference between horns and antlers?

The main difference between horns and antlers is that horns are permanent; antlers are shed every year.

How can you tell an African elephant from an Indian elephant?

The most obvious difference is in the size of the ears: African elephants have larger ears, which help them to keep cool in the hot African climate. The smaller Indian elephant may also be recognized by its more humped back and shorter tusks. African animals live wild on the grassy plains. They cannot be ridden or put to work by people. Indian elephants come from the rain forests of southern Asia and are trained to lift tree trunks and carry loads.

How smelly is a skunk?

Skunks themselves aren't smelly, but the liquid they eject from their stink glands is so repulsive that it can temporarily stop its victim from breathing. So confident are skunks of their defensive weaponry, that they wander around at dusk in search of their prey (insects, small animals, and berries) in a leisurely, almost brazen manner. Their bold black and white markings serve as a warning to potential predators, and they will erect their tails in a threatening posture if they sense danger.

Why do dogs bury bones?

In the wild, dogs and foxes have a natural tendency to store any leftover food. A red fox that has killed more food than it can eat will dig a hole and bury the surplus, returning to it later when it is hungry. The domestic dog's habit of burying bones is simply a natural urge that it has retained from its wild ancestors.

◀ Wolves live together in groups called packs. The pack hunts together, and this pack instinct is still found in domestic dogs today.

▲ The skunk defends itself by squirting a foul-smelling liquid at its attacker. The skunk's stripes are a warning: leave me alone!

▼ The cheetah is lean and very muscular and can sprint extremely fast for a short distance, covering the ground in huge bounds as it chases its next meal.

Are domestic dogs related to wolves?

Yes. Most scientists now believe that every breed of dog known today is descended from one wild species, the common wolf of Europe and Asia. It is possible that other wild species, such as jackals, have played a part in the origin of modern dogs, but this is unlikely. The oldest fossil remains of dogs, found in Europe and the Middle East, are about 9,000 to 11,000 years old. Dogs were probably domesticated long before that.

What is the fastest mammal?

The streamlined cheetah, with its long legs and supple body, is the fastest mammal on Earth, achieving speeds of over 62 miles (100 km) per hour. It can run fast only in short bursts, lacking the stamina for a prolonged chase. Its main prey are hares, small antelopes, and birds. Cheetahs usually hunt alone or in pairs. Unlike other cats, they cannot retract (draw in) their claws.

Why do tigers have stripes?

The tiger is the largest of the big cats, and usually hunts alone at dusk. Its coat is striped to enable it to blend in with the background vegetation as it stalks its prey—usually deer, wild cattle, or pigs. Often a tiger will pounce on its victim as it pauses to drink at a waterhole.

▲ The tiger is the biggest of the big cats. It hunts alone, often lying in wait in the undergrowth. A female tiger guards her cubs fiercely.

How are monkeys suited to a life in the trees?

Monkeys are adapted to their treetop life because they have a pair of forward-facing eyes (enabling them to judge distances) and long arms with grasping hands. Monkeys are therefore able to move about easily in the trees without having to descend. They move quickly and fluently through the treetops, swinging from branch to branch or climbing between trees in the dense forest canopy. They live in groups and keep in touch with howls, gibberings, and other noises.

▼ The spider monkey uses its strong tail, as well as its hands and feet, to cling to the branches of trees.

What is a primate?

A primate is the most highly developed of all mammals: it has a large brain and good hearing, touch, and vision. There are 179 species of primate, falling into two groups: the prosimians, or primitive primates, including lemurs, aye-ayes, and bushbabies, and the higher primates, including monkeys, apes, and humans.

▲ The chimpanzee is the most intelligent of the apes. Young chimps are playful and can learn simple skills.

Camouflage is used by animals to protect them from their enemies. Many are colored to match their background.

How do apes differ from monkeys?

Orangutans, gorillas, chimpanzees, and gibbons are apes. They look like monkeys but have no tails. Apes also walk in a more upright position than monkeys, though still on all fours.

BIRDS

How many species of birds are there?

There are about 8,600 species of birds, and they live in, on, or above almost every part of the Earth's surface, except for the deep oceans. Different from one another in size, shape, and color, birds are united by one characteristic: the presence of feathers. This is what makes birds unique. No other member of the animal kingdom has feathers.

Can all birds fly?

Not all birds can fly. Penguins cannot fly but use their wings as flippers for swimming underwater. Some species of cormorant, too, have lost the power of flight. Their bodies are so well adapted to swimming and diving that their wings have become too small to support their weight in flight. Some flightless land birds, such as the Australian emu, have powerful hind legs. These birds can walk great distances and flee rapidly from danger. The kiwi from New Zealand has such small wings they don't even show through its feathers.

Most birds can fold their wings close to their bodies. But penguins can't. They hold their wings stiffly out to the side.

▼ The penguin and kiwi are two examples of flightless birds. Penguins use their wings for swimming. Kiwis creep around in thick undergrowth.

Kiwi

Penguin

▲ The ostrich has long, powerful legs and can run very fast. It has wings but is not able to fly.

Which is the largest living bird?

The African ostrich, 8 feet (2.5 m) tall and weighing up to 300 pounds (136 kg), is the largest bird alive. It is too big to fly but is the fastest creature on two legs, achieving speeds of up to 43 miles (70 km) an hour.

Why do birds have feathers?

There are two main reasons why birds have feathers: to keep them warm and to help them fly. Feathers may also provide birds with beautiful plumage to make them attractive to the opposite sex.

Why do birds preen?

Birds keep their feathers in condition by preening. The bird smears its beak with oil from a gland and runs its beak through its feathers like a comb.

What are feathers made of?

Feathers are made of a horny protein substance called keratin. This is the same substance from which our hair and fingernails are made, the difference being in the way the feather is constructed. Keratin combines lightness with strength and flexibility, and this makes it an ideal building material for feathers.

Why do birds molt?

A bird drops worn-out feathers and replaces them with new ones. Most birds lose only a few feathers at a time, so they can still fly and keep warm. Winter coats are thicker for warmth. In the breeding season, birds tend to grow more brightly colored plumage.

How are birds able to fly?

Almost every part of a bird's body is designed for flight. Their wings and body shape are streamlined and their bones are light. Because flying uses up huge amounts of energy, their lungs have become very efficient and their internal digestive system is able to release energy from food very quickly.

How do birds keep flying without getting tired?

Birds use up lots of energy when they flap their wings. To reduce the amount of energy used, many have evolved ways of flying, such as soaring and gliding, which don't involve flapping. When they need to flap their wings, as during a rapid takeoff, their special breathing system ensures that they are supplied with extra oxygen.

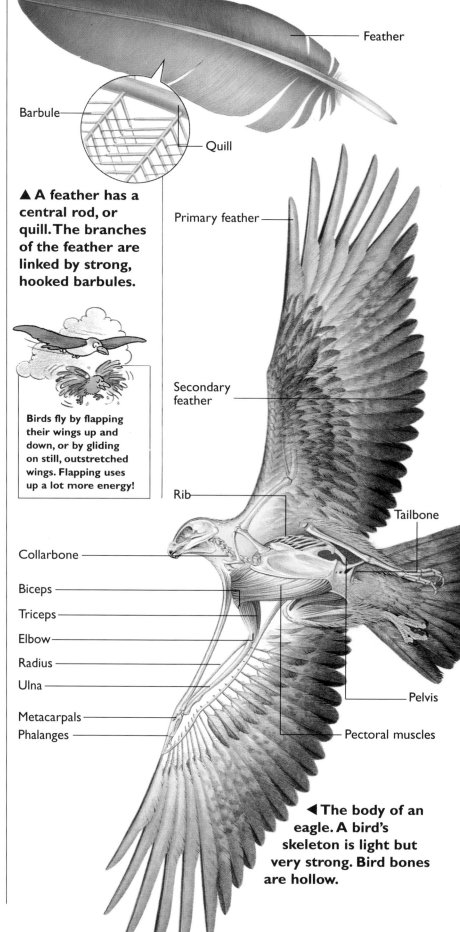

▲ **A feather has a central rod, or quill. The branches of the feather are linked by strong, hooked barbules.**

Birds fly by flapping their wings up and down, or by gliding on still, outstretched wings. Flapping uses up a lot more energy!

Feather

Barbule

Quill

Primary feather

Secondary feather

Rib

Tailbone

Collarbone

Biceps

Triceps

Elbow

Radius

Ulna

Metacarpals

Phalanges

Pelvis

Pectoral muscles

◄ **The body of an eagle. A bird's skeleton is light but very strong. Bird bones are hollow.**

Woodpecker
(drill)

Crossbill
(nutcracker)

Kestrel
(tearing)

Spoonbill
(detector/sieve)

Oystercatcher
(probe)

Why do birds lay eggs?

Birds lay eggs because their reptile ancestors laid eggs, and because it has suited them to retain this characteristic. If a female gave birth to live young or carried a developing egg around inside her body, she would probably be unable to fly because of the extra weight. So birds lay their eggs as soon as possible after mating.

Why do birds build nests?

Birds build nests to protect their eggs and young from the weather and from any marauding predators. Nests also help retain the warmth of the parent bird during incubation. Bird nests vary greatly in size and shape: they can be massive structures of loose branches, or tiny cuplike containers warmly lined with hair and feathers.

How do baby birds hatch?

A baby bird chips its way out of the shell using a special egg tooth on its beak. It pecks away from the inside until the shell cracks and it can escape.

▶ **The woodpecker makes a hole in a tree for its nest. The chaffinch makes a nest of moss and feathers. Storks build big nests of twigs.**

▲ **You can sometimes tell what kind of a food a bird eats from the shape of its beak. Birds use their beaks as tools; five different ones are shown here.**

BIRD FACTS

■ The ostrich lays the biggest egg of any bird; it weighs about 3¾ lb.

■ The smallest bird is the bee hummingbird of Cuba, which weighs less than 0.05 oz.

■ Depending on its species, a bird has between 940 and 25,000 feathers.

■ The world's fastest animal is a bird. The peregrine falcon can reach 186 mph in a dive.

■ The bird with the longest wings is the wandering albatross: nearly 90 feet across.

Why are birds' beaks all so different?

Birds' beaks are so different because they all eat different kinds of food. Seed-eaters tend to have short, strong, wedge-shaped beaks for picking and cracking seeds, while insect-eaters have thinner, pointed beaks which they use like tweezers to extract small prey. Birds that catch insects on the wing often have short beaks and wide gaping mouths which they use like fishing nets as they fly along. The beaks of flesh-eating birds are usually strong and hooked, suitable for ripping flesh off their prey.

Why do birds sing?

Birds sing to attract other birds of the same species or to warn them off. Males sing to attract females as mates. The song also warns other males that the singer has its own territory and will defend it. Parents and chicks recognize one another's voices.

Stork

Woodpecker

Chaffinch

◄ **Two great crested grebes dance to show that they are a pair. Many birds choose new mates (often more than one) each season, whereas others pair for life.**

Why do some birds dance?

Dances form part of the mating displays of certain birds. Great crested grebes perform an elegant courtship dance on the water to establish a firm pair bond. Often their display includes head-shaking and taking turns to preen each other. The display ends in an exchange of weed, in which two birds rise up out of the water facing each other and present their gifts.

Why do birds migrate?

Birds migrate as the seasons change in order to find the food and living conditions that suit them best at different times of the year. Each year songbirds, seabirds, waterfowl, and waders all make long, difficult journeys from their summer breeding quarters to their winter feeding grounds. They do this to take advantage of the seasonal variations in climate and food supply.

► **The Arctic tern is the champion long-distance flier. Its amazing migration takes it across the world and back again.**

DID YOU KNOW?

■ Treecreepers nest under the bark of trees. They find a loose piece of bark and make a nest behind it.

■ Perching birds, or songbirds, can sleep without falling off branches. They have three forward-pointing toes and one backward-pointing toe, for a firm grip.

■ Jays happily sit on ant nests. Angry ants crawl among the bird's feathers, squirting stinging formic acid. The acid gets rids of lice and fleas which make the bird itch.

■ Woodpeckers use their stiff tail feathers as supports when climbing trees.

■ Owls fly silently. Soft fringes on the feathers muffle the sound of the owl's wingbeats.

Which bird flies from the North Pole to the South Pole (and back again)?

Arctic terns spend months continuously on the wing at sea. They breed within the Arctic Circle during the summer months, and then head south for Antarctica to take advantage of the summer season there. They cover more than 22,000 miles on the round trip.

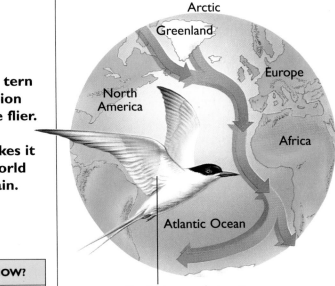

Arctic tern   Antarctica

Which birds carry water in their breast feathers?

Sandgrouse are birds that live in dry and desert areas in Africa and the Middle East. The males have special breast feathers that soak up water like a sponge. The males carry water to their chicks.

Why do woodpeckers peck wood?

They feed on insects which burrow in wood and under bark. They also nest in trees and will peck out holes if they can't find a suitable nest hole. Some woodpeckers drum their beaks loudly against trees to attract a mate.

REPTILES AND AMPHIBIANS

What is an amphibian?

An amphibian can be thought of as the halfway stage between a fish and a reptile. Most amphibians spend the first part of their life in water and the adult phase on dry land. They have soft, moist skins and lay their eggs in water or very damp surroundings. They live in wet places, such as swamps and marshes, although they cannot survive in the sea.

How many species of amphibians are there?

Compared to fish, reptiles, birds, and mammals, the total number of living amphibian species is rather small. Some 2,300 species are known, and these can be divided into three groups: frogs and toads (amphibians without tails); newts and salamanders (amphibians with tails); and caecilians (burrowing, limbless amphibians confined to the tropics).

What do frogs and toads eat?

All frogs and toads are flesh-eaters and, as a rule, eat only living prey. Their diet is usually made up of insects, spiders, slugs, and worms. Frogs and toads have long, sticky tongues which they shoot out to catch their prey. Some larger frogs, notably the horned frogs and bullfrogs, are able to eat small mammals, such as voles or shrews, and other amphibians.

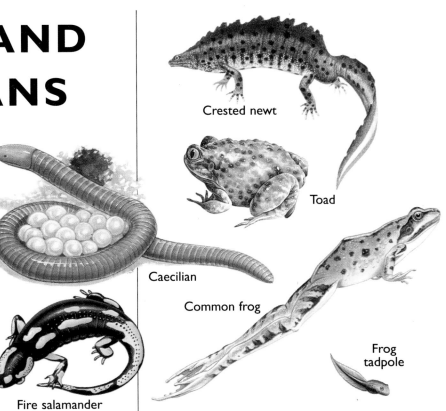

Crested newt

Toad

Caecilian

Common frog

Frog tadpole

Fire salamander

▲ Amphibians are found all over the world, except in places that are very dry or cold. Most amphibians have four legs, but caecilians are legless amphibians.

How do tadpoles turn into frogs?

When tadpoles first hatch out, they bear little resemblance to their frog or toad parents. Breathing through gills and swimming by means of fishlike tails, these tiny black creatures cannot leave the water. They grow back legs, and then front legs, and their tails shrink. They develop lungs and, now looking like frogs, leave the water.

Adult

Fertilized eggs

16 weeks old

2–3 days old

12 weeks old

6 days old

► The life cycle of the frog.

Why are some South American tree frogs so colorful?

A surprising number of frogs (some 500 species) spend their lives in the treetops. South American tree frogs are typically very brightly colored to warn predators that they are extremely poisonous to eat. All amphibians have mucous glands in their skin to keep them moist. In some frogs these glands also produce a poison so lethal that it can paralyze a bird or monkey instantly. South American Indians use secretions from golden poison-arrow frogs to poison the tips of their hunting arrows.

What are newts and salamanders?

Newts and salamanders are amphibians with long cylindrical bodies, long tails, and two pairs of equally developed, though often feeble, legs. Salamanders tend to be larger and spend less time in the water than newts. Salamanders are sometimes mistaken for lizards, but the salamander's rounded head and smooth skin (as opposed to the lizard's pointed head and very scaly skin) are a sure way to tell the two animals apart.

Marbled newt

Reptiles live almost everywhere on Earth. But these animals don't like the cold, so there are none living around the Poles.

▲ A poison-arrow frog. Bright colors can mean that a frog is poisonous.

▼ Newts and salamanders look fairly similar, but salamanders spend more time on dry land. Like all amphibians, they breed in water.

Spectacled salamander

How do reptiles differ from amphibians?

Unlike amphibians, reptiles have solved the problem of water loss from their bodies by developing a dry, scaly, watertight skin. Their eggs are protected within a leathery shell, so reptiles can lay their eggs on dry land. The 6,000 species of reptiles living today are the survivors of an age when reptiles dominated life on this planet. Of the 16 or 17 different groups known to have existed, only four remain: turtles and tortoises; crocodiles and alligators; snakes and lizards; and one reptile in a group of its own, the tuatara.

Why do most reptiles live in warm climates?

Reptiles are cold-blooded. This means that they can take their heat from their surroundings. Reptiles are most active in warm climates, where the plants and insects they eat are available all year round, but they can go for long periods without eating, because they need less energy to stay alive. When it gets cold, their body temperature drops and they become very sluggish.

What is a tuatara?

A tuatara looks like a large lizard, but is in fact a unique reptile. It is the only survivor of a widespread group of reptiles that arose some 200 million years ago and flourished before the dinosaurs. It is a stocky, strongly built animal with a large head and primitive backbone and sluggish movements. It survives only on a few remote islands of New Zealand.

Why does the green turtle travel such a long way to lay her eggs?

Green turtles feed in warm coastal waters all over the world, yet at nesting time will travel hundreds of miles to lay their eggs on the beach where they themselves were born. Turtles feeding off the coast of Brazil will travel over 1,200 miles (2,000 km) to the lonely island of Ascension in the middle of the Atlantic Ocean to lay their eggs. This is because South America was once joined to Africa, and as the continents slowly drifted apart, so the gap between Ascension Island and the coast of Brazil grew bigger. The turtles continue to make the journey there and back, crossing the ocean.

Why do tortoises move so slowly?

Tortoises have no need to move quickly because they carry their armor around with them! At the first hint of danger they withdraw their head and limbs into their shell until it is safe for them to come out again. Their slow lifestyle also means that they can keep going while using only a small amount of energy.

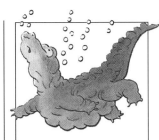

Crocodiles swallow stones to weigh themselves down in the water. This stops them from floating to the surface while hunting.

▼ **Cobras are poisonous snakes. A cobra spreads flaps of skin to make a hood to scare an enemy before it bites.**

◄ **This giant tortoise, like all tortoises, has no teeth. Its mouth is like a beak with a hard bite for chewing leaves, fruit, and grass.**

What is the difference between a crocodile and an alligator?

It is easy to mistake an alligator for a crocodile, as both have armor-plated bodies and long, powerful jaws. The most obvious difference between them is in the shape of the head. Crocodiles have narrower, more pointed snouts and their lower four teeth stick out when their mouths are closed, whereas alligators' snouts are broader and more rounded.

Are all snakes poisonous?

There are some 2,700 species of snakes, of which about a third are poisonous. Snake poison is known as venom, and is stored in special venom glands on the head. These venom glands are connected to hollow or grooved fangs, so that when the fangs sink into a victim's skin, venom gushes through the fangs into the victim's body.

Venom sac

Fang

How do rattlesnakes rattle?

The tail of a rattlesnake is made up of hard, bell-shaped, interlocking segments. When the snake feels threatened, it shakes its tail so the segments rub against each other and rattle. A completely new rattle segment forms every time the snake sheds its skin.

Why do snakes shed their skins?

In fact all animals, including humans, shed their skins, due to natural wear and tear. A snake's tough skin doesn't grow as the snake gets bigger, so the snake has to shed it from time to time, like taking off a tight coat.

How does a chameleon catch its food?

Chameleons are highly specialized tree lizards, and their ability to change color to match their surroundings is well known. They capture their prey by means of an extremely long and sticky tongue, which is catapulted out with such speed that few insects stand a chance of escaping. On spotting a suitable prey, both eyes then work separately to give the chameleon a clearer picture of its victim. In this way the chameleon can be said to have the best all-round vision of any reptile. Chameleons change color when angry or excited, as well as to hide from enemies. Some kinds go black with rage!

▶ **A snake's old skin begins to split at the lips, and the snake wriggles out head first, turning the skin inside out as it goes.**

Chameleons are masters of disguise. They can change their color to match their surroundings—well, almost!

Does the Komodo dragon breathe fire?

Unlike the fabulous winged monsters of popular myth, the Komodo dragon does not breathe fire, nor does it fly. This solidly built animal with a huge head and long thick tail is the largest of all living lizards. It lives on a few islands in Indonesia and preys on animals such as deer and wild pigs.

Komodo dragon

▲ **The chameleon's sticky tongue is longer than its body! It shoots it out in a twinkling and reels it back with an insect meal.**

FISH

Water out
past gills

Blood vessels

Water in
through mouth

Gill filaments

Gill arch

Water flowing past

Oxygen-rich
blood

Oxygen-poor blood

◄ **Feathery filaments in a fish's gills take in oxygen from the water. The oxygen passes into the fish's blood and is carried around the fish's body.**

How many fish are there?

Fish are the most numerous of all vertebrates. There are estimated to be about 21,000 different types of fish, of which about a third live in freshwater and two-thirds in the sea. Scientists classify fish into three groups: jawless fish (of which there are about 60 species); sharks and rays (about 600 species); and bony fish (more than 20,000 species). The bony fish are the most successful and have colonized almost every body of water on Earth.

How do fish swim?

Most fish swim using a side-to-side movement, the thrust forward being powered by a wave of muscular contraction spreading down the body. The strong muscles that run down either side of the fish's body may sometimes account for up to 75 percent of the fish's weight, and are the part of the fish we like to eat. The fish uses its fins for steering, braking, and balance. Some fish also fan their fins to keep themselves in one position. The fastest fish, the blue-finned tuna, can swim at 37 miles (60 km) per hour.

Seahorses are not strong swimmers, so they hang on to seaweed with their tails to avoid being swept away.

Why do fish die if taken out of water?

Like all animals, fish need oxygen to live. Unlike land-living animals, fish can take in oxygen only from water. When a fish is removed from water, it is removed from its source of oxygen and soon dies if not put back. Fish gulp in water through their mouths, forcing it over their pink gills and out through openings on either side of the head. The water keeps flowing over the gills, bringing fresh oxygen.

► **Fish swim by using their muscles to ripple their bodies along. Wiggling their tails from side to side gives them some extra push.**

Why do fish lay so many eggs?

Fish lay large numbers of eggs because the chance of each one surviving to adulthood is very small. The majority of fish lay tens of thousands of eggs, then have nothing more to do with them. Many eggs are eaten before they even have a chance to hatch out. Those fish that do exercise some form of parental care, such as the seahorse and stickleback, tend to lay fewer eggs.

Which fish can fly?

The South American common hatchetfish and its related species are the only fish in the world known to use powered flight (as opposed to gliding, like a flying fish). Its long pectoral fins act like wings, and you can hear them beating noisily when the fish is airborne. The hatchetfish rarely flies farther than 6 feet (2 m) and flies only when threatened.

Why do some fish swim in groups?

A collection of fish that live and swim together is called a school. The shape can vary from species to species. Herring form ribbonlike schools sometimes several miles long. Others, such as the Californian sardine, may rush together to form a compact ball if startled. Commercial fisheries rely on the fact that fish form schools —it is much easier to catch densely grouped fish than scattered individuals. So this good form of protection from other animals is actually a drawback when faced with a fishing net!

FISH FACTS

- There are about 250 kinds of sharks.
- Not all sharks are huge. The smallest is just 6 inches (15 cm) long.
- The longest bony fish is the oarfish, which can grow 49 ft (15 m) long.
- Sharks known to attack people include whites, blues, and hammerheads.
- Barracuda and moray eels have also attacked people.
- A female cod can lay up to 9 million eggs. But very few of the young survive.
- Flatfish—for example flounder, lie on their sides on the seabed.
- The African lungfish has feeble gills. It swallows air into a pair of simple lungs.
- The stonefish has 13 poisonous spines on its back. This ugly fish lies on the seabed and is extremely hard to spot.

How do sharks and rays differ from bony fish?

Sharks and rays live only in the sea and differ from other fish in having a skeleton made of cartilage instead of bone. Cartilage is similar to bone, but more rubbery and not so hard. Their skin is rough, like sandpaper, and they have no protective flap over their gills, which makes their gill slits easy to see. The most important difference is the absence of a swim bladder: sharks and rays have to keep swimming to keep afloat; otherwise they sink to the seabed.

Which is the biggest fish?

The biggest living fish is the whale shark, which can reach lengths of up to 59 feet (18 m). It is a filter feeder, feeding on small fish and plankton.

▲ A whale shark is a gentle giant. This enormous fish lays eggs as big as basketballs.

◀ Fish swimming in a school seem to move as one, coordinating their every movement with amazing precision.

◄ The giant manta cruises peacefully through the ocean. It eats tiny plankton, guiding them into its mouth with two fleshy flaps on its wide head.

Why is the giant manta also called a devil ray?

You only have to look at this fish to guess why! With large flapping "wings" (which are really huge pectoral fins) spanning over 20 feet (6 m), it glides effortlessly through the water like some ghostly bird. Seamen thought this sinister-looking fish was a harbinger of doom, and pearl-divers were afraid that they would be smothered by the ray's wings. They need not have worried, for giant mantas are completely harmless to humans. They feed mainly on plankton and small crustaceans.

How fierce are piranha fish?

The ferocity of the piranha fish is legendary. Its razor-sharp jaws are operated by huge muscles and are lined with large, pointed triangular teeth. These fearsome jaws are capable of chopping out a piece of flesh with the precision of a razor. Unlike most predatory fish, piranha hunt in schools, and their aggressive behavior is thought to be linked to the breeding season, when males are

▼ The piranha has razor-sharp teeth. These small fish hunt in large groups and usually eat other fish or dead animals.

guarding the eggs. Piranha are found in the streams and rivers of South America. They are attracted to any disturbance or hint of blood in the water. One reliable record tells of a 100-pound (45-kg) rodent being stripped down to a skeleton in less than a minute.

Are all sharks dangerous?

There are at least 250 species of sharks in the world, and of these, only about 25 are considered dangerous to human beings. These include the great white shark, the hammerhead shark, the tiger shark, and the mako shark. The largest of these, the great white shark, has a fearsome reputation, having been involved in many attacks on humans. Tropical beaches in areas known to be frequented by sharks are often protected by shark nets out at sea.

◄ One aggressive shark is the hammerhead. Having eyes and nostrils so far apart may help it track its prey.

Why do salmon leap up waterfalls?

Salmon have been known to leap as high as 10 feet (3 m) in their efforts to return upstream to their breeding grounds. The salmon is a remarkable fish. The mature adult, having spent several years at sea feeding and growing, returns to breed in the river or stream in which it was born. Once breeding has finished, many salmon die, their bodies wasted and exhausted by the journey.

How does the stickleback build its nest?

The male stickleback builds his nest using small pieces of water plants, gluing them together with a sticky secretion from his kidneys. Once he has assembled a small heap, he then burrows through the middle to make a tunnel, thereby completing the nest. Displaying a bright red belly, the male entices a female into the nest to lay eggs. The male stickleback guards the nest until the eggs hatch and the young are ready to leave. The males do not learn this behavior but all perform exactly the same actions.

How do some fishes make electricity?

About 250 kinds of fish can produce electric shocks. They do this to find their way in muddy water and also to kill their prey. The most powerful electric fishes can produce shocks of several hundred volts—enough to stun a person. Special muscles work like batteries.

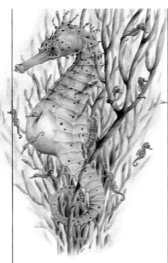

▲ The male seahorse looks after the eggs. He keeps them in a pouch on his body until the young hatch and can look after themselves.

▼ Deep-sea fish look weird, with gaping mouths, stomachs that stretch, and baitlike lures to attract a meal.

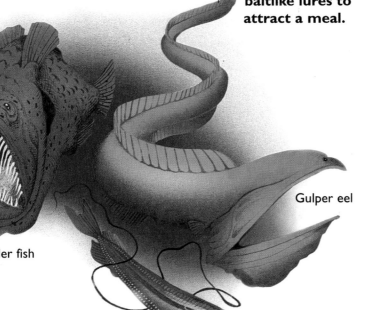

Angler fish

Gulper eel

Dragon fish

What kind of animal is a seahorse?

A seahorse is a very strange animal. It lives in the sea, and its head looks like a horse's head. But it is much smaller than a horse, being no more than 6 inches (15 cm) long. It has a curly tail and no legs and swims in an upright position, using a fin on its back. The fin gives it away, for the seahorse is in fact a very unusual kind of fish.

Why is the coelacanth called a living fossil?

Coelacanths are large, heavy-bodied fish which were thought to have died out 70 million years ago. When a living coelacanth was caught off the coast of South Africa in 1938, it was as if someone had discovered a living dinosaur! Living coelacanths bear close similarities to their fossilized ancestors. Their lobed fins have fleshy bases which look like the beginnings of limbs, and they are known to give birth to fully-formed live young. Scientists believe that some of the first vertebrates to live on land looked like coelacanths that walked on their fins.

What is life like for a deep-sea fish?

The world of the deep-sea fish is black and cold. Below 2,500 feet (750 m) no sunlight filters through, so no plants are able to grow. Food is scarce, and deep-sea fish have to rely on other animals for their food. To cope with these difficult conditions, deep-sea fish have evolved special mechanisms, which give them strange and often frightening appearances. Most have huge jaws.

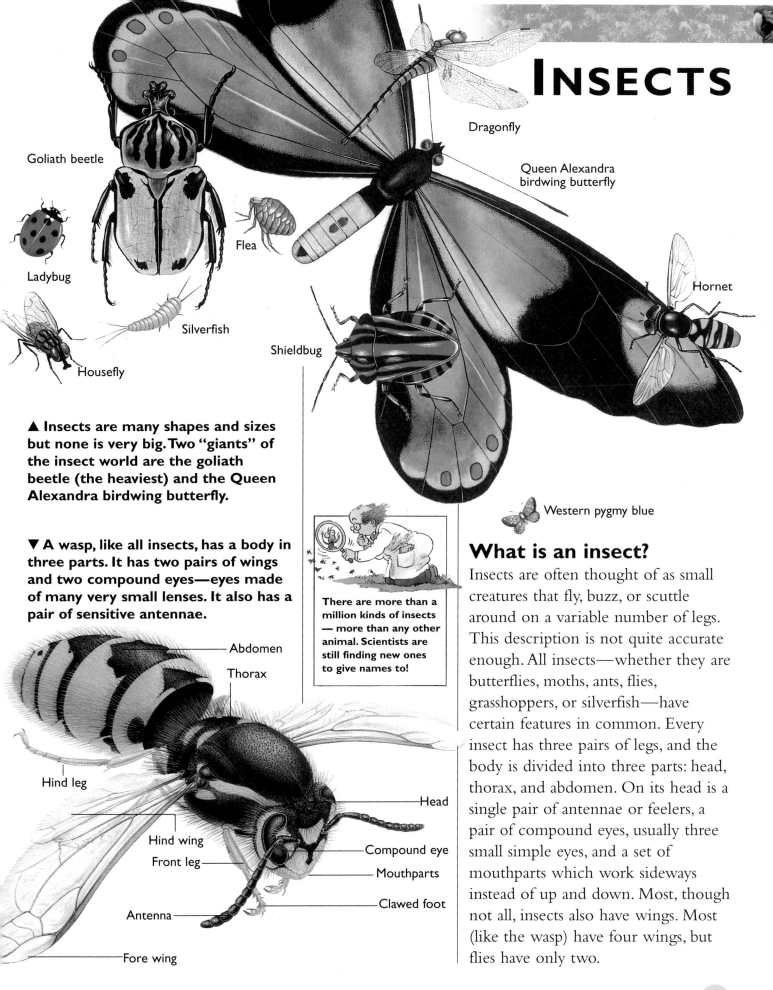

INSECTS

Goliath beetle

Ladybug

Flea

Housefly

Silverfish

Dragonfly

Queen Alexandra birdwing butterfly

Shieldbug

Hornet

Western pygmy blue

▲ Insects are many shapes and sizes but none is very big. Two "giants" of the insect world are the goliath beetle (the heaviest) and the Queen Alexandra birdwing butterfly.

▼ A wasp, like all insects, has a body in three parts. It has two pairs of wings and two compound eyes—eyes made of many very small lenses. It also has a pair of sensitive antennae.

Abdomen

Thorax

Hind leg

Hind wing

Front leg

Antenna

Fore wing

Head

Compound eye

Mouthparts

Clawed foot

There are more than a million kinds of insects — more than any other animal. Scientists are still finding new ones to give names to!

What is an insect?

Insects are often thought of as small creatures that fly, buzz, or scuttle around on a variable number of legs. This description is not quite accurate enough. All insects—whether they are butterflies, moths, ants, flies, grasshoppers, or silverfish—have certain features in common. Every insect has three pairs of legs, and the body is divided into three parts: head, thorax, and abdomen. On its head is a single pair of antennae or feelers, a pair of compound eyes, usually three small simple eyes, and a set of mouthparts which work sideways instead of up and down. Most, though not all, insects also have wings. Most (like the wasp) have four wings, but flies have only two.

Life cycle of a butterfly

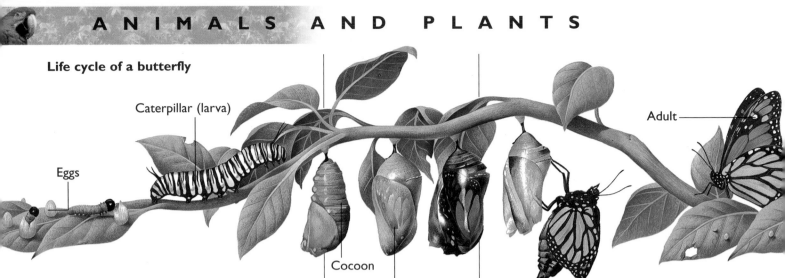

Caterpillar (larva)

Eggs

Cocoon

Pupa

Adult

How do insects grow up?

Insects go through changes as they grow from the egg to the adult. These changes are called metamorphoses. There are two types: insects such as grasshoppers pass through three stages, each resembling the adult more closely. This is incomplete metamorphosis. Complete metamorphosis, as in the butterfly, involves four stages: egg, larva, pupa, and adult. The intermediate stages bear no resemblance to the adult. You could not guess that a caterpillar would turn into a butterfly. Inside the pupa an amazing change takes place—and a butterfly comes out.

Which ant grows its own food?

Like other ants, leafcutter ants, of Central and South America, are "social" insects—they live together in groups called colonies. These ants strip leaves from trees and use them as a basis for growing fungi in underground "gardens." The workers chew the leaves and compress them into fungus beds, fertilizing the growth of the fungus with their droppings. The growing fungus is used to feed the whole ant colony.

▲ **Butterflies lay eggs that hatch into caterpillars. Each caterpillar spins itself a cocoon and becomes a pupa. Finally an adult butterfly emerges.**

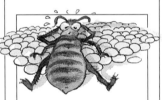

A queen bee lays up to 3,500 eggs a day for several weeks at a time. She is the only mother in the beehive!

▶ **A bee feeding from a flower becomes dusted with pollen. It carries the pollen to other flowers, perhaps a long distance away, and so fertilizes them.**

How do bees make honey?

Honey is made from nectar, the sugary liquid present in flowers. It is sucked up by bees using their long tongues and stored in their honey stomachs. When the bee's honey stomach is full, it returns to the hive and passes the nectar to other workers as a thin runny fluid. The hive bees then mix the nectar with secretions from their mouths before depositing it in open cells in the honeycomb. Within about three days the nectar compound is transformed into honey. The finished honey is then sealed with a wax cap until needed for future use, to feed young bees or as winter food for all.

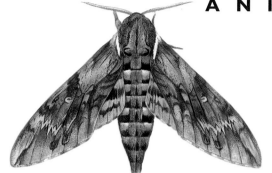

Hawkmoth

Peacock butterfly

What is the difference between a butterfly and a moth?

People tend to think of moths as dull colored, night-flying insects with fat, furry bodies, and butterflies as brightly colored, day-flying insects. In fact there are many brightly colored moths that fly by day. The six-spot burnet moth and the emperor moth are two examples. To a scientist, the real difference lies in the shape of their antennae and the linkage between the fore and hind wings. A butterfly's antennae are long and slender, and tipped with knobs, while the moth's antennae are thin and feathery. At rest, most butterflies fold their wings over their bodies, revealing their underside pattern, while moths hold their wings either spread out flat or at an angle to each other.

How does the grasshopper sing?

A grasshopper produces its familiar chirping sound by rubbing its hindlegs over the ribs of its fore wings. On the inner side of the femur, or "thigh" of each hindleg, is a row of tiny, evenly spaced pegs, and these are stroked over the prominent veins on the forewings. Usually it is only the male who sings.

▲ **Moths look like airplanes, with swept back wings. Most butterflies fold their wings when they are resting.**

▶ **The termite queen lays thousands of eggs, attended by the king. Soldiers defend the nest while workers gather food.**

INSECT WONDERS

■ Insects breathe through tiny holes in their bodies.

■ Many insects can drag an object 20 times their own body weight.

■ A caterpillar has from 2,000 to 4,000 muscles – six times as many as you!

■ A tiny midge holds the record for fast wingbeats: more than 62,000 times a minute.

■ Ants lay scent trails to food so other ants can follow them.

Why are termites called white ants?

Termites are pale, soft-bodied insects, and, like ants, they live in large, underground colonies. They also have a caste system to separate the different functions of its members. But those are the only similarities. Termites have straight antennae, but an ant's antennae are bent. An ant's body has a "waist" between the thorax and abdomen, but the termite does not. Ants and termites evolved along similar lines, but in fact termites are more closely related to cockroaches than to ants.

King

Worker

Queen

Soldier

Why are stick and leaf insects so called?

It is not hard to see why stick and leaf insects are named as they are. Practically indistinguishable from a background of twigs, leaves, and branches, the stick and leaf insects are camouflage experts. They rest motionless during the day, their long twiglike bodies blending perfectly with the surrounding branches, and move and feed only at night. Even their eggs are camouflaged to look like the seeds of the plant on which they live. These curious insects occur mainly in the tropical regions of Asia and live in trees and shrubs.

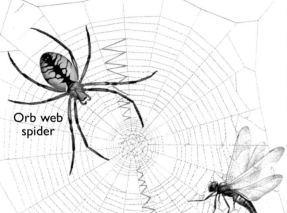

Orb web spider

Dragonfly

Is a spider an insect?

Spiders are not insects but arachnids. Unlike an insect, which has six legs, a spider has eight legs. Spiders do not have wings, nor do they have antennae, although a pair of slender palps at the front of the head may sometimes be mistaken for these. A spider's body is usually hairy and is divided into two main parts—a combined head and thorax, and an abdomen. The two are linked by a narrow waist. All spiders have a pair of poison fangs with which they kill their prey, and all are capable of producing silk, although they don't always use it to make webs.

Do all scorpions have a deadly sting?

Scorpions are related to spiders. The sting of a scorpion is located at the tip of its long curvy tail, which is either held to one side or arched over the scorpion's back. Some scorpions have only a mild sting, while others can be deadly to human beings. Scorpions live in hot, dry regions, and hunt at night.

◄ This orb web spider feels the dragonfly's efforts to escape and rushes to wrap its prey in silk to add to its food store.

▼ Lobsters and crabs are crustaceans. Hermit crabs take over the shells of other animals.

Lobster

▼ The scorpion is a relative of the spider. They use their stings for defense and to paralyze their prey.

Do centipedes really have a hundred legs?

Although "centipede" literally means "a hundred feet," no centipede has exactly that number. Some may have more, some less, but the most familiar garden centipedes have only 15 pairs of legs. Centipedes like to live in dark, damp places such as under logs and stones.

What are echinoderms?

The echinoderms are a group of spiny-skinned animals, which include such sea creatures as starfish, sea urchins, brittlestars, and featherstars. They are usually symmetrical and have their organs arranged in multiples of five. For example, starfish normally have five arms but some may have as many as 50.

Hermit crab

What is a crustacean?

Crustaceans have sometimes been described as the water-breathing insects of the sea. They do in fact belong to the same group (Arthropoda) as insects, and comprise an enormous variety of species, most of which live in the sea. All crustaceans have hard shell-like outsides, and two pairs of antennae, and some kinds have claws. Crabs, lobsters, crayfish, shrimps, waterfleas, and barnacles all belong to this group of animals.

ANIMALS IN DANGER

Why do animals die out?

When a species dies out, it becomes extinct. In the Earth's history there have been periods of mass extinctions —when the dinosaurs disappeared about 65 million years ago, for example. In the last 200 years people have become the most serious threat to animals. By destroying their habitat (the places in which they live) or by killing the animals themselves, humans have, since 1800, killed off more than 300 animal species. The rate at which animals are becoming extinct is increasing. Many hundreds of species are now in serious danger.

American alligators were once hunted for their skins. By the 1960s they were an endangered species and the hunting was stopped. Fortunately, now their numbers are rising again.

What is the greatest worldwide threat to animals?

The destruction of their habitats—the forests, prairies, coral reefs, swamps, or other places in which they live. Most of the animals that die out in the 21st century will do so because we have destroyed their homes. To reduce the damage, we need to protect animals' habitats and not destroy them for farming and buildings. We also need to restrict the growth of human populations.

Why did the dodo become extinct?

This flightless bird lived on the island of Mauritius in the Indian Ocean. Dodos were very tame and unafraid of humans. Sailors found it easy to kill the birds and stock their ships up with meat. Eventually, the dodos died out. On remote islands there are no large predators, such as cats, to pose a threat to birds. So birds, like the dodo, could lose the power of flight and still be safe. However, when sailors arrived, bringing cats and rats, the dodo was doomed. Surviving flightless birds such as the ostrich have defenses —powerful legs for running away and for kicking an enemy.

◄ The woolly mammoth was a relative of the modern elephant. It was hunted by early people, who may have speeded its extinction.

▼ The dodo could not fly to escape new enemies, like people and cats. Its eggs were eaten by rats.

Where are lemurs found?

On Madagascar, and nowhere else on Earth. Lemurs are an ancient group of animals, related to the ancestors of the monkeys and apes. They are less intelligent than the monkeys and died out in most parts of the world, as the monkeys evolved and took over their habitats. Only in Madagascar did the lemurs survive, because the monkeys never reached this island.

Why is tuna fishing a threat to dolphins?

Some types of dolphin like to swim with schools of tuna. Off the western coast of North America, fishermen use the dolphins to locate the tuna, which are usually swimming below them, out of sight. When the tuna are netted, the dolphins are also killed. To avoid this, many fishermen now use lines instead of nets.

Where do coral souvenirs come from?

From living coral reefs. These are either blown up with dynamite or broken up with iron bars dragged by ships. This shatters the coral into pieces that can be sold. Either process is very destructive. A reef takes thousands of years to build up and provides a home for thousands of different animals.

▶ The baby koala goes everywhere with its mother. It spends six months in her pouch and then six months clinging to her back.

◀ Lemurs now live only on the island of Madagascar. They look like monkeys but in fact are less advanced animals.

ANIMALS IN DANGER

■ Tigers in Asia are in danger. Their forest refuges are threatened, and many tigers are killed by poachers.

■ Parrots and other exotic birds are caught illegally and sold as caged pets.

■ Polluted seawater kills marine animals and seabirds.

■ Herring and cod, fish that once teemed in the oceans, are becoming scarce because we catch too many for food.

■ Many turtles cannot reach the beaches where they breed because hotels have been built there.

Why is there concern about the koala?

Koalas are suffering because Australian forests are being destroyed. If food is plentiful, koalas are great survivors. They managed to recover from intensive hunting between 1900 and 1930 and were, until relatively recently, expanding in most areas. But the increasing pace of forest destruction is a threat to them, as to many other Australian animals.

What is the wildlife trade?

Millions of wild animals are trapped or killed each year. Some are caught alive to be sold as pets. Birds and tropical fish in particular are in danger from this trade, but so are snakes and monkeys, among others. Many more wild creatures are killed for their skins. Most of this trade is against the law.

Are gorillas a national asset?

Rare animals can be saved only if local people benefit from their survival. In Rwanda, a small and war-troubled country in central Africa, foreign tourists could be invited to see the rare gorillas that live in Rwanda's forests. The money tourists spend is a useful addition to the national income of poor countries with valuable wildlife. Such countries can benefit from preserving wildlife as tourist attractions.

How many blue whales are there left?

Probably about 1,000. For a large animal like the blue whale, which breeds slowly, this is a dangerously low number. Blue whales have been completely protected from hunting since 1967, but there has been no marked increase in numbers, and the species is still endangered. Most whales are now protected from hunting, but some are still killed.

▶ Gorillas are immensely powerful but are peaceful animals. Left alone in their forest homes with their families, they harm no one.

The blue whale is so long that eight elephants could stand along its back.

▼ A few giant pandas live in zoos, but attempts to breed them in captivity have not often been successful.

◀ The blue whale is the largest animal that has ever lived. It is bigger than the biggest dinosaur. One whale can weigh as much as 150 cars!

Why is the giant panda so rare?

This panda was probably never common in China, and it is entirely dependent on bamboo for food. It needs enormous amounts of bamboo, so each panda has a very large territory. As the bamboo groves are cut down to make way for agriculture, the panda's habitat is slowly disappearing. Even where the bamboo remains, it is often in such small areas that only two or three pandas can live there. They will not cross open country, so they cannot reach other groups of pandas to find a mate. Small, isolated groups of this kind are destined to die out.

What kind of animal is the Tasmanian tiger?

This animal is not a tiger, but a marsupial mammal. It is more closely related to kangaroos and koalas than to the tigers of India. The first European to reach Australia called it a "tiger" because of the striped pattern on its hindquarters. The Tasmanian tiger—or thylacine, as it is often known—is thought to be extinct. But there are occasional reports of some of them still living in remote parts of Tasmania. It once inhabited the whole of Australia.

Why is the African elephant in danger?

Elephants in Africa are killed for their tusks, which provide ivory. Ivory is used only for decorative objects and piano keys. The search is on for an artificial substitute for ivory, to give the elephant a chance to survive in the wild. Elephants need a lot of space. If they stray into fields, they trample crops. The safest place for elephants is a game reserve, but even there poachers sometimes kill them.

▼ **Burning elephant tusks to try to stop the ivory trade. Poaching for ivory is the main threat to elephants.**

▶ **The black rhino is one of the world's most endangered animals. It is killed for its horn.**

Elephant herds are thriving so well in some parks that their overbrowsing is causing serious damage which is threatening many other African animals and plants.

How is the black rhinoceros being protected from poachers?

Rhinoceros horns are valued in Asia for use in traditional medicines and for making the handles of ceremonial daggers. All species of rhinoceroses are now dangerously low in numbers because of illegal hunting, or poaching. In some national parks in Africa, wardens are immobilizing rhinoceroses with tranquilizing darts, then sawing off their horns. This operation apparently does the rhinos no lasting damage, but it takes away all their value to poachers.

How did the oryx return home?

The Arabian oryx is a large antelope, whose numbers fell dangerously low due to uncontrolled hunting. By the early 1960s there were only about 100 to 200 animals left. In 1962, three oryx were captured and combined with zoo animals to form a captive breeding herd. Animals from this herd were later returned to live in the wild.

THE PLANT KINGDOM

What are the simplest plants like?

The first plants appeared about 3.5 billion years ago. They were single-celled algae and diatoms. Such plants are very tiny. A single drop of water can contain 500 diatoms.

Which are the most successful plants?

The flowering plants are the biggest and most successful plant group. There are more than 250,000 different kinds. They include grasses, cacti, trees, peas and beans, vines, potatoes, spices, and many garden and wild flowers. All these plants have flowers which play a part producing seeds to grow into new plants.

PLANT RECORDS

■ The oldest known plant is the creosote plant in California. It is around 11,700 years old.

■ The fastest-growing plant is bamboo. It can grow at 3 ft a day.

■ The Welwitschia, a desert plant of South Africa, lives for over 100 years but grows only two leaves.

■ A wild fig in South Africa had roots 394 ft (120 m) long—the longest roots ever measured.

■ The smallest plant is an Australian floating duckweed. This tiny water plant is just 0.02 inches long.

▼ Flowering plants color and scent the summer days. Their seeds are spread by animals or by the wind.

Why are flowers colored?

Many flowers have brightly colored petals to attract insects. These flowering plants rely on insects to carry pollen from flower to flower. Plants that flower at night often have pale-colored flowers so that they show up in the dark and the night-flying moths can see them. Many flowers give off scent to attract insects to pollinate them.

Why do most plants have flowers?

Flowers help plants to reproduce themselves. The flower produces male and female cells (pollen and egg cells). The egg cells must be fertilized with pollen from another flower of the same kind. Some plants, such as holly, have separate male and female flowers. The flower also protects the egg cells as they grow into seeds.

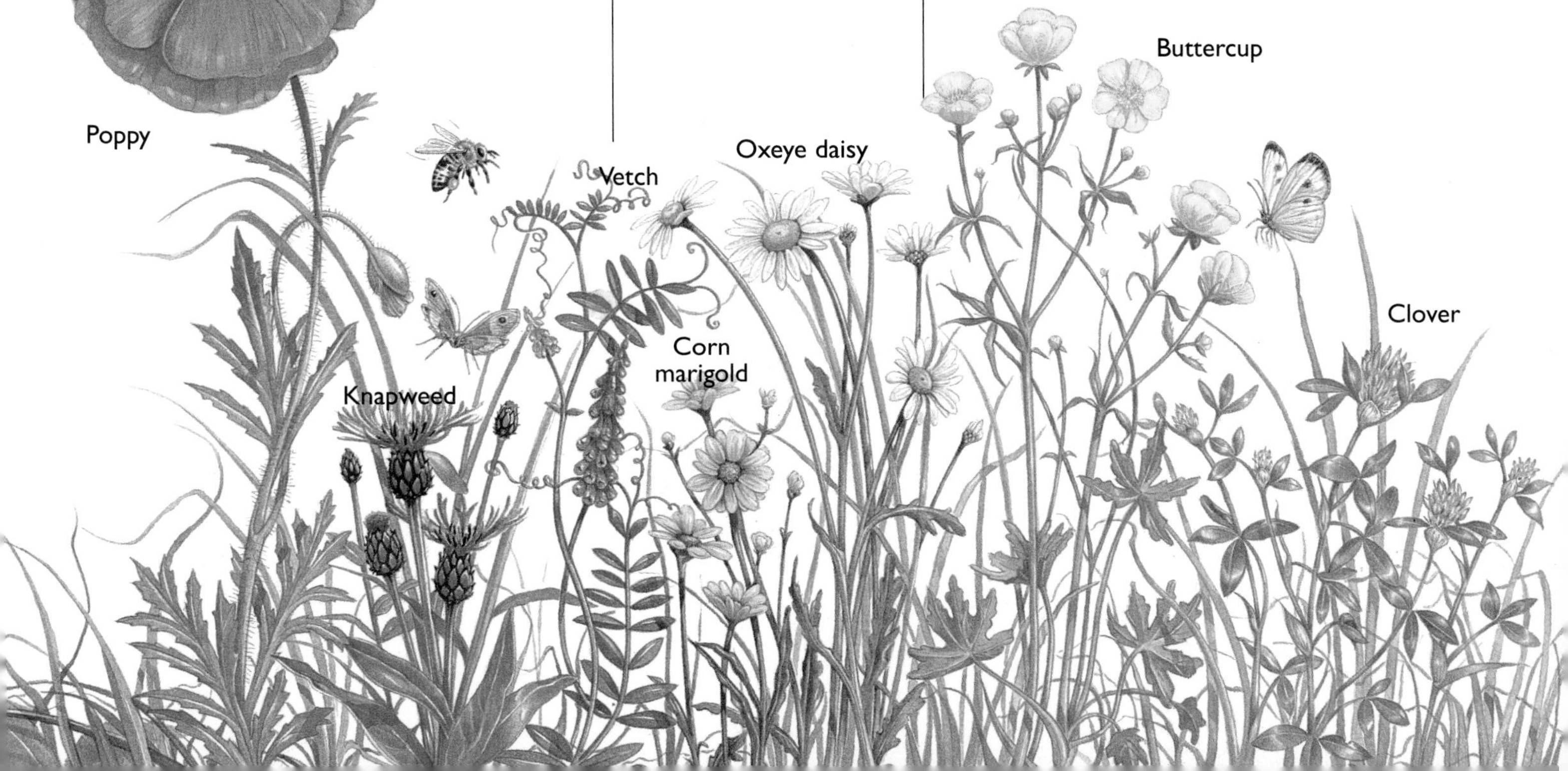

Petal
Stamen
Stigma

Poppy

Buttercup

Oxeye daisy

Vetch

Clover

Corn marigold

Knapweed

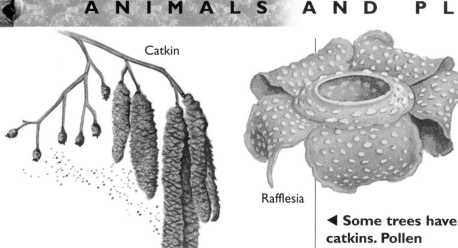

Catkin

Rafflesia

Do all flowers have petals?

No. Some plants are pollinated by the wind or by water. They do not need to attract insects and so their flowers often do not have petals. Many of these plants bloom in early spring, so that leaves do not get in the way of the wind blowing through the branches. The catkin flower of the hazel does not have petals, nor does the giant rafflesia.

Do all flowers close up at night?

Many, but not all, flowers close up at night or when the weather is cold. The daisy closes its flowers when the light begins to fade in the evening. Crocuses are even more sensitive and will open when the sun is shining and close when it goes behind a cloud. Wood sorrel even closes its leaves at night. Some flowers, like the evening primrose, close their petals during the day and open them at night.

Does grass have flowers?

Grass plants do have flowers, but they are not brightly colored because they do not need to attract insects to pollinate them. The flowers do not

◀ **Some trees have catkins. Pollen grains from male catkins are blown to the female catkins, so male sex cells and female egg cells are mixed. The giant rafflesia flower smells like rotting meat, to attract flies.**

▼ **Cacti soak up water during the rainy season and store it in their stems. The cactus shrinks as it uses up water during the dry season.**

have petals, and when the pollen is ready it is just blown away by the wind. Grasses, such as wheat, oats, and barley, are the most important source of food for people. The first farmers found that wild grass seeds scattered as easily as the pollen. Modern farmers have managed to grow crops with tighter flowering heads so that the seeds, or grain, do not fall out.

Do all plants have leaves?

Most, but not all, plants have leaves, though they do not always look like leaves. The blades of grass are leaves. Algae such as seaweed do not have leaves, but they have chlorophyll and can make their own food.

How do plants survive in the desert?

Desert plants such as cacti can live for months or even years without water. They have evolved ways of storing moisture in thick stems or swollen fleshy leaves. Other desert plants store water in their roots. A desert plant may remain dried up and appear dead for years. When rain eventually falls, the desert blooms. The plants spurt into growth. They flower, pollinate, make seeds, and spread them in only a few weeks.

Cactus after the rain

Shallow grooves

Water-filled tissue

Wide-spreading roots

Cactus during drought

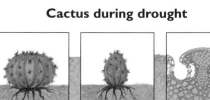

Why do some plants have wings and parachutes?

The wind can spread a plant's seeds over long distances. Some seeds are light enough to blow around easily. Dandelions and thistles have fruits crowned with hairy plumes that act like parachutes. The seeds drift away on the wind. The fruit of some trees such as the birch, maple, and ash have wings. These spin like the blades of a helicopter as they carry the seed away.

Which fruits explode?

A plant needs to spread its seeds to give each one the best possible chance of growing into a new plant. One way to spread seeds is to shoot them out from an exploding capsule or pod. Laburnum trees and other plants of the pea family have seeds in pods. When a laburnum pod dries out, it splits. The two halves twist, flinging out the seeds to spread them so the seedlings can find space to grow. Incidentally, never eat the seeds (or any part) of the laburnum tree, because they are poisonous.

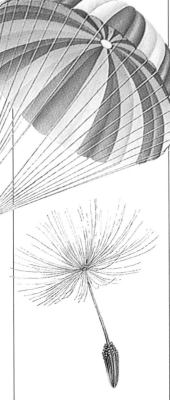

◄ Some plants parachute their seeds. The dandelion's plume of hairs slows its fall so it can drift on the wind.

Why do some plants have no flowers?

Mosses and ferns have no flowers because they do not produce seeds. Instead they produce spores. The spores of a fern form on its leaves and fall. The spore develops into a heart-shaped structure called a prothallus which produces male and female cells. When the female cell is fertilized, it grows into a new fern.

▶ There are about 10,000 kinds of ferns (like adder's tongue) and about 8,000 kinds of liverworts, small plants that grow in damp places (like *Marchantia polymorpha* and *Pellia epiphylla*).

Marchantia polymorpha

Adder's tongue

◄ The European squirting cucumber shoots out its seeds in a jet of water from its balloon-shaped fruit. Water pressure inside forces the seeds out suddenly.

Pellia epiphylla

Why are fungi not really plants?

Fungi are no longer classed as plants, because they contain no chlorophyll and cannot make their own food, as green plants do. Instead they take food from other plants, or scavenge on dead material such as old wood. Fungi produce chemicals which attack cellulose, which green plant cells are made of. In this way a fungus can feed on the plant cells.

Why does a puffball explode?

Puffballs are big, round fungi that look like balloons. The paper-thin wall of the ball bulges inward and bursts when a raindrop hits it, and a cloud of powdery spores escapes. The spores develop into new fungi.

Hang seaweed outside and it might forecast the weather! If it swells up, rain is on the way. If it dries out, it will be sunny.

▼ Seaweed looks like plants but it is really algae. Some seaweed clings to rocks. Some floats on or just below the surface of the sea.

▼ Most fungi produce fruiting bodies (the part we see) in the fall. The rest of the fungus is underground or in wood. Some fungi are good to eat, but others are poisonous.

Why does wet paper go moldy?

Fungi grow on anything made of cellulose—food, clothes, wooden furniture, old books. Anywhere that is damp is a suitable home for the spores of molds and mildews, which are kinds of fungus.

Which plants have no roots, leaves, or flowers?

Lichens are simple plants with no roots, leaves, or flowers. They are actually a combination of an alga and a fungus living closely together. Some grow as crusty patches on rocks, trees, and walls. Lichens grow very slowly and to a very great age (10,000 years old). They are among the oldest known living things and can survive in places that are too bare, dry, cold, or hot for other plants.

How does seaweed survive in the ocean?

Seaweed is tough. It is pounded by waves, and if it lives on the shoreline it is repeatedly soaked and dried out as the tides rise and fall. Many kinds of shore seaweed have branching feet that hold the seaweed fast to the rocks.

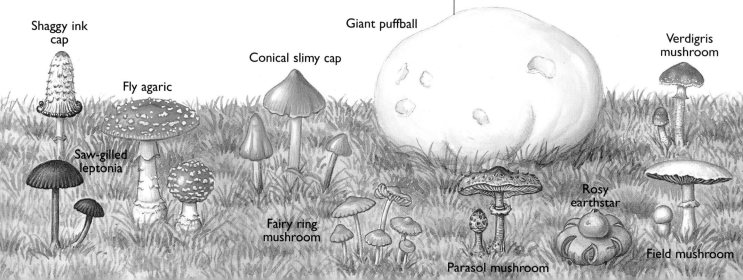

Shaggy ink cap

Fly agaric

Saw-gilled leptonia

Conical slimy cap

Giant puffball

Verdigris mushroom

Fairy ring mushroom

Parasol mushroom

Rosy earthstar

Field mushroom

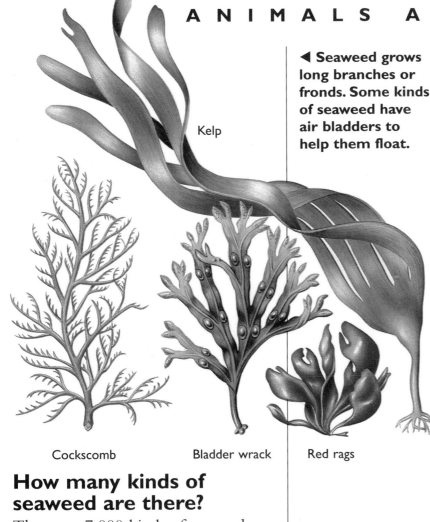

Kelp

◀ **Seaweed grows long branches or fronds. Some kinds of seaweed have air bladders to help them float.**

Cockscomb

Bladder wrack

Red rags

Why does bladder wrack have bladders?

Bladder wrack is a very common brown seaweed. It grows on rocks that are usually covered by water when the tide comes in. It has flat stems with pairs of bladders which are filled with air. These bladders help it to float up from the rocks when they are covered by the sea. Other types of seaweed also have bladders to help them float, and they will pop if you squeeze them.

What is giant kelp?

Giant kelp is the biggest seaweed of all. It can grow up to 200 ft (60 m) long, and grow together to form an underwater forest. The kelp makes an ideal shelter for many fish, lobsters, and other sea creatures. There are many different kinds of kelp. All are a kind of brown seaweed that grow in cool oceans. Kelp is not found in warm tropical waters.

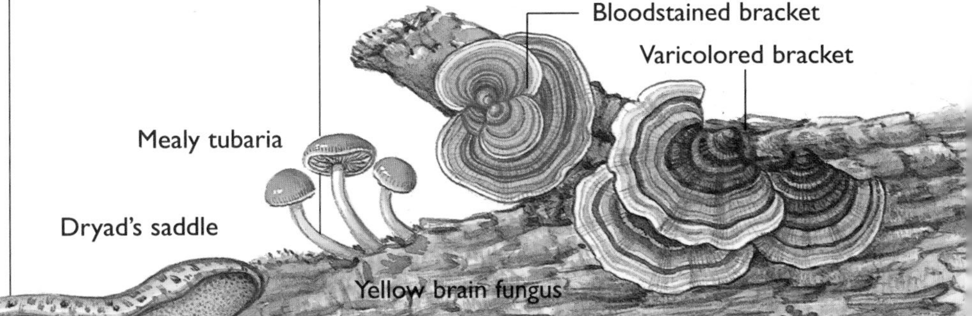

How many kinds of seaweed are there?

There are 7,000 kinds of seaweed, most of which grow near the shore where they can cling to the rocks or the seabed with a footlike "holdfast." Attached to the holdfast is a frond, which sways in the water. Most brown seaweed lives in cool seas, and some grow very large. Red seaweed is most common in warm seas. Green and blue-green seaweed is found in warm and cold seas.

Bloodstained bracket

Varicolored bracket

Mealy tubaria

Dryad's saddle

Yellow brain fungus

Coral spot fungus

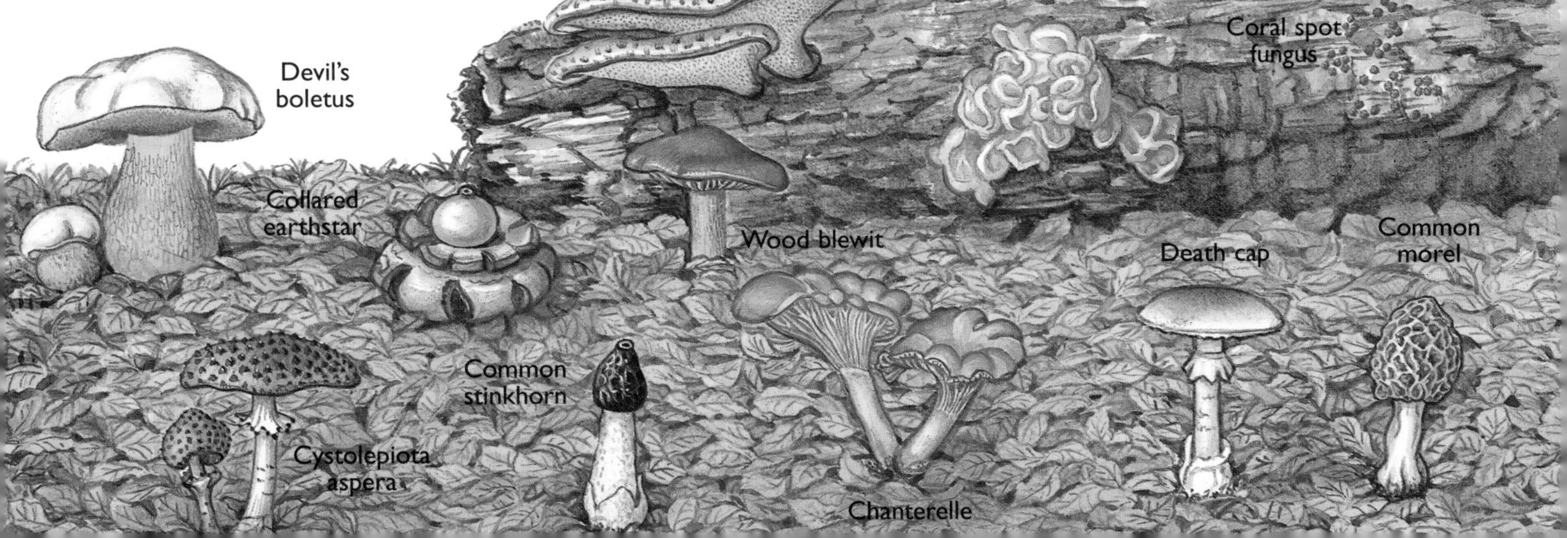

Devil's boletus

Collared earthstar

Wood blewit

Death cap

Common morel

Cystolepiota aspera

Common stinkhorn

Chanterelle

HOW PLANTS GROW

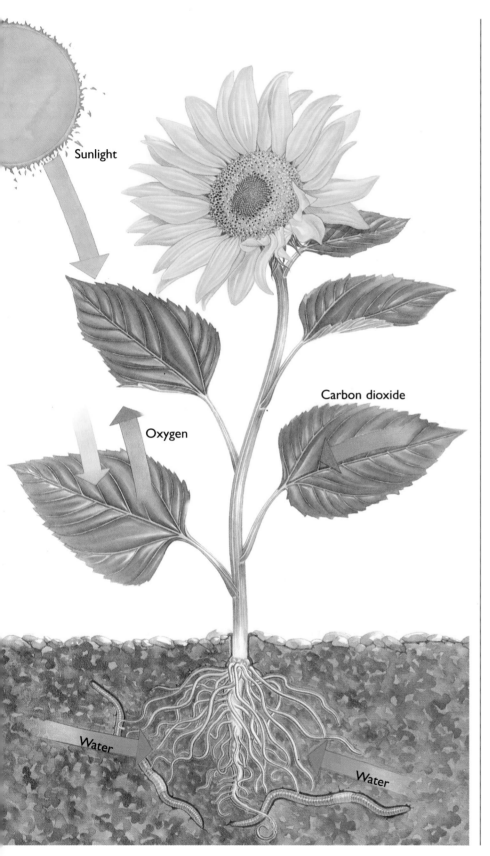

Sunlight

Oxygen

Carbon dioxide

Water

Water

Can plants live without sunlight?

All green plants need sunlight because they use the Sun's energy to make their food. The foodmaking process, called photosynthesis, takes place mainly in the leaves using a substance called chlorophyll. If a green plant is kept in darkness, it soon loses its green color, withers, and dies.

How do plants feed?

Plants have to feed themselves to stay alive, just as people and animals do. However, green plants are able to make their own food. They make sugars and starches by absorbing carbon dioxide through their leaves, and water from the soil and rain through their roots and leaves. They use energy from sunlight to change the gas and water into food, which they can store if necessary. This process is called photosynthesis. Oxygen is given off, which keeps the air supplied with oxygen. The plants also take up minerals through their roots. Fungi such as mushrooms and toadstools are not classed as plants because they do not make their own food. They feed on other plants, or the remains of plants, and can live in darkness.

◄ In photosynthesis, plants use energy from sunlight to turn water (from the soil) and carbon dioxide (from the air) into glucose. Leaves give off oxygen.

How are insects useful to plants?

Insects are useful to plants because they carry pollen from one flower to another. A plant must be pollinated before it can form seeds. Insects are attracted to flowers by their bright colors or by their scent, and by the sweet nectar many flowers produce. Some flowers even look like the insects they want to attract to them. As the insects reach for the nectar, they brush against the flower's stamens and stigmas and the pollen falls onto them. When they go to another flower, the pollen is brushed onto its stigmas.

Why do plants need water?

Over 90 percent of a plant is water. Without water a plant cannot make food by photosynthesis. Water helps to keep the plant's cells rigid. If there is not enough water, the cells become limp and the plant wilts. Most plants need a constant supply of water from their roots.

▶ When a bee lands on a flower, it dips its tongue into the flower to suck up the sweet nectar. At the same time pollen from the stamens sticks to its body and rubs off onto another flower's stigma.

MORE PLANT FACTS

■ Some giant water lilies of South America have leaves measuring 5 feet (1.5 m) across.

■ The giant saguaro cactus of the American desert reaches a height of well over 49 feet (15 m).

■ Plants usually need sunlight. But some plants manage to live at ocean depths where there is no sunlight.

■ The maidenhair tree or gingko of China is the oldest surviving plant species. It appeared about 160 million years ago.

■ The true fruit of an apple is the core, not the juicy part that you eat.

■ The taproot is a plant's main root, the part that is hard to pull up when you are weeding the garden!

◀ Cactus plants are adapted to life in hot deserts. They make use of the smallest drop of moisture.

Why do desert plants spread out?

Desert plants do not grow close together. If they did they would compete for the scarce food and water. Instead they spread out. Desert plants usually have long roots, which spread to catch as much moisture as possible. When it rains, the roots of the plant soak up all the water they can reach from the ground. The plant stores the water in its fleshy stem.

How do plants keep cool?

Plants lose water through tiny pores, or stomata, under their leaves. This loss is called transpiration. At the same time the plant draws up water from the soil into its roots. The water lost through the leaves helps keep the plant cool. The flow of water up the stem from the roots brings with it vital minerals from the soil.

Can a plant reproduce itself without making seeds?

Yes. Plants can reproduce in several other ways. They can split into two, they can grow buds that develop into new cells, they can make spores (as ferns do), or they can reproduce by vegetative propagation. This happens in strawberry plants. The plant sends out a long stem, called a runner, which sprouts roots. If the runner is then cut, its rooted part will grow into a new plant. Similarly, if you cut the eye, or bud, from a potato and plant it, it will send out a shoot to make a new potato plant.

Why are some plants parasites?

Some plants, such as ivy or tropical lianas, use other plants as supports. This avoids spending energy on making their own stem stiff. However, they make their own food. Mistletoe is a part-parasite. It takes some food from the tree it clings to by piercing the bark with rootlike tubes, but it also has green leaves to make some food on its own. Other parasites take all their food from the "host" plant and make none of their own. They are true parasites.

How do climbing plants climb?

Plants climb in different ways. Some, like clematis, are very weak and have twisting stems which climb up other stronger plants. As the stems touch the other plants they grow more quickly on one side and so curl around the other plant. Some plants, like ivy,

The first land plants evolved on Earth just over 400 million years ago. Unlike the limp aquatic seaweeds that they come from, they had tubes to draw up water and stiff stems to help them stand erect in the open air. But, unlike today's plants, they had no leaves, roots, or flowers.

Honeysuckle

Hop

Sweet Pea

Ivy

grow small roots on their stems, and these help them to grow up walls. Peas and squash have special coiled tendrils which wind around a support. Virginia creeper has little pads like suckers which cling to a wall or other surface. Climbing roses and blackberries use their sharp spines to hold onto surfaces or other plants.

How do the leaves of a water lily float?

Water lilies often have large leaves with many air spaces on the underside. The air trapped beneath the leaf makes it float on the water. Also, the leaves usually have strong stems which help them to keep upright. In this way, the water lily exposes its leaves to the light it needs to stay alive.

Why do some plants have thorns?

Thorns, prickles, and sharp spines help to protect a plant from hungry animals. They may also keep insects from boring into the plant. Cows in a meadow will eat grass but not thistles, because they have too many spines. Sometimes seeds are prickly so that they will cling to an animal's fur and so get spread around. They are carried by the animal to a new patch of ground, brushed off, and fall to the earth where they can start to grow.

Bramble

◄ **Some plants twist around stronger plants as they climb. Others have small roots or spines to cling on with.**

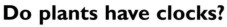

Why does a stinkhorn stink?

A stinkhorn is a kind of fungus which stinks in order to attract flies. It may smell bad to us, but flies like it. They feed on the slime which contains spores and then they carry the spores away on their legs. In this way stinkhorns can spread over a large area —aided by flies.

Why does moss grow in a thick mat?

Moss grows from spores. When the spore starts to grow, it sends out a thin green thread which grows branches. Buds form on the branches and grow into new moss plants. The young plants therefore grow very close together and soon form a mat. Moss leaves are not waterproof, and by growing in thick mats they keep moisture around themselves.

How do ferns grow?

Ferns do not have flowers, so they cannot produce seeds. Instead they have spores on the underside of the leaves. The spores fall to the ground and grow into little disks. The disks contain male and female cells, which later come together and grow into young ferns. Some ferns, like bracken, also spread from rhizomes, or underground stems.

▲ The stinkhorn is well named. Hungry flies swarm toward this smelly fungus, hoping for a meal. They fly off, carrying the stinkhorn's spores.

▼ Under the fern's fronds are sporangia, lined with spores. A spore is blown away and grows into a prothallus, from which a young fern soon develops.

Do plants have clocks?

Many plants know what time of year it is with amazing accuracy. Some flowering plants bloom at exactly the same time every year. Like many animals, plants prepare for winter by storing food in their underground stems and roots. Their "clock" is controlled by the length of day and night, which changes all year round.

Can plants eat insects?

Insect-eating plants, like the sundew and Venus flytrap, live in poor, often boggy soil. The soil has few minerals to feed the plants. The plants have therefore developed traps to catch insects as an extra food source. The sundew's leaves are covered in sticky-tipped tentacles. The Venus flytrap catches insects in traps on the end of its leaves. Each trap snaps shut when an insect touches one of its trigger hairs. The insect is crushed, and the plant breaks down its body with acid to obtain the food chemicals it needs.

Why do plant stems grow up and roots grow down?

Plants react to the Earth's gravity. No matter which way you plant a bean seed, the root always grows downward. The stem grows upward, seeking the light.

Fern   Sporangia   Prothallus   Young sporophyte   New fern

PLANT NAMES

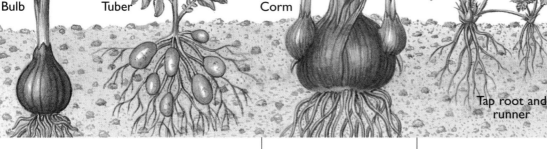

Bulb   Tuber   Corm   Tap root and runner   Rhizome

What is the difference between a bulb, a corm, and a tuber?

You can grow plants by planting bulbs, corms, or tubers in the ground instead of seeds. They are parts of the plant that form underground, and they store food for the new plant that will grow up. A bulb is an underground stem and leaves, a corm is an underground stem, and a tuber is an underground stem or a root. An onion is in fact a bulb of the onion plant, and a potato is a tuber of the potato plant. A rhizome is another kind of underground plant organ. It grows out sideways, and contains stored food. It also sends up new shoots to make new plants. Lilies grow like this, so one plant will soon grow into several.

What are annual, biennial, and perennial plants?

An annual plant grows from seed, flowers, fruits, and dies all in one year. A biennial plant grows from the seed one year, and flowers, fruits and dies the next year. A perennial plant grows up, flowers, and fruits every year.

▲ Bulbs, tubers, corms, and rhizomes store food for plants. These underground organs are also able to make new plants.

▼ The tasty nuts of the beech tree are a good source of food for animals such as mice and squirrels in the fall.

Which plant is named after the Persian word for turban?

The tulip is named after the Persian word for a turban. People thought that the flower looked like a turban, which is a headdress made from wrapped cloth.

What is beech mast?

The triangular brown nuts of the beech tree are sometimes called beech mast when they are lying on the ground. Beech mast is a useful source of food during the winter, especially for some birds.

Why is bird's-foot trefoil so called?

Bird's-foot trefoil is a clover. It gets this name because the seed-pods look like the claw of a bird. The word "trefoil" comes from Latin words meaning "three" and "leaf." Like all clovers, the leaves of bird's-foot trefoil are made of three leaflets. Clovers with four or more leaflets are sometimes found. Some people think they are lucky.

What is belladonna?

Belladonna is another name for the very poisonous plant known as deadly nightshade. *Belladonna* means "beautiful lady" in Italian, and the plant was probably given this name because it contains the drug atropine. If atropine is squeezed into the eye, it makes the pupil larger. At one time, ladies used it because they thought it made their eyes beautiful. Nowadays only eye doctors use atropine, to help them examine the inside of the eye.

Which pretty wild flower has a name meaning "cow dung?"

This flower is the cowslip, which is from the old English word for cow dung. It got this name because the flowers always grow in bright yellow clumps in fields, scattered like patches of cow dung.

How does bracket fungus get its name?

Bracket fungus is a kind of fungus that grows on living and dead trees. It has this name because it grows somewhat like a bracket or shelf, sticking out from the bark of a tree.

▲ **Belladonna, or deadly nightshade has been used as a medicine plant for several hundreds of years. Eating the berries, however, can kill you.**

In 1768, Captain James Cook's first landfall in Australia was named Botany Bay, in honor of the plant collections made there by Joseph Banks, a famous botanist who accompanied Cook in the *Endeavour*. Botany Bay is now surrounded by the airport and suburbs of Sydney.

▶ **Fly agaric is one of the most deadly of poisonous fungi. Its reddish cap makes it easily seen and avoided.**

How did the dandelion get its name?

The name dandelion comes from three French words *dent de lion*, which mean "tooth of the lion." It got this strange name because the outline of the leaves was thought to look like a lion's teeth.

Why is the fly or bug agaric toadstool so named?

The fly agaric or bug agaric toadstool is very poisonous. Its juice was once used to make preparations for killing flies or bugs. The name "agaric" comes from a Greek word, meaning a kind of fungus.

Why should you avoid a destroying angel?

Because it is a deadly poisonous toadstool. It is a close relative of the death cap or death cup, which can also be called the destroying angel. All wild fungi are best left untouched unless you know exactly which kinds are harmful and which aren't.

PLANTS AND PEOPLE

What are the most important foods?

Staple foods are those that make up the biggest part of a person's diet. People in western countries eat a wide range of foods, but most people's diet includes such foods as bread, potatoes, rice, or pasta. In Africa and Asia people depend on staple foods such as rice, cassava (manioc), and yams. Poorer people may eat little except their staple food. Children need a wide range of food.

The average 12-year-old needs about 2,500 calories of food energy each day. A portion of french fries will give about 270 calories, a broiled steak 520, an apple 70, a portion of lettuce 5.

How do subsistence farmers live?

A subsistence farmer has a small plot of land. On it the farmer grows several crops and perhaps keeps a cow or chickens. He or she can grow just enough food to feed a family for a year. In a good year, there may be some food left over to sell at the local market. Once all farmers were subsistence farmers. Today many have gone over to "monoculture"—that is they grow only one crop to sell (such as wheat or coffee) or keep one kind of animal (such as chickens or cattle). They buy the rest of their food.

Potatoes

Rice

French fries

Bread

Spaghetti

Flour

Polished rice grains

Pasta

Wheat

◄ **Carbohydrates are formed in green plants during photosynthesis. About half the food we eat should be made up of carbohydrates, a vital source of fuel.**

What is cassava?

Cassava, or manioc, is an important food plant grown in many tropical countries. People use its root to make flour, bread, and tapioca. The roots look like the tubers of a dahlia flower. There are many varieties of cassavas. The plant contains cyanide, so it is not harmed by insects such as locusts. The cassava must be cooked to remove the poison. Cassava is also used to make glues and explosives.

▼ **Cassava plants grow in warm regions of Africa and Asia. Cassava grows quickly.**

Why can modern farmers grow more food?

A farmer today can grow more food than a farmer 100 years ago on the same amount of land. This is because today there are improved disease-free plants and chemicals that enrich the soil and others that kill harmful pests. Modern farmers grow far fewer kinds of plants than farmers in the past. One disadvantage of modern farming techniques is that many chemicals wash into rivers, polluting the water.

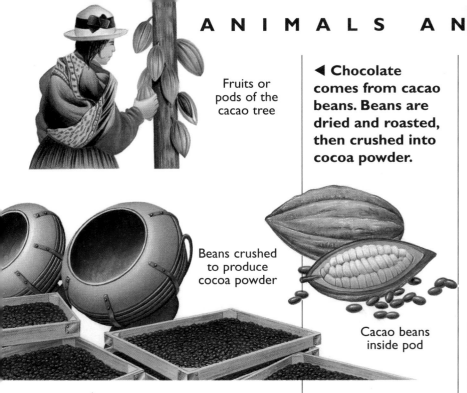

Fruits or pods of the cacao tree

◄ **Chocolate comes from cacao beans. Beans are dried and roasted, then crushed into cocoa powder.**

Beans crushed to produce cocoa powder

Cacao beans inside pod

Does chocolate grow on trees?

Chocolate comes from a tropical tree, the cacao tree. Cacao trees are grown in western Africa, Brazil, and Malaysia. The tree first grew in South America, for we know the Maya and Aztec peoples grew cacao before Europeans began settling in the New World in the 1500s. The cacao tree has long, melon-shaped seeds. Inside are the beans, which are made into the chocolate we eat.

Why do farmers use fertilizers?

Farmers add fertilizers to soil to restore nutrients and feed plants to make them grow better. Some fertilizers are organic, made from animal dung, sewage, or other plants. Other fertilizers are made from chemicals. The most common factorymade kinds are nitrogen, phosphorus, and potassium fertilizers. Fertilizers boost harvests, helping to increase the world's food supply.

▶ **Ripe coffee beans are picked by hand. They are dried and roasted before being sold whole or ground into a powder.**

FARM FACTS

■ Besides being good to eat, beans enrich the soil with nitrogen from the air.

■ It was in the 1800s that farmers began using chemical fertilizers.

■ A fertilizer called super-phosphate, made from rock, was discovered in 1842.

■ Before the 1800s, farmers used only animal dung and plant compost to restore nutrients to the soil.

■ Guano, the piled-up droppings of seabirds, is an excellent fertilizer. So is bat guano, from the floor of caves.

What are cash crops?

A farmer who grows just one crop (such as potatoes, apples, or bananas) is growing a cash crop. When the crop is harvested, the farmer sells it for money. Farmers in some countries rely almost entirely on one such crop —such as coffee, cocoa, or tea— which is raised on enormous farms or plantations. People who once had their own farms often now work for wages on plantations.

Which crop grows in flooded fields?

Young rice plants are planted in a flooded field because they need lots of water to grow. The fields are surrounded by mud banks and drainage channels. The water is drained away when the rice is ready for harvesting. One kind of rice, called upland rice, can be grown on dry hillsides.

Why are beans useful plants?

The beans we eat are the seeds or pods of various bean plants. Beans are very nourishing. They are rich in proteins, carbohydrates, and vitamins.

TREES

Why do trees have bark?

The bark of a tree is a tough covering that protects the living wood inside. It stops the tree from losing too much water. It also stops too many insects and parasites from attacking the wood. The bark also helps to protect the tree from very cold or very hot weather. Bark is actually made up of two layers. The inside layer is a soft, living, corklike material. The outer layer, which you can see, is a hard, dead shell.

Why do some trees produce sticky gum or resin?

The sticky gum or resin produced by many trees helps to protect the tree from attacks by insects. It also seals any wounds in the bark such as those caused when a branch is torn off.

What are deciduous trees?

Deciduous trees are trees that lose their leaves in the fall. Evergreen trees, such as most conifers, lose their leaves gradually all year round. Deciduous trees are also called broad-leaved trees, because their leaves are broader than those of conifers. All deciduous trees have flowers, although the flowers are not always obvious. Leaves are green in summer because they contain chlorophyll. In the fall, the leaf's supply of water is blocked. As the leaf dries out it turns different colors before it falls.

▲ The bark of a London plane tree (top) and a silver birch. Bark is there to protect the living wood inside the tree.

Deciduous

▶ A deciduous tree loses its leaves in the fall. This helps the tree conserve water through winter by sealing off all its food "pipes." Evergreens, however, have leaves all through the year.

Evergreen

◀ **Tree roots take in water and minerals. Some trees have as many roots below ground as they have branches above it.**

▼ **Each year, a layer of new wood grows just beneath the bark and makes a ring. Counting the rings shows how old a tree was.**

What is a conifer?

A tree is called a conifer if it produces its seeds in cones and has needlelike or scalelike leaves. Conifers are almost always evergreen trees. They lose, and replace, their leaves periodically but never all at the same time.

Why do conifers have needlelike leaves?

The leaves of conifers are usually thin and needlelike, and are very tough, so that they do not lose much water. This allows the tree to grow in places where there is not very much water, at least for part of the year. Conifers grow in the very cold parts of the world and high up mountains. They also grow in places where there are hot, dry summers but damp winters.

How can you tell the age of a tree?

If you look at a tree stump or a cut log, you will see that it is made up of rings of different-colored wood. If you count the rings, you can tell how old the tree is in years. A layer of new wood grows every year. When the trunk or a branch is cut across, you can see the rings.

What kind of tree is used for making baskets?

Many baskets are made from the thin branches of the willow or osier. The bark is taken off to give white wood, or the branches may be boiled with the bark on, which dyes the wood. The branches are soaked so that they will bend easily for weaving into baskets. When they dry, they become firm but are still pliable, so that they do not easily break. Willow wood has many other uses because it is both light and strong.

What is a pollarded tree?

If the top of a young deciduous tree is cut off about 6 feet (2 m) from the ground, it will send out fresh shoots from the new top. This is called pollarding. Willows may be pollarded to encourage the growth of suitable branches for basketmaking.

Why should cattle not graze near yew trees?

Farmers stop cattle, horses, and sheep from grazing under yew trees because their leaves, bark, and fruit are poisonous. The animals do not try to graze on the yew trees themselves. But they will eat pieces that have fallen off the trees.

How do trees act as the Earth's "lungs?"

Trees play a vital part in keeping the Earth's atmosphere fit for animals and people to breathe. Tree leaves take up carbon dioxide gas from the air and give off oxygen. We could not live on Earth if the air had too much carbon dioxide or not enough oxygen.

TREE FACTS

■ Travelers in Madagascar can take a drink from the traveler's tree. This tree stores water at the base of its long leaf stalks.

■ The trunk of the General Sherman tree in Sequoia National Park is 90 feet around. It is the world's thickest trunk.

■ The ombu tree of Argentina is very hardy. It needs little water. Its wood is so moist it will not burn, and so spongy that it is impossible to chop down!

■ The coco-de-mer palm tree of the Indian Ocean has the largest seeds of any tree. The nuts of the coco-de-mer can weigh as much as 44 lbs. (20 kg).

■ In Arizona's Petrified Forest there are logs of prehistoric trees turned to stone millions of years ago.

▼ The spindle tree gets its name because its wood was used to make spindles. It has attractive flowers.

How is a palm different from most other trees?

Palms are unlike most other trees because they do not grow side branches. They do not grow thicker, but only taller. A pattern of scars can be seen all the way up the trunk of a palm tree. The scars mark the places where old leaves once grew. New leaves grow in a cluster at the top of the trunk. If this cluster is cut off, no more new leaves can grow, and the palm will die. The trunk of a palm tree does not have growth rings like other trees. Palm trees are very useful. They provide nuts for food and leaves for use as building materials.

Why is a spindle tree so named?

The spindle tree grows in Europe and North America, where it is sometimes called the wahoo. The wood of this tree was once used to make spindles. The spindle was used to wind wool, which was spun by hand. This method of spinning is still used in some parts of the world.

How does a banyan tree grow so big?

A banyan tree is a kind of fig tree that grows in India and Sri Lanka. The seeds of banyan trees are often dropped into the tops of other trees by birds. As the seeds start to grow, they send roots down through the air to the ground. Branches start to develop, and supports grow down from them. These supports take root as soon as they reach the ground. The supports grow into new trunks and send out more branches. These branches send down more supports, and so on. After a while the tree that first supported the banyan will die. It is possible for one banyan tree to be the size of a small forest. There is a tree in Sri Lanka that is said to have 350 large trunks and more than 3,000 smaller ones!

Why do leaves turn yellow, red, and brown in the fall?

During the summer the leaves of a tree are busy making food for the tree. They contain chlorophyll, which makes them green. When fall comes, the stalks of the leaves are sealed off and the chlorophyll decays. The leaves lose their green color and turn yellow, red, or brown before they fall off.

◀ **A banyan tree sends down new roots from scattered seeds, forming a small forest of new stems all around the parent tree.**

Bonsai trees are planted in shallow containers and starved of plant food. The roots and shoots are pruned as the young tree grows, and the branches are twisted and bent with wire so that the adult tree may be less than 20 in. (50 cm) tall. The full-grown plant will look like an aged, gnarled tree.

▶ **A bonsai tree. Bonsai trees are shaped by being trimmed and tied with wires, so that they never grow up into mature trees.**

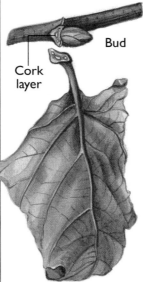

Bud

Cork layer

Dead leaf

Once the leaves have fallen, the tree rests until the following spring, using food stored during the summer. Some trees do not lose all their leaves, and these are called evergreens. Most trees that have cones (conifers) are evergreen.

What is an arboretum?

An arboretum is a collection of living trees, just as a zoo is a collection of living animals. The collection has been planted and taken care of to show many different kinds of trees. Such collections give people the chance to study different trees easily without having to travel to find them.

What is a bonsai?

A bonsai is a tree in a pot, like a plant. It is specially cultivated so that it is a perfect miniature of a full-size tree. Most bonsai come from Japan, but the trees are sold worldwide.

◀ **When a dead leaf falls in autumn, the stem is sealed, to conserve water and to prevent infection. Next year's new bud forms at the point where the old leaf grew.**

PLANT RECORDS

How rare can a plant become?

Plants can become very specialized, living only in one small area. For example, there is only one cafe marron tree in the world. It grows on Rodriguez Island in the Indian Ocean. Scientists have taken cuttings of the tree to propagate it (make new trees), and so conserve it.

How high up can plants grow?

Many kinds of mosses, shrubs, and wild flowers can lie on high mountains amid the cold, wind, and snow. Most grow close to the ground, clinging to the rocks and thin soil. Flowering plants have been found growing over 20,000 feet (6,000 m) up in the Himalayas of Asia.

What are the biggest living things on Earth?

The biggest living things on Earth are giant sequoia trees in California. The biggest one is 275 feet (84 m) tall and measures 100 feet (30 m) around its trunk. It is probably 2,000 years old.

▶ The rafflesia plant produces an enormous flower with five fleshy lobes, but it has no stems or leaves.

▼ Giant sequoia trees can grow as tall as a 25-story skyscraper. The tallest trees are more than two thousand years old.

Which plant has the biggest flowers?

The largest flowers belong to the rafflesia, or stinking corpse lily, of Southeast Asia. They measure 3 feet (1 m) across. This flower smells like rotting meat, unpleasant to people but attractive to lots of insects which visit the flower and pollinate the plant. The rafflesia flower grows as a parasite on the stems and roots of shrubs.

Which plant has the largest fruit?

The jackfruit, which grows in India and Sri Lanka, probably has the largest of all fruits. One fruit may be as heavy as 55 pounds (25 kg). It is an oval, yellow, spiny fruit with a sweet or sour brown pulp inside. The pulp can be eaten raw or it can be cooked in different ways.

Which plant has the longest leaves?

In Madagascar there is a palm tree called the raffia palm. Its leaves grow more than 39 feet (12 m) long and there have been trees with leaves 65 feet (20 m) long and over 6 feet (2 m) across. Slightly smaller are the fan-shaped leaves of the talipot palm.

Which plant lives the longest?

The oldest known plant is the desert creosote plant which grows in California and which is estimated to be 11,700 years old. The bristlecone pine trees of Nevada, California, and Arizona are believed to be the oldest trees in the world. The oldest known one that is still living is about 4,600 years old.

Which tree grows fastest?

The eucalyptus tree of Australia can grow as much as 33 feet (10 m) in a year. There are more than 600 kinds of eucalyptus, and they include the tallest hardwood trees in the world, more than 330 feet (100 m) high. Eucalyptus trees have been planted in many other countries.

Which is the most poisonous fungus?

The death cap or death cup toadstool is probably the most poisonous fungus in the world. Even a very small piece of it can kill. People do not start to feel ill until about ten hours after they eat it. Nothing can be done to help, because there is no cure for the poison. The death cap is poisonous to all animals.

▲ The creosote plant is the oldest known plant. This plant was already old when the pyramids of Egypt were being built!

AMAZING PLANTS

■ Few plants can live in the bitter Arctic cold. Two that do are the yellow poppy and Arctic willow.

■ A record-breaking rose tree in Arizona is so huge it has to be held up by posts and piping. 150 people can sit beneath its blooms!

■ The fruit with the greatest food value (in kilocalories) is the avocado.

■ The most leaves ever counted on a clover is 14.

■ The world's most massive tree—the General Sherman giant sequoia in Sequoia National Park, California—weighs 2,000 tons.

■ Flowering plants have been found growing at a height of 21,000 feet (6,400 m) in the Himalayas.

■ The largest of all the flowering plant families is the grass family.

Which tree grows most slowly?

A cycad with the scientific name of *Dioon edule* probably holds the record for the slowest growth. One of these trees studied in Mexico in the 1980s grew less than ³⁄₁₀₀ inch (0.76 mm) each year. A tree 120 years old has grown only 4 inches (10 cm) high!

Which plant has jaws?

A few plants that live in boggy places where food is scarce have added insects to their menu. They digest the bodies of their captives to gain extra nourishment. Some, like the sundew, have sticky tentacles. Butterworts have sticky leaves. The pitcher plant traps insects in a vase-shaped funnel. The most spectacular carnivorous plant is the Venus flytrap. It has hinged spiky leaves that close like jaws around any insect that lands on them.

Which were the first farm crops?

Roots, bulbs, and tubers were probably the first plants grown by people. Peas and beans were eaten 10,000 years ago.

ANIMALS AND PLANTS QUIZ

BODY BASICS

What is the human body made of?

About two-thirds of the human body is water. The remaining third is an extremely complicated mixture of chemicals. The water-and-chemical mix is arranged into structures called cells. These are tiny, but you can see them using a microscope. Each part of the body is made of a completely different kind of cell. Heart cells, skin cells, bone cells, and blood cells all are different. Brain cells are among the very smallest.

▼ This is what a cell's inside looks like. All cells are made up in the same basic way, though they are different shapes and sizes.

What is a cell?

Cells are the small building blocks of the body. They have a very thin outer layer, called the cell membrane, which lets in food and oxygen and lets out waste. Much of the cell is a jellylike substance called cytoplasm. Activity inside the cell is controlled by the nucleus. There are over 50 trillion cells in the human body. There are tubular, round, flat, and square cells. Female egg cells are the largest, just big enough to be seen without a microscope.

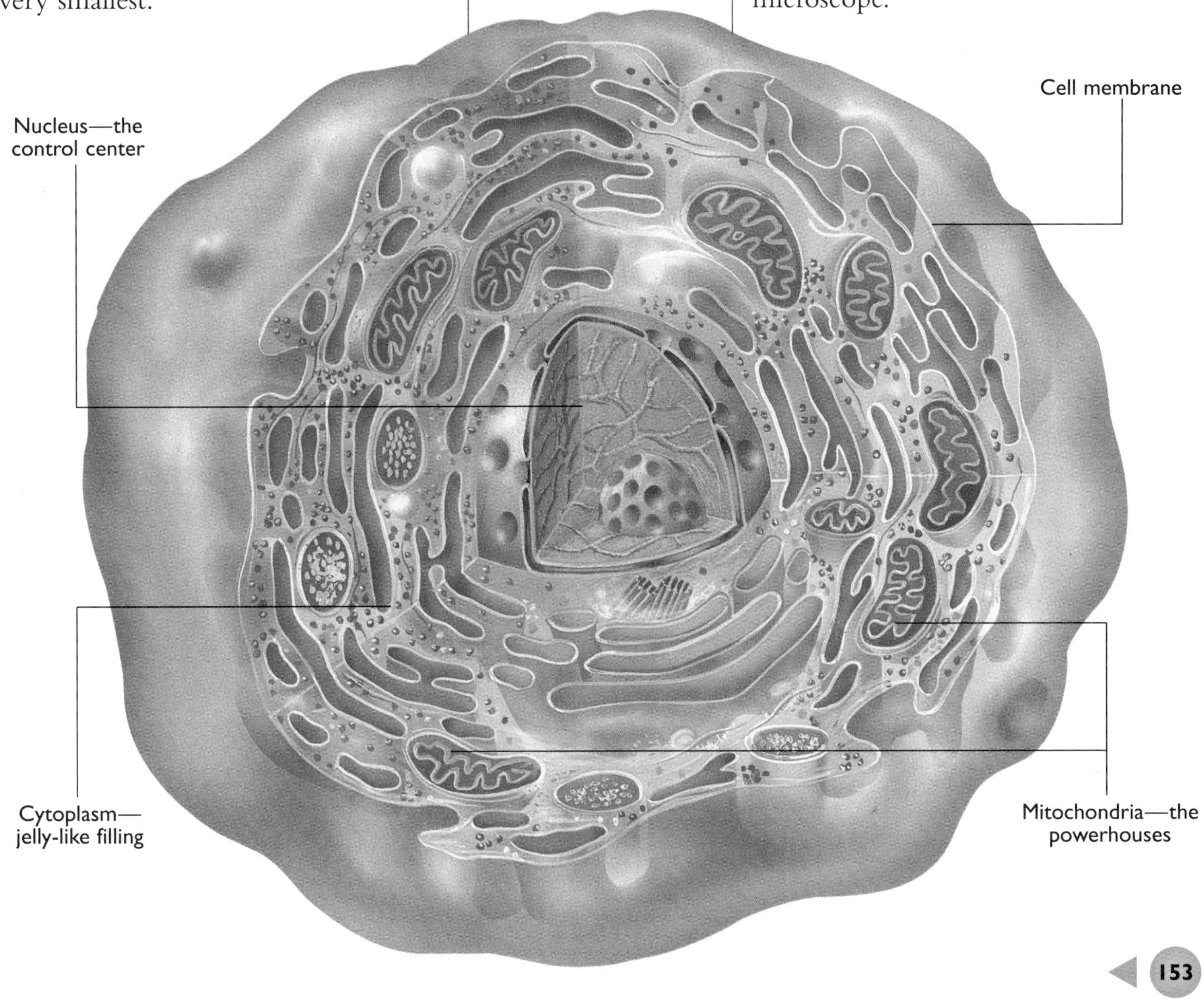

Nucleus—the control center

Cell membrane

Cytoplasm— jelly-like filling

Mitochondria—the powerhouses

153

What happens inside a cell?

Within the cytoplasm are tiny structures called organelles. Each organelle has a different job to do. For example, materials for growth and repair (proteins) are made on tiny round grains called ribosomes. These are found along a folded membrane called the endoplasmic reticulum. Round organelles, called lysosomes, contain chemicals that break down harmful substances or worn-out parts of the cell that need to be replaced.

Do all cells look the same?

Although all cells have things in common, they do not all look the same. In fact, there are several hundred different kinds of cell in the body. Their shape and size relate to

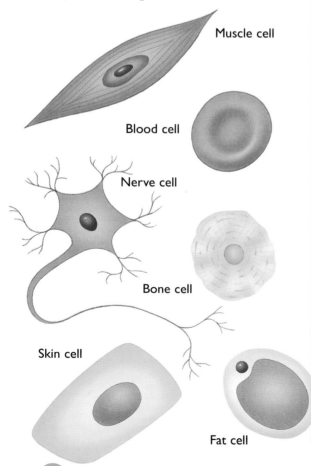

Muscle cell

Blood cell

Nerve cell

Bone cell

Skin cell

Fat cell

CELL FACTS

■ There are more than 50 trillion cells in your body!

■ There are several hundred different kinds of body cells.

■ Some of the cells in the gut live only a few days.

■ Many brain cells last a lifetime.

■ You have more red blood cells than any other kind of cell—about 30 trillion. Red blood cells are constantly being made in the bone marrow.

Blood contains a substance called hemoglobin, which contains iron and gives blood its red color. Insects have blue, green, or colorless blood. Insect blood has no hemoglobin.

◀ **Different body cells look different and act in different ways. For example, a muscle cell is long and thick. It uses up a lot of energy. A nerve cell has very long, wirelike arms, along which nerve signals pass from one part of the body to another.**

---

the job they do. Nerve cells are long and thin, to carry messages from one part of the body to another. The largest human cell is the egg cell, found in women. It is about 0.2 millimeters across. The smallest cells are red blood cells, which are less than 0.01 millimeters across. Human sperm cells, found in men, are also very small. The head of a human sperm is about 0.005 millimeters across.

What do cells need to stay alive?

Cells need three basic things to stay alive: food, oxygen, and a "friendly," watery environment with a careful balance of the right chemicals, so that the cell can carry out its tasks properly. The cell also gets rid of its waste into this watery environment, from where it is carried away.

Food and oxygen are carried to the cells by blood, which also takes away waste. Blood also provides the tissue fluid in which cells live.

What is an organ?

An organ is a structure made of different tissues, collected together to do a particular job. We have nine organ systems in all. The skeletal and muscular systems support, protect, and move parts of the body. The nervous system and endocrine system coordinate the body's actions. The circulatory (transportation) system carries blood; the respiratory system is responsible for breathing. Food is broken down by the digestive system, the urinary system removes waste from the body, and the reproductive system produces children.

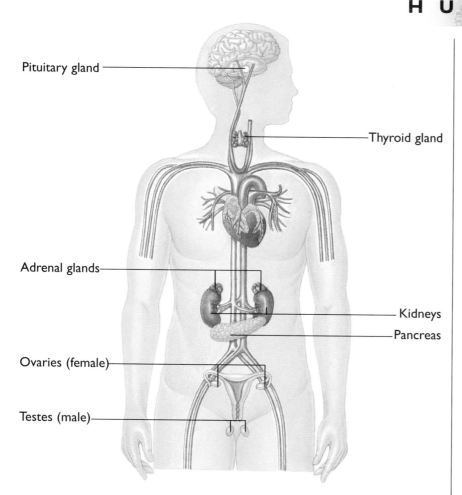

Pituitary gland

Thyroid gland

Adrenal glands

Kidneys

Pancreas

Ovaries (female)

Testes (male)

What is a gland?

A gland is a structure that produces a fluid that the body needs to work properly. An entire organ can be a gland; examples are the liver and kidneys. On a much smaller scale, tiny glands in the skin produce sweat.

How do glands affect growth?

How tall we are is controlled by a growth hormone, a chemical made by the pituitary gland. Too much can make a person very tall, and too little can stunt their growth. Children with abnormal levels can be treated so that they grow to a more average size. The pituitary gland is the most important in the body because it produces hormones that have effects on other parts of the body.

▲ **The endocrine glands are in the neck, head, and torso. They help to coordinate the body's activities by releasing chemical messengers called hormones into the bloodstream.**

▶ **This diagram shows some of the activities included in metabolism— the changes that convert food into energy.**

What is your metabolism?

Metabolism is a general term that covers all the activity inside your body. This includes the chemical reactions in the cells to produce energy or materials for growth.

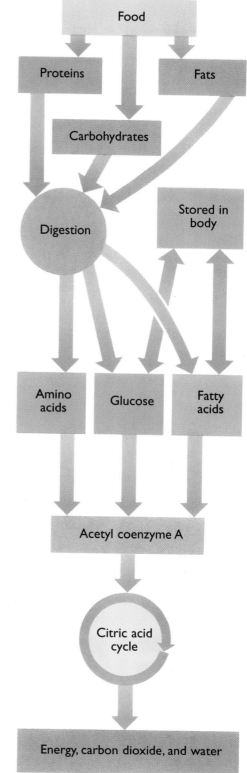

Food

Proteins

Fats

Carbohydrates

Digestion

Stored in body

Amino acids

Glucose

Fatty acids

Acetyl coenzyme A

Citric acid cycle

Energy, carbon dioxide, and water

SKELETON AND MOVEMENT

How many bones are there in the body?

Adults have about 206 bones. The number may vary slightly from person to person because some people have an extra pair of ribs, and some have more bones in their hands and feet.

Bones support the soft parts of the body. Without bones, we would

Your funny bone isn't a bone at all. It's a nerve just under the skin in each elbow. If you bang your elbow, the nerve sends a message to your brain, and you get a funny feeling!

Which is the largest bone?

The largest bone is the thighbone, or femur. Its special design also makes it the strongest bone. A man who is about 6 feet (1.8 m) tall will have a femur about 20 inches (50 cm) long, accounting for almost a third of his height. Our bones grow as we do. When you were born, you had about 350 bones. But by the time you finish growing, there will be only 200 or so bones inside you! As you grow, some of the smaller bones in your body join together to make bigger ones.

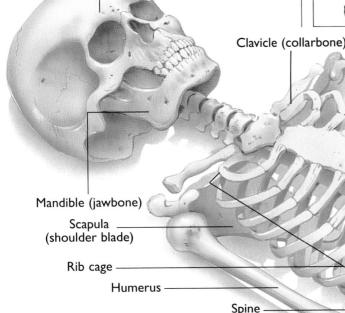

Cranium (skull)

Clavicle (collarbone)

Costa cartilage

Sternum (breastbone)

Pelvis (hipbone)

Femur (thighbone)

Mandible (jawbone)

Scapula (shoulder blade)

Rib cage

Humerus

Spine

Ulna

Radius

Coccyx

Metacarpals (hand bones)

be a messy heap. They also protect vital organs in our body from physical damage. For example, the skull protects the brain and eyes, and the rib cage protects the lungs and heart.

Which is the smallest bone?

In the middle ear is a tiny bone called the stirrup. It is only ⅛ inch (3 mm) long and weighs about 3 milligrams. It passes sound vibrations to the liquid in the inner ear.

▲ The skeleton is made up of different kinds of bones. Strong bones protect important organs, like the brain and the heart.

What is inside a bone?

The outer layer of bone is called compact bone. This is hard and very strong. The inner layer of bone contains lots of spaces, and so is called spongy bone. This bone is also strong but is fairly light, so it keeps down the overall weight of the skeleton, and makes it easier to move. In the middle of bone there is a cavity, filled with a substance called bone marrow. The marrow inside a child's bones is red. As it ages, the marrow in some bones becomes yellowish.

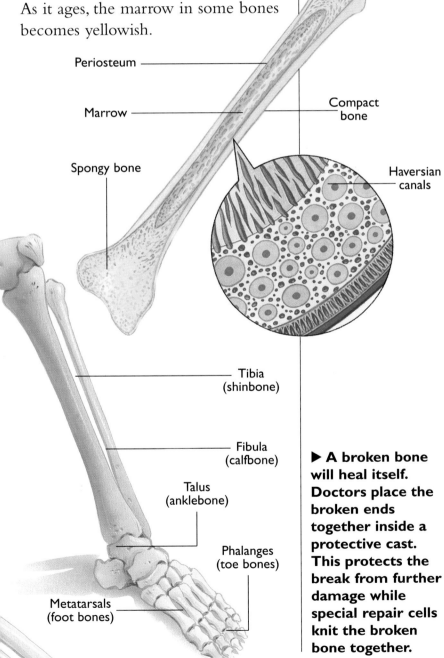

Periosteum

Marrow

Spongy bone

Compact bone

Haversian canals

Tibia (shinbone)

Fibula (calfbone)

Talus (anklebone)

Phalanges (toe bones)

Metatarsals (foot bones)

▼ **A bone has a hard outer layer, or periosteum. Beneath this is the compact bone, where food and oxygen move along blood vessels in the Haversian canals.**

▶ **A broken bone will heal itself. Doctors place the broken ends together inside a protective cast. This protects the break from further damage while special repair cells knit the broken bone together.**

How strong is bone?

For its weight, bone is as strong as steel and four times stronger than the same amount of reinforced concrete.

The hard part of bone is made up mainly of the mineral calcium phosphate. Through this run fibers of a protein called collagen. Calcium phosphate gives bone its strength, and collagen gives bone its bendiness. If you boil a chicken bone, the collagen is removed so that the bone becomes brittle. If a chicken bone is put in strong vinegar, the calcium dissolves and so the bone becomes rubbery.

How do broken bones mend?

When a bone is cracked or broken, bone cells at the injury grow and multiply, spreading through the damaged region to close up the break. If the two broken ends of the bone are lined up and held still inside a plaster cast, the bone will heal. In children and young adults, this healing process takes 12 weeks or less for bones in the arm or leg. More complicated breaks, known as compound fractures can be more serious. Doctors sometimes insert pins into the bone to hold the broken parts together.

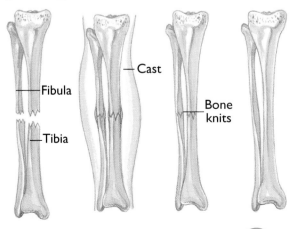

Fibula

Tibia

Cast

Bone knits

Where are the vertebrae?

The vertebrae (just one is a vertebra) are the bones that make up the spine. There are 33 altogether, linked in a flexible chain that runs from the neck to the lower back (the bottom nine vertebrae are fused). The top two vertebrae, the atlas and axis vertebrae, have a different structure from the others, so they can work as a pair to let the head nod and turn. Between each pair of vertebrae a cartilage disk cushions against any jarring. If a disk slips out of place, it can be painful until it is replaced.

Atlas vertebra

Axis vertebra

▲ **The atlas vertebra twists on the axis vertebra. This allows you to turn your head sideways.**

Your bones are made partly of a mineral called calcium. It's a little like stone, but your bones are very much alive. They get bigger as you grow.

◄ **Your backbone is a flexible column, held upright in its S-shaped curve by muscles and ligaments. There are 33 vertebrae in the spine.**

What are ribs for?

The ribs form a protective cage around the heart and lungs. You can feel your rib cage extending from the flat bone in the middle of your chest, right around your sides to your spine. The ribs also swing up and down when you breathe to inflate and deflate your lungs.

How do bones grow?

In a fetus (unborn child) the bones are made of cartilage. By the time the baby is born, most of the cartilage has turned to bone, in a process called ossification. Growth areas still remain near the ends of the bone. This is where new bone cells are formed. These growth areas disappear when the skeleton reaches full size. Even then, the bone can still alter its shape slightly and repair itself.

Why do people shrink as they grow old?

As people get older, the cartilage pads that protect the bones of the spine become thinner, and this leads to height loss. Because people's muscles become weaker with age, their posture changes and this makes them look smaller too. Bones are probably at their strongest when we are in our late twenties. Many people over 60, women in particular, suffer from a condition known as osteoporosis. The bones lose some calcium and become more brittle. A diet that includes plenty of fresh green vegetables, milk, and milk products should supply enough calcium for most people, but in some cases taking extra calcium may be recommended by a doctor.

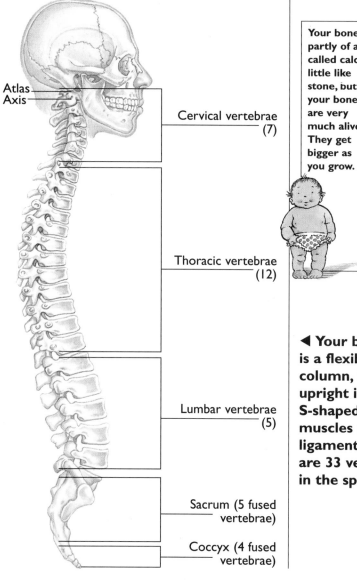

Atlas
Axis

Cervical vertebrae (7)

Thoracic vertebrae (12)

Lumbar vertebrae (5)

Sacrum (5 fused vertebrae)

Coccyx (4 fused vertebrae)

What is a joint?

A joint is a place where two or more bones meet. A joint may be fixed (the skull), or movable (the knee). Joints allow us to twist, turn, and move our bones. Muscles are attached to and move the bones across a joint. Usually only one bone at a joint moves, relative to another. Strong, elastic straps of tissue called ligaments hold bones together at joints.

What is cartilage?

Cartilage is a slippery, bluish-white substance found at the ends of bones, which allows bones to move against one another without causing damage. Cartilage is more slippery than ice. It is flexible and gives when bones are jarred, so it makes a good shock absorber. The knee has two extra pieces of cartilage, because the knee joint is always under a substantial amount of stress.

▼ **This is how your hip joint works. The synovial fluid lubricates the joint, to reduce rubbing between bones.**

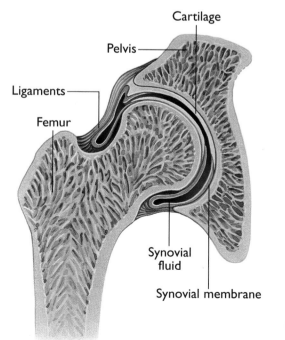

Cartilage

Pelvis

Ligaments

Femur

Synovial fluid

Synovial membrane

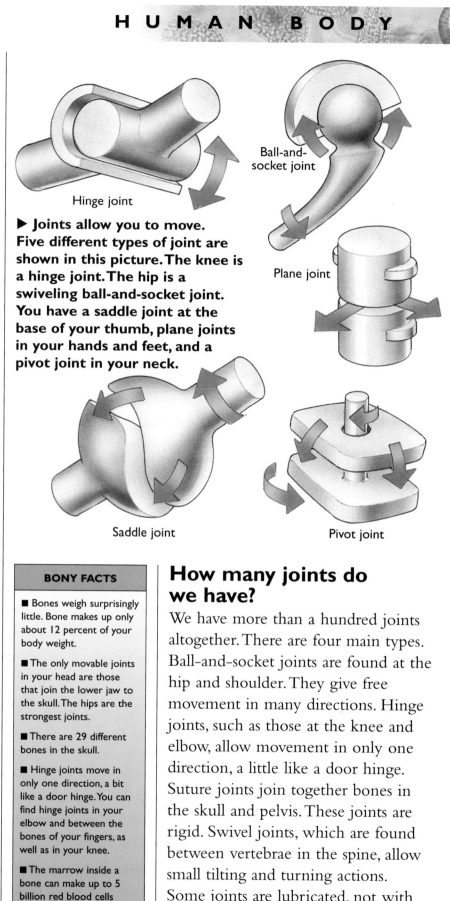

Hinge joint

Ball-and-socket joint

Plane joint

Saddle joint

Pivot joint

▶ **Joints allow you to move. Five different types of joint are shown in this picture. The knee is a hinge joint. The hip is a swiveling ball-and-socket joint. You have a saddle joint at the base of your thumb, plane joints in your hands and feet, and a pivot joint in your neck.**

BONY FACTS

■ Bones weigh surprisingly little. Bone makes up only about 12 percent of your body weight.

■ The only movable joints in your head are those that join the lower jaw to the skull. The hips are the strongest joints.

■ There are 29 different bones in the skull.

■ Hinge joints move in only one direction, a bit like a door hinge. You can find hinge joints in your elbow and between the bones of your fingers, as well as in your knee.

■ The marrow inside a bone can make up to 5 billion red blood cells each day. It also makes the white blood cells.

How many joints do we have?

We have more than a hundred joints altogether. There are four main types. Ball-and-socket joints are found at the hip and shoulder. They give free movement in many directions. Hinge joints, such as those at the knee and elbow, allow movement in only one direction, a little like a door hinge. Suture joints join together bones in the skull and pelvis. These joints are rigid. Swivel joints, which are found between vertebrae in the spine, allow small tilting and turning actions. Some joints are lubricated, not with oil as in an engine, but with a liquid called synovial fluid which is sandwiched between the bones.

How do muscles help us move?

Joints allow the skeleton to move, but muscles produce the movement, by pulling the bone into a new position. Here is what happens when you bend your elbow. The biceps muscle is attached to your shoulder blade at one end and to a bone in the forearm at the other. The triceps muscle is also connected to the shoulder blade and forearm. When the biceps contracts (shortens), the triceps is relaxed (lengthens) and the elbow bends. When the triceps contracts and the biceps is relaxed, the elbow joint straightens and so does your arm.

What are muscles made of?

Muscles are made of thousands of cells called muscle fibers, which shorten when a muscle contracts. The cells are held together by a layer of connective tissue. The pulling power of a muscle varies, since not all the fibers shorten at once.

How many muscles do you have?

You have about 650 muscles, with over 50 in your face alone. You use 17 muscles to smile, over 40 to frown.

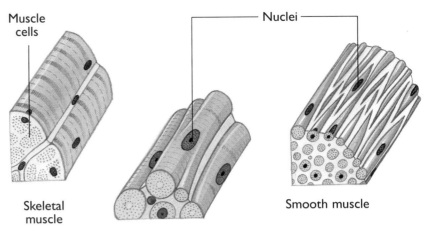

Muscle cells

Skeletal muscle

Cardiac muscle

Nuclei

Smooth muscle

▲ The three types of muscle are made up of different muscle cells. Skeletal muscle cells are the longest, and have several nuclei, whereas cardiac and smooth muscle cells have only one nucleus.

Is there more than one kind of muscle?

There are three main muscle types: skeletal, smooth, and cardiac. Skeletal muscles are voluntary, which means we can control them by thinking. The other two types of muscle are involuntary, which means they work automatically. Smooth muscle moves food along the digestive system. Cardiac muscle produces the pumping of the heart and never stops working.

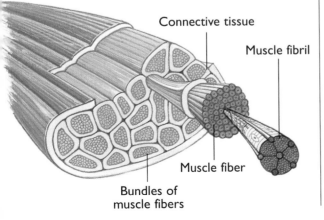

Connective tissue

Muscle fibril

Muscle fiber

Bundles of muscle fibers

◄ Muscles consist of bundles of fibers. The fibers contain rods, which slide over each other to shorten the fiber when the muscle contracts.

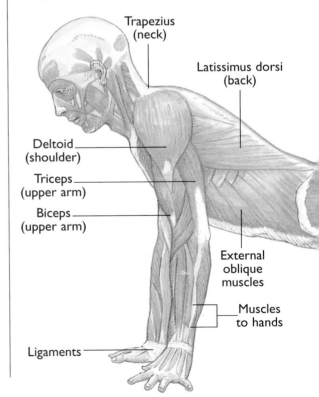

Trapezius (neck)

Latissimus dorsi (back)

Deltoid (shoulder)

Triceps (upper arm)

Biceps (upper arm)

External oblique muscles

Muscles to hands

Ligaments

Why do most muscles work in pairs?

Muscles can only pull or contract, they cannot push. Either another muscle or gravity must pull a muscle out into a longer shape when it is relaxed. That is why most muscles come in pairs and work against each other. We call such muscles an antagonistic pair.

Which is the strongest muscle?

Size for size, the strongest muscle in your body is the masseter. One masseter is located on each side of the mouth. Together they give a biting force of about 155 pounds (70 kg).

Which is the largest muscle?

This is the gluteus maximus, the muscle that runs from the buttock to the back of the thigh. However, in women, one muscle may show a dramatic increase in size. During pregnancy, the uterus (womb) increases in weight from about 1 ounce (30 g) to more than 2 pounds (1 kg).

You get a cramp when your muscles are tired. You may have to stamp, stretch, or rub the leg to get rid of the pain.

MUSCLE FACTS

■ Muscles account for around 40 percent of your body weight.

■ You use about 200 different muscles when you walk.

■ Even when you are not moving, some of your muscle fibers have to contract to keep you standing up or sitting down.

■ The smallest muscle is the stapedius, in the middle ear. It is less than $\frac{1}{100}$ in. (0.27 mm) long.

Your biggest muscles are the ones you sit on.

Which is the most active muscle?

It has been estimated that the eye muscles move more than 100,000 times a day. Many of these movements take place during dreaming. Cardiac muscle keeps contracting 70 or so times a minute, while the smooth muscle in your gut moves all the time.

Why do muscles get tired?

When a muscle works very hard, it makes some of the energy it needs by breaking down stored food without using oxygen. This process is called anaerobic respiration. It causes a waste substance called lactic acid to build up inside the muscle, stopping it from working properly.

What causes a cramp?

When too much lactic acid builds up, it causes the muscle to contract strongly and painfully. This is a cramp. A cramp occurs when your start to exercise a little-used muscle, or if you have been sitting or standing in an uncomfortable position. The best way to deal with a cramp is to massage and gently stretch the painful muscle.

What are the benefits of regular exercise?

Exercise helps you to look good, feel good, and stay healthy. It strengthens your muscles and helps to maintain good muscle tone. It can improve your body shape and posture. Exercising strengthens the cardiac muscle, helps to keep good circulation, and can also relieve stress.

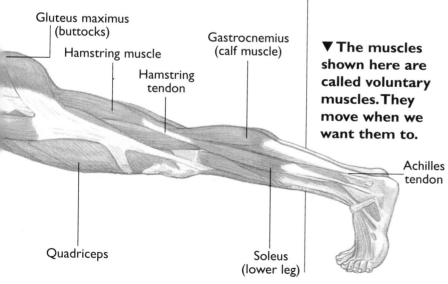

▼ The muscles shown here are called voluntary muscles. They move when we want them to.

Gluteus maximus (buttocks)

Hamstring muscle

Hamstring tendon

Gastrocnemius (calf muscle)

Quadriceps

Soleus (lower leg)

Achilles tendon

LUNGS AND HEART

What happens when we breathe?

When we breathe in, we draw air in through our nose or mouth. The air is mainly nitrogen (78 percent), with about 21 percent oxygen and 0.04 percent carbon dioxide. This mixture of gases travels down the windpipe, or trachea, into two large tubes called bronchi, one leading to each lung. From here the air travels into a system of smaller air passages called bronchioles and finally reaches millions of tiny air sacs, called alveoli, inside each lung.

Fold your arms across your chest. Now breathe in. You'll feel your lungs getting bigger as they fill up with air.

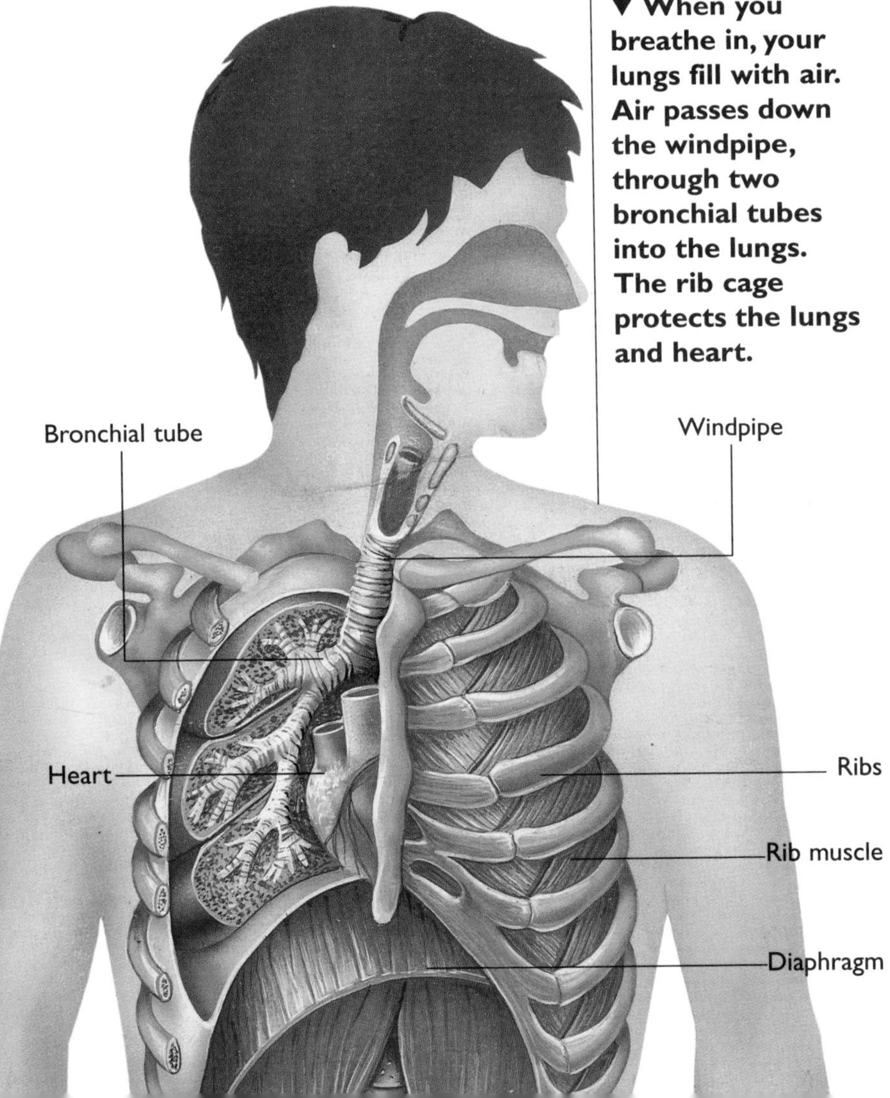

▼ **When you breathe in, your lungs fill with air. Air passes down the windpipe, through two bronchial tubes into the lungs. The rib cage protects the lungs and heart.**

Bronchial tube

Windpipe

Heart

Ribs

Rib muscle

Diaphragm

When we breathe out, air takes the reverse route from the air sacs to our nose or mouth. But the content of the air is slightly different. The air we breathe out contains much less oxygen than before and more carbon dioxide and more water vapor. A large sheet of muscle called the diaphragm, situated just below the lungs, contracts and expands to pull air in or push air out of the lungs.

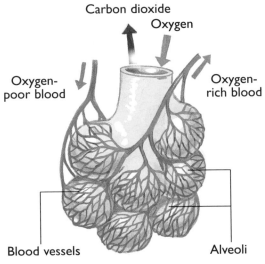

Carbon dioxide

Oxygen

Oxygen-poor blood

Oxygen-rich blood

Blood vessels

Alveoli

▲ **Inside the lungs, oxygen from the air is exchanged with waste carbon dioxide gas from the blood. The oxygen is carried to the body cells in the blood.**

Why do we breathe faster when we exercise?

When we exercise, our muscles do more work and therefore need more energy. They get this energy from food, which is broken down during respiration. Respiration uses up oxygen and so we breathe faster to supply the extra oxygen our muscles need when we exercise.

When we are sitting or standing, we breathe in and out only about 10 percent of the air in our lungs. When we exercise hard, this figure goes up to about 60 percent.

Why is it better to breathe through your nose?

Air breathed in through your nose is warmed to a comfortable temperature for your lungs and moistened and cleaned more effectively than air breathed in through your mouth. Small hairs in the nose filter out dirt. Mucus inside the nose traps some of the dirt, and tiny hairs called cilia push this to the throat where it is swallowed. Like the nose, the air passages in the lungs have mucus and cilia to help clean the air breathed in.

Why is breathing harder on top of a mountain?

The higher up you climb, the thinner the air becomes. This means that with each breath you are taking in much less oxygen than you would normally. Breathing is therefore more difficult on a high mountain. Exercise becomes difficult because you have to breathe much more heavily to get the oxygen you need.

What can a chest X-ray show?

Doctors use chest X-rays to look for signs of disease in the lungs. The infections that cause bronchitis, pneumonia, or tuberculosis, or more serious conditions such as lung cancer, can show up on the X-ray picture as dark patches.

DID YOU KNOW?

■ A baby is born with pink lungs. As we get older, our lungs darken because we breathe dirty air.

■ A person at rest breathes in and out about 13 times a minute. With each breath, about 30 cu. in. (500 cc) of air is taken in.

■ On average, the lungs of an adult man can hold about 5½ qts. (6 l) of air.

■ A woman's lungs hold slightly less air, about 4 qts. (4.5 l).

■ In ancient times, people thought that a person's breath was the life spirit.

▲ It is almost impossible to stop yourself from yawning. Animals yawn too.

▶ An X-ray photo of a person's lungs, showing the ribs and spinal column. Doctors use X-rays to check for signs of lung disease.

Why do we pant after running fast?

When you pant after a sprint, you are paying the "oxygen debt." Exercise that helps your body take in more oxygen causes a build-up of lactic acid, a waste product. Once the exercise is over, the liver processes the lactic acid, using oxygen to break it down. The oxygen debt is the amount of oxygen you must take in to process the lactic acid that has built up.

Why do we yawn?

A yawn seems to be the body's way of getting more oxygen to the brain to make us feel more lively. When we yawn we take in air slowly and deeply and then breathe it out. We seem to yawn most when tired or bored, or sitting in a stuffy room. Yawning can be a sign that a person needs more air. Drinking or washing the face in cold water can stop us from yawning.

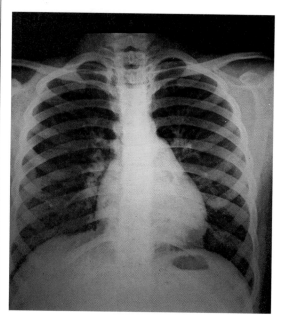

What happens when you cough?

Just before you cough, you tightly close your vocal cords and tense your chest muscles. Then, when you release your vocal cords, the air comes shooting out of your lungs. Coughing is important because it removes irritating particles from your throat and air passages.

Why do we sneeze?

Sneezing is a way of getting rid of something that is irritating the sensitive parts of the nose. Air is forced out of the lungs through the nose. Sneezing helps stop dust or pollen from reaching our lungs.

What makes a lump in the throat?

It feels like a lump, but it is actually a tightening of muscles in the throat, a side effect of the hormone adrenaline, which is released when we feel sad.

THROATY FACTS

■ Your Adam's apple is the lump in the front of your throat. It is formed by the voice box, or larynx.

■ Inside the larynx are two bands of cartilage called vocal cords.

■ People snore when soft tissues in the throat collapse during deep sleep. The soft tissues partly block air passing in and out of the lungs. Vibrations are set up, producing the snores.

▶ Blood circulates around the body. Arteries take blood from the heart to the cells of the body. Veins carry blood back to the heart.

Air can shoot out of you as fast as a motorcycle! When you sneeze, air rushes out of your lungs at about 100 mph (160 km/h).

◀ If dust or germs get into your nose, your body makes you sneeze to get rid of them. Your lungs shoot out air.

How does the voice work?

When you speak or sing, air from your lungs passes out across your vocal cords and makes them vibrate. If you almost close the space between your vocal cords, you get a high-pitched sound. If you open the space, you get a lower-pitched sound. A fast outbreath produces a loud note.

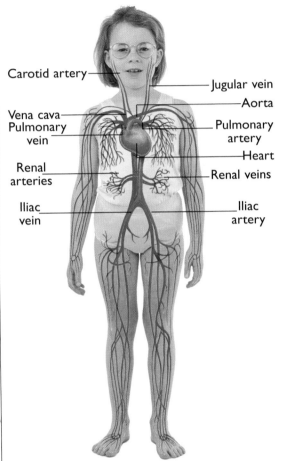

Carotid artery
Jugular vein
Aorta
Vena cava
Pulmonary vein
Pulmonary artery
Heart
Renal arteries
Renal veins
Iliac vein
Iliac artery

What is your circulation?

Your circulation is the system that carries blood around your body. It consists of a pump, called the heart, and a branching system of tubes, called blood vessels. There are three main types of blood vessels. Arteries carry blood away from the heart. Veins carry blood back to the heart. Capillaries are the tiny blood vessels that connect arteries with veins. They go to every part of the body.

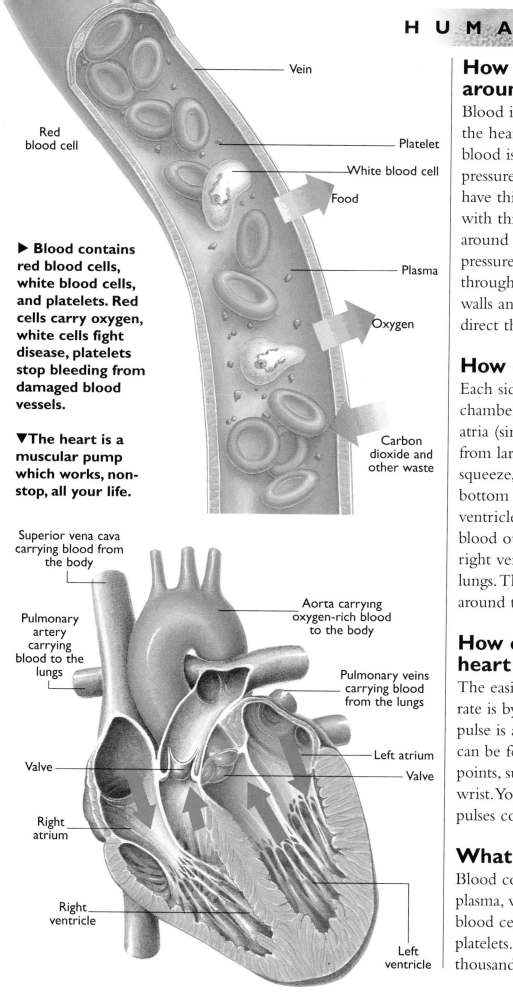

Vein

Red blood cell

Platelet

White blood cell

Food

▶ **Blood contains red blood cells, white blood cells, and platelets. Red cells carry oxygen, white cells fight disease, platelets stop bleeding from damaged blood vessels.**

Plasma

Oxygen

▼**The heart is a muscular pump which works, non-stop, all your life.**

Carbon dioxide and other waste

Superior vena cava carrying blood from the body

Pulmonary artery carrying blood to the lungs

Aorta carrying oxygen-rich blood to the body

Pulmonary veins carrying blood from the lungs

Valve

Left atrium

Valve

Right atrium

Right ventricle

Left ventricle

How does blood get around the body?

Blood is pumped around the body by the heart. When the heart squeezes, blood is pushed out under high pressure into the arteries. Arteries have thick muscular walls to cope with this pressure. As the blood travels around the body, it gradually loses its pressure and so flows more slowly through the veins. Veins have thinner walls and contain one-way valves to direct the blood back to the heart.

How does the heart work?

Each side of the heart has two chambers. The top chambers, called atria (singular "atrium"), receive blood from large veins. When the atria squeeze, they pump blood into the bottom chambers, or ventricles. The ventricles then squeeze, pumping blood out along large arteries. The right ventricle sends blood to the lungs. The left ventricle sends it around the body.

How can I measure my heart rate?

The easiest way to measure your heart rate is by measuring your pulse. The pulse is a regular throb or beat which can be felt beneath the skin at certain points, such as the inside of your wrist. Your heart rate is the number of pulses counted in one minute.

What is blood made of?

Blood consists of a liquid called plasma, which contains red and white blood cells, and cell fragments called platelets. Dissolved in the plasma are thousands of different substances.

What does blood do?

Blood carries useful materials around the body and takes away waste products. Blood helps with communication, by delivering chemical messengers, called hormones, to parts of the body. Blood protects the body from germs, by sealing cuts with thickened, or clotted, blood and by attacking germs with white blood cells. Body temperature can be controlled by directing blood to or away from the skin to warm or cool it.

What do red blood cells do?

The main function of red blood cells is to deliver oxygen around the body. The hemoglobin in red blood cells combines with oxygen, which is picked up in the lungs and then delivered to all body tissues. Hemoglobin is a very efficient oxygen-carrier. It allows blood to carry 60 times more oxygen than could be dissolved in the blood plasma. Red blood cells are packed full of hemoglobin.

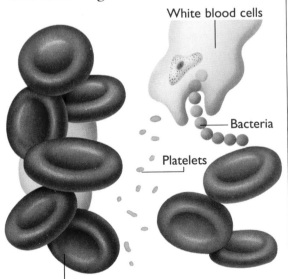

White blood cells

Bacteria

Platelets

Red blood cells

A baby has less than 1 quart (1 l) of blood, not quite enough to fill a milk carton. When you grow up, you will have enough blood to half-fill a bucket— about 4½ quarts (5 l).

FACTS ABOUT THE HEART AND BLOOD

■ Your heart is only roughly similar in shape to a "love heart."

■ The left side of the heart is bigger than the right.

■ A heartbeat is the sound the heart makes when the heart valves open and close. A doctor can listen to the sounds by placing a stethoscope on your chest.

■ There are four blood groups: A, B, AB, and O.

■ It takes about a minute for a drop of blood to travel from the heart to your toes and back again.

◄ Red blood cells look like doughnuts. They carry oxygen to all parts of the body. White cells fight harmful bacteria. Platelets stop bleeding and seal wounds.

What do white blood cells do?

White blood cells help to protect the body from disease. About two-thirds of white blood cells are phagocytes, which defend the body by eating up invading germs. The remaining white cells are lymphocytes. They produce chemicals called antibodies, which destroy harmful germs. White blood cells are much larger than red blood cells, but they are far fewer in number (approximately 1:600).

Where in the body gets the most blood?

Size for size, the kidneys get more blood than other organs. The kidneys have a vital role in filtering and cleaning the blood. However, during hard exercise muscles get more blood. The body supplies the muscles with up to five times more blood than they get when the body is at rest. Blood is diverted from other organs to feed the muscles. Only the blood supply to the brain is constant throughout.

Why do cuts stop bleeding?

Cuts stop bleeding because blood quickly forms a clot that plugs the wound and seals off the damaged vessels. At the site of an injury, the platelets in the bloodstream stick together, as well as to the edges of the cut, making a thin seal. The platelets, and cells damaged by the injury, release substances that react with clotting factors in the blood to form fibers. Blood cells get caught up in the tangle of platelets and fibers, and form a clot that plugs the leak.

How does blood deal with germs?

When we cut or graze our skin, blood vessels are broken. Blood leaks out and helps to wash away harmful germs from the site of the injury. Platelets help to form a clot, which then becomes a scab and seals up the injury. At the same time, the phagocytes (the white blood cells) move in and eat up any germs that may have entered the body, while other white cells called lymphocytes knock out the germs by producing disease-fighting chemicals, which are called antibodies.

What is a blood group?

A blood group is the name given to a type of blood. Blood groups vary from person to person. The two main systems for grouping blood are the ABO and Rhesus systems. There are four blood groups in the ABO system, the most common system of blood grouping. They are O, A, B, and AB.

What is a blood transfusion?

A blood transfusion is the transfer of blood from a healthy person (the donor) into the body of someone who lacks enough blood, either because of disease or injury. The donor's blood must be matched to the patient's blood group.

A blood donor volunteers to give blood so that hospitals can have a supply stored, ready for operations and emergencies. A donor can give about 1 pint (0.5 l) of blood without any ill effects, and many people who are blood donors give blood regularly.

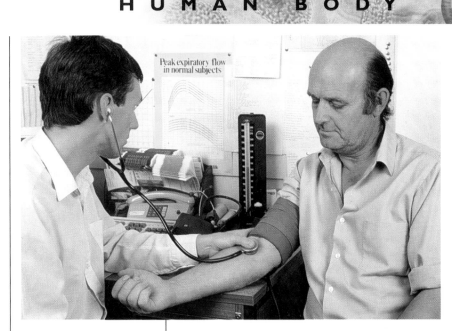

▲ Taking a person's blood pressure is a routine method for checking that the heart and circulation are working properly.

Most germs won't hurt you, but some will make you ill if they get inside you. If they do, your blood gets to work on the germs and kills them.

What is blood pressure?

Blood pressure is the pushing force given to blood by the heart. A doctor usually measures blood pressure using a special arm-cuff attached to the gauge. The first reading gives blood pressure during heartbeats; the second, pressure between heartbeats.

What is a heart attack?

A heart attack happens when the heart can no longer cope with the demands made upon it. Heart attacks are usually caused by a blood clot blocking a coronary artery. Some heart muscle cells become starved of food and oxygen, and die. Many people recover from heart attacks.

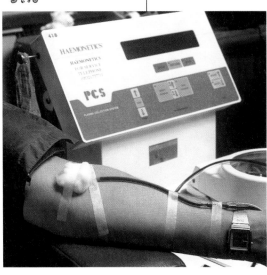

◄ People who give blood are called donors. They attend donor centers where blood is taken from the arm and then stored until it is needed for a transfusion.

FOOD AND WASTE

Why do we need food?

Food contains different kinds of substances, which our bodies need, but they are not in a form that the body can use. They must first be broken down in a process called digestion. The food is first chewed into smaller pieces, then broken down chemically in the stomach and intestines by acids and proteins called digestive enzymes.

Your body tells you it needs food by making you feel hungry. Food smells, or just thinking about food, can make your mouth water.

▼ The digestive system starts in the mouth. Food passes through the stomach and the intestines. Finally, waste leaves the body.

Teeth

Salivary glands

Esophagus

Gall bladder

Duodenum

Colon

Liver

Stomach

Pyloric sphincter

Pancreas

Ileum

Rectum

Which foods give us energy?

Foods that contain carbohydrates are a good source of energy. Sugars, and a substance called starch, found in bread and potatoes, are carbohydrates. Fats give us energy too. Butter, margarine, and oils are very rich in fats, and are best eaten in small amounts.

Why do we need vitamins and minerals?

Although we need only tiny amounts of vitamins and minerals, they are essential for many functions in the body. Lack of the mineral iron, for example, leads to a shortage of red blood cells, causing anemia. Vitamin B helps wounds to heal and keeps the gums healthy. Calcium and vitamin D help to make bones strong. Vitamin D is found in fish and cheese and is made by the skin in sunlight.

What is a balanced diet?

A balanced diet is one that supplies the different types of foods that you need in the right amounts—not too much and not too little of each. It gives you the raw materials and energy for a healthy, active life. The amount of food you need each day depends on your age, size, and sex, as well as your general level of activity. A tall teenage boy who plays a lot of tennis will need a lot more food each day than a small elderly woman. In general, adult men need more food-energy than women.

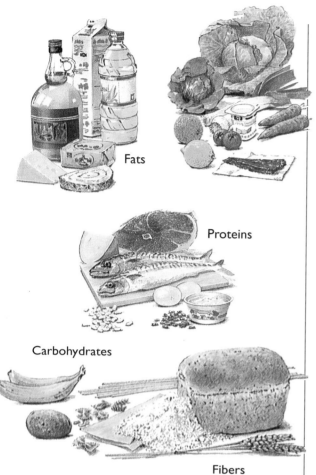

Fats

Proteins

Carbohydrates

Fibers

◀ **For good health, it is important to eat a balanced diet, including some of each of the foods shown: fruit, vegetables, carbohydrates (for fuel), fiber (to aid digestion), fats (for energy), and proteins.**

Why do we get hungry?

Our eating is controlled by an area deep in the brain. When this "hunger center" receives signals from parts of the body saying that we need to eat, we get hungry. Painful sensations, such as stomach cramps, can also sometimes prompt us to eat.

How much water do we need every day?

An adult needs about 1½ to 2 quarts (1.5 to 2 l) of water a day. Much of this will come from food. For example, bread is about 40 percent water.

We feel thirsty when the normal amount of water in the blood starts to drop, and the blood gets very slightly thicker. Part of our brain senses this and sends signals to the body that tell us we need more fluid.

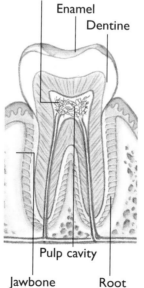

▲ **The center of a tooth is a space full of nerves and blood vessels. Around it is a wall of dentine and on top, a layer of hard enamel.**

Why are teeth different shapes?

Teeth are different shapes because they have different jobs to do. The incisor teeth at the front of your mouth are shaped like chisels. They are used for biting and gnawing. The canines, just behind the incisors, are pointed teeth used for tearing food. The premolars and molars at the back are shaped for grinding food.

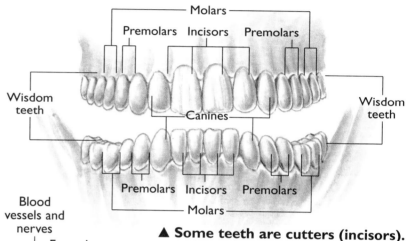

▲ **Some teeth are cutters (incisors). Others are grinders (molars). The wisdom teeth are the last to appear.**

What are teeth made of?

Each tooth consists of a visible part, called the crown, and a root, which attaches it to a socket in the jawbone. The outer, off-white part of the tooth is made of enamel, the hardest substance in the body. Underneath the enamel is dentine, which is similar to bone, but harder.

How do teeth grow?

Teeth grow from small patches of tissue covering the bone of the upper and lower jaws. Teeth start growing before we are born, but they begin to come through the gum only about six months after birth.

Why does your mouth water?

The taste, smell, and sometimes even the thought of food causes the salivary glands to send saliva (a colorless fluid) along little ducts into the mouth. Sometimes jets of saliva squirt out into your mouth, so that your mouth "waters." Saliva is mostly water, with some mucus. It also contains an enzyme, which starts off the digestive process by breaking down starch, a carbohydrate.

What happens when you swallow?

Swallowing is a complicated process. When you swallow, your tongue squeezes against the roof of your mouth and pushes the food or drink up and back. At the same time, the soft part at the top of your mouth moves up, closing off the nasal passages so that nothing goes up your nose. Finally, your epiglottis flaps down and your larynx (voice box) moves forward and upward. This closes off the windpipe and opens up the gullet, or esophagus. The food or drink is squeezed into your throat and down the esophagus to the stomach.

What happens in the stomach?

The stomach looks like a bag. It has muscular walls, and is closed by valves. In the stomach, food is churned up and mixed with stomach juices containing digestive enzymes and acid. The acid also kills most of the germs in food. The mushy food is then delivered gradually to the small intestine.

If air comes back up the tube from your tummy, you make a sound called a burp. Carbonated drinks can make people burp.

MORE BODY FACTS

■ An average person eats 50 tons of food and drinks more than 40,000 quarts (liters) of liquid in a lifetime.

■ When you are resting, about a quarter of your blood is in your liver. When you begin to move around, some of this blood is immediately sent to other organs.

■ Indigestion is a pain in the stomach. It can be caused by eating too fast, or by the stomach producing too much acid.

■ If you eat food that is spoiled, or just eat too much, you may vomit. Muscles in your diaphragm and stomach contract and force the contents of your stomach back up and out of your body.

■ About two thirds of your body is water. You might live 2 to 3 weeks without food, but you could die in 2 or 3 days without water.

▶ The liver is the body's largest organ. Its activity produces enough heat to keep your insides warm. The pancreas makes the hormone insulin. Bile is stored in the gall bladder.

Why does your tummy sometimes rumble?

The stomach and intestines are very active—the stomach churns food and the intestines squeeze it along. All this activity means that your stomach makes noises most of the time. When you are hungry your stomach contains a little liquid and a lot of gas. Because there is a lot of gas in your stomach, its rumblings are louder.

What does the liver do?

The liver has many different roles. It checks the amount of digested food in the blood. If there is more food than the body needs, it changes the extra into sugar and stores it. The liver also stores some vitamins and iron. It helps the body to get rid of some poisons and cleans the blood by removing dead red blood cells. The liver makes bile, which is stored in the gall bladder before being pumped into the digestive system, where it breaks down fats.

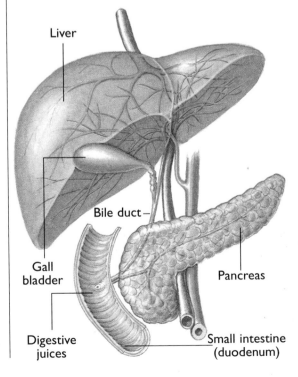

Liver

Bile duct

Gall bladder

Digestive juices

Pancreas

Small intestine (duodenum)

How long does it take to digest a meal?

It takes about 24 hours to completely digest a typical meal. Food spends about four hours in your stomach. This is followed by up to six hours in the small intestine, six or seven hours in the colon, and six or seven hours in the rectum, before the residue is expelled as feces (solid waste).

What are the body's waste substances?

The body's main waste substances are the gas carbon dioxide (produced during respiration), urea (from breaking down excess proteins), and water and salts that the body does not need. The excretory organs excrete waste. They are the lungs, the kidneys, the liver, and the skin. The lungs, for example, get rid of carbon dioxide. The kidneys get rid of water and other substances, such as salts. Waste products from the liver are taken to the kidneys and excreted in urine, or they are excreted in bile, and expelled through the gut.

Why do we have an appendix?

No one knows. The appendix is a dead-end tube at the point where the small and large intestines join. It is not used in human digestion, although it is an important organ in animals that eat grass. The appendix can sometimes cause trouble, if it becomes infected and inflamed. This condition is known as appendicitis, and the appendix may have to be removed in the hospital. People without their appendix never notice any difference.

▶ **You have two kidneys. These organs filter the blood, remove waste (urea) made in the liver, and send it as urine to the ureter.**

When you go to the bathroom, your body is getting rid of water it doesn't need. This waste water is called urine. Urine is usually a yellowish color.

DID YOU KNOW?

■ Diarrhea may be caused by food poisoning or by an infection in the intestines. You need to drink a lot to make up for the water you lose when you have diarrhea.

■ You can swallow upside-down, though it isn't a good idea. It is possible because food is pushed along the esophagus by bands of muscles.

■ The walls of the stomach are protected by a layer of mucus. This prevents the enzymes and strong acid from trying to digest the stomach itself!

■ Your kidneys filter all the blood in your body about 300 times each day.

■ People can live with one kidney. If one kidney is diseased or damaged, it can be removed and the other kidney will do the job of two kidneys.

■ Urine is yellow because it contains substances formed by the liver when it breaks down hemoglobin from old blood.

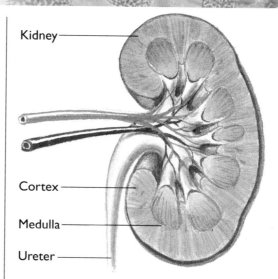

Kidney

Cortex

Medulla

Ureter

What do the kidneys do?

The kidneys are a pair of very hard-working filters. They purify the blood, taking out waste substances and making sure that useful substances are kept in. The kidneys produce urine, a fluid that contains waste substances filtered from the blood. Urine is passed to the bladder, where it is stored until it leaves the body through a tube called the urethra.

How does a kidney machine work?

A kidney machine filters blood by a process called dialysis. It is used to help people whose own kidneys are not working properly. A tube inserted into an artery in a patient's arm carries blood to the machine, where it is pumped through cellophane tubing in a container of liquid. Wastes in the blood pass through the walls of the tubing into the liquid, and substances that the body needs pass from the liquid into the blood. The clean blood is then returned to the patient through a tube connected to a vein in their arm. Blood must pass through the machine 20 times or more.

SKIN AND HAIR

Why do we have skin?

Skin is a waterproof, flexible covering that protects us from the outside world and helps to keep out harmful germs. Our skin is sensitive to touch, heat, cold, and pain, and so it allows us to sense what is happening around us. Skin helps protect us from harmful rays in strong sunlight, and uses some sunlight to make vitamin D. Skin contains sweat glands, body hairs, and tiny blood vessels which help to control our body temperature.

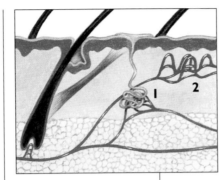
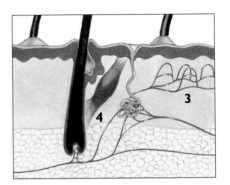

▲ Beneath the skin: sweat glands (1); skin capillaries which widen (2) to let heat escape and narrow (3) to reduce heat loss; hair erector muscles (4) which make "goose pimples."

Hair—
Pore
Dermis
Granular layer
Epidermis
Hair root
Erector muscle
Hypodermis
Sweat gland
Blood vessel
Sebaceous gland

▲ The skin has two main layers: a tough outer layer called the epidermis and, beneath it, the dermis. Sebaceous glands give off oil to stop the skin from drying out.

Why are people's skins different colors?

Melanin is a dark brown substance, or pigment, that protects the skin from the Sun's harmful ultraviolet rays. The color of skin depends on how much melanin there is in the epidermis.

Where does sweat come from?

Sweat is a saltwater liquid, which also contains small amounts of the body's waste substances. Sweat is produced by glands in the dermis and is released onto the skin through tiny openings called pores. As the sweat dries, it cools the body. There are many sweat glands under the arms, in the groin, and on the hands, feet, and face. Stale sweat smells. It is important to wash regularly to remove it.

Why do bruises change color?

A bruise is a purplish mark that appears when tiny blood vessels in the skin break, generally after a hard knock. Bruises are first dark purple, then change through blue, green, and yellow before fading away altogether. These color changes are a result of the blood being broken down and reabsorbed as the damage heals and the normal skin color returns.

How does skin heal itself?

Cut or injured skin heals itself automatically. If someone cuts themselves and starts to bleed, the blood soon forms a clot that stops further bleeding. The clot dries to form a scab, which prevents germs from entering the damaged skin. Beneath the scab, new skin cells grow across the wound, and when the skin is healed the scab drops off.

How does skin tan?

In strong sunlight, the skin produces extra melanin to protect it from harmful ultraviolet rays. This melanin spreads through the epidermis, in the form of tiny black grains. Eventually skin turns darker, producing a tan. Every skin color turns darker with exposure to sunlight.

What are nails made of?

Nails are made of dead cells that contain keratin, the protein found in the outer layer of skin. Nails grow by being pushed out of a pit in the skin called the nail bed, which lies horizontal to the skin. As the nail grows it slides along the surface of the nail bed to the fingertip. Most of the nail is pink, because the blood vessels underneath it show through.

HAIR FACTS

- Most people have about 100,000 hairs on their head alone.
- Hair turns gray because as we get older some hairs lack pigment.
- Hair is very strong. A rope made from about 1,000 human hairs could support an adult.
- The average person loses 50 to 100 hairs a day, but these are continually replaced.
- Some men go bald because the male hormone, testosterone, seems to affect the hair follicles so that lost hair is not replaced.
- Dandruff is dead skin that flakes off the scalp.

▲ **Whether your skin is pale or dark, too much sunlight can burn you. When you are in the sun, wear a hat and put on a layer of suitable suntan lotion.**

What is hair for?

Hair helps to prevent heat loss from the body, because it is able to trap a layer of warm air next to the skin. Hairs in our nostrils filter out dirt, to keep our lungs clean. Hair has two parts: the root and the shaft. The hair root is embedded in the skin and is enclosed in a tiny pit, called a hair follicle. The hair shaft contains the pigment that gives hair its color. Hair is made of keratin, the same substance found in nails and skin.

Why is hair different colors?

Hair color is determined by the mixture of pigments that it contains. Hair-producing cells can produce a mixture of black, red, and yellow pigments. For example, dark-haired people have predominantly black pigment and fair-haired people have mostly yellow pigment.

What makes hair curly?

Hair is curly, wavy, or straight depending on the shape of the follicles it grows from. Straight hair grows from round follicles, wavy hair from oval follicles, and curly hair from flat follicles.

Why do we have eyelashes?

Eyelashes act as protection for our eyes. Our eyelashes help stop dust and other particles from reaching the delicate surface of the eye and irritating it. Our eyebrows, however, are probably used to make signals, as a means of nonverbal communication, rather than as protection for our eyes.

NERVES AND SENSES

How are the body's actions coordinated?

Coordination is the way different activities in the body are linked together. The body relies on two systems to coordinate its actions. The nervous system sends messages to and from the brain as electrical signals along nerves. The hormonal (endocrine) system sends chemical messengers called hormones around the body. The hormones travel in the bloodstream through the arteries.

What are hormones?

Hormones are chemicals produced in one part of the body that have an effect on another part. For example, the hormone insulin is produced by the pancreas and affects the functioning of the liver and other tissues in the body.

There are over 30 hormones. They are produced by structures called endocrine glands, which are found in the head, neck, and torso. Hormones have an enormous effect on many bodily processes, from our growth to the workings of our reproductive system.

Which is the most important gland?

The pituitary gland is the most important, because it produces hormones that control most of the other endocrine glands. Height is controlled by a growth hormone produced by the pituitary gland. Too

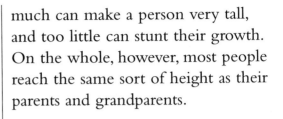

BRAIN FACTS

■ The brain contains over 10 billion nerve cells.

■ Each of these cells can have as many as 25,000 connections to other cells.

■ It is estimated that the brain can store as many as 100 million bits of information in a lifetime.

■ Brains are getting heavier. In 1860 the average man's brain weighed 48 oz. (1,370 g). Today it weighs 50 oz. (1,420 g).

■ Messages travel along large nerves at more than 300 ft. (90 m) a second (about 200 mph/320 km/h).

■ Messages go much more slowly through the smaller nerves, such as those in the digestive system.

People's brains are different sizes. Bigger brains don't make people more clever—any more than big feet make them better runners!

much can make a person very tall, and too little can stunt their growth. On the whole, however, most people reach the same sort of height as their parents and grandparents.

What makes up the nervous system?

The nervous system is made up of billions of nerve cells, which carry electrical messages all around the body. It has two main parts: the central nervous system (CNS), made up of the brain and the spinal cord; and the peripheral nervous system (PNS), made up of all the nerves that run through the central nervous system to the rest of the body.

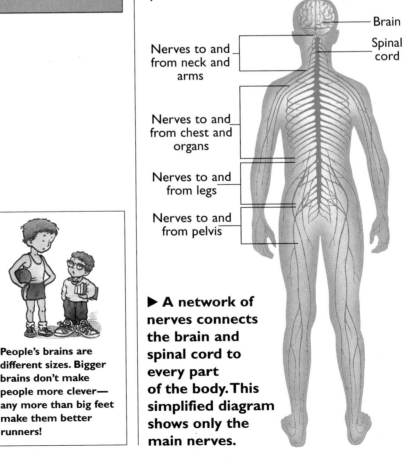

Nerves to and from neck and arms

Nerves to and from chest and organs

Nerves to and from legs

Nerves to and from pelvis

Brain

Spinal cord

▶ **A network of nerves connects the brain and spinal cord to every part of the body. This simplified diagram shows only the main nerves.**

How many nerves do you have?

Running between your brain and the sense organs and muscles in your head are 24 large nerves—the cranial nerves. These include nerves from your eyes, nose, and ears. Your 62 spinal nerves run from your spinal cord to the rest of the body.

▼ **A typical muscle nerve cell, or neuron, has a star-shaped control center. The axon carries messages. Dendrites receive messages. Neurons communicate with one another at synapses.**

What is a reflex?

When you react to something without thinking, your action is a reflex. For example, if your hand touches something hot, you will jerk it away without stopping to think about it. Most reflexes are controlled by your spinal cord and hardly involve your brain at all.

How do nerves pass on messages?

One nerve cell does not actually touch the next. The message has to be carried by chemicals across a gap called the synapse. The branched ends of axons send out chemicals called neurotransmitters when triggered by a nerve impulse. The chemicals stimulate the next-door cell, setting up a new nerve impulse so that the message carries on its way.

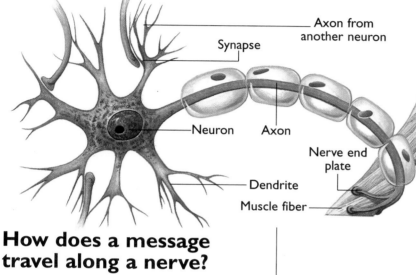

Axon from another neuron

Synapse

Neuron

Axon

Nerve end plate

Dendrite

Muscle fiber

How does a message travel along a nerve?

A message is picked up by a nerve cell at its dendrite end. The message travels through the cell as a small electrical current, called a nerve impulse. When the message gets to the end of the axon it is then passed to the next cell.

▼ **We use our five senses all the time. They tell us what is going on and help us communicate.**

What are our five senses?

Our five senses are sight, hearing, smell, taste, and touch. Our sense organs, such as our eyes, contain special cells called sensory receptors. These cells pass information about the outside world to nerve cells, which then transmit a message to the brain. Sensory receptors in the eye receive information in the form of light rays.

Hearing

Taste

Touch

Smell

Sight

How do our eyes work?

The eyes are two tough balls of tissue containing transparent jelly. At the front of each eye is a transparent covering called the cornea. The colored part of the eye is called the iris. It surrounds the pupil, a dark hole through which light enters the eyeball. Six muscles connect the eyeball to the bones in the eyesocket and move the eyeball around. The optic nerve runs out of the back of the eye and goes to the brain.

Light rays enter the eye and pass through the pupil to the lens. Both the curved surface of the eye and the lens bend the rays and focus them into a clear image on the retina. Cells in the retina send messages along the optic nerve to the brain.

EYE FACTS

■ You blink on average about 6 times a minute.

■ The human eye can detect 10 million different color shades.

■ In bright light, muscles in the iris make the pupil shrink, protecting the sensitive retina.

■ Tears keep our eyes shiny and moist. Tears are made by a gland above the eyeball.

■ Tear fluid also contains a chemical that kills germs.

■ Two-thousandths of a second after light hits the retina, your brain has formed an image!

■ We all have one eye that we use more than the other—just as people are right-handed or left-handed.

What gives your eyes their color?

Your eye color is produced by a pigment called melanin. Eyes can be brown, blue, gray, green, or somewhere in between. The color depends on how much melanin is present in the iris—brown eyes contain much more than blue eyes.

How do we see colors?

There are three types of cone cell, each sensitive to one of three colors: red, blue, or green. We see other colors when a combination of cone cells is triggered. For example, when both red and green cones are stimulated, we see yellow.

Are two eyes better than one?

Yes. Two eyes see over a bigger area, and because our eyes are set slightly apart, they see objects from slightly different angles. The brain fits the two images together to give a 3-D image, which helps us judge distances better.

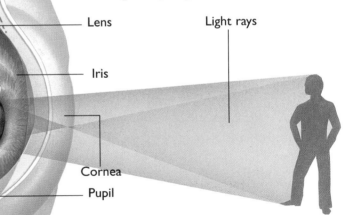

Blood vessels

Retina

Image

Lens

Light rays

Iris

Blind spot

Cornea

Pupil

Optic nerve

Eye muscle

Lens muscle

◄ **Light rays pass through the pupil and are focused by the lens as an upside-down image on the retina, a layer of light-sensitive cells at the back of the eye. Your brain turns the image the right way up.**

What makes our eyes water?

Crying makes our eyes water when we are upset, or our eyes may water to wash away dirt or an irritation, such as smoke. Normally, tear fluid drains away at roughly the same rate that it is produced. However, if tear fluid forms more quickly than it is drained away, it wells up, forming tears, and our eyes water.

Why do some people need glasses?

People need glasses if the lenses in their eyes cannot focus the light rays properly on the retina. The image they see looks fuzzy. Wearing glasses can help correct their sight. People can also wear contact lenses—thin plastic disks that rest on the surface of the eye and act like the lenses of glasses—to correct their vision.

How do our ears hear?

Sound is made up of pressure waves, which can travel through air, liquid, and solid objects. When these waves strike the outer ear, they are funneled down the ear canal to the eardrum, which starts to vibrate. Its vibrations are magnified by the three bones in the middle ear. The stirrup acts like a piston, transferring these vibrations to the fluid of the inner ear. As the fluid moves, it excites special hair cells in the cochlea. These hair cells send signals along the auditory nerve to the brain, which interprets the signals as sound. The brain is able to concentrate on the sounds that it wants to listen to and hold back the rest of the sound-signals.

Middle ear   Semicircular canal   Auditory nerve

Cochlea

Hammer   Stirrup

Anvil

Eustachian tube

Ear canal   Eardrum

▲ The ear flap on the outside helps to funnel sounds into the ear canal. The middle ear contains the hammer, anvil, and stirrup bones. The cochlea is in the inner ear.

If you hold a shell to your ear, you'll hear the sound of the blood flowing around inside your head. It sounds a bit like the sea.

What causes deafness?

There are two kinds of deafness. In one type, sounds do not reach the inner ear. This could be caused by a blockage in the outer ear, such as a buildup of wax, or by an infection in the middle ear that stops the three bones from working properly. In the second type of deafness, sounds reach the inner ear, but no electrical signals are sent to the brain. Noise damage to the cochlea can cause such deafness.

How do our ears help us balance?

Above the cochlea in the inner ear are three tiny, fluid-filled, semicircular canals. These loops are the organs of balance. Each contains small pieces of chalky substance that are in contact with sensitive cells. When we move, the chalk triggers these cells to send signals to the brain. One loop detects up-and-down motion, another forward-and-backward motion, the third side-to-side movement. So whichever way we move, even if our eyes are shut, the brain is informed.

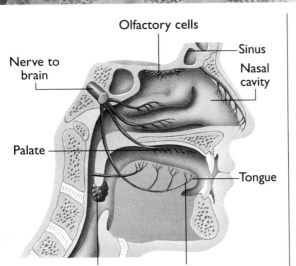

Olfactory cells

Nerve to brain

Sinus

Nasal cavity

Palate

Tongue

Tonsils   Nerves for tasting

▲ **Nerve fibers for smell are on the roof of the nasal cavity.**

What is the nose for?

Obviously, the nose is for smelling and for breathing. Inside the nose are patches containing millions of sensitive olfactory cells, which can tell one smell from another. The nose also cleans, warms, and moistens the air that you breathe into your lungs, and it makes your voice sound pleasant.

How many things can we smell?

Most people can recognize about 4,000 different scents. Someone with an extremely sensitive nose, such as a chef, wine taster, or perfumemaker, can detect 10,000 different smells.

How does a cold spoil our sense of smell?

When we have a cold, our nasal membranes defend themselves against the cold virus by producing large amounts of mucus. This blocks the nose and stops the chemicals in air from reaching the sensitive and delicate olfactory cells.

Your tongue tastes things, but it also helps you to speak and sing. Tiny bumps called tastebuds send messages to your brain, telling you if what you're eating tastes good or awful.

▶ **You taste the four main tastes (sweet, salty, bitter, and sour) on different parts of your tongue.**

SENSE FACTS

■ Put your finger on your tongue and try to say "Hello." See how your tongue helps you to speak?

■ Your nose helps you taste, as well as smell things. Microscopic particles of food are carried by air into your nose. Nerves detect them and send messages to the brain.

■ You have about 10,000 tastebuds on your tongue.

■ Tastebuds don't last for ever. Most people have lost half their tastebuds by the age of 60.

■ Tastebuds are good at detecting natural plant poisons, which taste very bitter. However, they cannot detect chemical poisons that taste sweet or have no taste at all.

What is taste?

Taste is a combination of the tongue sensing the chemicals in food, and the nose smelling them. Smell is more important in tasting food. On the upper surface of the tongue are small collections of cells, called tastebuds. The tastebuds pick out four different tastes: bitter, sweet, sour, and salty. The way food tastes is a combination of these basic tastes.

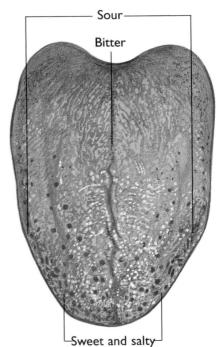

Sour

Bitter

Sweet and salty

How is skin able to sense things?

The skin has five different kinds of sensory receptors. These cells are sensitive to heat, cold, pressure, texture, and pain. The receptors are connected by sensory nerves to the spinal cord and brain. They are continuously sending signals about the state of our surroundings and what is happening on the surface of the skin. Light pressure and cold receptors are near the surface of the skin. The sensory receptors for heat and deep pressure are buried deeper.

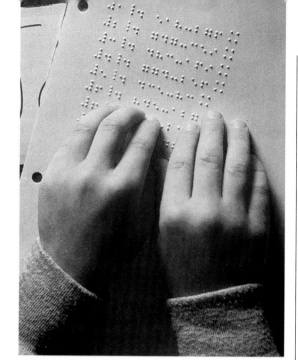

How do blind people read with their fingers?

Blind people often compensate for their lack of sight by developing other senses—hearing, smell, and touch in particular. They may learn to read by touch, using a system called Braille, in which small dots raised from the surface of the paper represent letters and punctuation. Blind people can read about 100 words a minute by passing their fingertips over the page.

What causes pain?

Any stimulus that is strong enough to cause tissue damage is likely to trigger pain; for example, strong pressure, swelling, muscle spasm, and the presence or absence of certain chemicals. Other sensory receptors will also give pain signals if the stimulus they respond to is strong enough. For example, temperature receptors will give a feeling of pain if the temperature is too hot or too cold. Pain can be useful—it tells us that something is wrong and stops us from hurting ourselves more seriously.

◄ Blind people can read using Braille. The tips of the fingers are especially sensitive, and a skilled blind reader can read a Braille book as fast as most sighted people can read a printed page.

Pain tells you if something is wrong. It warns your body to take care and protect itself. It hurts when you stub your toe because your body is telling you to stop—something is in the way!

▶ Some parts of your body have more nerve cells than others. If the size of the various parts of your body corresponded to the number of nerve cells in them, this is what you would look like!

Which are the most sensitive parts of the body?

The lips are most sensitive to touch and texture, while the small of the back is the least sensitive. The most sensitive parts for pressure are the fingertips, and the least sensitive is the bottom! The lips and fingertips are so sensitive because they have more nerve endings. Our fingers and toes need to be more sensitive, as we use them to explore the world around us. Our lips are very sensitive too, as you can see from the picture below.

Why do we itch sometimes?

Little is known about why we itch. Sometimes we can see a cause, such as a scab or an insect bite. Stimulating pain receptors can cause itching, but no nerve endings have been specifically connected with itching alone. Thinking about an itch can bring on the urge to scratch, but the reason for this is a mystery.

REPRODUCTION AND GROWTH

How does a new life begin?

Every baby begins life when a single egg cell from the mother and a tiny sperm cell from the father join together inside the mother's body. This is called fertilization. The fertilized egg grows and divides, and after nine months the baby is born.

Where do eggs come from?

Eggs are made in two almond-shaped organs in the woman's body, called the ovaries. About once a month, from puberty (10 to 14 years) until the age of 45 to 50, an egg is released from one of the two ovaries.

Where do sperm come from?

A man's reproductive organs are the penis and testes (singular "testis"). Sperm are made in the testes. They are manufactured in tiny tubes and are then stored in a long tube called the epididymis, which is coiled on the surface of the testis. The sperm travel to the urethra inside the erect penis through two tubes called sperm ducts to pass into the woman's body. Sperm look like microscopic tadpoles. Only one sperm can fertilize the egg. Each sperm has a head containing a nucleus, which fuses with the egg when fertilization takes place. The tail stays outside.

SPERM FACTS

■ About 50 million sperm are made in each testis every day.

■ 300 million sperm may be released, but only a few hundred get close to the egg and only one will fertilize it—if fertilization happens.

■ Some sperm reach the Fallopian tube in only about five minutes. Others may take hours.

■ A sperm lashes its tail to push itself along as it moves toward the egg.

▼ The female and male reproductive organs. During sexual intercourse, sperm travel from the penis through the vagina and uterus to the Fallopian tube to reach the egg.

Where does fertilization take place?

Sperm enter the woman's body during sexual intercourse. The man's penis becomes stiff and is put inside the woman's vagina. Semen, a fluid containing the sperm, is squirted from the penis into the woman's vagina. An egg may be fertilized as a result. The sperm fertilizes the egg in a tube called the Fallopian tube which joins each ovary to the uterus. The fertilized egg travels on to the uterus, where the baby grows.

What is the menstrual cycle?

Women have a monthly cycle, or period. Every month a mature egg is released from the ovaries, and the lining of the uterus develops so that it can receive a fertilized egg. If the egg is not fertilized the lining of the uterus breaks down. This is called the

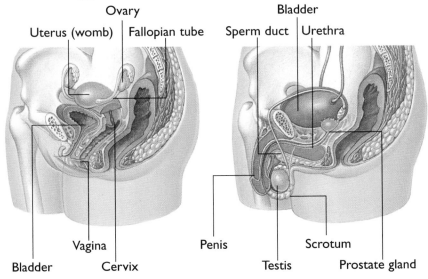

Ovary
Uterus (womb) | Fallopian tube
Vagina
Bladder | Cervix

Bladder
Sperm duct | Urethra
Penis | Scrotum
Testis | Prostate gland

Day 1: uterus lining shed—period begins

Day 5: uterus lining starts to build up, ready to receive a fertilized egg

Day 14: mature egg released from ovary

menstrual cycle. It usually takes about 28 days, although the length of time varies from person to person. The cycle is controlled by hormones from the pituitary gland and the ovaries.

What happens if the egg is fertilized?

If the egg is fertilized, its outer membrane swells into a jellylike barrier to keep out other sperm. The fertilized egg travels down the Fallopian tube to the uterus. As it does so it divides, first into two cells, then four, then eight. It arrives in the uterus as a ball of about 100 cells.

When is a baby an embryo?

An unborn baby is called an embryo for up to eight weeks after fertilization. The embryo forms from part of the ball of cells implanted in the mother's uterus. Its life-support system is the placenta, a disk-shaped organ with many blood vessels joined to the baby by the

◀ A girl begins to have menstrual periods at puberty. Every month, the ovaries release an egg cell. The most likely time for an egg to be fertilized is between the fourteenth day and the eighteenth day of her cycle.

LIFE FACTS
■ At 4 weeks, the embryo is no bigger than a grain of rice. It has a head and a tail.
■ At 16 weeks, the mother feels the baby kicking.
■ By the 20th week, it has eyebrows and fingernails.

▶ The fetus grows inside its mother's uterus. It gets food and oxygen from its mother through the umbilical cord. By 12 weeks, it looks human and has fingers and toes. At 38 weeks, the baby's head is near the opening of the uterus. The baby is ready to be born.

umbilical cord, through which the baby feeds.

How quickly does the embryo develop?

The embryo develops very quickly. At four weeks, it is no bigger than a grain of rice, and has a head. Between the fourth and eighth week of pregnancy, its hands, feet, and facial features develop. After the twelfth week of pregnancy, the embryo looks human and its major organs are starting to develop. After sixteen weeks, the mother will start to feel the baby kicking. By the twentieth week, the baby has eyebrows and fingernails. After thirty-eight weeks, the baby is usually ready to be born.

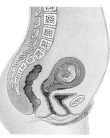

8 weeks

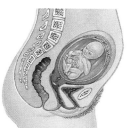

12 weeks

28 weeks

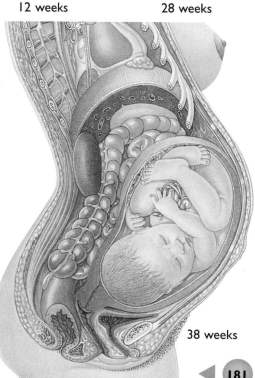

38 weeks

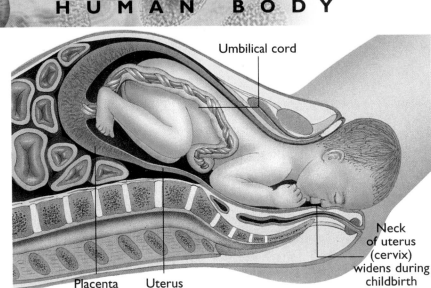

Umbilical cord

Placenta   Uterus

Neck
of uterus
(cervix)
widens during
childbirth

What happens when a baby is born?

Birth usually takes place around the 38th week of pregnancy. The process of giving birth usually lasts between six and twelve hours. The mother pushes hard with her abdominal muscles, and the baby is gradually pushed through the cervix and vagina (birth canal), out into the world.

What are twins?

If two eggs are released by the mother's ovaries and both are fertilized, two fetuses develop with separate placentas. These are called fraternal twins. Identical twins come from the same egg and sperm, and so have exactly the same genes. The single fertilized egg splits at an early stage, producing two fetuses that can grow into identical twins.

▲ **When a baby is ready to be born, the neck of the uterus stretches and opens, and the baby is pushed out. The baby starts to breathe and the umbilical cord is cut.**

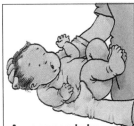

As soon as a baby is born, it takes a big gulp of air and begins to breathe. The umbilical cord is cut, leaving a small scar—the belly button.

◀ **Identical twins come from one egg, which splits to produce two fetuses that grow into two babies that look alike.**

What is a multiple birth?

When a pregnant woman gives birth to two or more children, it is called a multiple birth. The highest number of children ever produced from a multiple birth is ten.

What is a test-tube baby?

The world's first test-tube baby was born in England on July 25, 1978. A test-tube baby does not grow inside a test tube. Eggs are taken from the woman and mixed in a small glass dish with sperm from the man. The eggs are fertilized and the young embryos are kept alive for a few days before they are placed in the woman's uterus. The resulting babies are called test-tube babies. Such treatments are used to help people who cannot have children normally.

What can a newborn baby sense?

A baby has a good sense of smell, much better than its sense of hearing or sight. It first learns to recognize its mother by smell.

What happens in the first week of life?

In the first week of a baby's life many changes are taking place. For example, the blood, which originally flowed through the umbilical artery, is re-routed through the lungs, liver, and heart. A hole between the two sides of the heart seals up so the heart can function properly. A newborn baby has several reflex actions. It automatically turns its head toward the breast and will grasp any object placed in its palm.

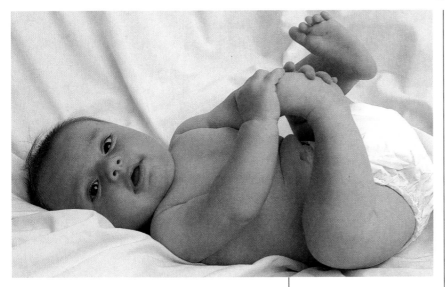

What can a baby do at three months?

At three months, a baby usually spends most of its time lying on its back. It can raise its head slightly, smile at its parents, and will turn toward a noise. It can hold a rattle and will try to reach for toys, but its movements are jerky.

What is a baby like at twelve months?

The baby is now three times its weight at birth. It crawls mainly, but can usually stand with support and walk a little while holding onto furniture. It is able to pick up objects carefully between finger and thumb, and has learned to let go of objects. The baby can now recognize its name and say a few simple words.

▲ A baby has a large head to hold its brain. It needs a large brain to learn about its surroundings and respond to them.

GROWTH FACTS

■ At 6 months a baby has doubled its birth weight and can sit propped up.

■ Children grow very quickly during the first two years of life.

■ From age 3 to 10 growth is slower. A new growth spurt begins at puberty.

■ Boys may carry on growing until they are 23.

■ Most girls are fully grown by the age of 20.

◄ At 12 months, a toddler is beginning to stand and to take a few steps with assistance.

How do we grow?

Most of our growth is due to an increase in the number of cells in our body. Cells divide to form other cells. This process continues until we are full-grown. Growth is controlled by a hormone produced by the pituitary gland. You actually grow a little faster at night, since this is when levels of the growth hormone are highest.

What is puberty?

Puberty is the period in our life when the sex organs mature and other physical changes occur so that we develop into men and women.

At puberty, a girl's ovaries mature and her menstrual cycle begins. Her breasts develop and her hips widen. Body hair develops under the arms and in the groin area. Her voice becomes lower. Boys and girls may start to lose "baby" fat.

At puberty, a boy's penis and testes get larger and he starts producing sperm. His body shape changes and his torso gets larger. He can grow a beard, and his body hair becomes thicker, particularly under his arms and in the groin area. His voicebox (larynx) develops and his voice gets deeper, or "breaks."

What triggers the changes of puberty?

In both boys and girls, puberty is triggered by the pituitary gland in the brain. This gland stimulates other glands to release sex hormones. In boys, the changes are triggered by testosterone, which is produced by the testes. In girls, they are triggered by estrogen, produced by the ovaries.

When are we at our physical peak?

We are at our physical peak in our twenties. This is when we have stopped growing and are at our strongest physically.

What is ageing?

Ageing is a natural process in which some of the body's cells gradually become less efficient and eventually die. This process happens to us all, but its rate varies from person to person.

Our senses and our bodies' defenses all deteriorate to some extent as we grow old.

Does long life run in families?

Yes. How long a person lives, barring accidents, seems to be inherited, though only to some extent. Some families seem less prone to disease and the effects of ageing. So if your grandparents live to a ripe old age, you may do the same.

Scientists still do not know why the human female outlives the male by about 8 years. The age to which people live is increasing in the West. About 13 percent of the population is over 65.

▼ Our appearance and the shape of our bodies change as we grow older. We grow until we are about 20. As we get older, it takes longer to repair and replace damaged parts of the body.

What are chromosomes?

Chromosomes are microscopic, threadlike structures found in the nucleus of every cell, although they become visible only when the cell is dividing. Chromosomes contain all the necessary information for the cell to develop. Human cells normally contain 46 chromosomes, which come in 22 matching pairs, plus a special pair that determines the sex of the individual.

What is a gene?

A gene is a short section of a chromosome. The gene carries a set of instructions that determines one of the individual's characteristics, such as eye color. About half our genes have come from each of our parents.

Age 6

Age 4   Age 8   Age 15   Age 40   Age 60

Which features do we inherit from our parents?

We are a mixture of our parents. The male sperm cells and female egg cells contain only 23 chromosomes each, half the number found in any other cell. When the nuclei of these two cells come together in a fertilized egg, the chromosomes combine to make 46 chromosomes in total. Half the genetic information in every cell has come from our father, and half from our mother. We inherit features such as skin color, hair color, and overall body shape. Our features may be a combination of both parents, or we may look more like one parent.

What is a dominant gene?

Most of our characteristics are controlled by two genes—one from each parent. Often these genes are not identical. For example, genes for eye color can be different. If you have a gene for brown eyes from one parent and a gene for blue eyes from the other, the brown-eye gene will override the blue-eye one. You will have brown eyes. The gene for brown eyes is said to be "dominant."

How is a baby's sex decided?

A woman has two X chromosomes in the 23rd pair of chromosomes. A man has one X and one Y. All the mother's eggs carry an X chromosome. About half the father's sperm carry an X and half carry a Y. If a Y-carrying sperm fertilizes the egg, the baby will have an X and a Y and will be a boy. If an X-carrying sperm fertilizes the egg, the baby will be XX—a girl.

X-shaped chromosome

Nucleus

Cell containing DNA

Double helix

Genes

▶ **The DNA molecule forms chromosomes, some of which form X-shapes as they duplicate themselves. DNA is packed tightly inside the chromosomes.**

What is DNA?

DNA (short for deoxyribonucleic acid) is the complicated chemical substance that makes up our genes and chromosomes. DNA contains the genetic information that is passed from one generation to the next. The DNA molecule is in the cell nucleus. Chromosomes look like long threads, but they form X-shapes in cells that are about to divide. DNA consists of two long strands wound around each other like a twisted ladder. The arrangement of the "rungs" makes up the genetic code.

BODY FACTS

■ We have 22 matching pairs of chromosomes, plus a special pair that determines our sex.

■ On average, women tend to live longer than men.

■ Some diseases, such as hemophilia, are inherited.

■ No two human beings are exactly alike in looks or in personality.

■ The oldest known person lived for nearly 121 years.

■ About 18 percent of your body is made of carbon, which is the same material that diamonds and pencil leads are made of!

■ More men are color-blind than women—about 1 in 12. Only one woman in 250 is affected.

BRAIN AND MIND

What does the brain look like?

From above, the brain looks somewhat like a giant walnut, pinkish-gray in color and wrinkled.

What is the brain made of?

The brain is a mass of more than 10 billion nerve cells. These are surrounded and supported by cells called glia, which supply them with nutrients.

What does the brain do?

The brain is the body's control center. It sends messages to and receives them from organs and tissues all over the body. The brain gives us our ability to learn, reason, and feel. Besides our voluntary, or conscious, activities it controls involuntary activities, too. For example, it controls heartbeat and digestion.

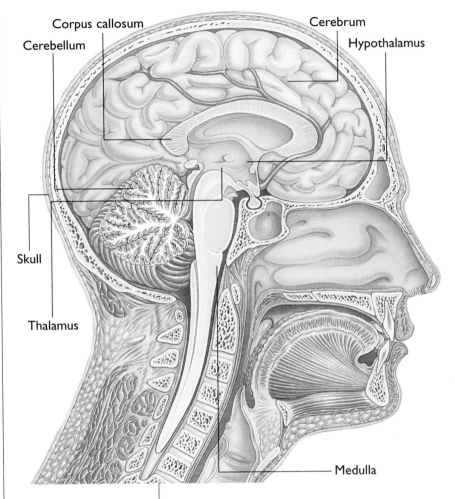

Corpus callosum
Cerebellum
Cerebrum
Hypothalamus
Skull
Thalamus
Medulla

▲ The brain is protected by the bony skull. The biggest part of the brain is the cerebrum. This is the conscious part of the brain.

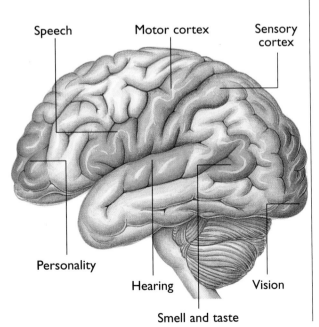

Speech
Motor cortex
Sensory cortex
Personality
Hearing
Vision
Smell and taste

◄ Different parts of the brain process different types of information.

How is the brain protected?

The skull protects the brain from most physical injuries. The brain is also protected by three layers of tissue called meninges, which are wrapped around it. The inner layer acts as a barrier to prevent bacteria from reaching the brain. The middle layer contains cerebrospinal fluid. This supplies the brain with food and oxygen and acts as a shock absorber, cushioning the brain against damage. The outer layer lines the cranium. The skull itself consists of several bones which are fused together.

How is the brain like a computer?

Like a computer, the brain is made up of circuits that carry electrical signals, but these circuits are made up of nerve cells. As in a computer, some of the circuits in the brain form a memory to store information, and others are used to process incoming information and respond to it.

What are the main parts of the brain?

The three main parts are the cerebrum at the top, the medulla on the underside, and the cerebellum at the back. The largest part is the cerebrum (about 85 percent of the brain's weight). It gives us intelligence and emotions. We use it to think, feel, and remember.

Why are most people right-handed?

The left side of the brain is connected to the right side of the body. The nerve cells that carry messages from the brain cross over at the base of the brain. Signals from the left go to the right side of the body, and vice versa. In most people, the left side of the brain is dominant over the right side. Because the left brain controls movement in the right side of the body, most people therefore have better control with their right hand.

Do the right and left halves do different jobs?

Yes, they do. In most people the left side seems to control speaking, writing, and logical thinking. The right side is more artistic and creative.

Our brain is so important that a quarter of all the blood pumped by the heart is pushed into the brain. The brain's capacity for storing information is quite extraordinary. A person of 80 can often remember with great accuracy an event that happened in their early childhood. Scientists still do not know how the billions of cells in our brain manage this remarkable feat.

BRAIN FACTS

- A human brain weighs on average 3 lbs. (1.4 kg); that's about 2.5 percent of body weight.

- By the age of 5, a child's brain has reached 90 percent of its full weight.

- The brain is shaped roughly like a cauliflower.

- The brain has more than 10 billion nerve cells.

- The outer edge of the cerebrum (the "thinking zone") is about the size of a newspaper page, but is all scrunched up.

- Gray matter is the part of the brain and spinal cord that contains the nerve cell bodies.

Are girls' brains different from boys'?

There is evidence that girls' and boys' brains are slightly different. As a general rule, most boys are better at tasks that require "spatial ability"— picturing the shape and position of objects or patterns. Girls are better at using words and usually learn to read at an earlier age than boys.

What is the mind?

The mind is the part of us that gives rise to our thoughts, memories, and feelings. Most people believe that the mind is situated in the brain.

How many things can we remember?

We can remember a list of about seven things at the same time. This is why most people have difficulty in remembering a telephone number with more than seven figures. If the numbers are grouped, it makes them easier to remember because your memory can hold about seven "packets" or groups of information at one time. Memory is located in more than one area of the brain.

How do we learn?

We learn in many different ways. When we learn facts for a classroom test, we may soon forget them. When we learn a skill like riding a bicycle or swimming, it may stay with us for a lifetime. Much of our early learning comes from copying other people. Animals learn in the same way, from their parents. Humans also learn from passed-on information—for example, from books.

What is instinct?

An instinctive action is something we can do without having to learn it. A newborn baby will automatically turn its head to suck its mother's breast. This instinctive behavior helps the baby survive, as it needs to be able to feed at once and cannot afford to spend time learning how.

What are conditioned reflexes?

Conditioned reflexes are movements that we coordinate consciously at first but learn to perform automatically. Learning to play tennis or to ride a bike develops many conditioned reflexes.

What is intelligence?

Psychologists (scientists who study the mind) cannot agree on a definition of intelligence. Put simply, intelligence is mental ability—the ability to reason, learn, and understand. There are many different ways in which we can show intelligence, from writing an original story, to solving a math problem. Intelligence covers many different mental skills, and most people are better at some skills than others.

▲ **A chimpanzee infant watches an adult probe a termite nest with a stick. It is learning to use a simple tool.**

How do you do

Dolphins have a great ability to learn complex tasks and to communicate with each other. They can also be trained to get close to the sounds of a few human words. Some experts think that they are capable of learning the beginnings of a true human language.

◄ **To play chess well, a player needs to use strategy— working out possible moves in advance and calculating the likely results of each move.**

Why are humans so intelligent?

Humans are more intelligent than other animals because we have a much larger cerebrum. This gives us a greater ability to reason and allows us to communicate our ideas using language. In this way, knowledge is spread rapidly and can be passed from one generation to the next. Our ability to stand on two legs frees our hands for toolmaking, enabling us to do far more than other animals.

Which is the most intelligent animal?

After humans, the most intelligent animals may be either chimpanzees or dolphins. Both these animals have good problem-solving and communication skills.

Is intelligence inherited?

There is evidence that intelligence is inherited to some degree. But the environment you are brought up in— how you are encouraged to play, read, and learn—plays a very important part. This helps you to make the most of the abilities you have inherited.

What is personality?

Personality includes an individual's particular characteristics—for example, whether they are loud or quiet, serious or happy-go-lucky. Personality is sometimes measured in terms of whether a person is an extrovert or introvert. Most of us are neither completely one type nor the other.

Where do our feelings come from?

When we go about our everyday lives we respond to the pictures, sounds, and smells around us. Our feelings, or emotions, are a particular response to what we experience. Feelings are produced in the brain. They involve many areas, particularly the hypothalamus and the cerebrum. Feelings arise as a result of nerve signals from the senses, or from the cortex, in response to our thoughts.

▼ **Babies can make all the sounds used in every language in the world. But they learn to select and use the sounds they hear most often.**

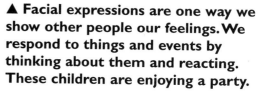

TALKING FACTS

■ There are about 600,000 words in the English language.

■ On average, a person who speaks English uses fewer than 10,000 words.

■ There are about 5,000 languages in the world. The most common is Mandarin Chinese, followed by English.

■ Dr. Harold Williams (1876–1928) of New Zealand spoke 58 languages.

▲ **Facial expressions are one way we show other people our feelings. We respond to things and events by thinking about them and reacting. These children are enjoying a party.**

How do babies communicate?

Babies begin to communicate by crying. A mother or father can soon distinguish different types of crying. The cry a baby makes when it is hungry is different from that when it is tired or frustrated. Facial expressions are important too. After a few months, babies can communicate their moods by smiling or frowning.

How quickly do we learn language?

As babies, we start to babble. We are learning to make the sounds used in language. By the age of about one year or so, we say our first words. By two years we have a vocabulary of several hundred words and can speak in short phrases. By three we speak in sentences, and by four we have learned basic rules of grammar.

What is body language?

Body language is nonverbal communication; that is, everything other than what we say. This includes the pitch of the voice, our facial expression, our gestures and hand movements, and posture. Hand gestures can mean different things in different cultures. The thumbs-up sign means "OK" in English-speaking countries. In France it also means "zero" and in Japan it means "money." In some countries it is a rude gesture.

What is social behavior?

Social behavior is the way we act when we are with other people. In particular, it is the behavior of someone in a group, such as a family, a group of friends, or a class at school. Group, or peer, pressure is the pressure a group of people put on an individual to behave in a particular way. For example, in a group of friends you may feel under pressure to like the same music and clothes as the others, or to go to the same places. It is fun to be one of the crowd sometimes, but it's also good to have your own ideas and values.

SLEEP FACTS

■ On average, most people sleep about 8 hours a day. So in your lifetime, you will probably spend about 20 years sleeping!

■ Our bodies grow and repair themselves during 3- or 4-hour periods of deep sleep, called orthodox sleep.

■ We dream during rapid eye movement (REM) sleep (about 2–3 hours a night).

■ During REM sleep our eyes flick back and forth under our eyelids.

■ Some people suffering from a rare condition called total insomnia have gone without proper sleep for many years.

■ Babies sleep most of the time because they are growing so quickly.

■ We sleep more when we are ill, because our bodies need time to rest and get better.

Why do we need to sleep?

No one is exactly sure why we need to sleep. Of course, sleeping rests the body, and it is thought that during sleep we repair our tissues, grow new cells, and recover from the day's activities. Our brains are still very active while we sleep, and some people think that the brain sorts through the day's events during this time, organizing new information and fitting it in with previous information. This may help us to learn from new experiences. A newborn baby needs 16 hours of sleep each day; a person aged 65 needs only 6 hours.

Some people sleepwalk. Nobody knows what causes sleepwalking. Parts of the brain that control movement and speech stay awake. The person may speak, sit up, and even walk, but they do not recall anything when they wake up.

▲ When you're asleep, you breathe more slowly and your heart beats less quickly. You shift position about 40 times during the night, and you dream for about a quarter of the time.

Why do we dream?

Everyone dreams every night, but we do not remember most of what we dream. According to the psychoanalyst Sigmund Freud, dreams can show our secret wishes and fears but in a disguised form. Other dreams may simply be the brain's way of sorting through and organizing the day's events.

What is an optical illusion?

An optical illusion is an image that your brain interprets wrongly or strangely. For example, when you see a full Moon low on the horizon, it appears to be much larger than when it is high in the sky. But if you measured its apparent size with a ruler held at arm's length, you would see that it is the same in both positions.

What causes mental illness?

There are many causes of mental illness—illness of the mind. Social factors like poor housing, unemployment, family difficulties, or pressures at school or work, can result in stress that brings on mental illness. Much mental illness is believed to be caused by an imbalance of chemicals in the brain.

Mental handicap or severe learning difficulty should not be confused with mental illness. It results from permanent damage to the brain and may be caused (as in Down's syndrome) by a genetic disorder. Such conditions cannot, as yet, be cured, but people with mental handicaps can achieve a great deal.

▶ **This picture is an example of an optical illusion. The water looks as if it is flowing uphill, as well as downhill. But it can't be— or can it?**

DID YOU KNOW?

■ Four out of five dreams are in color, but people describe most dreams as being in black and white.

■ As dreams fade from memory, they lose their color. If you wake up more than 10 minutes after dreaming, you will remember nothing.

■ Animals dream too. Dogs sometimes look as if they're hunting and make excited noises.

■ Irrational fears are called phobias.

■ Some people are scared of open spaces (agoraphobia).

■ Others dislike enclosed spaces (claustrophobia).

■ Some people fear spiders (arachnophobia), even though they know a spider can't hurt them.

Dreams can be frightening or sad, but they are happening only inside your head. A scary dream is called a nightmare. You may cry out while still asleep, and feel unable to move until you are properly awake.

What is depression?

Depression is the most common form of mental illness. A depressed person has feelings of deep sadness and hopelessness. He or she has very low self esteem. A depressive often cannot eat, sleep, or work properly. Many people who suffer from depression can be helped by antidepressant drugs and therapy.

Can phobias be cured?

A phobia is a deep and irrational fear —such as fear of open spaces, snakes, heights, or confined spaces. Behavior therapy can help a person learn about their fear and slowly become accustomed to it. Someone who is frightened of spiders, for example, would gradually get used to seeing spiders up close and even to touching them. Airlines take fear of flying very seriously and often give courses to help people overcome it.

HEALTH AND MEDICINE

Baseball

Cycling

Tennis

Gymnastics

Basketball

▲ Keeping fit helps your body grow strong and keeps you healthy. There are many ways to enjoy keeping fit, by yourself or with friends.

What do we need to do to keep fit?

Regular exercise helps our bodies to function better. Fitness experts recommend we do at least 15 minutes of stamina training three times a week to develop a healthy heart and lungs. Swimming, jogging, cycling, and aerobics classes all help develop stamina. If you have a special health problem you may need to check with your doctor before doing this type of exercise.

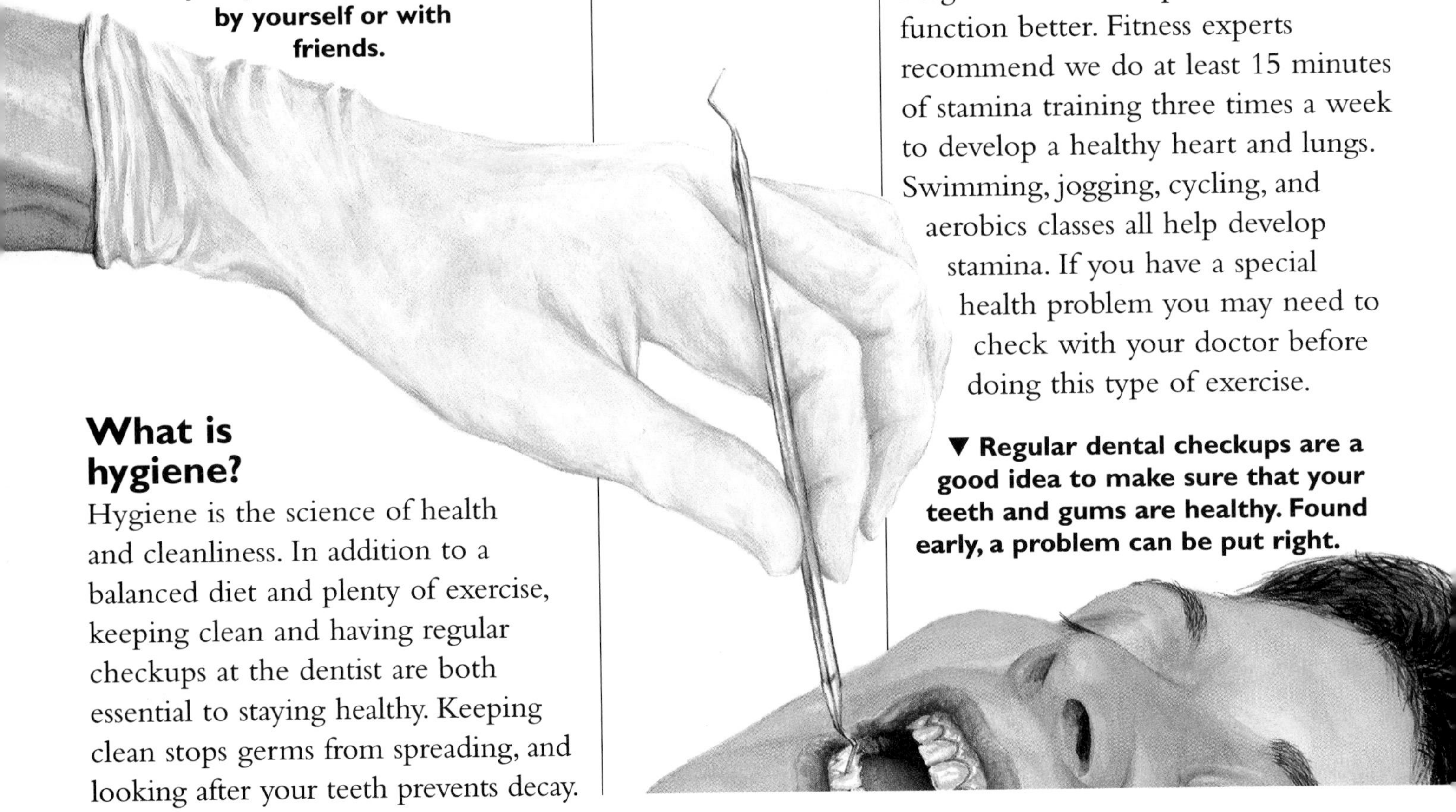

▼ Regular dental checkups are a good idea to make sure that your teeth and gums are healthy. Found early, a problem can be put right.

What is hygiene?

Hygiene is the science of health and cleanliness. In addition to a balanced diet and plenty of exercise, keeping clean and having regular checkups at the dentist are both essential to staying healthy. Keeping clean stops germs from spreading, and looking after your teeth prevents decay.

Vitamins A, B, D
calcium, iron

Vitamins A, C, E, K
calcium, iodine, potassium

Vitamins B, D, E
zinc, magnesium

Vitamins A, B, D, E
iron, sulfur, iodine

Are too many vitamins bad for you?

In most cases no, but there are some exceptions. Regular large doses of vitamin D, over one hundred times the recommended amount, can cause kidney failure. In a pregnant woman, very large amounts of vitamin A can cause defects in the unborn baby. If you eat a well-balanced diet, you should not need vitamin pills.

Which foods should we avoid?

We should cut down on salt and animal fats, since they may both increase the risk of heart disease. Too much sugar and fat makes us overweight, making heart disease, kidney problems, and diabetes more likely.

▶ Eating too much can make a person overweight. People usually try to lose weight by cutting down on carbohydrates and fats. Also, a new routine of sensible eating and regular exercise helps.

▲ Different foods contain different vitamins and minerals. A well-balanced diet will give you all the vitamins and minerals you need.

▶ Brushing your teeth after meals and using floss to clean between teeth help to keep your teeth and gums clean and healthy.

What is a vegetarian?

A vegetarian is someone who does not eat meat or fish. Most vegetarians eat dairy products, such as eggs and milk, but vegans avoid all animal products. They eat only food that comes from plants. A vegetarian diet includes less fat than the diet of someone who eats meat.

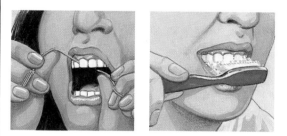

Why is tooth-brushing so important?

Tooth-brushing is important because it helps remove plaque, which causes tooth decay. To get rid of as much plaque as possible you should brush your teeth after every meal, and use dental floss to clean the gaps between your teeth. Using special plaque-disclosing tablets, which turn plaque red or blue, allows you to check how well you brush your teeth. Fluoride is sometimes added to water supplies because it helps to strengthen the enamel in children's teeth.

What is a disease?

A disease is a condition, (not an injury), that prevents your body from working properly. Some diseases are caused by micro-organisms called microbes entering your body and then feeding and reproducing inside it. They may damage the body, or poison it by releasing toxic waste substances. Other diseases are caused by a fault in one of the body systems.

Which microbes cause disease?

Four main types of microbes cause disease: viruses, bacteria, protozoa, and fungi. Disease-causing microbes are often known as germs.

What are bacteria?

Bacteria are living things that each consist of just one cell. They are smaller than our body cells. Bacteria are all around us, in the air, in soil, and on our skin. Bacterial diseases include cholera, tetanus, tuberculosis (TB), whooping cough, typhoid, and most kinds of food poisoning.

What is a virus?

Viruses are the smallest living things. Most are more than a thousand times smaller than a period at the end of a sentence. They are only really alive when they enter the cells of another living creature (organism) and start to multiply inside them. On their own, viruses cannot feed or grow, and show no signs of life.

▶ **Bacteria are everywhere and most do us no harm, but some do. Salmonella bacteria are a common cause of food poisoning.**

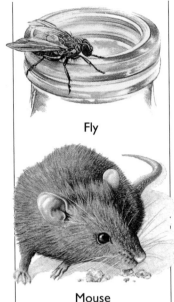

Fly

Mouse

▲ **Simple rules of hygiene can prevent infectious diseases. Keep food protected from flies and mice, which leave harmful bacteria.**

How are diseases spread?

Germs, or pathogens, are spread in many ways. The viruses that cause colds and flu are spread in droplets of saliva coughed, sneezed, or breathed out by an infected person. Some diseases are spread in food and drink —for example by the food-poisoning bacteria Salmonella. Some animals carry diseases that they give to people. For example, the fleas of black rats carried the germ responsible for the plague in the Middle Ages.

How do our bodies deal with germs?

Our bodies have various ways of dealing with germs. If the skin is damaged, a blood clot will soon seal up the cut. The nose, mouth, air passages, and gut are all lined with mucus, which stops germs from getting through. Tears, sweat, and earwax kill them with chemicals, and strong acid in the stomach kills most germs in our food.

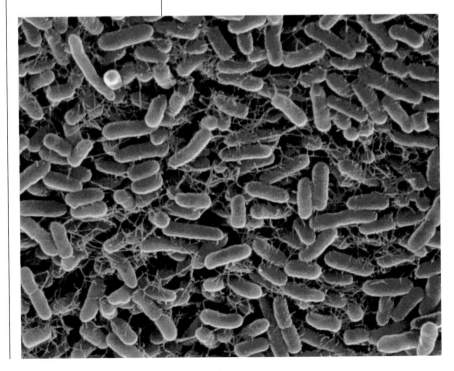

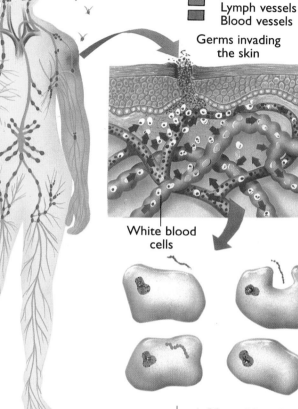

◀ The lymph system is the body's defense against germs. Germs are carried in air and water, as well as by animals and insects.

Lymph node

Lymph vessels

Lymph vessels
Blood vessels

Germs invading the skin

White blood cells

▲ Your blood contains white blood cells to fight diseases.

▶ Doctors and nurses use germ-free gloves and instruments. They cover their faces so they do not breathe germs in or out.

What are antibodies?

The immune system is our defense against infection. Two kinds of white blood cells react and neutralize harmful germs. Lymphocytes produce antibodies that destroy the germs and phagocytes which eat them. Antibodies are chemicals that stop germs from multiplying or slow them down so they can be eaten by phagocytes. Once the lymphocytes have defeated a germ, they are ready for action the next time they meet it and can make more of the right antibody. This is how we become immune to a disease, either naturally or after we have a vaccination.

Who was the first doctor?

The first doctor known by name was Imhotep, an Ancient Egyptian who lived around 2650 B.C. After his death the Egyptians worshiped him as a god for his healing powers.

Who discovered that germs cause disease?

Louis Pasteur (1822–1895), a French professor of chemistry, demonstrated that germs enter wounds and cause disease, proving that the germs did not simply grow out of the wound as had been thought previously.

Why do hospital staff wear gowns and masks during operations?

Gowns and masks prevent bacteria and other germs from traveling from the body or clothes of the staff into the patient's wound during the operation. Other precautions are also taken. The clothes the staff wear are sterilized so they are completely free of bacteria. The whole operating room itself is a sterile environment—even the air is cleaned to remove bacteria.

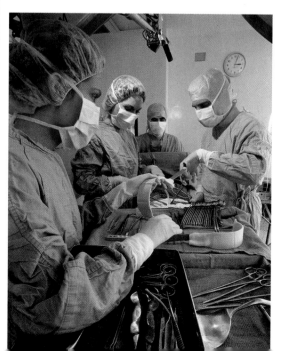

Why do people have operations?

Usually operations involve cutting into the body, to remove damaged or diseased tissues, such as the removal of someone's tonsils or appendix. Exploratory operations are performed so that the surgeon can find out what is wrong with the patient. Some operations are carried out to replace body parts with artificial parts, such as a hip, or a heart valve. Emergency operations may save someone's life—for example, after a serious accident.

What does an anesthesiologist do?

An anesthesiologist specializes in giving patients drugs that make them either unconscious or insensitive to pain. An anesthetic is given by injection just before the operation. If a further anesthetic is needed during the operation it can be inhaled as a gas. The anesthesiologist also carefully monitors the patient's breathing and heartbeat.

What are antibiotics?

Antibiotics are drugs that are used to kill bacteria or keep them from reproducing inside the body. Antibiotics are taken as tablets or by injection. Most antibiotics, such as penicillin, come from molds. They take a few days to work.

What are antiseptics?

Antiseptics are chemicals that kill bacteria. They are used to clean wounds and to help treat mouth or throat infections. Many antiseptics can be poisonous if swallowed.

▶ Surgery is made safe by modern methods of asepsis (sterilization to kill germs) and anesthesia. Every year new advances are made.

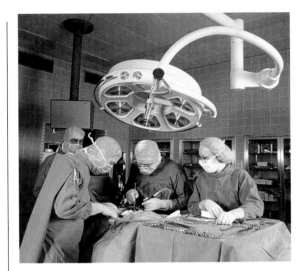

MEDICAL FACTS

■ The first person to study the body in detail by cutting up dead bodies was Vesalius (1514–1564), a doctor born in what is now Belgium who taught anatomy in Italy.

■ The English physician William Harvey (1578–1657) showed that the heart pumps blood around the body.

■ Lady Mary Wortley Montagu, who had traveled in the East, introduced vaccination against smallpox to Britain in 1771. Vaccination was known in China in the 10th century.

■ An early anesthetic was nitrous oxide or "laughing gas." A patient was conscious but laughing!

■ In 1846 an American dentist named William Morton was the first to give his patients ether as an anesthetic.

■ The first heart transplant was in 1967 and was performed by Dr. Christiaan Barnard in South Africa.

How do X rays work?

X rays are invisible waves of energy that can pass through soft tissues like skin and muscle but are stopped by heavier tissue such as bone. Passing X rays through the body and onto a light-sensitive plate produces an image, which shows damage such as broken bones. Where X rays pass through the body, the plate is blackened; where they do not, the plate remains light. In addition to bone damage or disease, fluid on the lung can be detected.

▼ X rays are high-frequency waves that pass through most living tissue, but not heavier material such as bone.

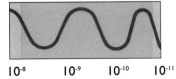

Gas discharge tube

Ultraviolet rays   X rays   Gamma rays

10^{-8} 10^{-9} 10^{-10} 10^{-11}

X ray

What is a C.A.T. scan?

C.A.T. stands for Computerized Axial Tomography, an X-ray technique that takes photographs of slices through a patient's body. The X-ray source is rotated around the patient, so that they are scanned from all sides. A C.A.T. scanner shows up soft tissues as well as bones. Using a series of images, a computer generates a three-dimensional picture of the body.

Which body parts can be replaced with artificial ones?

A whole range of artificial parts are now available to replace existing tissues that are damaged or diseased. These include artificial heart pacemakers and valves, blood vessels, and various joints, such as artificial replacements for the hip and knee.

▶ A patient having a C.A.T. scan has X rays fired through the body at different angles. A computer picture then shows "slices" through the body.

What is genetic engineering?

Genetic engineering is the process of adding, removing, or transferring individual genes. Much of this work is done using bacteria and viruses, into which human genes are inserted. The gene then makes the microbes produce a particular substance that can be extracted and used. Insulin is produced in this way.

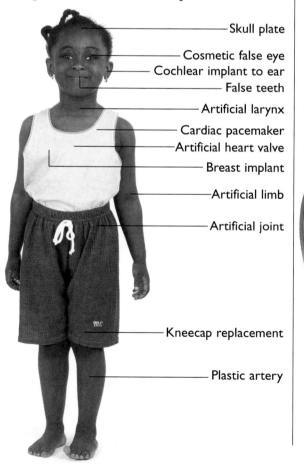

◀ Thanks to the miracles of modern medicine, this little girl could have a number of body parts replaced during her lifetime.

▶ Three kinds of implant

- Skull plate
- Cosmetic false eye
- Cochlear implant to ear
- False teeth
- Artificial larynx
- Cardiac pacemaker
- Artificial heart valve
- Breast implant
- Artificial limb
- Artificial joint
- Kneecap replacement
- Plastic artery

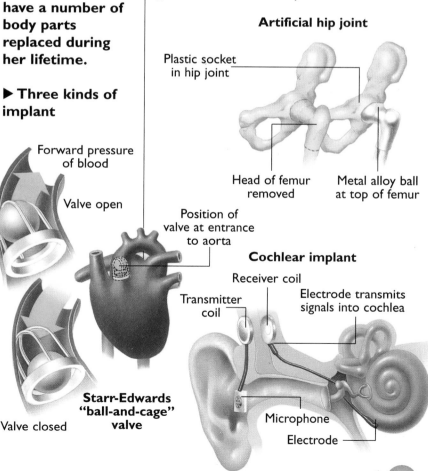

Forward pressure of blood
Valve open
Position of valve at entrance to aorta
Starr-Edwards "ball-and-cage" valve
Valve closed

Artificial hip joint
Plastic socket in hip joint
Head of femur removed
Metal alloy ball at top of femur

Cochlear implant
Receiver coil
Electrode transmits signals into cochlea
Transmitter coil
Microphone
Electrode

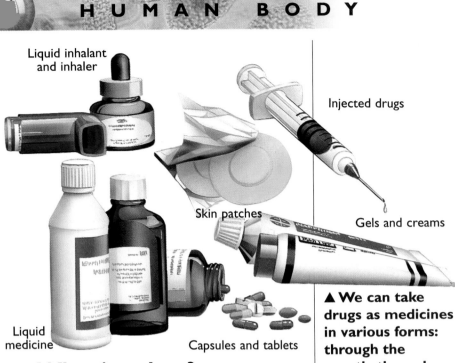

Liquid inhalant and inhaler

Injected drugs

Skin patches

Gels and creams

Liquid medicine

Capsules and tablets

▲ **We can take drugs as medicines in various forms: through the mouth, through the skin, or as an injection into the bloodstream.**

▶ **Diabetics cannot produce energy from sugars in the body because they lack insulin. They must inject themselves with the hormone.**

What is a drug?

A drug is a chemical substance that alters the way your mind or body works. Many drugs are in everyday use as medicines, either on prescription from a doctor or for sale over the counter. Some drugs, such as heroin and marijuana, are illegal.

What is meant by drug abuse?

Someone who abuses drugs takes them for a purpose for which they were not originally intended, or in amounts that are dangerous. The drug is usually taken for the temporary pleasurable effects it gives, or as a way of escaping from problems. The person often becomes addicted, or dependent, on the drug and will suffer withdrawal symptoms such as muscle cramps, headaches, and shivering when they stop taking it. This is because their body is used to the drug being present. Dependency on a harmful drug can ruin a person's life. Treatment centers and therapy can help drug-abusers quit.

DRUG FACTS

■ Tea contains a drug—caffeine. So do coffee and some soft drinks. Like other stimulants, caffeine is habit-forming.

■ Alcohol is a drug too. Drinking it in large amounts can affect judgment, coordination, and behavior, and damage the body.

■ Quinine was the first effective drug against malaria. It comes from the bark of the cinchona tree in South America.

■ Many plants contain substances that can be used as drugs to combat diseases.

How do drugs keep people well?

Sometimes the body makes too much of one chemical or too little of another. Doctors prescribe drugs to restore the balance of the body's chemistry. A person may have a too-fast heartbeat and high blood pressure. This can be caused by the body releasing too much adrenaline. Drugs called beta-blockers stop adrenaline from reaching the heart muscles and causing these problems. Drugs given to a patient by a doctor must never be taken by anyone else.

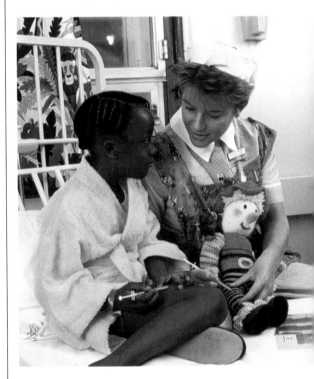

Why do some children need drugs?

Some children need drug treatment to fight disease or help them grow properly. They may have to visit the hospital regularly and miss classes or sports while they are treated. Cancer sufferers receiving chemotherapy, drugs to kill harmful cancer cells may feel sick and lose their hair.

What is alternative medicine?

Alternative, or complementary, medicine is a type of treatment not usually given by family doctors. Alternative medical treatments often involve treating the person as a whole, rather then treating a specific condition or symptom.

What is acupuncture?

Acupuncture is a form of Ancient Chinese treatment based on the idea that energy flows through the body in channels called meridians. Disease or pain occurs where the flow of energy is blocked. To unblock the flow, an acupuncturist inserts needles into various parts of the body. This does not hurt and gives relief in many cases. Acupuncture is also used in China as an anesthetic.

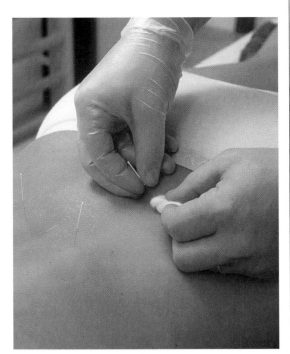

▲ In acupuncture, needles are stuck into the body at precise points. This ancient form of treatment comes from China, but it is now finding its place in modern Western medicine.

ALTERNATIVE MEDICINE

■ Reflexology is based on the theory that all parts of the body correspond to zones on the hands and the soles of the feet. Reflexologists massage these zones to help relieve pain, reduce stress, and improve circulation.

■ Aromatherapy is used to treat physical problems and stress by rubbing the body with essential plant oils.

■ Chiropractic is the manipulation of the spine and other parts of the body. It is based on the idea that aches and pains, such as backache, are caused by problems with the nervous system.

■ Herbal medicines have been used for thousands of years. Various plants are picked wild or grown for their natural medicines. Experts in plant medicine are called herbalists.

■ Holistic medicine is based on the idea that many factors affect our health—such as genetics, nutrition, family relationships, stress at work, and so on.

■ Homeopathy is based on the idea that substances that produce certain symptoms in a healthy person will cure those symptoms in a sick person. Very weak doses of the substances are given.

▶ Kosher food is food that has been prepared according to Jewish Law. Often meat is salted, and the cooking and eating of milk products with meat is forbidden.

What are eating disorders?

Sometimes people become ill because they avoid eating. They may do so because they have a fear of becoming too fat. Some young people may suffer from eating disorders because they either fear growing up or seek attention. Anorexia nervosa is an eating disorder. Sufferers may feel hungry but refuse food. Sufferers from the condition known as bulimia have a tremendous craving for food and stuff themselves with huge meals. Then they make themselves sick.

Why do some people eat special diets?

Special diets are needed by people suffering from certain diseases. For instance, people with diabetes must limit the amount of sugar they eat. Some people suffer allergic reactions to certain food (such as peanuts, milk, wheat, or eggs) and so avoid them. Members of some religious groups also have rules about food.

HUMAN BODY QUIZ

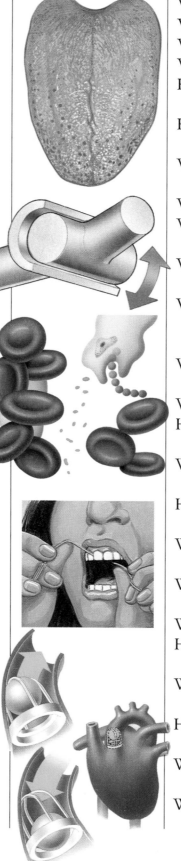

AFRICA

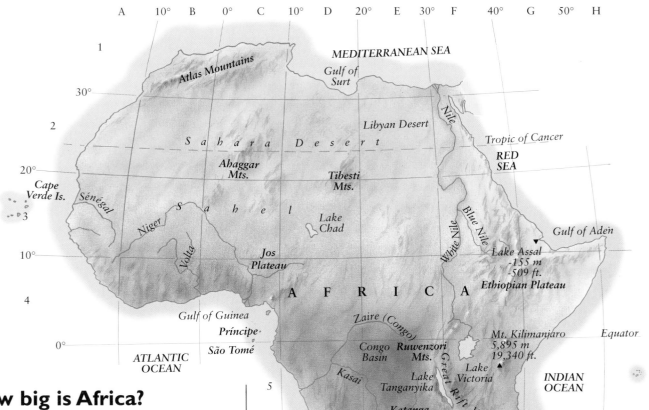

How big is Africa?

North America would fit into Africa with an area half the size of Europe to spare! Africa has a land area of 11½ million square miles (30 million sq km). It is more than 5,000 miles (8,000 km) long from north to south, and more than 3,700 miles (6,000 km) wide from east to west.

Africa is mostly a huge jungle: true or false?

False. Most of Africa is either desert (40 percent) or grassy savannah (40 percent). Forests cover less than a fifth of Africa.

Where are the Mountains of the Moon?

The Ruwenzori Mountains are on the border between Uganda and

▲ The map of Africa shows how much of the continent is desert. There are also large expanses of grassland. The rain forests are in central and western Africa.

Zaire (Dem. Rep. of Congo) in central Africa. These peaks are over 16,400 feet (5,000 m) high. They were named the Mountains of the Moon by the early geographer Ptolemy, who in A.D. 150 drew a map showing the Nile River that began in these mountains. The river has several sources, including Lake Victoria.

◀ **201**

◄ **Tourists walk along the crest of a huge sand dune in Namibia. The Namib is one of Africa's driest deserts.**

Is there much desert in Africa?

About 40 percent of Africa is desert. The Sahara Desert covers much of the northern third of the continent. Other deserts are the Namib and the Kalahari in the southwest.

What is the Great Rift Valley?

The Great Rift Valley is one of Africa's outstanding natural features: a series of valleys that cuts through eastern Africa. The Great Rift Valley is the result of enormous volcanic movement. In places, the rift in the Earth is over 1 mile (1.5 km) deep and 25 miles (40 km) wide. In other places, the rift has filled with water, creating some of Africa's greatest lakes (Mobutu Sese Seko, Edward, Nyasa, and Tanganyika), as well as the Red Sea.

▲ **Boats carry goods and passengers along the Nile River. This mighty river is the lifeblood of Egypt, and has been for thousands of years.**

Which are Africa's greatest rivers?

Africa's biggest rivers are the Nile (the longest river in the world), followed by the Zaire (Congo), the Niger, and the Zambezi.

Where is Tugela Falls?

Tugela Falls is a series of five waterfalls on the Tugela River in South Africa. The highest fall is 1,350 feet (410 m) high and the total drop is 3,106 feet (950 m). Tugela is the second highest waterfall in the world.

How high is the land in Africa?

Compared to Asia or North America, Africa is fairly flat. The north, west, and center of the continent are mostly less than 2,000 feet (600 m) above sea level. Most of northern Africa is the plateau of the Sahara. The highest land is in the east and south. This area includes the Great Rift Valley and the grassy plains of the Eastern Highlands.

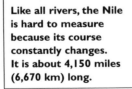

Like all rivers, the Nile is hard to measure because its course constantly changes. It is about 4,150 miles (6,670 km) long.

► **Tugela River tumbles over a series of falls, creating a spectacular, natural wonder.**

Is there any snow in Africa?

Africa's highest mountain is in Tanzania in eastern Africa. It is Kilimanjaro or Uhuru ("Freedom") and is 19,340 feet (5,895 m) high. Kilimanjaro is an extinct volcano. Although very near the Equator, the summit is always covered with snow.

Which is Africa's largest island?

The island of Madagascar, off the eastern coast of Africa, covers 226,640 square miles. It is the fourth biggest island in the world and is separated from the mainland by the Mozambique Channel. Madagascar has animals found nowhere else in the world, such as lemurs and rare birds. Most of its people rely on agriculture.

▲ Kilimanjaro's snowcapped peak can be seen from far away. The mountain towers above the vast plains where elephants and many other animals roam.

◄ Central Madagascar is a high plateau. There are lowlands in the east and south. Many of the island's natural forests have been cut down.

On the island of Madagascar, a man makes a speech to his bride-to-be before she will marry him. If the speech is no good, he pays a fine and starts all over again!

When did people first live in Africa?

Africa is where human beings are first thought to have evolved. Scientists have found bones and other remains of humanlike creatures that are older than remains found elsewhere. These creatures lived more than 4 million years ago. About 2 million years ago the first true humans lived in Africa, hunting animals, gathering plants, and making the first stone tools. These people are known as *Homo habilis* ("skillful human").

▼ The humanlike creature *Australopithecus* lived in Africa over 4 million years ago, and may have used sticks and stones as tools.

What is the "smoke that thunders?"

Near the Zambia–Zimbabwe border the Zambezi River plunges over the Victoria Falls. This is Africa's most spectacular waterfall, 350 feet (108 m) high and 1 mile (1.5 km) wide. As the river pours over the falls, a great mist of spray rises into the air and the thunder of the water can be heard far away. The African name for the falls is *Mosi-oa-tunya*, which means "the smoke that thunders."

Why is drought a problem in Africa?

Rainfall in Africa is very uneven. Some parts of the continent, such as the western rain forests, get rain all year round. Drier areas may go for years without a shower. Much of Africa has one or two wet seasons each year. If these rains fail, crops do not grow and people starve. Drought

◀ **The Victoria Falls are one of the most impressive sights in the world. Clouds of spray are thrown up by the water crashing down into the gorge below.**

▶ **Lack of water is a big problem in several countries of Africa, such as Ethiopia. Nomadic people often carry water with them.**

In the Sahara, sand blown by the driving wind can strip paint off a car—like a giant sheet of sandpaper. Camels need their tough skins!

(lack of rain) has been a cause of famine in the lands fringing the Sahara and in Ethiopia in northeast Africa.

What is the harmattan?

The harmattan is an African wind. It blows from the Sahara westward and southwestward from December to February. The harmattan is dry and also cool, because the desert is cooler at this time of year. It carries dust from the Sahara across neighboring countries.

Why is Africa a warm continent?

The Equator runs across the middle of Africa, and all but a tenth of Africa is within the tropics. Temperatures are high all year round, and there is little difference between summer and winter. The Sahara in the north is one of the hottest places in the world.

Which is Africa's largest country?

The biggest country in Africa is the Sudan. It has an area of nearly 1 million square miles (2.5 million sq km). The north is bleak desert, but in the south are grassy plains. The Nile River creates a big marshy area, the Sudd.

How do Bushmen survive in the desert?

The Bushmen, or San, are people of southwest Africa. A few still roam the Kalahari Desert, where there is little water and few trees. The Bushmen are skillful hunters and trackers and gather foods such as insects, roots, and berries. They can find drinking water underground in roots and wet sand. They can live in a land so harsh that outsiders would soon die of thirst and hunger. Like many Africans, the Bushmen are now giving up their traditional ways.

Which African men wear veils?

The Tuareg are nomads of northern Africa. They roam in or around the Sahara Desert. The Tuareg are Berbers, a people who lived here long before Arabs settled northern

AFRICA FACTS

- Area: 11,704,000 sq. mi. (30,313,000 sq km).
- Population: about 750 million people.
- Number of countries: 53.
- Longest river: Nile 4,150 miles (6,670 km).
- Largest lake: Lake Victoria 26,828 sq. mi.
- Highest mountain: Mt. Kilimanjaro 19,340 feet (5,900 m).
- Largest country: Sudan.
- Country with most people: Nigeria.
- Largest city: Cairo.
- The oldest nation in Africa is Ethiopia, which has been independent for about 2,000 years.

▼ Desert nomads like the Tuareg wander from place to place with their animals. They know where to find food and water.

Africa. They are Muslims, but it is the Tuareg men, not the women, who hide their faces behind veils. Once the Tuareg raided and traded across the Sahara, but most have now abandoned their old desert life.

How do Africa's nomads live?

Some Africans still follow traditional ways of living like the nomads of the Sahara region and northeast Africa. These people wander with herds of camels, sheep, and goats. They have no settled homes but keep moving in search of fresh pasture for their animals.

Was the Sahara once green?

About 10,000 years ago, the Sahara was much wetter than it is now. Where there are now only rocks and sand, there were lakes and streams. Trees and grass were able to grow, and animals such as elephants, giraffes, and antelope were plentiful. About 6,000 years ago the climate began to change and the Sahara became drier. People and animals were forced to move away as green land began to turn into desert. The Sahara is still spreading.

Where did Benin people live?

The Benin people lived in West Africa, south of the Niger River. Four hundred years ago, they made beautiful objects out of ivory, wood, and bronze. From about A.D. 1000, powerful African states such as Benin, Kanem–Borno, and Songhai ruled large territories in West Africa.

Which northern African country is famous for leather goods?

Morocco in northern Africa. Ancient cities such as Fez and Marrakesh have tanneries where goat skins are treated and dyed to make leather. Most Moroccans are poor and own small plots of land on which they graze sheep, cattle, and goats. Morocco is an ancient Islamic kingdom and most of its people are Arabs, but about a third are Berbers. Morocco has been ruled by the kings of the Alawi dynasty since the 1600s.

◀ Benin is famous for its art, such as these bronze figures of a king and two kneeling subjects. African artists have influenced the ideas of modern Western artists, such as Picasso.

In which African country, besides Egypt, can you see pyramids?

The Sudan is a huge, dry country in northeast Africa. At Meroë, east of Khartoum, you can see the ruins of pyramids built more than 2,000 years ago. Between 592 B.C. and A.D. 350 Meroë was a powerful kingdom. The people of Meroë worshiped the gods of Ancient Egypt.

▲ These ruined pyramids are at Meroë, east of Khartoum in the Sudan. The people of Meroë would have seen and admired the pyramids of Egypt, to the north.

◀ At a Moroccan tannery, workers soak and treat animal skins to turn them into leather. Tanning is a messy and smelly business!

Which countries share the Kariba Dam?

This hydroelectric scheme was completed in 1959 with the building of a dam across the Zambezi River. The dam provides power for Zambia's copper industry and also for Zimbabwe. The damming of the Zambezi created an artificial lake, Lake Kariba.

Where is Table Mountain?

Table Mountain is South Africa's most famous landmark. For many visitors, the first sight of South Africa is the city of Cape Town, beneath the backdrop of Table Mountain.

Where can you visit a gold mine beneath a city?

In Johannesburg, South Africa. The city began in the gold boom of the late 1800s, and is now a center of commerce. Visitors can explore a gold mine beneath the city and a museum showing life in the gold rush.

▼ **A view of Cape Town from Signal Hill. In the background rises Table Mountain. Visitors can ride the cableway to the top.**

▶ **The Kariba Dam was built to provide a source of energy for both Zambia and Zimbabwe. Behind the dam is Lake Kariba.**

AFRICA'S WEALTH

■ Africa exports petroleum, gold, and diamonds, and other minerals, such as cobalt.

■ South Africa is the world's largest producer of gold.

■ Crops grown in Africa include corn, cocoa, cassava, palm kernels, vanilla beans, yams, bananas, coffee, cotton, rubber, sugar, and tea.

■ Africans raise two-thirds of the world's camels!

■ Africans raise a third of the world's goats. They also keep cattle and sheep in large numbers.

■ Africa has about a quarter of the world's forests.

■ About 40 percent of Africa's factory-made goods are made in South Africa.

Which is the biggest city in Africa?

Cairo, the capital of Egypt, is the biggest city in Africa. It is a bustling, dusty city full of hooting taxis and hurrying crowds. Modern hotels and office blocks rise up next to old mosques and basic housing where the city's poor people live. About 9.7 million people live in Cairo.

▲ **Cairo, Africa's largest city, has grown at a rapid pace in modern times, with many new buildings. These provide an interesting contrast with the traditional bazaars and cafés.**

ASIA

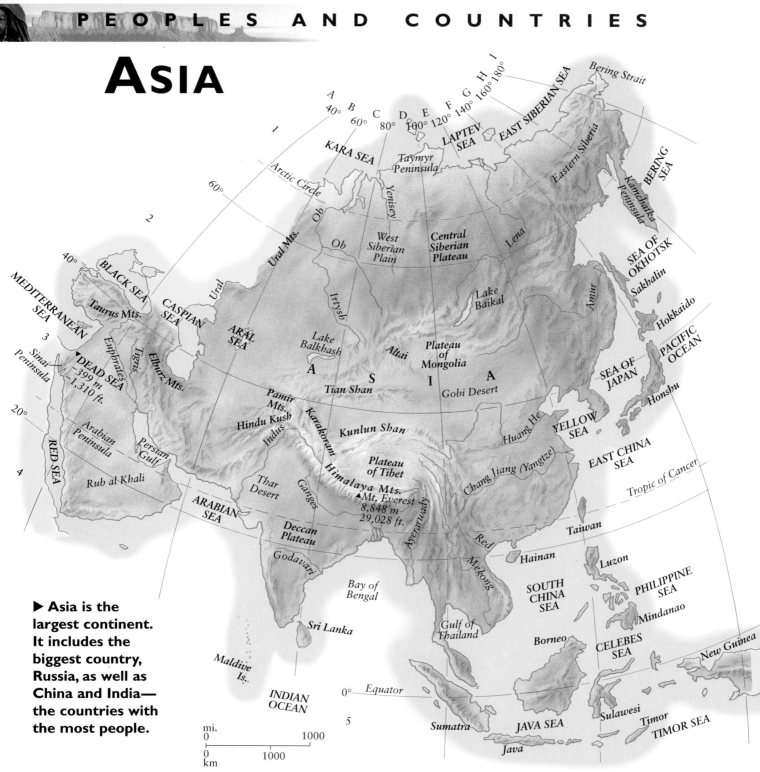

A 40° B 60° C 80° D E 100° 120° F G 140° H I 160° 180°

Bering Strait

KARA SEA

LAPTEV SEA

EAST SIBERIAN SEA

Arctic Circle

Taymyr Peninsula

Eastern Siberia

BERING SEA

Kamchatka Peninsula

Ob

Yenisey

West Siberian Plain

Central Siberian Plateau

Lena

SEA OF OKHOTSK

Sakhalin

Ob

Ural Mts.

Irtysh

Lake Baikal

Amur

Hokkaido

MEDITERRANEAN SEA

BLACK SEA

CASPIAN SEA

Ural

Lake Balkhash

Altai

Plateau of Mongolia

PACIFIC OCEAN

Taurus Mts.

ARAL SEA

A   S   I   A

SEA OF JAPAN

Honshu

Euphrates

Tigris

Elburz Mts.

DEAD SEA -399 m -1,310 ft.

Tian Shan

Gobi Desert

Sinai Peninsula

Pamir Mts.

Hindu Kush

Karakoram

Kunlun Shan

Huang He

YELLOW SEA

EAST CHINA SEA

Arabian Peninsula

Persian Gulf

Indus

Plateau of Tibet

Himalaya Mts.

Chang Jiang (Yangtze)

RED SEA

Rub al Khali

Thar Desert

Ganges

▲Mt. Everest 8,848 m 29,028 ft.

Ayeyarwady

Tropic of Cancer

ARABIAN SEA

Deccan Plateau

Red

Taiwan

Godavari

Bay of Bengal

Mekong

Hainan

Luzon

SOUTH CHINA SEA

PHILIPPINE SEA

Sri Lanka

Gulf of Thailand

Mindanao

Borneo

CELEBES SEA

New Guinea

Maldive Is.

INDIAN OCEAN

0° Equator

Sumatra

JAVA SEA

Sulawesi

Timor

TIMOR SEA

Java

▶ Asia is the largest continent. It includes the biggest country, Russia, as well as China and India— the countries with the most people.

mi.
0   1000
0   1000
km

How big is Asia?

Asia is the biggest continent. Its area of 17 million square miles (44 million sq km) is greater than North and South America put together, and four times greater than Europe. The coastline of Asia is almost 81,000 miles (130,000 km) long—more than three times the distance around the world.

Some mountains get smaller all the time as they are worn away. The Himalayas are getting higher, pushed up by movements in the Earth's crust.

What are Asia's main features?

Asia's natural features are very varied, from the world's highest mountains (the Himalayas) to long rivers (such as the Chang Jiang), lakes as big as seas (the Caspian), and deserts like the Gobi. There are hot jungles, cold forests, grasslands, and snowy tundras.

Which country has the most languages?

India has 14 major languages and more than 160 others. There are also 700 dialects (local or regional variations). Hindi is the official language of India, and many Indians also speak English.

Where is the Khyber Pass?

The Khyber Pass is in northwest Pakistan. Here the land is rugged and hilly. The pass is a route through the mountains to Afghanistan.

What is the Tonlé Sap?

The Tonlé Sap is a large lake in Cambodia, in Southeast Asia. During the summer floods, its waters cover 3,900 square miles (10,000 sq km). The lake is formed by water from the Mekong River, the longest river in Southeast Asia (2,800 miles) and the fifth longest in Asia.

▼ The Tonlé Sap is a large lake in Cambodia. People in this region use the rivers and the lakes for transportation and fishing.

▲ In the Dead Sea, you can float while reading the paper! This is because the water is unusually salty and supports your weight.

Where are Asia's high and low points?

Asia has the highest and lowest points on the Earth's land. Mount Everest (over 28,000 [8,800 km] feet above sea level) is the highest point. The shores of the Dead Sea (about 1,310 feet [400m] below sea level) are the lowest points to be found anywhere on land.

Where are Asia's deepest gorges?

The deepest gorges cut by rivers are those made by the Indus, Brahmaputra, and Ganges, which flow through India and Pakistan. In places, these rivers cut gorges that are more than 3 miles (5 km) deep.

Does Asia have more people than any other continent?

Yes. Besides covering one third of the Earth's land surface, Asia has about three-fifths of the world's people. More than 3.5 billion people live in Asia, in 49 countries.

ASIA FACTS

■ Area: 17,135,000 sq. mi. (44,380,000 sq km).

■ Population 3.5 billion.

■ Number of countries: 49.

■ Longest river: Chang Jiang (Yangtze), 3,900 miles (6,300 km).

■ Largest lake: Caspian Sea, 144,000 sq. mi. (372,000 sq km).

■ Highest mountain: Everest 29,000 feet.

■ Largest country: Russia (partly in Europe).

■ Country with most people: China.

■ Largest city: Tokyo, over 26 million people.

◀ **Climbers from all over the world come to the Himalaya Mountains to climb Mount Everest and the other peaks.**

Some people also call Tibet the Roof of the World because it is so high and remote. Tibet was once a free country but is now controlled by China.

Which is the highest mountain in India?

To the north of India rise the mighty Himalayas, the highest mountains in the world. The highest peaks, including Mount Everest itself, are in Nepal, but India, too, has some towering peaks. The highest mountain in India is Nanda Devi, which is 25,410 feet (7,817 m) high.

Where is the Roof of the World?

The Roof of the World is the name given to a region north of India where several mighty mountain ranges meet. Here are the highest mountains on Earth, including the peaks of the Himalayas, the Tien Shan, the Kunlun Shan, the Karakoram, and the Pamirs.

In which country do people live longest?

Every country has a few people who live to an exceptionally great age—100 or more. In Japan the average life expectancy (the age a newborn baby can expect to live) is 77. This is higher than in Europe or the United States. In some poor countries of Africa the life expectancy is only 45 to 50.

How many islands make up Japan?

Japan is a bow-shaped chain of islands which stretches for about 1,200 miles (1,900 km). There are four main islands, called Honshu (the biggest), Hokkaido, Shikoku, and Kyushu. There are about 3,000 smaller islands.

Which is Japan's most famous mountain?

Japan has more than 160 volcanoes, about a third of which are active. The most famous is Fujiyama, or Mount Fuji. It is the highest mountain in

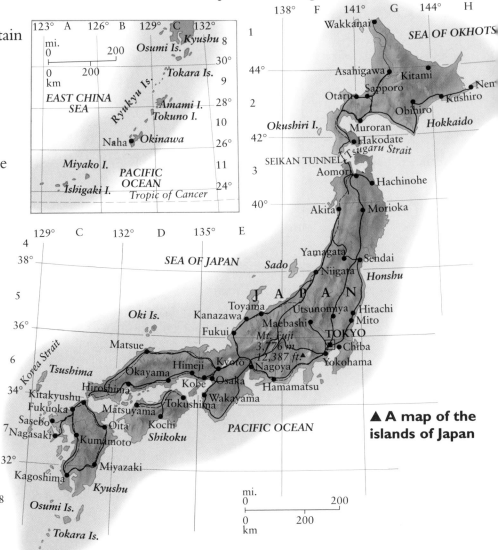

▲ **A map of the islands of Japan**

Japan (12,400 feet [3,780 m]). This cone-shaped volcano last erupted in 1707. To the people of Japan, Fujiyama is a sacred mountain. Every year thousands climb to the top of the mountain, as a spiritual pilgrimage.

What are the Maldives?

The Maldives are a chain of low-lying coral islands in the Indian Ocean. Some of the islands belong to India. The rest make up the republic of the Maldives, a separate country. There are more than 2,000 islands, but fewer than 200 are big enough for people to live on.

Where is Angkor Wat?

Angkor Wat is a temple in Cambodia and the biggest religious building in the world. It was built by the Khmer people of Southeast Asia in the 1100s in honor of a Hindu god. Later Buddhists added to the temple buildings. Angkor Wat was abandoned by the 1500s. Wooden buildings rotted away and the stone temple was overgrown by forest. In the 1860s a Frenchman discovered the ruins.

▲ **Mount Fuji is crowned with snow, which melts in summer. The top of the mountain is often hidden by clouds.**

DID YOU KNOW?

■ The smallest Asian nations are tiny, like Bahrain which covers only 240 sq. mi. (622 sq km).

■ Although China has more than a billion people, most of the country is deserts or mountains with very few people.

■ All the world's major religions—Judaism, Christianity, Islam, Hinduism, and Buddhism —began in Asia.

■ Asians speak many languages. In India alone, there are hundreds of local dialects.

■ The most prosperous countries of Asia include oil-rich Saudi Arabia and manufacturing giants such as Japan, Korea, Taiwan, and Singapore.

■ Indonesia has 13,000 islands, more than any island group in the world.

▼ **The Maldives are a string of coral reef islands in the Indian Ocean, south of the Indian subcontinent. Only the larger ones are shown here.**

A   73°   B
Eight Degree Channel

Ihavandiffulu Atoll   Tiladummati Atoll
1   *Miladummadulu Atoll*
Makunudu Atoll
Malosmadulu Atoll   *Fadiffolu Atoll*
5°   *Kerdiva Channel*
INDIAN OCEAN   *Male Atoll*
Wilingili I.   Male I.
Ari Atoll   *South Male Atoll*
                         Felidu Atoll
M A L D I V E S
Nilandu Atoll   *Mulaka Atoll*
2   *Kolumadulu Atoll*
                         Haddummati Atoll
One and Half Degree Channel
mi.   INDIAN
0   100   OCEAN
                         Suvadiva Atoll
0   100
km
0°   Equator
Equatorial Channel
                         Addu Atoll
3   *Gan I.*

Where is Siberia?

East of the Ural Mountains lies Siberia, a wilderness of 5½ million square miles (14 million sq km) stretching to the Pacific Ocean. Siberia is a region of vast forests, rivers, and frozen plains. Here are the coldest inhabited places in the world; winter temperatures drop to −42°F (−67°C).

▼ Traveling by reindeer sled is a good way to get around in Kamchatka, Siberia, where winters are long and cold.

Which is Asia's longest river?

The Chang Jiang, or Yangtze Kiang, in China is the longest river in Asia. It flows into the South China Sea.

Which Asian city is sacred to three religions?

Jerusalem is a holy city for people of three faiths: Jews, Christians, and Muslims. Jerusalem was divided between Israel and Jordan until 1967. Since then Israel has held all of the city. For Jews, Jerusalem is the ancient Hebrew capital, where King Solomon built the Temple. For Christians, the city is where Jesus Christ preached and was crucified. Muslims believe that Muhammad rose to heaven from a rock in Jerusalem.

Some Asian cities are very crowded. Many people live in high-rise blocks, which squeeze a lot of homes into a small space.

Which rivers are known as the "cradle of civilization?"

Ancient civilizations grew up near rivers. Rivers were trade routes and provided water for farming. Several great civilizations arose in Asia. The rivers Tigris and Euphrates in Mesopotamia (now Iraq) gave rise to the civilizations of Sumer and Babylon over 5,000 years ago. The Indus river valley in Pakistan was the center of another great ancient civilization, known for its cities.

Where is Asia's biggest island?

The island of Borneo is the biggest island in Asia. Its 284,200 square miles (736,000 sq km) are shared by three countries: Malaysia, Indonesia, and Brunei. Borneo is a mountainous island, and much of it is covered in dense rain forest, although logging companies are steadily cutting down the trees for timber.

▲ The Dome of the Rock in Jerusalem is a Muslim shrine, or holy place. The city is sacred to Muslims, Christians, and Jews.

Where are Asia's richest countries?

A country's wealth is measured in different ways. One way is to work out the average wealth per person (supposing that all the country's wealth could be divided equally between all its people). The oil-producing countries of the Middle East, such as the United Arab Emirates, have small populations, but enormous national wealth from selling oil.

Which is the only city situated on two continents?

Istanbul in Turkey lies in Europe and Asia. It is built on both banks of the Bosporus, the strait that separates these two continents, and is sometimes called the "Gateway to Asia." This great city has had three names. Founded by the Ancient Greeks, it was first called Byzantium, but was renamed Constantinople by the Romans in A.D. 330. In 1453 the Turks captured the city and it became known as Istanbul. It is the largest city in modern Turkey.

◄ **Dubai is one of the oil-rich United Arab Emirates. In this shop, people can buy gold.**

The world's biggest gas station is in Jeddah, Saudi Arabia. It has more than 200 pumps!

▼ **Japanese children learn calligraphy— writing with a brush and ink.**

Why is Bahrain a true desert island?

The island of Bahrain in the Persian Gulf has hardly any rain. For several months of the year no clouds are seen, and the average annual rainfall is less than 4 inches (100 mm). Despite being mostly desert, Bahrain is rich, because it sells oil abroad.

What is it like learning to write Chinese?

In China, and in Japan too, writing can be an art. People sometimes write words slowly and beautifully using a brush instead of a pen. About 50,000 symbols can be used to write Chinese. Fortunately, children only have to learn about 5,000 of them.

Where is the longest wall on Earth?

The Great Wall of China is the longest structure ever built. It is about 1,500 miles (2,400 km) long and was built in about 210 B.C. to keep out invaders on China's northern borders.

◄ **The Great Wall of China was built by linking old walls with new ones. Thousands of workers toiled to build the wall.**

Which city has the most crowded commuter trains?

Japan has a highly efficient rail system including high-speed electric trains and the world's longest rail tunnel, the Seikan Tunnel (34 miles [54 km] long). People going to work in Tokyo cram into the city's commuter trains. Trains can be so crowded that railroad staff, called crushers, push in the passengers while the doors close. Tokyo is huge, and people travel from suburbs to work in offices, shops, and factories.

▼ **In Tokyo, Japan, station staff push commuters onto crowded trains during the rush hour.**

When did North Korea become a communist state?

North Korea is a communist country where all factories and farms, and even cars, are owned by the government. North and South Korea formed a single country from the 1300s until 1910, when Japan occupied Korea. This occupation ended in 1945 when Japan was defeated in World War II. After this the country was divided, and in 1948 North Korea became a communist state. Ever since the Korean War (1950–1953), there have been tensions between North and South Korea. South Korea has a free-market economy, and many people earn high wages in factories.

◄ **Buddha Park in Laos is famous for its statues. The park is near the country's capital, Vientiane.**

▶ **Many people think the Taj Mahal is the most beautiful building in the world. Tourists from many countries come to see it.**

What is Buddha Park?

Buddha Park lies about 12 miles (20 km) from Vientiane, the capital of Laos. It is a site built in the 1950s to honor the Buddhist and Hindu religions, and the park contains Hindu and Buddhist sculptures. Many people in Laos are Buddhists, although during the 1970s the country had a communist government.

Where are the ruins of Mohenjo-Daro?

In Pakistan. Mohenjo-Daro was an important center of the Indus valley civilization which flourished about 4,000 years ago. It was one of the earliest examples of a planned city, with streets laid out to a grid pattern and good drains.

Where do people live in stilt houses?

Many island people in Indonesia and the Philippines live on boats or in wooden houses built on stilts over the water. The Philippines has over 7,000 tropical islands. Indonesia has more than 13,000!

Where is the Taj Mahal?

This beautiful tomb stands in a garden outside the city of Agra in India. The Mogul Emperor Shah Jahan had the Taj Mahal built in memory of his favorite wife, Mumtaz Mahal. It was built from the 1630s to the 1650s.

Why do people bathe in the Ganges River?

Hindus from all over India come to the Ganges River to bathe in its waters. They visit the holy city of Varanasi, to worship in the city's 1,500 temples and wade into the Ganges at bathing places called ghats.

Where is Singapore?

Singapore is a tiny island country in Southeast Asia. The name means "city of the lions." The city of Singapore has grown from a small fishing village in the 1820s to become one of Asia's chief trading and banking centers.

Which is the biggest city in Asia?

Tokyo in Japan has grown so large that it and nearby Yokohama, now form a huge metropolis of more than 26 million people.

MORE FACTS ON ASIA

- People in Japan, as well as China, eat with chopsticks.
- The most popular sport in Japan is baseball.
- In some Asian cities, you can ride in a pedicab—a taxicab pulled by a driver riding a bicycle.
- Indian music sounds different from that of the West because it uses a different scale.
- In Bali, dancers tell stories without words, relying on movements.
- Among Asia's rarest animals are the giant panda, snow leopard, and Indian rhinoceros.

NORTH AND CENTRAL AMERICA

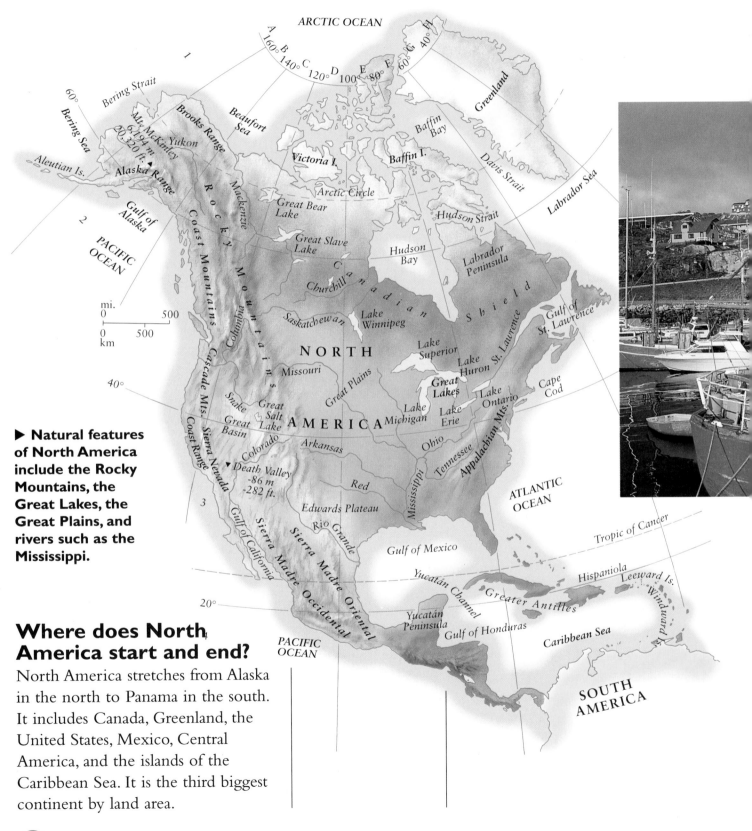

ARCTIC OCEAN

A 160° B 140° C 120° D 100° E 80° F 60° G 40° H

1

Bering Strait

60°

Bering Sea

Aleutian Is.

Brooks Range

Beaufort Sea

Greenland

Baffin Bay

Davis Strait

Labrador Sea

Mt. McKinley 6,194 m 20,320 ft.

Yukon

Alaska Range

Victoria I.

Baffin I.

2

Gulf of Alaska

PACIFIC OCEAN

Rocky Mountains

Mackenzie

Great Bear Lake

Arctic Circle

Great Slave Lake

Hudson Strait

Hudson Bay

Labrador Peninsula

Churchill

Canadian Shield

Gulf of St. Lawrence

mi. 0   500

0   500 km

Coast Mountains

Columbia

Saskatchewan

Lake Winnipeg

Lake Superior

Lake Huron

St. Lawrence

NORTH

Missouri

Great Plains

Great Lakes

Lake Ontario

Cape Cod

40°

Cascade Mts.

Sierra Nevada

Coast Range

Snake

Great Salt Lake

Great Basin

Colorado

Arkansas

AMERICA

Lake Michigan

Lake Erie

Ohio

Tennessee

Appalachian Mts.

ATLANTIC OCEAN

▶ **Natural features of North America include the Rocky Mountains, the Great Lakes, the Great Plains, and rivers such as the Mississippi.**

▼ Death Valley -86 m -282 ft.

Red

Edwards Plateau

Rio Grande

Mississippi

Gulf of California

Sierra Madre Occidental

Sierra Madre Oriental

Gulf of Mexico

Yucatán Channel

Tropic of Cancer

Hispaniola

Leeward Is.

Greater Antilles

Windward Is.

20°

3

PACIFIC OCEAN

Yucatán Peninsula

Gulf of Honduras

Caribbean Sea

Where does North America start and end?

North America stretches from Alaska in the north to Panama in the south. It includes Canada, Greenland, the United States, Mexico, Central America, and the islands of the Caribbean Sea. It is the third biggest continent by land area.

SOUTH AMERICA

Which is North America's largest country?

Canada at more than 3,849,000 square miles (9,970,000 sq km). The United States is smaller, covering 3,619,000 square miles (9,373,000 sq km). Yet only 29 million people live in Canada compared to over 268 million in the United States.

Mexico City's population is growing rapidly. The United Nations calculates that by the year 2000, Mexico City will have more than 19 million people.

◄ Julianehaab is a port in southern Greenland. Ice covers 80 percent of this northern island.

▼ This map shows the different climate regions of North America, from the Arctic north to the tropical south.

Is Greenland part of North America?

Greenland is a self-governing part of Denmark, a country in Europe. Yet geographically this enormous island is part of North America.

Which is North America's biggest city?

Mexico City, with over 16.5 million people, is the biggest city in North America. The largest city in the United States is New York, with a population of 16 million.

Which is North America's smallest country?

Of the 23 independent North American countries the smallest is St. Kitts and Nevis, an island state in the Caribbean. The islands have a combined area of 104 square miles (269 sq km) and only 44,000 people live there. There are even smaller island states in the region, but they are not self-governing.

What is the climate of North America like?

North America has every kind of climate. The far north is ice-covered all year round. The interior has mostly cold winters and either warm or mild summers. The southeast is warm and moist. The southwest is mostly dry with great ranges of temperature and areas of desert. In the far south, in Central America, there are hot, wet tropical forests.

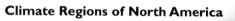

Climate Regions of North America

Key
- Polar
- Cold Continental
- Wet Continental
- Semi-arid
- Desert
- Wet Subtropical
- Wet and Dry Tropical

Which is North America's hottest spot?

The highest temperature ever recorded in North America was 135°F (57°C) at Death Valley in California, in 1913.

Where is Yosemite Falls?

Yosemite Falls, the highest waterfall in North America at 2,420 feet (740 m), is in Yosemite National Park, California.

▲ **Pioneers found Death Valley difficult to cross because of the heat and lack of water.**

▶ **Visitors to the Everglades can take a boat trip to watch alligators and other wild animals.**

◀ **Yosemite Falls in California, where a mountain creek falls in three stages, linked by a cascade.**

Where is the world's longest frontier?

The boundary between Canada and the United States stretches for 4,000 miles (6,400 km)—the longest in the world. The border was established in the 1800s, when the newly independent United States was expanding across the western territories and Canada was still governed by Britain. Today, the two nations are friendly neighbors and share much in common. Canadians are greatly outnumbered by Americans.

What are badlands?

Badlands are areas of steep hills and gullies cut by rushing streams. Soil is thin, and few plants can grow there. The climate is usually dry. Sudden heavy rainstorms cause floods which wash away soil and wear the rocks. The Badlands National Park in South Dakota has a spectacular rocky landscape.

What are the Everglades?

The Everglades are subtropical swamps in the south of Florida. The Everglades cover more than 2,700 square miles (7,000 sq km). In places, saw grass grows almost 13 feet (4 m) tall. Elsewhere there are salt marshes and mangrove trees. No one lived in the swamps until the 1840s, when the Seminole Indians took refuge there. Some of the swamps have been drained for farming, and part forms a U.S. National Park, where visitors can see turtles, alligators, and many different kinds of birds. Like all wetlands, the Everglades need protecting to preserve their wildlife.

NORTH AMERICA FACTS
■ Area: 9,350,000 sq. mi. (24,211,000 sq km).
■ Population: 458,000,000.
■ Number of countries: 23 (including Central America and Caribbean).
■ Longest river: Mississippi, 2,350 mi.
■ Largest lake: Lake Superior, 31,700 sq. mi. (82,103 sq km).
■ Highest mountain: Mount McKinley (Alaska), 20,320 ft. (6,194 m).
■ Largest country: Canada.
■ Country with most people: United States.
■ Largest city: Mexico City; population of 16.5 million in 1996.

▶ The St. Lawrence Seaway is one of the major transportation routes in North America, carrying manufactured goods and raw materials.

A Florida alligator can sometimes be mistaken for a floating log—until it opens its mouth!

What is the Canadian Shield?

This is not a defensive weapon, but the biggest geological landform in Canada. It covers half the country. The Shield is an area of rock almost 600 million years old. It has rounded hills, many lakes and, in the south, thick conifer forests. Farther north it is too cold for trees. The Canadian Shield is an important mining region.

Where can ocean-going ships sail far inland?

Along the St. Lawrence Seaway, big ships can carry cargoes from the Atlantic Ocean as far inland as the Great Lakes—a distance of over 2,170 miles (3,500 km). The Seaway is made up of deepened and widened stretches of the St. Lawrence River and canals. It was opened in 1959.

What is the largest state in the United States?

The largest state is Alaska, which has an area of 586,500 square miles (1,519,000 sq km). That's four times the size of Germany.

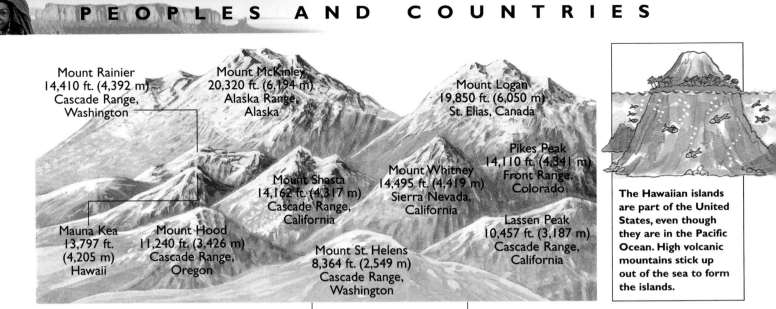

Mount Rainier
14,410 ft. (4,392 m)
Cascade Range,
Washington

Mount McKinley
20,320 ft. (6,194 m)
Alaska Range,
Alaska

Mount Logan
19,850 ft. (6,050 m)
St. Elias, Canada

Pikes Peak
14,110 ft. (4,341 m)
Front Range,
Colorado

Mount Whitney
14,495 ft. (4,419 m)
Sierra Nevada,
California

Mount Shasta
14,162 ft. (4,317 m)
Cascade Range,
California

Mauna Kea
13,797 ft.
(4,205 m)
Hawaii

Mount Hood
11,240 ft. (3,426 m)
Cascade Range,
Oregon

Lassen Peak
10,457 ft. (3,187 m)
Cascade Range,
California

Mount St. Helens
8,364 ft. (2,549 m)
Cascade Range,
Washington

The Hawaiian islands
are part of the United
States, even though
they are in the Pacific
Ocean. High volcanic
mountains stick up
out of the sea to form
the islands.

Where is the highest mountain in North America?

Mount McKinley, in the Alaska
Range, is in the northwest of the
continent. It has two peaks, the
higher rising to 20,320 feet (6,194 m).
The mountain was named for William
McKinley, the 25th President of the
United States. Its original name is
Denali, "the high one."

Where are the Rocky Mountains?

The Rocky Mountains form the
largest mountain system in North
America. They extend over 3,000 miles
(4,800 km) from Canada into the
United States. Most of the mountains
were formed millions of years ago by
movements of the Earth's crust.

Which river is known as the Big Muddy?

The Missouri is the second longest
river in the United States. It carries
vast amounts of mud, hence its
nickname "Big Muddy." The Native
American name Missouri is said to
mean "town of the large canoes."

▲ The highest
mountains in
North America.
Also included
is Mauna Kea,
in Hawaii.

▼ A Mississippi
paddlewheel
steamboat has a
flat bottom, so it
doesn't get stuck
on sand banks.
Steamboats
used to carry
passengers and
cargo up and down
the river. Today
they carry tourists.

What is unusual about Mount Rushmore?

Mount Rushmore is a granite cliff in
the Black Hills of South Dakota. Into
the rock are carved four huge faces of
U.S. presidents: George Washington,
Thomas Jefferson, Theodore
Roosevelt, and Abraham Lincoln. The
head of George Washington is as high
as a five-story building. A complete
figure on this scale would be about
460 feet (140 m) high.

Where is the Panama Canal?

The Panama Canal cuts across the
Isthmus of Panama (an isthmus is a
narrow neck of land). The canal is 50
miles (80 km) long and was opened
in 1914. Digging began in 1881, but

work stopped in 1889 because so many workers died of tropical diseases. In the early 1900s the United States took on the task, having leased the surrounding land from the new republic of Panama. Ships using the canal are saved a long journey around South America to sail from the Atlantic to the Pacific Ocean. After 2000 Panama will run the canal.

What are the Antilles?

There are two main groups of Caribbean islands—the Greater Antilles and, farther east, the Lesser Antilles. The islands of the Lesser Antilles are smaller; they include the Windward and Leeward Islands which curve southward.

Which is the largest island in the West Indies?

Cuba, the most westerly of the Greater Antilles islands, is the largest West Indian island. Next comes Hispaniola, which is divided into two countries: Haiti and the Dominican Republic (which occupies the eastern part of the island).

▼ Native Americans made these leather moccasins and a pipe decorated with colorful, patterned weavings.

Where do the Chippewa live?

The Chippewa are a group of Native Americans living in North Dakota and Minnesota. They originally lived around Lake Superior, in both the United States and Canada. The name of Manitoba (a province in Canada) is thought to have come from the Chippewa word *manitou*, meaning "great spirit."

What are moccasins?

Moccasins are traditional shoes made by Native Americans in North America. The Eastern Woodland tribes made moccasins from a single piece of leather, and often decorated them. Today, craftworkers continue these traditional skills for tourists.

Which Native Americans are famous weavers?

The Navajo people of the Southwest weave colorful wool blankets. They are the second largest tribe in the United States, second in numbers only to the Cherokee. They are successful in farming and business, earning money from coal mining, lumber, and manufacturing as well as from weaving and other craftwork.

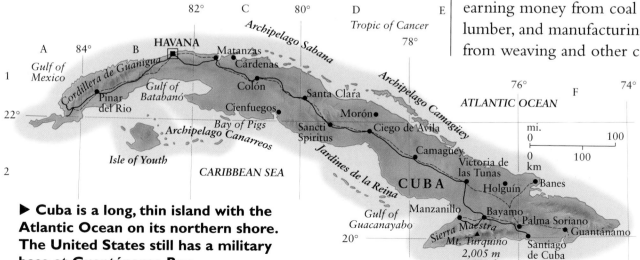

► Cuba is a long, thin island with the Atlantic Ocean on its northern shore. The United States still has a military base at Guantánamo Bay.

221

Where is the Capitol?

The Capitol Building is in Washington, D.C. Both the Senate and the House of Representatives meet here. Work began on the building in 1792, but the dome was not completed until 1865.

Which U.S. cities have the tallest buildings?

New York City and Chicago are rivals in the skyscraper contest. New York has the World Trade Center and the Empire State Building, while Chicago (which claims to be the home of the skyscraper) has the taller Sears Tower, the second highest building in the world.

Where are yellow cabs a familiar sight?

Visitors to New York City can travel around the city in one of its famous yellow cabs. Or they can ride on one of the city's three subway systems. New York City also has two of the best-known railroad stations in the nation: Grand Central Terminal and Pennsylvania Station. Thousands of commuters travel to the city each day.

The President of the United States lives in the White House in Washington, D.C. It earned its name after the building was burned by British troops in 1814 and the smoke-stained walls were painted white.

▼ An Inuit. The name Eskimo (also used for the Inuit) is a Native American word meaning "eaters of raw meat."

◄ New York's brightly lit Times Square is one of the city's many famous sights. Many Broadway theaters are located in this area.

In which part of North America is French more common than English?

In the Canadian province of Quebec. Most of the people of Quebec are French Canadians. Montreal, the largest city in Quebec, has more French-speakers than any other city in the world after Paris in France.

Why do people come to watch the Calgary Stampede?

This is one of the most exciting rodeo shows in the world. It takes place in July every year in Calgary, a city in Alberta, Canada. Large crowds pack the arena to watch the famous chuck wagon race, which is one of the highlights of the rodeo.

Where do the Inuit live?

The Inuit are people who live in the Canadian Arctic. Here, most of the ground is covered by snow in winter. The Inuit traditionally lived by hunting and fishing, but the modern world has brought changes, including the mining of oil and gas. Many Inuit now have regular jobs or make craft goods to sell to tourists. They want more control over their ancient lands.

Where do people store corn in pyramids?

In Mexico. Cone-shaped silos looking somewhat like pyramids can store a year's corn harvest. The Mayan people grew corn as their main food crop in Mexico as early as 3,000 years ago, and it is still an important source of food, forming the basis of many Mexican dishes.

◄ The stone Chacmool, or messenger of the gods, at Chichén Itzá was used in sacrificial ceremonies.

Where is Chichén Itzá?

Chichén Itzá is an ancient city in Mexico, built by the Mayan people over 1,000 years ago. The city's ruins include a tall limestone pyramid with a temple on top, and a huge plaza or open space where there was a steam bath and a ball game court. The ruins are now an important archaeological site and tourist attraction.

Where do people celebrate the Day of the Dead?

The Day of the Dead is a Mexican holiday which takes place every year on November 2nd, All Souls' Day. People remember dead friends and relatives, taking flowers and candles to their graves and having picnics there.

FACTS ABOUT NORTH AMERICA

- Mexico's most popular sport is soccer. Mexicans also enjoy bullfights.

- A favorite dish in Newfoundland, Canada, is flipper pie (made from fish).

- The first people to settle North America came from Asia more than 15,000 years ago.

- The first Europeans known to have visited North America were Vikings, about the year A.D. 1000.

- The United States is the fourth biggest country by area—after Russia, Canada, and China.

- The national bird of the U.S. is the bald eagle, shown on the Great Seal of the United States.

▼ Mexicans make painted papier-mâché skeletons to celebrate the Day of the Dead. The skeletons wear hats, too!

Where is Central America?

Central America is the narrow land bridge joining North and South America. It extends from Guatemala and Belize in the north as far as Panama in the south. There are seven countries in Central America, the largest being Nicaragua.

Who built pyramids in Central America?

The native peoples of Central America developed remarkable civilizations. The Mayan people built great stepped pyramids. On top of each pyramid was a small temple. They also built cities such as Tikal, in what is now Guatemala. The great age of Mayan civilization lasted from A.D. 250 to 900.

How did the Caribbean Sea get its name?

The Caribbean Sea is to the east of Central America. Its name comes from the Caribs, a people who lived on some of the islands of the West Indies and in South America. When Christopher Columbus sailed to the Americas, in 1492, the Spanish sailors called the sea *Mar Caribe*— Caribbean Sea.

Where is cigar-rolling an important industry?

Cuba is famous for its cigars. Workers roll Havana cigars by hand. These cigars are named after the capital city of Cuba. Cuba has had a communist government since 1959, when Fidel Castro overthrew the dictator Fulgencio Batista.

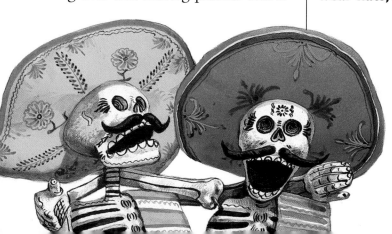

SOUTH AMERICA

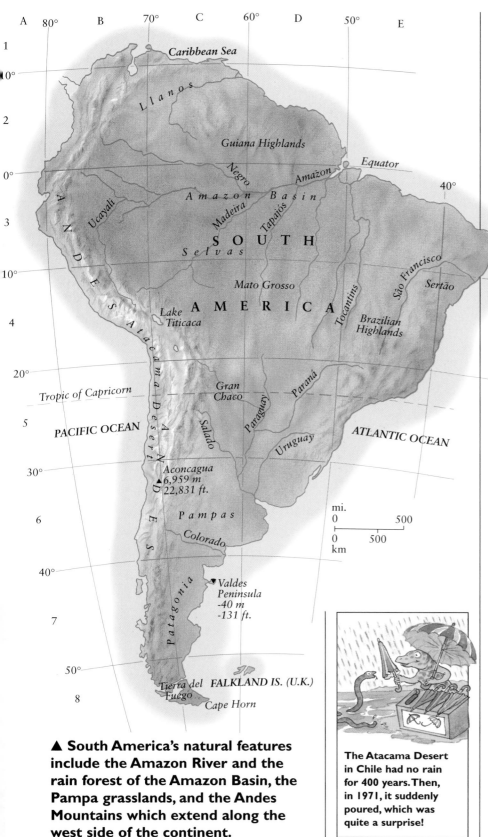

A South America's natural features include the Amazon River and the rain forest of the Amazon Basin, the Pampa grasslands, and the Andes Mountains which extend along the west side of the continent.

The Atacama Desert in Chile had no rain for 400 years. Then, in 1971, it suddenly poured, which was quite a surprise!

Is South America south of North America?

The South American continent is actually southeast of North America, not directly south. New York, on the east coast of North America, is farther west than Valparaiso, Chile, on the west coast of South America.

How big is South America?

South America covers an area of nearly 7 million square miles (18 million sq km), so it is roughly twice as big as Canada. South America has the world's biggest rain forest, in the Amazon River Basin and the high Andes Mountains.

Where is Cape Horn?

Cape Horn is at the southernmost tip of South America. Most of South America lies within the tropics, yet Cape Horn is less than 620 miles (1,000 km) from Antarctica.

Who were the first people to live in South America?

When Europeans arrived in South America in the late 1400s, they discovered that people had been living there for thousands of years, including the great Aztec, Inca, and Mayan civilizations. Today, most South Americans are of mixed ancestry. They share many traditions, but local cultures reflect their African, American Indian, and European background.

▶ **La Paz in Bolivia holds the record as the world's highest national capital.**

Which are South America's most important rivers?

There are four mighty river systems in South America. They are the Magdalena, Orinoco, Amazon, and Paraná–Paraguay.

A 81°   B   78°   C
1   Esmeraldas
    Tulcán COLOMBIA   75°
    Ibarra
0° Equator   E C U A D O R
PACIFIC   ■QUITO
OCEAN   Río Napo
    Manta Quevedo   Latacunga
2   Portoviejo   Chimborazo   Ambato
    6,267 m▲
    20,561 ft.
    Babahoyo   Riobamba
2° Guayaquil Milagro
    PAN AMERICAN
    HIGHWAY   PERU
3   Puna I. Cuenca
    Gulf of
    Guayaquil Machala
4°   Loja
    mi.
4   0   100
    0   100
    km

SOUTH AMERICA FACTS

- Area: 6,800,000 sq. mi. (17,817,000 sq km).
- Population: 323,000,000.
- Number of countries: 12.
- Longest river: Amazon, 4,005 miles (6,448 km).
- Largest lake: Maracaibo, 5,217 sq. mi. (13,512 sq km).
- Highest mountain: Mount Aconcagua (Argentina), 22,831 ft. (6,959 m) above sea level.
- Largest country: Brazil.
- Country with most people: Brazil.
- Largest city: São Paulo (Brazil).

Why is Quito not so tropical?

Quito is the capital of Equador. It is only 15½ miles (25 km) south of the Equator so it should be hot. However, it is almost 10,000 feet (3,000 m) above sea level, which means it has a mild climate—higher means cooler.

Where is Patagonia?

Patagonia is a bleak desert region at the very southern tip of Argentina. When Spanish explorers reached it in the 1500s they met local Indians who stuffed their boots with grass for extra warmth. The name Patagonia comes from a Spanish word meaning "big feet."

Which is the highest capital city in the world?

La Paz, the capital of Bolivia, is 11,800 feet (3,600 m) above sea level. High in the Andes, it is the world's highest capital. Lhasa in Tibet is higher by about 165 feet (50 m), but Tibet is no longer an independent country.

Which is the biggest lake in South America?

South America has fewer large lakes than other continents. The biggest lake is Lake Maracaibo (5,217 square miles [13,512 sq km]) in Venezuela. This lake has valuable oil reserves beneath it and is also a busy waterway.

▶ **Glaciers flow down from the Andes Mountains. This is a glacier in Patagonia, seen from a viewing platform.**

225

How big is the Amazon rain forest?

The Amazon rain forest is one of the wonders of the natural world. The Amazon River Basin, in which the rain forest grows, covers about 2¾ million square miles (7 million sq km). That's twice the size of India. Although much of the forest has been destroyed by logging and burning, it is still by far the biggest forest anywhere on Earth. Conservationists are trying to save as much as possible of the remaining rain forest from destruction.

What is the Selva?

The Selva is a region of tropical rain forest in the Amazon River Basin. It is one of four regions in the central plains of South America. The other three are the Llanos grasslands of the north, the Gran Chaco scrub-forest, and the southern Pampas grasslands.

Where do gauchos live?

Gauchos are South American cowboys. Huge herds of cattle roam the grassy plains of Brazil, Uruguay, and Argentina. The gauchos used to be horsemen who rounded up wild cattle. Now they are ranch workers.

▶ The Amazon rain forest is amazingly rich in plant and animal life. Each layer of the forest teems with life, from the dark forest floor to the sunlit treetops.

Liana

▼ Gauchos look after enormous herds of cattle on the grassy plains of South America. They ride tough, well-trained horses.

Monkey

Frog

Toucan

Macaws

Butterfly

Ants

MORE FACTS ABOUT SOUTH AMERICA

■ Much of South America is thinly populated but cities such as São Paulo are fast-growing, with many poor people.

■ Coastal Peru and northern Chile are among the driest places on Earth.

■ Cape Horn at the tip of South America is only 600 mi. (970 km) from Antarctica.

■ Spanish is spoken in most of South America, except in Brazil where Portuguese is spoken.

■ The Amazon holds 20 percent of the world's fresh water.

■ Lake Titicaca in Bolivia is the highest lake in the world used by boats. It is 12,533 ft. (3,821 m) above sea level.

Why is South America a youthful continent?

South America has more than 450 million people. The population now is three times greater than 50 years ago. Many people have large families and about a third of all South Americans are under 15 years old.

Which is the biggest city in South America?

São Paulo, in Brazil, with a population of more than 16 million, is the largest South American city, yet it is not Brazil's capital. Brasilia, a new city with 400,000 people, replaced Rio de Janeiro as the capital in 1960.

Is South America rich in minerals?

Yes, the continent has large reserves of metals such as copper, iron ore, lead, zinc, and gold. Venezuela is the chief South American oil producer. Bolivia has tin mines. Guyana, Suriname, and Brazil mine bauxite (which is aluminum ore).

What does Cotopaxi do?

From time to time it erupts, for Cotopaxi is one of the world's largest active volcanoes. It has erupted 25 times in the past 400 years, the last time in 1975. Cotopaxi is in Ecuador and is 19,342 feet (5,897 m) high.

Where is South America's lowest point?

On the east coast of Argentina. The Valdés Peninsula is about 130 feet below sea level.

Why do some South American places have Dutch names?

In Suriname, on the northeast coast, the official language is Dutch. Suriname was once a Dutch colony. Most people in South America speak Spanish or Portuguese, the languages of Europeans who settled and conquered most of South America from around 1500. In French Guiana and Guyana, the people speak French and English.

Which part of South America has the hottest weather?

The Gran Chaco region of Argentina. Here it can get as hot as 109°F (43°C). Most of South America has its hottest weather in January, which is a summer month south of the Equator.

Climate
- Subpolar
  Very cold winter
- Mountainous
  Altitude affects climate
- Temperate/Marine
  Mild and wet
- Subtropical
  Warm with mild winter
- Tropical
  Hot with high rainfall
- Steppe
  Warm and dry
- Savannah
  Hot with dry season
- Arid
  Hot and very dry

Where does the Orinoco River flow?

This South American river flows through Venezuela in the north of the continent and empties its waters into the Atlantic. It forms the border between Venezuela and Colombia.

The Amazon rain forest is bigger than similar tropical forests in Africa and Asia. It spreads on either side of the enormous Amazon River.

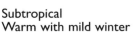

▲ A map of the climate regions of South America. Most of the continent is warm with good rainfall.

Where is Sugar Loaf Mountain?

The Brazilian city of Rio de Janeiro is famous for its white sandy beaches, its carnival, and two mountain landmarks, known as Sugar Loaf (1,325 feet [404 m] high) and Corcovado (2,309 feet [704 m]). Sugar Loaf is a curious egg shape; on top of Corcovado is a 98-foot (30 m) statue of Jesus Christ.

▲ The statue of Jesus Christ above Rio de Janeiro, with Sugar Loaf Mountain in the background.

Where is the finest natural harbor in South America?

Despite having a very long coastline, South America has few bays suitable for use as harbors. The finest natural harbor is at Rio de Janeiro in Brazil.

Where are the world's longest mountains?

The Andes stretch more than 4,340 miles (7,000 km) along the western side of South America. They form the world's longest mountain range (not counting undersea mountains). Aconcagua in Argentina (22,831 feet [6,959 m]) is the highest peak.

Where is Machu Picchu?

The Inca city of Machu Picchu, high in the mountains of Peru, was never discovered by the Spanish invaders who conquered the Inca empire in the 1500s and 1600s. Today, the ruins of Machu Picchu are one of the most impressive monuments to the civilization of the Inca people.

Where is the world's highest waterfall?

The Angel Falls plummet down a cliff on Mount Auyantepui in southeast Venezuela. These falls are the highest in the world, with a total drop of 3,211 feet (979 m). The first sighting of the falls by a white person was by an American pilot named Jimmy Angel in 1935.

Who listened greedily to tales of El Dorado?

El Dorado ("The Golden Man") was a legendary Indian king. He was said to be so rich that he covered himself in gold dust. Tales of El Dorado encouraged explorers from Spain to travel across Central and South America in the 1500s and 1600s, seeking gold. They found gold, but did not find El Dorado.

▲ The ruins of the Inca fortress-city of Machu Picchu were discovered in 1911 by an American archaeologist.

▲ Kamayura of the Amazon.

Where do the Kamayura people live?

The Kamayura are just one of the many native peoples who live in the rain forests of South America. The Kamayura live in Brazil, hunting and fishing in a way of life that remained unchanged for thousands of years until the 1900s.

Which Latin American countries grow coffee?

Coffee is a major crop in Colombia, Brazil, and Ecuador. The coffee beans are exported all over the world.

In which country do women wear distinctive hats?

In the Andes Mountains of Peru, women still wear traditional clothes, including shawls and highly distinctive hats that look somewhat like derbies. Men wear embroidered hats with ear flaps.

◀ Dusted with gold, El Dorado made a ritual voyage in a raft. This small gold raft is a reminder of a now-forgotten magical ceremony.

EUROPE

Where do Europe and Asia join?

Europe is part of the Asian landmass, because no sea divides it from Asia. In the east, several natural land barriers form a boundary between Europe and Asia. These barriers include the Ural Mountains, the Ural River, and the Caspian Sea. Since Europe and Asia are joined, the two together are sometimes referred to as Eurasia. Europe is smaller than all the other continents except Australia.

▲ The map of Europe shows how the continent has water on three sides. Its natural features include mountain ranges such as the Pyrenees, Alps, Carpathians, and Urals. Europe's rivers include the Danube, Rhine, and Volga.

Which is Europe's longest river?

The longest river in Europe is the Volga. It flows for over 2,190 miles (3,530 km) across Russia and empties into the Caspian Sea.

Why is western Europe ice-free in winter?

Although much of the coast of Norway lies in Arctic waters, it is not ice-bound in winter. Norway, like the rest of northwest Europe, has milder winters than places in North America that are equally far north. This is because the Gulf Stream's warm waters flow across the Atlantic. The warm ocean current warms the winds blowing from the sea across western Europe, keeping winters in coastal areas (such as Britain) mild, with ice-free oceans.

Where is Scandinavia?

Scandinavia is a region of northern Europe. Three countries are in Scandinavia, though not all of them are on the Scandinavian peninsula: Denmark (the most southerly), Norway, and Sweden. Sometimes Iceland (an island in the Atlantic Ocean), and Finland are also included.

Where is Lapland?

Lapland is the part of Scandinavia and Finland north of the Arctic Circle. It is not a country, but takes its name from the Lapps (or Sami), a people who traditionally roam the area with their herds of reindeer.

◀ The Lapps still herd reindeer. These hardy people use the animals to draw sleds across the snow-covered ground.

▶ The Black Forest in Germany is a reminder that in the past much of western Europe was covered by dense forest.

EUROPE FACTS

- Area: 4,067,400 sq. mi. (10,534,600 sq km).
- Population: 713,000,000.
- Number of countries: 47.
- Longest river: Volga, 2,193 mi. (3,531 km).
- Largest lake: excluding Caspian Sea (Europe–Asia border) Lake Ladoga in Russia, 6,835 sq. mi.
- Highest mountain: Mount Elbrus, 18,508 ft. above sea level.
- Largest country: Russia (partially in Asia).
- Country with most people: Russia.
- Largest city: Moscow (Russia), 8,957,000 people.

Where is the Black Forest?

The Black Forest, or *Schwarzwald* in German, is a region of mountains and coniferous forest in southwest Germany. The Danube River rises there and the Rhine River flows along its western edge. The Black Forest, with its dark-leaved trees, is a remnant of the much larger forests that once covered most of northern Europe.

Why has the Mediterranean Sea been so important?

The Mediterranean Sea has been a trading area for thousands of years. Civilization spread across the sea from Egypt and Mesopotamia. Greece and Rome became powerful, and later Italian city-states such as Venice grew rich from Mediterranean trade. Today the Mediterranean is still important for trade, especially with the oil fields in the Middle East, and is also a popular tourist area. Around its sunny shores are busy ports, picturesque villages, and modern vacation resorts.

A 8° **B** 10° **C** 12° **D** 14° **E** 16° **F** 18° **G**

SWITZERLAND · AUSTRIA
1
46° · Monte Bianco 4,807 m 15,771 ft. · *Lake Maggiore* · *Lake Como* · Bolzano · *Dolomites* · Trento · Udine · SLOVENIA
Como · *Lake Garda* · Trieste
Bergamo · Verona · Padua · Venice
Milan · Ferrara · *Gulf of Venice* · CROATIA
2 · Turin · *Po* · Parma · Reggio · Modena · Ravenna
44° · Genoa · Bologna · Imola · Rimini
FRANCE · La Spezia · *Arno* · Florence · SAN MARINO · Ancona
San Remo · Pisa · Arezzo · Perugia · ADRIATIC SEA
LIGURIAN SEA · Leghorn · Siena · Assisi
3 · *Lake Trasimeno* · Terni · Pescara
Corsica (France) · *Elba* · Tivoli · Térmoli
42° · Civitavecchia · VATICAN CITY · ROME · I T A L Y · Foggia · Barletta
4 · Strait of Bonifacio · *Ponza* · Naples · POMPEII · Bari
Sassari · Olbia · *Ischia* · Salerno · Brindisi
Capri · Amalfi · Taranto · Lecce
40° · *Sardinia* · Oristano · *Gulf of Taranto* · Cape Santa Maria di Leuca
5 · Cagliari · TYRRHENIAN SEA · Cosenza
· *Stromboli* · Catanzaro
38° · MEDITERRANEAN SEA · *Ustica* · *Lipari Is.* · Messina · IONIAN SEA
6 · Trapani · Palermo · Reggio di Calabria
Marsala · Caltanissetta · Catania
Sicily · Syracuse
Pantelleria · Ragusa
Cape Passero

mi. 0 — 100
km 0 — 100

◀ **Italy is shaped somewhat like a boot. The north is cooler than the south, and more industrialized. The islands of Sicily and Sardinia are part of Italy.**

Is all of Italy warm?

Parts of Italy have a Mediterranean climate with mild winters and hot, dry summers. The south, especially Sicily, can be very hot. However, areas of northern Italy around the Po Valley and in the Alps have cold winters.

How high are the Scottish Highlands?

In the Highlands of Scotland are the highest mountains in Britain. They are ancient and have been worn and weathered over many millions of years, giving them a smooth, rounded appearance. The highest mountain, Ben Nevis, is only 4,406 feet (1,343 m) high.

▼ **Cannes is a quiet town when its famous film festival is not going on.**

Where is the Côte d'Azur?

In the south of France the summers are dry and hot, and there are usually many sunny winter days. The French call part of their Mediterranean coast the "sky-blue coast," or Côte d'Azur, for this reason.

Which European country has reclaimed nearly half its land from the sea?

The Netherlands. The name Netherlands means "low countries," and this part of Europe is very flat and low-lying. Sea walls called dykes hold back the sea. Pumps drain the flat land, and a network of canals carry the water away. Large areas of marsh have been reclaimed from the sea and turned into good farmland.

Which countries share the Iberian Peninsula?

Spain and Portugal. This square-shaped peninsula is in the southwest corner of Europe.

▲ The Netherlands is sometimes known as Holland. Its capital is Amsterdam.

Where is the Camargue?

The Camargue is the delta, or mouth, of the Rhône River in southeastern France. Formed by sedimentation, it is flat, lonely marshland, with numerous shallow lagoons. Rich in bird life, it was once known for its herds of horses and fighting bulls. Today farmers grow vines and rice there.

How many countries make up the British Isles?

Two: the United Kingdom and the Republic of Ireland. The United Kingdom consists of Great Britain (England, Wales, and Scotland) and Northern Ireland.

◀ This map shows the main natural features and cities of the United Kingdom. The capital is London.

Where does the Po River flow?

The Po flows in Italy, across the broad Lombardy plain south of the Alps. It is Italy's longest river.

Where are the Carpathian Mountains?

These mountains are in central Europe. They form part of the boundary between Slovakia and Poland, and extend into Romania. They are lower than the Alps, with a high point of 8,710 feet (2,655 m), and have fewer lakes, glaciers, and waterfalls. The Carpathians in Romania are said to be the home of the legendary Count Dracula!

Where is the land of a thousand lakes?

Finland, in northwest Europe, has about 60,000 lakes and thousands of offshore islands. Europe's biggest freshwater lake is not in Finland, however. It is Ladoga, in Russia.

Where is St. Petersburg?

This Russian city was made the capital of Russia by Emperor Peter the Great in 1712. In 1914 its name was changed to Petrograd and in 1924 it was renamed Leningrad, after the Soviet communist leader Lenin. It returned to its old name in 1991 after the fall of communism.

How long is Britain's longest river?

The rivers in Britain are not very long. The Severn, about 220 miles (350 km), is the longest. The Thames is slightly shorter, at 215 miles (346 km).

It takes eight days to cross Russia by train! As children go to school in Moscow (west), children in Vladivostok (east) are going home. Russia is so large it straddles both Europe and Asia.

EUROPE FACTS

■ Vatican City in Rome, Italy, is the smallest state in the world.

■ About one-eighth of the world's people live in Europe.

■ After Russia, Ukraine is Europe's largest country. Next comes France.

■ Europe takes its name from Europa, a princess in Ancient Greek mythology.

▶ Finland is a country in Scandinavia. Lapland is in the northern part of Finland.

Where are the Balkans?

The Balkans are a group of countries on the Balkan Peninsula in southeast Europe, including Albania, Greece, Macedonia, and Bulgaria. To the east of the Balkans is the Black Sea and to the south is the Mediterranean. There are several mountain ranges in the area.

Where is the Corinth Canal?

This canal connects the Gulf of Corinth in southern Greece with the Aegean Sea. It was opened in 1893 and is the deepest canal ever cut. Its walls are 1,505 feet (459 m) high.

◀ The Leaning Tower of Pisa is one of the world's curiosities. The problem facing engineers is how to keep it in one piece but still leaning!

What makes the Leaning Tower of Pisa lean?

The Leaning Tower is one of Italy's most remarkable landmarks. It is a marble bell tower built in Pisa between 1173 and the 1360s. Unfortunately, the builders chose ground that was too soft to carry such a weight, and the tower soon began to lean. It is already 16½ feet (5 m) out of vertical, despite efforts to hold it up, and engineers are considering new ways to stop it from falling.

What is Florence famous for?

Florence is a city in Italy with beautiful old buildings, paintings, and sculptures. It is a treasure-house of art and architecture. Tourists from all over the world come here to admire the art galleries, museums, and churches— including the Cathedral, known as the Duomo. Florence has a famous old bridge, the Ponte Vecchio, built across the Arno River in 1345.

Where is Venice?

Venice is an elegant city of islands and canals in Italy. It was once a rich city-state, whose rulers were known as *doges*. Venice is a unique city, where people travel by boat rather than by car, and is famous for its palaces and churches. Its annual carnival was at its grandest in the 1700s, and at carnival time people still dress up in costumes based on designs from that period. The city is endangered by seasonal floods which threaten its buildings and works of art.

▲ Michelangelo's statue of David is one of the many art treasures to be seen in Florence.

Why are houses in Amsterdam tall and narrow?

Amsterdam is a city in the Netherlands, also known as Holland. In the 1600s land for building was so scarce, and therefore prices so high, that merchants in the city built narrow but extremely tall houses— still a feature along the many canals of the attractive old city.

Where would you see stave churches?

In Norway. Stave churches are wooden churches, so-called because of the four wooden staves, or corner posts, around which they were built. Between 1000 and 1300, wooden stave churches were built all over Norway—not long after the Vikings who lived there were converted to Christianity.

◀ This stave church in Norway is almost 1,000 years old. It was built by Vikings.

AUSTRALASIA AND THE PACIFIC

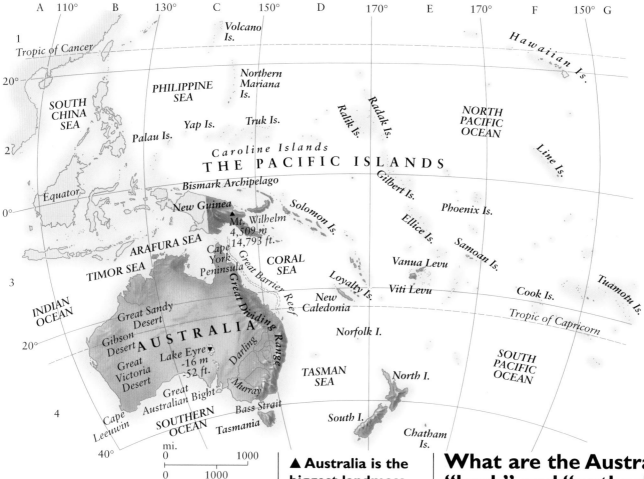

A 110°   B   130°   C   150°   D   170°   E   170°   F   150° G

1 Tropic of Cancer

Volcano Is.

Hawaiian Is.

20°

PHILIPPINE SEA

Northern Mariana Is.

SOUTH CHINA SEA

NORTH PACIFIC OCEAN

Yap Is.   Truk Is.

Ralik Is.

Radak Is.

Palau Is.

Line Is.

2   Caroline Islands
THE PACIFIC ISLANDS

Gilbert Is.

Equator

Bismark Archipelago

New Guinea

Solomon Is.

Phoenix Is.

0°

Mt. Wilhelm
4,509 m
14,793 ft.

Ellice Is.

Samoan Is.

ARAFURA SEA

Cape York Peninsula

CORAL SEA

Vanua Levu

TIMOR SEA

Great Barrier Reef

Loyalty Is.

Viti Levu

Cook Is.

Tuamotu Is.

3

New Caledonia

Great Dividing Range

INDIAN OCEAN

Tropic of Capricorn

Great Sandy Desert

Gibson Desert   AUSTRALIA

Norfolk I.

20°

Great Victoria Desert

Lake Eyre
-16 m
-52 ft.

Darling

SOUTH PACIFIC OCEAN

Murray

TASMAN SEA

North I.

Great Australian Bight

Bass Strait

4   Cape Leeuwin   SOUTHERN OCEAN   Tasmania

South I.

Chatham Is.

40°

mi.
0   1000
0   1000
km

Where is Australasia?

Australia, New Zealand, and neighboring islands in the Pacific Ocean make up Australasia. Papua New Guinea is also included. Australia is sometimes treated as a continent on its own because it is so big. The islands excluding Australia are called Oceania. The whole area covers vast parts of the Pacific Ocean, from the warm seas north of the Equator to the icy waters around Antarctica.

▲ Australia is the biggest landmass in the island region of the southern Pacific. There are thousands of other islands.

What are the Australian "bush" and "outback?"

Most Australians today live in towns and cities. They call the countryside the bush and the vast, near-empty interior of their country the outback. The outback has a few mining and farm settlements, but no large cities. Most outback farms are cattle or sheep ranches, called "stations." Some are huge, covering more than 965 square miles (2,500 sq km)—bigger than a city the size of New York or London. Ranchers use trucks and helicopters and keep in touch with the outside world by radio.

Where is Tasmania?

Tasmania is an island about 125 miles (200 km) off the coast of southern Australia. The Bass Strait separates the island from the mainland. Tasmania was part of the mainland until about 12,000 years ago. It became an island when the sea rose, filling what is now the Bass Strait.

Which lake in Australia disappears?

A map of Australia shows Lake Eyre, an apparently large lake in South Australia. Yet most years the lake is dry. It fills with water only after unusually heavy rains. Most of the time it is a bed of salt. The salt forms a crust over 13 feet (4 m) thick.

The prickly-pear cactus, introduced to Australia, escaped from gardens and spread over thousands of miles. The caterpillars of the Cactoblastis moth finally destroyed it.

▶ **The bed of Lake Eyre is a thick coating of salt. The salt forms lumps and patterns on the surface of the lake, which is usually dry.**

Which is Australia's longest river?

The Murray (1,610 miles [2,589 km]) is Australia's longest permanently flowing river. The Darling is 1,700 miles (2,740 km), but much of it is dry in the winter. Early explorers had hoped to find greater rivers flowing from the vast heart of the country.

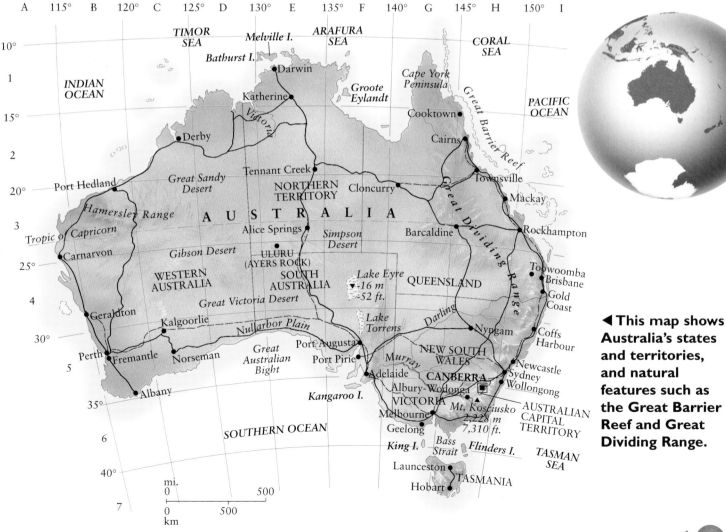

◀ **This map shows Australia's states and territories, and natural features such as the Great Barrier Reef and Great Dividing Range.**

After whom is Sydney, Australia, named?

In 1778 a party of British sailors and convicts landed in a bay in south Australia. They named it after Viscount Sydney, a British government minister. Sydney is now the largest city in Australia, and the harbor is famous for its bridge and opera house (an arts center).

Are there winter sports in Australia?

Mount Kosciusko in southeast Australia is the highest mountain of the country. It is a peak in the Snowy Mountains range in the Australian Alps and is 7,310 feet (2,228 m) high. In winter it is snow-covered and good for skiing.

Where are the Sutherland Falls?

The Sutherland Falls is one of New Zealand's many impressive waterfalls. Water plunges 190 feet (580 m) down a mountain near Milford Sound on South Island. The falls are the fifth highest in the world.

▲ The kiwi is an unusual bird of New Zealand. Kiwis live in burrows, coming out at night to look for grubs and worms to eat.

UNCHARTED TERRITORY

Even though Australia was not known in the Western world, it did exist in old myths. Terra Australis even appeared on early maps as a large round mass long before any European had seen it.

◄ Although much of Australia is too warm for snow, Mount Feathertop, one of the peaks running south from the Great Dividing Range, is high enough for snow.

▶ A waterfall in Milford Sound, a sea inlet on the west coast of South Island, New Zealand.

Where are people called "Kiwis?"

New Zealanders are often referred to as "Kiwis." The kiwi, a flightless bird, has become one of New Zealand's national emblems. New Zealand's wildlife includes a number of plants and animals found nowhere else in the world. It has some of the oldest plant forms known.

Which country has more sheep than people?

One of New Zealand's most important industries is sheep farming. There are about 71 million sheep in New Zealand—that's over 20 times the number of people. Australia has even more sheep, about 135 million, compared to over 17 million people. The wool industry in Australia was started in the late 1700s when settlers from Britain introduced merinos (a breed of sheep with fine wool).

Where in New Zealand do rocks produce steam?

The North Island of New Zealand is a region of volcanic rocks. Heat from deep beneath the Earth warms underground water, which forces its way to the surface as geysers, jets of steam, and bubbling hot springs.

Why are some Pacific islands high, and others very low?

The high islands of the Pacific (such as Fiji) were made by volcanic activity on the ocean floor, which pushed up mountains. The low islands, such as Tuvalu, are coral reefs and atolls. Most are small, and some are so low that flood waves easily sweep over them.

◀ A geyser near Rotorua in New Zealand gushes steam and spray. Volcanic energy produces these hot waterspouts.

AUSTRALASIA FACTS
■ Area: 3,285,700 sq. mi. (8,510,000 sq km).
■ Population: 29,000,000.
■ Number of countries: 11.
■ Longest river: Murray (Australia), 1,610 mi. (2,589 km).
■ Largest lake: Lake Eyre (Australia), 3,700 sq. mi. (9,583 sq km).
■ Highest mountain: Mount Wilhelm (Papua New Guinea), 14,793 ft. (4,509 m) above sea level.
■ Largest country: Australia.
■ Country with most people: Australia (over 17 million).
■ Largest city: Sydney.
■ Many marsupials live in Australia. The best known of these pouched animals is the kangaroo.
■ Bats were the only mammals to reach New Zealand before people introduced domestic animals.

◀ In the warm, clear waters around the Pacific islands, coral reefs thrive. Many fish and plants live on or around the coral where there is safety and plenty of food to eat.

Where is Oceania?

Oceania is the name given to the thousands of islands scattered across the Pacific Ocean. Not all Pacific islands are part of Oceania. Indonesia, the Philippines, and Japan are part of Asia. Australia is either treated as a separate continent or grouped with nearby islands of Oceania under the name Australasia.

Which is the largest Pacific island?

New Guinea is the largest island in the Pacific and the third largest island in the world, with an area of 300,000 square miles (777,000 sq km). New Guinea and New Zealand together make up more than 80 percent of all the land in the Pacific islands. Many other Pacific islands are tiny.

▼ Islands of Palau in Micronesia, seen from the air. There are thousands of islands scattered across the ocean.

How many islands are there in the Pacific?

No one knows exactly how many islands there are in the Pacific Ocean. There may be as many as 30,000. Some are tiny islets or coral atolls just high enough to break above water.

Where is Polynesia?

The islands of the Pacific form three main groups. These are Melanesia in the southwest Pacific; Micronesia in the northeast Pacific; and Polynesia in the central and south Pacific. Polynesia means "many islands" and this group is the largest. The distance across Polynesia from Midway Island in the north to New Zealand in the south is over 5,000 miles (8,000 km).

Where do people throw boomerangs?

The boomerang is a wooden throwing stick used mainly by the Aborigines, the native people of Australia. Some boomerangs are shaped in a special way so that they return to the thrower. Others are made to stun or kill an animal being hunted for food.

What is mysterious about Easter Island?

Easter Island is an island in the Pacific Ocean, 2,200 miles (3,540 km) west of Chile. It is famous for very large stone statues of people. These huge carvings were made with stone axes by people who once lived on Easter Island but then moved away. Exactly why the statues were set up remains something of a mystery. The statues were probably made after A.D. 400 by people who came either from South America or Polynesia by boat. In the 1700s, following a war on the island, many statues were broken.

▶ One of the mysterious huge stone heads found on Easter Island. Some 600 statues like this were carved from volcanic rock.

Polynesian sailors explored the vast South Pacific Ocean in wooden canoes. The ancestors of the Maoris reached New Zealand by canoe about 1,000 years ago.

▲ A shield and boomerang made by Aborigines, the first inhabitants of Australia.

Where do people in neighboring villages speak different languages?

Papua New Guinea is a land of many languages. Most of the people live in small villages, deep in the forest or high up in the mountains. Some remote villages are so cut off from each other that their languages are quite different. People need a translator to speak to their neighbors on the other side of the mountain!

How do South Sea Islanders live?

The Pacific islands are small and isolated, and people depend mostly on farming, mining, and tourism. Islanders have traditionally lived from the sea, by fishing and trading.

Where are the Friendly Islands?

Tonga, an island kingdom in Polynesia, was given this name by the British explorer Captain James Cook. He landed there in 1773 and received a warm welcome.

What is pidgin English?

English is widely spoken throughout the Pacific, though French is used on some islands. In Melanesia, many people speak pidgin, a mixture of English and local words.

Which Pacific island group is part of the United States?

Hawaii. It was taken over by the United States in 1898 and became a state in 1959. Two of the volcanoes on Hawaii are still active.

GOVERNMENT

What is the United Nations?

The United Nations Organization, usually called the UN, is a group of many countries that joined together in 1945 to try to encourage peace in the world. The UN has 184 member countries, and its headquarters are in New York. The UN sometimes sends special forces to try to settle quarrels between countries. There are also several UN agencies, or international organizations, that deal with international social and economic problems around the world.

What is the Commonwealth?

When people talk about the Commonwealth, they usually mean the British Commonwealth of Nations. This is an association of nations that were once part of the British Empire. The British monarch is head of the Commonwealth, but the member countries are independent and govern themselves.

What is a republic?

A republic is a country in which the electorate (people allowed to vote) have the power to govern the country. The country is ruled by elected leaders. The head of a republic is usually called the president.

▶ **The flag of the United States has stars for each state and 13 stripes (for the original 13 British colonies).**

▲ **Canadian troops arrive as UN peacekeepers in Sarajevo, one of the war-torn cities of the former Yugoslavia.**

How many states are there in the United States?

The United States of America is a federal republic consisting of fifty states. Most of the states are next to each other in North America, but Alaska is separated from the rest by Canada, and Hawaii is an island group in the Pacific Ocean. The American flag has fifty stars on it. Each star represents one state.

What does an ambassador do?

An ambassador is a person chosen by a country to represent it in another country. The ambassador lives in an embassy. He talks to the rulers and other important people in the country on behalf of the government of his own country.

What is a dictator?

A dictator is a ruler of a country who has total power over its people. In a country ruled by a dictator, called a dictatorship, there is usually only one official political party and no opposition is allowed. A dictatorship is often ruled by the army.

What is the European Union?

An organization of a number of European countries. The Union began in 1957 as the European Economic Community, also known as the Common Market. Its members seek to trade more freely with one another, and the Union also has a joint European Parliament and a Court. There are plans for a common currency, too.

▲ Colonel Muammar Gadaffi has led Libya since 1969, as all-powerful president.

▼ Expensive stores like Tiffany's in New York City attract rich customers.

Which countries belong to the European Union?

There are 15 members of the European Union. They are (with the dates they joined): Germany, France, Italy, Belgium, Netherlands, Luxembourg (all 1957); United Kingdom, Ireland, Denmark (all 1973); Greece (1981); Spain (1986); Portugal (1987); Austria, Sweden, and Finland (all 1995).

What is GNP?

GNP stands for Gross National Product. This means the amount of money a country earns in a year, minus its outgoings—such as imports and foreign debts. Divide by population to find the per capita (per head) figure.

◄ Early designs for coins and travellers' checks for the new money system proposed for the European Union.

Are people getting richer?

Some are, some aren't. Taking the world as a whole, average income per person has doubled since 1950. But while an American is three times richer today than in 1950, a person living in Ethiopia is no better off. The world's wealth is unfairly shared.

Which country has the most gold?

The United States has about a quarter of the world's gold reserves. These are stored in gold bars at the U.S. Army base at Fort Knox in Kentucky under tight security.

Which is the richest country?

In terms of GNP per capita (per head), the answer is Switzerland, with a figure of $35,000. The poorest country is probably Mozambique where per capita GNP is less than $100.

Which is the world's biggest bank?

The World Bank, or the International Bank of Reconstruction and Development. It was founded in 1945. The Bank is an agency of the United Nations and lends money to countries for essential projects such as irrigation schemes to provide water for drinking and farm crops.

◀ **Gold ingots (bars) are kept in strongrooms under guard. Gold has been highly valued since ancient times and is still used as a measure of wealth.**

Every country has a national anthem. This is a special song which is sung to show respect for a country and its history.

DID YOU KNOW?

■ Many countries besides the U.S. use the name "dollar" for their money.

■ But only Japan uses the *yen*. And only Poland uses the *zloty*.

■ The Chinese were the first to use paper money, in the A.D. 800s.

■ In Brazil, the richest 20 percent of the population earn 28 times more than the poorest 20 percent.

■ There are more than 170 self-governing countries.

■ There are about 60 colonies or other small territories ruled by larger nations.

■ The Ancient Greeks were the first people to experiment with democracy, or rule by the people.

What is communism?

A system of government and economics based on the ideas of Karl Marx (1818–1883), a German philosopher. The central idea of communism is that the government should run most businesses and own property for the good of all the people. In practice, communist states have usually been undem8cratic and badly managed, and by the 1990s only China, among the major nations, had a communist government.

What is federalism?

A union of self-governing states who agree to accept a single central government's rule in certain matters. Such a union is also known as a federation. Countries with federal systems of government include the United States, Canada, Australia, and Switzerland.

Which is the world's biggest democracy?

India, which has more than 500 million electors. The 1996 elections in India were the largest ever held in a democratic country.

Which country elects its king?

Malaysia. The king of Malaysia is the only elected monarch in the world. Other countries have kings, queens, sultans, sheikhs, or other rulers who hold the title through succession— which means each new ruler is a relative of the previous one. The eldest child of a hereditary ruler usually succeeds, but it can be the eldest son who takes over.

RELIGION AND CUSTOMS

Which Christian religion has the most followers?

The Roman Catholic Church has more followers than any other Christian religion in the world. Roman Catholics believe that the Pope is the successor of St. Peter, the apostle appointed by Jesus Christ to be head of the Church. The center of the Roman Catholic Church is Vatican City, in Rome, Italy. The Pope governs the Church from there.

▲ **Vatican City-State in Rome is the center of government of the Roman Catholic Church. It includes the great domed church of St. Peter.**

◀ **Siva is an important god in Hinduism. Hindus believe Siva is both creator and destroyer. Statues of the Buddha, founder of Buddhism, can be seen in many countries of Asia.**

Siva

The Buddha

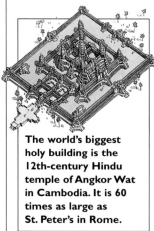

The world's biggest holy building is the 12th-century Hindu temple of Angkor Wat in Cambodia. It is 60 times as large as St. Peter's in Rome.

Which religions teach that people return to Earth after death?

Some religions teach that, after death, the soul or spirit of a human being enters another body, either human or animal. This belief is called reincarnation. Buddhists and Hindus, who live mainly in India, believe that their behavior in this life decides in what form they will be reborn. Some people believe that a person may be reborn many times until the soul is ready to enter heaven.

Which religion follows the teachings of the Koran?

The Koran is the holy book of Islam. In Islam, there is one god called Allah, and the Koran is believed to be the word of Allah which was revealed to Muhammad by the Angel Gabriel. Followers of Islam are known as Muslims. At least a million Muslims travel as pilgrims to the holy city of Mecca every year. This city in Saudi Arabia was the birthplace of Muhammad, and all Muslims try to go there once in their lives.

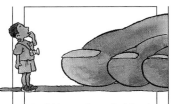

Who was Buddha?

Buddha, or "the enlightened one," is the title given to Siddhartha Gautama, an Indian holy man who lived in the 500s B.C. Buddha is believed to have sat under a tree called the Bo-Tree and come to understand the cause and cure of suffering. The followers of Buddha are called Buddhists. They live mainly in Southeast Asia, China, and Japan.

In 803, workers finished carving a statue of Buddha in cliffs near Leshan, in China. The statue is so big that two people can sit on one of its toenails!

Who is the head of the Church of England?

The king or queen of Great Britain is head of the Church of England (associated with the Episcopal Church). When Henry VIII quarreled with the Pope, he declared that the sovereign was head of the English Church, and this was later established by law.

BELIEF FACTS

■ The Jews were the first people to believe in one god, whom they called Yahweh.

■ Taoism, an ancient religion of China, has many gods. Some are famous people, others are ancestors.

■ Hindus celebrate a lively spring festival called Holi. People light bonfires and throw colored powder at one another.

■ Christmas trees are a reminder of old midwinter festivals, which have become part of Christmas.

What is a rabbi?

A rabbi is a specially ordained official who decides upon questions of law and ceremony in the Jewish religion, or Judaism. The rabbi performs marriages and other ceremonies and is similar to a priest.

▶ At Carnival time in Rio de Janeiro, Brazil, people in amazing costumes parade through the streets.

◀ Before his bar mitzvah, a Jewish boy receives instruction from a rabbi. The bar mitzvah marks acceptance into adulthood.

Why do people celebrate Halloween?

Halloween, on October 31st, is when children in the United States and some other countries dress up as witches, ghosts, skeletons, and scary monsters. Halloween comes from an old pagan festival that later became the Christian festival of All Saints' Day on November 1st. The religious mass (service) held on that day was called Allhallowmass and the evening before came to be known as Allhalloween. All Saints' Day is still a religious feast day in many Christian countries.

Why do people parade at Carnival time?

Carnival, or Mardi Gras, marks the start of Lent, a period of fasting for many Christians when they try to give up something (such as eating chocolate). In the past, Carnival was a celebration feast when people ate their last meal with meat before the solemn time of Lent began. Today people in bright costumes fill the streets for Carnival parades.

Why do we eat Easter eggs?

The eggs Christians exchange at Easter represent the renewal of life. Easter was originally a pagan spring festival, to celebrate the end of winter. Christians took it over and associated Easter with the resurrection, or rising from the dead, of Jesus Christ.

French children enjoy a special dinner on January 6th. Three kings from the East are said to have visited the baby Jesus on that day.

◀ **On Good Friday, Christians remember the death of Jesus on the cross. People in Ecuador parade a tableau of the event.**

▼ **Chinese people dance in dragon costumes to celebrate their New Year.**

What are saints' days?

In the Christian calendar some days are associated with saints. Examples are days named for patron saints of a country, such as St. Patrick's Day (Ireland) or St. David's Day (Wales).

What is Yom Kippur?

This is a Jewish festival. It is a day when people fast and express their regret for faults in their lives. It is also known as the Day of Atonement.

Which religion celebrates Diwali?

Hinduism. The festival of Diwali is a happy occasion when people enjoy parties, light candles, and give one another presents. It is a New Year festival dedicated to the god Vishnu and the goddess Lakshmi.

Who name their years after animals?

The Chinese New Year starts in January or February. In the Chinese calendar, which according to tradition begins in 2637 B.C., the years run in cycles of 60 and are named for 12 animals. 1997 was the year of the Ox, for example. The sequence continues as follows: Tiger, Hare (Rabbit), Dragon, Snake, Horse, Sheep (Goat), Monkey, Rooster, Dog, Pig, Rat.

▲ Muslims pray every day, often five times a day, turning to face toward Mecca as they do so.

What is Ramadan?

The month of fasting for Muslims. The end of Ramadan is marked by a holiday called the Eid, when people go to the mosque to perform special prayers of thanksgiving and entertain friends and family with enormous meals in their homes.

Why do Americans have parties on the Fourth of July?

Every July 4th, Americans celebrate Independence Day. All over the United States, people enjoy parades, picnics, pageants, and fireworks to mark the anniversary of the founding of the United States. Americans living abroad join in the celebrations.

What is Thanksgiving?

Thanksgiving Day is a national holiday in the United States and Canada. The first Thanksgiving was in 1621, when the Pilgrims in Plymouth Colony gave thanks to God for their first harvest. It is a time for family get-togethers and good food.

FURTHER FACTS

■ Since 1941, Thanksgiving Day has been on the fourth Thursday in November.

■ Easter is more important than Christmas to Christians in the Orthodox Churches.

■ December 26th is a holiday in some countries. It was traditionally a day for giving gifts, and so in Britain is called Boxing Day.

■ Scots celebrate Hogmanay on New Year's Eve, December 31st.

■ In many countries April Fool's Day, April 1st, is a day for playing jokes on one another.

■ St. Valentine's Day, February 14th, is a bonanza for the greeting card industry!

When is Bastille Day?

On July 14th, a special day for the people of France. French people celebrate Bastille Day in memory of an event during the French Revolution in 1789 when crowds stormed the Bastille prison in Paris. The prison was a hated symbol of the old, harsh government. Bastille Day is nowadays marked by a large military parade in Paris.

Is Buddha's birthday a festival?

In Japan, the Flower Festival is a colorful festival to mark the birth of Buddha. In Sri Lanka and Thailand, Buddhists celebrate Wesak or Vesakha-puja, a feast that marks not only Buddha's birth but also his enlightenment and death. Buddhism has largely disappeared from its country of origin, India.

▲ Japanese people celebrate Buddha's birthday with flowers.

PEOPLES AND COUNTRIES QUIZ

Which valley created some of Africa's greatest lakes? *(page 202)*

Which is Africa's highest mountain? *(page 203)*

What is the African name for the Victoria Falls? *(page 204)*

Where do Bushmen, or San, people live? *(page 205)*

What were the Benin people famous for? *(page 206)*

In which country is Africa's biggest city? *(page 207)*

What are the Huang He and Chang Jiang? *(page 208)*

In which country is the Tonlé Sap Lake? *(page 209)*

In which ocean are the Maldive Islands? *(page 211)*

Which king built the Temple in Jerusalem? *(page 212)*

Why are the United Arab Emirates so rich? *(page 213)*

Which is the longest structure ever built? *(page 214)*

Which city's name means "city of the lions"? *(page 215)*

Which is the biggest city in the United States? *(page 217)*

In which U.S. state is Death Valley? *(page 218)*

What year was the St. Lawrence Seaway opened? *(page 219)*

Whose faces are carved into Mount Rushmore? *(page 220)*

What craft are the Navajo people famous for? *(page 221)*

In which city is the Sears Tower? *(page 222)*

Why do Mexicans make papier-mâché skeletons? *(page 223)*

Who were the first South Americans? *(page 224)*

In which South American country is Patagonia? *(page 225)*

What are the Llanos and Pampas? *(page 226)*

Which South American country produces the most oil? *(page 227)*

Where is Rio de Janeiro? *(page 228)*

Who built Machu Picchu? *(page 229)*

Into which sea does the Volga River flow? *(page 230)*

What animals do the Lapps herd? *(page 231)*

Which is Britain's highest mountain? *(page 232)*

What does the name Netherlands mean? *(page 233)*

Which European city was once called Leningrad? *(page 234)*

Where is the famous bridge called the Ponte Vecchio? *(page 235)*

What is a "station" in the outback of Australia? *(page 236)*

What would you taste if you licked Lake Eyre? *(page 237)*

Which bird has become an emblem of New Zealand? *(page 238)*

Which is the third largest island in the world? *(page 239)*

What were boomerangs used for? *(page 240)*

Why are there 13 stripes on the U.S. flag? *(page 241)*

What is stored at Fort Knox? *(page 243)*

In which country is the Vatican? *(page 244)*

What is the date of Halloween? *(page 245)*

Who is the patron saint of Ireland? (page 246)

In which month do the French celebrate Bastille Day? *(page 247)*

FIRSTS

When was the first voyage around the world?

In 1519 five ships left Spain. Three years later, one returned. It had sailed around the world. The leader of the historic expedition was Ferdinand Magellan (1480–1521), a Portuguese sailor. Like most of his seamen, he did not live to see its end. After crossing the Pacific, he was killed in a fight with local people in the Philippines.

Which European sailor first reached India?

In 1498 a Portuguese named Vasco da Gama arrived in India. Guided by an Arab sea captain, he was the first European seaman to land there.

Where was the Northwest Passage?

By the 1500s many people guessed that the world was round. By sailing west, across the Atlantic Ocean, a ship ought to be able to reach Asia. Even after the Americas were discovered, many tried to find the Northwest Passage. Finally, in 1906, a Norwegian ship commanded by Roald Amundsen (1872–1928) made the journey, from east to west, north of Canada.

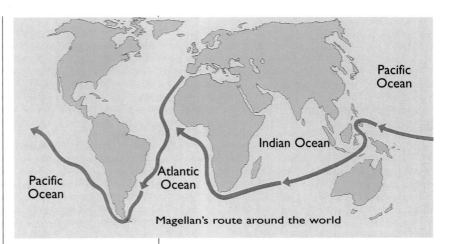

Pacific Ocean

Indian Ocean

Atlantic Ocean

Pacific Ocean

Magellan's route around the world

▲ A map of Magellan's historic voyage. His ships sailed around the tip of South America and across the Pacific Ocean. The survivors finally crossed the Indian Ocean on their way home.

We can't flap our arms fast enough to fly like birds. Our arm muscles are too weak. But people tried in vain to copy birds in the days before planes were invented!

Who made the first powered flight?

A balloon can fly only where the wind takes it. In 1852 a French aviator tried fitting an engine to a balloon. The aviator's name was Henri Giffard (1825–1882). His "airship" was a cigar-shaped balloon filled with hydrogen gas. It was powered by a small steam engine.

Who built the first successful airplane?

In the late 1800s many inventors tried to build a machine with wings and propellers that would fly under its own power. Pioneer fliers such as Otto Lilienthal (1848–1896) of Germany proved that a glider would carry a person into the air. Orville and Wilbur Wright built their own gliders, then added a homemade engine. In 1903 they made the first controlled flights in a heavier-than-air machine.

◄ The Wright brothers built their *Flyer* airplane themselves. It flew for just 12 seconds on its first flight.

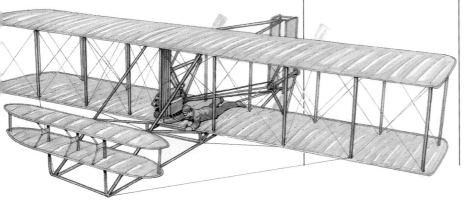

Who first flew from France to England?

In 1909 Louis Blériot (1872–1936), a French pilot, landed his airplane near Dover. He had made the first ever flight from France to England. Without a map or compass, Blériot got lost in a mist. His engine overheated, but a rain shower cooled it, and also cleared the mist. Spotting the Dover cliffs below, Blériot flew down to make a very bumpy landing after his 37-minute flight.

Who first used an aqualung?

Jacques Cousteau (1910–1997), a French naval officer, wanted to be able to swim freely under water. To do this, he and his team invented the aqualung. The diver carried air-tanks on his back, and swam with flippers on his feet. Cousteau proved that people could explore and even work under the sea.

Who were the first people to leave the Earth?

The first person to fly into space was the Russian Yuri Gagarin in 1961. In 1968 three U.S. astronauts flew around the Moon in *Apollo 8*. They were the first to escape from Earth's gravity.

▲ **Louis Blériot flew across the English Channel in a plane that he had designed and built. His flight made him famous in Britain and France.**

In 1958 the USS *Nautilus*, the first nuclear-powered submarine, sailed from the Bering Strait to Iceland, crossing directly under the North Pole. The journey took four days.

▶ **The first team of explorers to reach the South Pole was led by the Norwegian Roald Amundsen. Using huskies to pull their sleds, they reached the South Pole in Dec 1911.**

◀ **Russian cosmonaut Yuri Gagarin flew once around the Earth inside this *Vostok* spacecraft.**

Who first reached the North Pole?

The American explorers Frederick Cook and Robert Peary both claimed to have reached the North Pole—the first in 1908 and the second a year later. However, it is possible that their claims are not true and that they turned back before getting to the Pole. The first person definitely to reach the North Pole was the American explorer Richard Byrd, who, with his co-pilot Floyd Bennett, flew over the Pole in an airplane on May 9, 1926. The first explorer definitely to travel over the ice to the North Pole was the American explorer Ralph Plaisted. He arrived there on April 19, 1968.

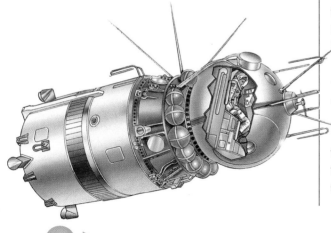

Who were the first people to cross Australia?

The center of Australia is desert, and it is dangerous to cross it overland. The first to make the journey, from south to north, were Robert Burke, William Wills, Charles Gray, and John King in 1860 and 1861. On the return journey, the explorers suffered hunger, thirst, exhaustion, and

sickness. They failed to make contact with other members of the exhibition and Gray, Burke, and Wills died. King lived with Aborigines and was rescued.

Who first swam the English Channel?

A British sea captain, Matthew Webb (1843–1883), first swam across the Channel from England to France, a distance of 21 miles (34 km) in a straight line. His swim, in 1875, took 21¾ hours.

▶ **New Zealander Edmund Hillary and Nepali Tenzing Norgay were the first to climb Everest, or *Chomo-Lungma* as the Tibetans call Everest.**

EXPLORING FIRSTS

■ Roald Amundsen of Norway led the first expedition to reach the South Pole in 1911.

■ In 1993 Erling Kagge of Norway walked alone to the South Pole.

■ From 1979 to 1982 explorers traveled to the South Pole, the North Pole and back to London —34,700 mi. (56,000 km).

■ The longest recorded swim was 1,825 mi. (2,938 km) down the Mississippi River in 1930.

■ The first European sailor to see the Indian Ocean was Bartholomeu Diaz of Portugal, who in 1487 sailed to the southern tip of Africa.

■ Around A.D. 800 the Maoris sailed in canoes across the Pacific from Polynesia to New Zealand.

◀ **The explorers crossing Australia used camels. These desert animals could survive in the hot, dry conditions of the Australian interior.**

Who first flew nonstop across the Atlantic Ocean?

Two British pilots, John Alcock (1892–1919) and Arthur Brown (1886–1948), made the first nonstop flight across the Atlantic Ocean in 1919. It lasted nearly 16½ hours, and Brown had to crawl out onto the wings of the airplane to remove ice that was forming there. The American pilot Charles Lindbergh (1902–1974) made the first solo crossing, in 1927.

Who first sailed around the world alone?

An American sailor, Captain Joshua Slocum (1844–*c*.1910), made the first solo voyage around the world in a small sailing boat called *Spray*. It took three years and two months, from 1895 to 1898.

Who first climbed Mount Everest?

Many people had tried and failed to climb the world's highest mountain before 1953. Two members of a British Commonwealth expedition reached the top on May 29, 1953.

EXPLORERS

Who discovered the Americas, but thought it was Asia?

The first European explorer known to have reached the Americas was Christopher Columbus, who was born in Italy but explored for the Spanish. He sailed from Spain to the Bahama Islands, off the coast of North America in 1492. Columbus was trying to find a new route to India or the Indies (then a name for the East), and thought he had arrived there. He therefore called the people he found there "Indians."

Who sailed across the Pacific on a raft?

In 1947, a team of scientists led by the Norwegian Thor Heyerdahl (born 1914) sailed across the Pacific Ocean on a raft called the *Kon-Tiki*. The raft was of an ancient design, and the trip showed that the people of the South Sea Islands could have gotten there by raft from South America.

Who are the Americas named after?

The Americas are named after the Italian explorer Amerigo Vespucci (1451–1512). Vespucci explored South America after Columbus reached the Americas. Vespucci believed that a new land had been discovered, and it was named "America" after him. The name was given to the two new continents— North and South America.

Christopher Columbus

▲ **Columbus set out with three small ships across the Atlantic. The journey to the New World took 30 days.**

In Columbus's time, many people believed the world was flat. They feared that he and his ships would sail too far west and fall over the edge!

▶ **Marco Polo followed the ancient trade routes across Asia to China. Travelers rode horses and camels over mountains and deserts.**

Where did Marco Polo travel?

Marco Polo (1254–1324) and his family were the greatest European travelers of the Middle Ages. Marco was born in Venice, Italy. His father and uncle were traders and had visited China, where they met the Emperor Kublai Khan. In 1271, they set off again with Marco. The travelers did not return until 1295. During all this time, they traveled throughout China and southern Asia. They were amazed by the sights they saw.

Who named a huge country after a village?

This was the French explorer Jacques Cartier (1491–1557) and the country is Canada. Although he was not the first European to reach Canada, Cartier was the first to explore much of it. From 1534 onward, he made three voyages to Canada. He tried to find out what the Native American name for the country was. However, the people he asked thought he was inquiring about their village. So they said "*kanada*," which meant "village."

▶ James Cook visited Pacific islands where local people came out to meet his ship in huge canoes.

▼ The Aztecs of Mexico thought Cortés was a pale-skinned god and welcomed him with gifts.

Who first explored the South Seas?

The South Seas are the southern part of the Pacific Ocean, and are dotted with many tropical islands. This part of the world was first thoroughly explored by Captain James Cook (1728–1779), a British explorer who made three voyages there between 1768 and 1779. He also explored Australia and New Zealand, and he realized that a great unknown continent (Antarctica) must exist to the south, though he never reached it. Cook was a great explorer. He made maps of the coastlines he sailed along, and on his ships were artists who drew the people, animals, and plants they saw. On his third voyage, Cook was murdered by islanders in Hawaii.

Who were the conquistadors?

The conquistadors were the Spanish invaders who conquered the Indian civilizations in Central and South America in the 1500s. *Conquistador* is the Spanish word for "conqueror." The conquistadors sought the gold treasures made by the Indians but destroyed their civilizations. The best known of the conquistadors are Hernando Cortés, who plundered Mexico, and Francisco Pizarro, who destroyed the Inca Empire of Peru. The invaders ruined the way of life of the peoples they conquered.

DID YOU KNOW?

■ Magellan had 277 men under his command when he set sail in 1519.

■ One ship and 19 men returned home in 1522 after the historic around-the-world voyage.

■ The first European to see the Pacific Ocean was the Spaniard Vasco Nuñez de Balboa.

■ In 1513 Balboa crossed Panama from the Atlantic coast and saw the Pacific.

■ Europeans had been to North America before Columbus. In A.D. 1000, the Viking Leif Ericsson sailed from Greenland to Newfoundland.

Who was Abel Tasman?

In 1642 sailors on board a Dutch ship sighted New Zealand. The ship's captain was Abel Janszoon Tasman (1603?–1659), the first European explorer to reach New Zealand and the island of Tasmania (named after him). Tasman was searching for an unknown "south land." He actually sailed around Australia without realizing it, and thought neither New Zealand nor Tasmania worth further voyages.

Who was Ibn Battuta?

Ibn Battuta was a great Arab traveler. During the 1300s, he visited many lands. He was shipwrecked, crossed the Sahara, and was entertained by kings and princes. He visited Egypt, Africa, Persia (Iran), India, Russia, Mongolia, and China. He went wherever there were fellow Muslims, including Spain (then partly under Moorish rule). Ibn Battuta was a scholar, curious always to see new sights, and his travels lasted 30 years.

Who first explored Louisiana?

In the 1500s and 1600s, French explorers in North America opened up routes westward and south, into what is now the United States. Robert de la Salle (1643–1687) explored the Great Lakes by boat, and in 1682 he sailed down the Mississippi River to claim Louisiana for the French king, Louis XIV.

When did the Vikings reach North America?

North America was probably first sighted in about A.D. 986 by a Viking named Bjarni Herjolfsson, but the

Ibn Battuta was so famous that he was welcomed everywhere he went. He wrote a best-selling book about his journeys to many lands.

► A cathedral window shows David Livingstone, explorer and fighter against slavery in central Africa.

▼ The Vikings who landed in Vinland ("Vineland") hoped it would be a good place to settle and build new homes.

first visit was by Leif Ericsson in A.D. 1000. Leif reached the coast of Labrador and cruised south until he came to a land where wild grapes grew. He called it Vinland, after these vines. Vikings who tried to settle were driven out by Native Americans.

Where did Jedediah Smith explore?

In the early days of the American West, fur trader Jedediah Smith (1799–1831) made long trips into the wilderness.

Smith followed Native American trails from the Great Salt Lake west to the Rocky Mountains and on to California.

Who was David Livingstone?

In the 1800s Africa was still largely unexplored by Europeans. A Scottish missionary named David Livingstone (1813–1873) was a great African explorer. He also did much to end the evil slave trade. In 1866 Livingstone set off to search for the source of the Nile. Nothing was heard of him until 1871, when an expedition led by Henry Morton Stanley (1841–1904) found him near Lake Tanganyika. Though ill, Livingstone explored until the end of his life.

Who was Alexander von Humboldt?

Humboldt (1769–1859) was a German traveler and scientist, whose work was an example to other geographers. He trained as an engineer, but in 1799 he went off to South America. With him went his friend, the French botanist (plant expert) Aimé Bonpland (1773–1858). Humboldt and Bonpland hacked their way through the Amazon jungle and climbed the Andes Mountains.

Where did Lewis and Clark explore?

Two U.S. Army officers, Meriwether Lewis and William Clark, made a pioneer mapmaking journey across North America from 1804 to 1806. They led an expedition from St. Louis up the Missouri River and across the Rocky Mountains. They then explored the Columbia River westward to the Pacific Ocean, before returning to the East. Lewis and Clark mapped much new territory in the West, blazing trails for future settlers who went to California and other western territories.

▶ The bathyscaphe *Trieste* made its recordbreaking dive in 1960 with two people aboard. They rode in the cabin beneath the huge float.

DID YOU KNOW?

■ Marco Polo was only 17 when he made the long, difficult journey from Europe to China.

■ Livingstone was the first European to see the Victoria Falls in Africa.

■ Livingstone and other explorers searched for the source of the Nile River.

■ In 1863 John Hanning Speke proved that the river's source was Lake Victoria.

■ The farthest any explorers have traveled is to the Moon. The first to land on the moon were U.S. astronauts Neil Armstrong and Edwin Aldrin in 1969.

■ The first Europeans to reach the Rocky Mountains were probably two French brothers, the Vérendryes, in the 1740s.

■ The name Sacagawea means "Bird Woman." Sacagawea was captured as a young girl and sold to a fur trader, later employed by Lewis and Clark.

Where did Jacques Piccard explore?

Jacques Piccard (born 1922), a Swiss scientist, dived into the deepest part of the Pacific Ocean. He used a special diving craft known as a bathyscaphe, and with a U.S. Navy officer, Don Walsh, made a record-breaking descent of 35,800 feet (10,900 m) into the Mariana Trench, the deepest valley on the ocean floor.

Who first crossed Antarctica?

In 1957 and 1958, an expedition crossed Antarctica using snow tractors instead of dog sleds as earlier explorers had. The expedition was led by a British scientist, Sir Vivien Fuchs (born 1908), and the journey took 99 days.

◀ Meriwether Lewis and William Clark were helped by a Shoshoni named Sacagawea. She acted as interpreter whenever they met other Native Americans.

RULERS AND LEADERS

Who was Julius Caesar?

Gaius Julius Caesar (100–44 B.C.) was a brilliant Roman general and writer who became the ruler of Rome. Caesar was a member of an aristocratic Roman family. He became joint ruler of Rome, and won greater fame by his success as a soldier. He conquered Gaul (France) and twice landed in Britain.

In 49 B.C. Caesar returned to Rome and made himself dictator. He campaigned in Egypt, where he fell in love with its queen, Cleopatra. Although he ruled Rome wisely, he had enemies who were jealous of his success. In 44 B.C. they assassinated him, claiming that he planned to make himself king of Rome.

▲ Boudicca led her people into battle against the Roman armies. After early successes, the Celtic Britons were defeated.

When Muhammad was fleeing from Mecca to Medina, he hid from his pursuers in a cave. While he was in there, a spider spun a web across the entrance. His pursuers saw the intact web and decided Muhammad could not be in the cave.

He went that way

◀ Julius Caesar was Rome's most successful general. His political enemies feared he would become all-powerful, and killed him.

Who was Queen Boudicca?

Boudicca—sometimes called Boadicea—was ruler of the Iceni, a Celtic British tribe, in about A.D. 60. She led a rebellion against Roman rule in southern Britain. The rebels captured several towns including Londinium (London), but were then defeated by the strong Roman army. Boudicca poisoned herself rather than risk capture.

Who was Muhammad?

Muhammad was the founder of the Islamic religion. Its followers, the Muslims, call him the Prophet of God. The Prophet was born in Mecca, now in Saudi Arabia, in about A.D. 570.

In 595, Muhammad married a rich widow, Khadija. He led a peaceful life as a merchant in Mecca. When he was about 40 he had a vision of the Archangel Gabriel, calling him to preach the word of God. He began preaching in 613. In

620 Khadija died. By this time Muhammad had made many enemies and he was forced to flee. He took refuge at the oasis of Yathrib, now Medina, city of the prophet.

By 630 Muhammad had established his new religion. He died in 632. His teachings were recorded in the Koran, the sacred book of Islam, as revelations from God.

▶ This medieval picture shows William the Conqueror and the next three Norman kings: William II, Henry I, and Stephen.

◀ Muslims believe the Archangel Gabriel was Allah's (God's) messenger. This painting shows Gabriel.

▼ A statue of Charlemagne. He led the most powerful empire in Europe.

Who was Charlemagne?

Charlemagne, born in 742, was king of the Franks (French) from 771 to 814. He made himself ruler of much of western Europe and attempted to revive the Roman Empire. On Christmas Day 800 Pope Leo III crowned Charlemagne Emperor of the West. Charlemagne was a great admirer of learning. He encouraged literature and the arts at the Frankish court, and founded a school at Aachen (now in Germany). He was a wise ruler. His empire, later called the Holy Roman Empire, lasted in various forms for about 1,000 years.

Who was William the Conqueror?

William (c.1028–1087) was Duke of Normandy, in France. In 1066 he conquered England. William had a slight claim to the English throne. It is said that he was promised it by the Saxon king, Edward the Confessor, who had no heir, but when Edward died the English chose instead a Saxon earl, Harold, as king. So William invaded England and defeated the Saxons at the Battle of Hastings. Harold was killed in the battle.

Who was Saladin?

Saladin (1138–1193) was the greatest Saracen (Muslim) general at the time of the Third Crusade. He became sultan of Syria and Egypt, and in 1187 he captured the holy city of Jerusalem. When news of his victory reached western Europe the Third Crusade was proclaimed.

Who was Good Queen Bess?

Queen Elizabeth I of England is sometimes called Good Queen Bess. She was born in 1533, the daughter of King Henry VIII and Anne Boleyn, and became queen when her half-sister Mary I died in 1558. During Elizabeth's reign England became a great nation. She died in 1603.

Who was known as the Sun King?

Louis XIV of France was known as the Sun King. He became king in 1643 when he was only five years old. He was called the Sun King because his court was so splendid. He had a magnificent palace and gardens built at Versailles, near Paris. He remained king of France for 72 years and died in 1715.

▲ **Queen Elizabeth reviews her troops at Tilbury, near London, before the sea battle against the Spanish Armada. Her fighting words inspired the English.**

Who built the Taj Mahal?

One of the most beautiful buildings in the world, the Taj Mahal, was built at Agra in northern India by Emperor Shah Jehan. It took 20,000 workers about 18 years to complete (from 1630 to 1648) and was a tomb for his wife Mumtaz Mahal. She was Shah Jehan's favorite wife but died in childbirth. He was buried beside her beneath a great white dome which, on the inside, is 79 feet (24 m) high.

▼ **King Louis XIV ruled France from his palace at Versailles. He approved plans for the lavish building and the costly entertainment put on there.**

Which king of England had six wives?

Henry VIII. In 1509, he married Catherine of Aragon. He divorced her in 1533 and married Anne Boleyn. In 1536, he had Anne beheaded and immediately married Jane Seymour. She died the following year. His fourth wife was Anne of Cleves. He married her in 1540, and divorced her six months later. In the same year he married Catherine Howard, only to have her beheaded less than two years later. His sixth wife, Catherine Parr, managed to outlive him.

GREAT RULERS

■ Solomon (from about 1015 B.C. to about 977 B.C.), king of Israel. Famous for his wisdom.

■ Alfred the Great (849–899), king of the West Saxons in England. Fought the Vikings, made good laws, encouraged learning.

■ Genghis Khan (1162–1227), Mongol conqueror, founder of the largest land empire ever seen.

■ Akbar (1542–1605), Mogul emperor of India. Famous for his justice and religious tolerance.

■ Abraham Lincoln (1809–1865), President of the United States. Opposed slavery and led the Union to victory in the Civil War.

◄ **Henry VIII desperately wanted a son to rule England after him. If a wife failed to give him one, or displeased him in some way, he got rid of her.**

▼ **George Washington had fought on the same side as the British. Now he fought against them, to win independence for the United States. After the war, he was elected president.**

Who drafted the Declaration of Independence?

The first draft of the Declaration was made by Thomas Jefferson, a delegate to the Continental Congress of the 13 American Colonies in 1776. Jefferson was born in 1743 and became a lawyer. He began his political career in the Virginia Assembly. In 1783 he was elected to Congress; that same year he devised America's decimal currency. Jefferson then followed Benjamin Franklin as U.S. Ambassador to France; four years later he became Secretary of State. After that he was elected vice-president (from 1797 to 1801) and president (from 1801 to 1809). As president, he bought Louisiana from France. He died in 1826.

Who was the first President of the United States?

The first president was George Washington, who had led the armies of the American Revolution. He served from 1789 to 1797. Washington was born in Virginia in 1732. He worked as a land surveyor, fought in the French and Indian War, and then became a gentleman-farmer. When war started between Britain and its 13 American colonies, Washington was chosen as the American commander-in-chief. After the war was won, Washington helped draw up the U.S. constitution.

Who was known as "the grandmother of Europe?"

Queen Victoria was born in 1819 and became queen of Great Britain and Ireland in 1837. She reigned for nearly 64 years until her death in 1901. In 1840, Victoria married Prince Albert of Saxe-Coburg. Through her own marriage and those of her children, she was related to most of the royal families of Europe. For this reason, Victoria became known as "the grandmother of Europe."

Who crowned himself emperor of France?

Napoleon Bonaparte (1769–1821) was a Corsican soldier who crowned himself emperor of France in 1804. He was eventually defeated by British and Prussian forces at the Battle of Waterloo in 1815 and was exiled to the island of St. Helena in the South Atlantic.

Which king tried to make the waters obey him?

King Canute of Denmark and Norway became king of England in 1016. In order to demonstrate to his lords that his power was limited, he once took them to the seashore and commanded the tide to turn back.

Which ruler once worked as a shipbuilder?

Peter the Great (1672–1725) of Russia visited several European countries in his youth. He had a passion for ships and worked in shipyards in Holland and England.

Sitting Bull

▲ **A painting of Napoleon by Jacques-Louis David, showing him as a heroic war leader. Napoleon came to power as a defender of the French Revolution against foreign enemies. He went on to bring other parts of Europe under French rule.**

Who was Sitting Bull?

Sitting Bull was a fierce leader of the Sioux. He lived from about 1834 to 1890. So that they would not lose all their lands, Sitting Bull persuaded the Sioux to fight and kill the white settlers. This led to the famous Battle of the Little Bighorn in 1876, when the Sioux killed Colonel George Custer and his troops. This was the Native Americans' greatest victory. Sitting Bull survived the battle, but he was driven into Canada. He later returned to the United States and, still rebellious, was killed while resisting arrest.

Who was known as the Iron Chancellor?

Prince Otto von Bismarck, who created the nation of Germany, was known as the Iron Chancellor. He was born in 1815, when Germany was not one country but a league of separate states, and became chief minister of Prussia, the most powerful state. Then, after a series of wars, he united the states in 1871 into one Germany, of which he became Chancellor (prime minister). Because Bismarck said that problems should be settled by "blood and iron," he became known as the Iron Chancellor. He led Germany until 1890 and died in 1898.

Prince Otto von Bismarck

Who was elected President of the United States four times?

Franklin D. Roosevelt, born in 1882, was elected President of the United States four times—in 1932, 1936, 1940, and 1944. He died in 1945, having served as president for twelve years, a record. Roosevelt was a remarkable man. He led the United States through the Depression of the 1930s and through World War II, yet he was crippled by polio and could not walk unaided. Now, no president may serve for more than eight consecutive years.

Who led Germany in World War II?

The German leader in World War II was Adolf Hitler (1889–1945). Hitler came to power in Germany in 1933 as the head of the National Socialist party. He and his followers were known as Nazis (short for National Socialists). They set up a dictatorship in Germany, killing their enemies, and invading other European countries. This caused World War II.

◄ **Franklin Roosevelt was famous for his radio broadcasts to the American people. He suggested the name United Nations for the allies during World War II.**

▲ **Martin Luther King was a fearless campaigner for civil rights.**

▼ **Adolf Hitler dreamed of world domination. He led Germany into war, and ordered the killing of millions of innocent people.**

Who led Britain in World War II?

The British leader in World War II was Winston Churchill, who lived from 1874 to 1965. Churchill became prime minister in 1940, soon after the outbreak of war. By then, Germany had invaded most of Europe, and Britain stood virtually alone against the enemy. The British forces fought strongly under Churchill's powerful leadership, and the country was not invaded. The U.S.S.R. and the United States entered the war in 1941, and four years later the war was over.

Which country was led by General de Gaulle?

Charles de Gaulle was the greatest French leader of this century. Born in 1890, he became a general early in World War II. When the Germans occupied France, de Gaulle refused to collaborate with them. He left, and commanded the Free French forces outside France. De Gaulle returned after the war, and was president of France from 1945 to 1946 and from 1958 to 1969.

Who was Martin Luther King?

Martin Luther King, Jr., led the civil rights movement in the United States, and won international acclaim for his campaign to win equal rights for African-Americans. King was a Baptist minister. He began his protests in 1955 when he led a boycott of buses in Montgomery, Alabama, because black people were made to sit in the rear seats. King believed in nonviolent protest.

THE ANCIENT WORLD

What is Stonehenge?

Stonehenge is an ancient monument in southern England. It was constructed at various times between 1750 B.C. and 1500 B.C. It was probably used as a temple, or to observe the movements of the Sun and Moon to make calendars.

Why were the pyramids of Egypt built?

The pyramids were built as tombs for the pharaohs (rulers) of Ancient Egypt, and they had chambers that contained the remains of the pharaohs. However, these chambers were later robbed of their treasures. The biggest pyramid, the Great Pyramid at Giza, was 480 feet high when built, around 2600 B.C.

▼ The Seven Wonders of the World were listed by writers in ancient times. They were visited by travelers who marveled at their size and magnificence. The pyramids were the oldest and by far the biggest of the Wonders.

What were the Seven Wonders of the World?

The Seven Wonders were structures of the ancient world. They were considered to be the seven most wonderful ever built. The Great Pyramid in Egypt is the only one still standing. The other six were the Hanging Gardens of Babylon; the Temple of Diana at Ephesus; the Tomb of Mausolus at Halicarnassus; the statue of Zeus at Olympia; the Pharos Lighthouse at Alexandria; and the Colossus of Rhodes, a statue beside the harbor entrance. There are no reliable pictures of the six vanished Wonders, only descriptions by historians and travelers.

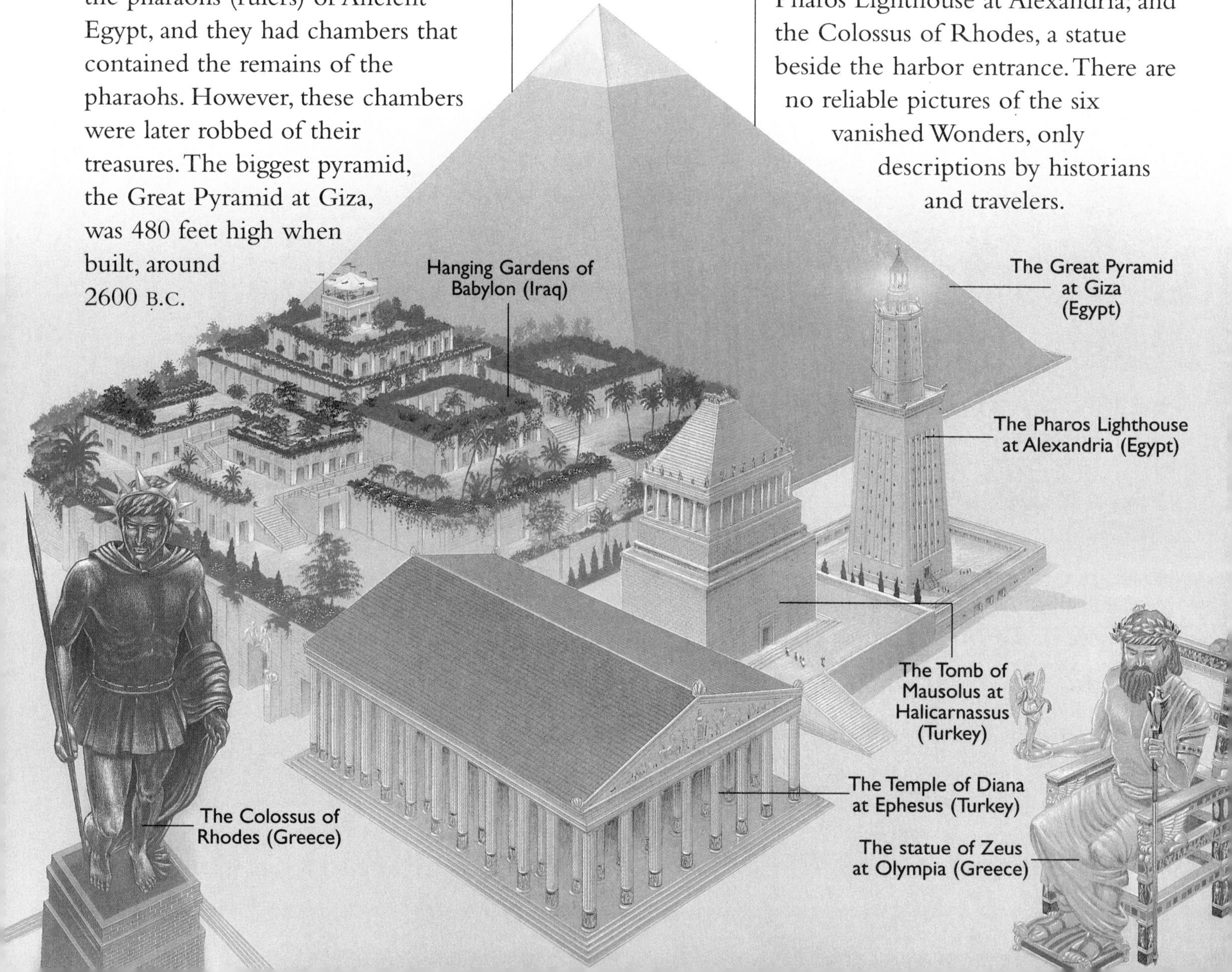

Hanging Gardens of Babylon (Iraq)

The Great Pyramid at Giza (Egypt)

The Pharos Lighthouse at Alexandria (Egypt)

The Tomb of Mausolus at Halicarnassus (Turkey)

The Colossus of Rhodes (Greece)

The Temple of Diana at Ephesus (Turkey)

The statue of Zeus at Olympia (Greece)

◄ Alexander the Great led his armies as far east as India. In a short but brilliant life, he was never defeated in battle.

Who founded the ancient city of Alexandria?

The city of Alexandria in Egypt was founded in 331 B.C. by the Greek emperor Alexander the Great (356–323 B.C.). By conquest, Alexander built up a great empire that extended from Greece as far as India and Egypt and was as big as the United States. The empire brought Greek civilization to the ancient world, and Alexandria became its center of learning.

Who was the first Roman emperor?

Augustus, who lived from 63 B.C. to A.D. 14, was the first emperor of Ancient Rome. Before Augustus, Rome was a republic governed by elected consuls. After the death of Julius Caesar, Augustus—then called Octavian—held power with Mark Antony (c.83–30 B.C.). Octavian defeated Mark Antony, and in 27 B.C. declared that Rome would be an empire with himself as the first emperor. He took the name Augustus, and Rome reached its greatest glory under his rule. The month of August is named after him.

▼ Cleopatra lived in great splendor in Egypt. She was a descendant of one of Alexander the Great's generals.

DID YOU KNOW?

■ The Greek philosopher Aristotle was Alexander the Great's tutor.

■ Cleopatra married two of her brothers, sharing the throne with them.

■ She had a son by Julius Caesar, and twins by Mark Antony.

■ Hadrian's Wall had gates where soldiers kept a check on all people traveling in and out of Roman Britain.

Who was Cleopatra?

Cleopatra was an extremely beautiful queen of Egypt. She was born in 69 B.C. The Roman leader Julius Caesar, fascinated by her, made her queen. After Caesar's death, Cleopatra captivated Mark Antony, his successor. Antony left his wife, Octavia, for Cleopatra, provoking a battle for control of Rome with Octavian, who was Octavia's brother. Octavian met Antony and Cleopatra in battle in 31 B.C. and won. Defeated, Antony killed himself and Cleopatra soon also took her own life, possibly with an asp (a poisonous snake).

Why did the Romans build a wall across England?

Hadrian's Wall is a famous landmark in the north of England. It is a huge wall, 73 miles (118 km) long, which runs across the whole country from coast to coast. It was built by the Roman emperor Hadrian between A.D. 123 and 138 to keep Scottish raiders from invading England, then a province of the Roman Empire.

Who took elephants across the Alps?

Hannibal (247–182 B.C.) led the forces of Carthage against Rome and used elephants in war to scare his enemies. He took the Romans by surprise by marching over the Alps in 218 B.C., taking the elephants with him. Once in Italy, Hannibal harassed the Romans for years, but he did not defeat them.

▼ Hannibal's army and war elephants crossed the Alps.

Who were the Incas?

The ancestors of the Incas lived among the mountains of Peru possibly as long as 4,000 years ago. The Incas began building up their country in about A.D. 1200.

From 1438 to 1493, two kings, Pachacuti and his son Topa Inca, expanded the Inca Empire. It eventually covered large parts of present-day Ecuador, Bolivia, Chile, and Argentina.

Who were the Celts?

The Celts were a group of peoples living in central Europe in the 500s B.C. Many migrated west. They were warriors and farmers. Their language survives in Welsh, Gaelic, and Breton.

The Mayan people of Central America chewed gum. The rubbery gum was called chicle, and they collected it from the sapodilla tree. Chicle is still used to make chewing gum.

When did the Mayan Empire flourish?

The Mayan Empire was at its height in southern Mexico and Central America from about A.D. 250 to 900. The Maya built huge stone cities, had elaborate religious ceremonies, and developed a system of picture writing. The great Mayan cities were abandoned in the late 800s. Nobody knows why.

Who was China's first emperor?

For 260 years the states of eastern China fought each other for control of the whole country. The struggle was eventually won by Ch'in, one of the westernmost states. Its leader was Prince Cheng, known as the "Tiger of Ch'in." When Ch'in won, Cheng proclaimed himself Shih Huang-ti, which means "the first emperor." Shih Huang-ti also ordered the building of the Great Wall of China to keep out invaders from the north.

▶ The Inca ruler Pachacuti led his army into battle to expand his empire.

When was the Han dynasty founded?

The Han dynasty overthrew the Ch'in dynasty in 202 B.C. It ruled China for more than 400 years. During the Han dynasty the Chinese Empire expanded. Han scholars studied higher mathematics and astronomy. Paper was invented during this period, and Han traders visited Persia and Rome.

▼ **The Ancient Chinese built large cities. People from the countryside brought vegetables and farm animals into town to sell in the market. Travelers from the West were amazed by Chinese cities, and the orderly life that went on in them.**

▼ **Vikings fighting at sea. Their wooden longships were fast and easy to steer.**

Who was Attila?

Attila (c.406–453) was the leader of the Huns, a warlike group of tribes from central Asia that terrorized Europe in the A.D. 400s. He forced the rulers of the eastern Roman Empire to pay him a large annual fee to leave them alone. He then led a large army of Huns into Gaul (France). The Romans defeated Attila at Châlons-sur-Marne in 451. He died two years later.

Who was Confucius?

Confucius was a Chinese philosopher who lived 2,500 years ago (551–479 B.C.). The real name of Confucius was K'ung ch'iu. He became known as K'ung-fu-tzu, which means great master Kung; Confucius is a Westernized form of that title.

DID YOU KNOW?

■ The Vikings were feared as warriors. They hired themselves out as paid soldiers.

■ Much of what we know about Ancient China comes from tombs. Clay models of houses, soldiers, and horses have been found in Chinese tombs.

■ The Holy Roman Empire lasted until the early 1800s. But it was never very powerful after the Middle Ages.

■ Confucius believed in order, family, and good government. His ideas had a great influence on Chinese life.

■ The Huns were one of a number of "barbarian" peoples who attacked the Roman Empire. The Romans regarded these people as uncivilized.

Who were the Vikings?

The Vikings were pirates from Scandinavia. They were bold and skillful navigators, who sailed the European seas in their long ships. Each ship had a large, square sail, but could also be driven by oars.

From A.D. 793 onward, Vikings from Norway raided England. They began to settle there in the late 800s. Other Vikings attacked France and settled there. They were known as Northmen, or Normans, and gave their name to Normandy. Other Vikings reached Spain, Sicily, Italy, and Russia, leaving their mark.

What was the Holy Roman Empire?

The Holy Roman Empire was a group of small German and neighboring states that were powerful in the Middle Ages. It was intended to be a second Roman Empire built of Christian states. The empire was founded by Charlemagne, or Charles the Great, who was crowned the first Holy Roman emperor by the Pope in Rome on Christmas Day, A.D. 800.

FAMOUS EVENTS

What does the Bayeux Tapestry show?

The Bayeux Tapestry is a very long piece of embroidery. It shows in pictures the invasion of England by Duke William of Normandy (William the Conqueror) in 1066. Bayeux is a small town in northern France, and the tapestry is in a museum there. It is something like a comic strip. It starts with King Harold of England's visit to Duke William, probably in 1064. It ends with the Battle of Hastings in 1066 when Harold was killed by an arrow that pierced his eye, and his troops were defeated.

► Disguised as Native Americans, colonists threw British tea into the water. This was one of the acts that lead to the American Revolution.

What was the Boston Tea Party?

In 1773, when the U.S. was still a group of British colonies, a Tea Act was passed in Britain that allowed the East India Company to send tea directly from London to America without using American merchants. In Boston, a group of patriotic Americans boarded the tea ships and threw the tea into the harbor in protest. This defiant act became known as the "Boston Tea Party."

Sheep were brought to Australia by the early settlers. Today there are about 135 million sheep, nearly nine times the number of people in Australia!

▲ Norman soldiers on horseback charge into battle. This scene is part of the long Bayeux Tapestry, which tells the story of William's invasion of England in 1066.

Why is the year 1901 important in the history of Australia?

On January 1, 1901, the Commonwealth of Australia came into being. Before this, Australia consisted of a number of separate colonies. With the Commonwealth Act of 1900, the colonies became a federation. The formation of the Commonwealth marked the beginning of Australia as a full nation.

What was the charge of the Light Brigade?

Between 1854 and 1856 the Crimean War was fought between Russia on one side and Turkey, England, France, and Sardinia on the other. In October 1854 the Russians tried to seize the British base at Balaklava. Because of a misunderstanding of orders, the Light Brigade, an army division, charged the main Russian position. The soldiers were heavily outnumbered by the Russians and many were killed, but the brave survivors got through and captured the enemy position.

What caused the Civil War?

Political differences between the northern states (the Union) and the southern states (the Confederacy). The turning point came in 1860 when Abraham Lincoln became president. The South, which depended on slaves for labor, feared that Lincoln would abolish slavery. In 1861, 11 southern states separated from the Union because they thought that states, not Congress, should decide their own laws. After four years of fighting, the South surrendered, preserving the Union.

When was the Battle of Gettysburg?

The Battle of Gettysburg was a turning point in the Civil War. It lasted from July 1 to July 3, 1863. Gettysburg is a little town in Pennsylvania. The Confederates, led by Robert E. Lee (1807–1870), were defeated by the Union army under George Meade (1815–1872).

▲ During World War I, recruiting posters urged men to join the army. Many died in trench warfare in France and Belgium.

▼ The Battle of Agincourt (1415) was an English victory over a larger French army during the long Hundred Years' War.

Which war became known as the Great War?

World War I (1914–1918) became known as the Great War. This was because, at the time, there had never been a war in which so many different countries took part. More people were killed than ever before in a war, and more buildings were destroyed. But when World War II took place (1939–1945), it was even bigger and more destructive.

What was the Hundred Years' War?

France and England were at war from 1337 to 1453. This is more than a hundred years, but the period is known as the Hundred Years' War. It was eventually won by France.

Which event does the Eiffel Tower commemorate?

The Eiffel Tower, designed by A. Gustave Eiffel (1832–1923), was built for the Paris Exhibition of 1889. This exhibition commemorated the French Revolution, which began a century before. The Revolution started on July 14, 1789, when a mob of angry Parisians attacked the Bastille, a prison. They pulled the building down stone by stone. The anniversary of the destruction of the Bastille is a national holiday in France.

Which "unsinkable" ship sank on its first voyage?

This ship was the *Titanic*, a British passenger liner. At the time, the *Titanic* was the world's largest ship, and experts believed that it was unsinkable. But on the night of April 14, 1912, during its first voyage, it hit an iceberg in the middle of the Atlantic Ocean and sank. Out of more than 2,200 people on board, some 1,500 were drowned.

▲ In Paris, on July 14, 1789, crowds attacked the Bastille prison and freed all of the prisoners.

▶ Sitting beside his wife, Jacqueline, President Kennedy was driven through the streets of Dallas to meet the cheering crowds. Moments later he was shot by an assassin. People still argue about who killed him.

In the 1780s French people were angered by a new tax on salt, which they used to keep meat fresh. The tax made salt too expensive.

Who was shot at Ford's Theater in 1865?

Abraham Lincoln, sixteenth President of the United States, was fatally shot on April 14, 1865, at Ford's Theater, Washington, D.C. His assassin was John Wilkes Booth (1838–1865), a southern actor, who hated Lincoln for having defeated the Confederacy. He got into the presidential box, shot the president, then leaped onto the stage and fled. He was later captured.

When was President Kennedy assassinated?

President John F. Kennedy was assassinated by a gunman in Dallas, Texas, on November 22, 1963. The President was being driven in an open car.

Who won the Battle of the Little Bighorn?

The battle was fought on June 25, 1876, between the Sioux and a U.S. cavalry column led by Colonel George A. Custer. Trouble had begun in 1874 when the United States government sent miners and soldiers into the Black Hills of South Dakota, a region sacred to the Sioux. The Sioux refused to sell the land, so the government decided to drive them out. Custer split his force of 650 troops into three columns. His own column fell into a Sioux ambush led by Chief Sitting Bull. Custer and his men were all killed.

▼ On D-Day, June 6, 1944, Allied troops landed in France. The massive air, sea, and land invasion was the biggest in history.

When did World War II start?

World War II began with the German invasion of Poland on September 1, 1939. On September 3, Britain and France declared war on Germany. Australia, New Zealand, India, Canada, and South Africa supported Britain. By 1940 Germany had overrun much of Europe. Japan and Italy joined in on Germany's side. Italy invaded Yugoslavia, Greece, and much of North Africa. Germany then attacked Russia in 1941, the year the United States entered the war. In 1944 Allied forces invaded western Europe while Russia attacked from the east. Germany was defeated by May 1945. Japan surrendered in August 1945.

▼ Genghis Khan's Mongol warriors rode into battle on horseback. Each man was a skilled rider and fighter.

What happened at Pearl Harbor?

On the morning of December 7, 1941, Japanese bombers attacked the United States naval base at Pearl Harbor, Hawaii. They destroyed six warships, damaged 12 others, and destroyed 174 aircraft. The Japanese attacked while their officials were negotiating in Washington, D.C. about causes of dispute between Japan and the United States. The Pearl Harbor attack took the United States into the war against Japan and its allies, Germany and Italy.

Which empire was ruled by Genghis Khan?

Genghis Khan (1162–1227) was the leader of the Mongols, a warlike group of people from central Asia. He was one of the greatest conquerors in history, leading a vast army against China in 1211 and into Russia in 1223, and threatening to overrun eastern Europe. Genghis Khan created a Mongol empire. His grandson Kublai Khan (1215–1294) ruled China.

What was the Spanish Armada?

The Armada was an invasion fleet of galleons packed with soldiers sent from Spain to attack England in 1588. Spain was then Europe's mightiest power. The English fleet fought off the Armada in a series of battles in the English Channel, but did not seriously damage it. However, the Spanish could not join forces with an invasion army waiting in the Netherlands, and their ships were driven north around Britain by strong winds. Many were wrecked in storms off the coasts of Scotland and Ireland.

When did the Pilgrim Fathers land in America?

In 1620 a group of Puritans left England on a ship called the *Mayflower*. They were bound for new lives in America. They sailed from Plymouth in England and landed in Massachusetts. The Pilgrim Fathers, as they became known, founded

▲ The great galleons of the Spanish Armada were out-sailed by the smaller English ships at the Battle of Gravelines in the English Channel.

the second English colony in North America (after Jamestown, Virginia, 1607)—the first was founded by people seeking religious freedom. Those who survived the hard winter gave thanks for their first harvest with a feast—the first Thanksgiving.

When did France become a republic?

In 1792, after revolution had overthrown the monarchy. The French Revolution began in 1789, as a movement to make government in France more democratic. But the revolution rapidly became more extreme and violent. People accused of being enemies of the republic were executed. In 1799, a soldier named Napoleon Bonaparte seized power, and he soon made himself emperor.

◀ The Pilgrim Fathers were helped by Native Americans as they built homes and planted crops in their new land.

When was the Russian Revolution?

In 1917, revolutionaries forced the czar (emperor) of Russia to give up his supreme power. A group of communist extremists, known as Bolsheviks, seized power from the liberal democratic politicians. Their leader was Vladimir Lenin (Vladimir Ilyich Ulyanov; 1870–1924). By 1921, Lenin had made Russia a communist state, the largest of the new Union of Soviet Socialist Republics.

Who led India to independence?

Mohandas Karamchand Gandhi (1869–1948) was the most influential leader of the movement that won India's independence from British rule in 1947. Gandhi was a lawyer, who preached a policy of nonviolence as he campaigned for India's freedom. After independence, Gandhi tried to stop the fighting that broke out between India's Hindus and Muslims. He was assassinated in 1948 by a Hindu who disliked Gandhi's tolerance of all religions.

GREAT EVENTS

■ Greece fought a war for freedom against Turkey from 1821 to 1829.

■ Spain's colonies in South America won their independence between 1809 and 1825.

■ 1848 became known as Europe's Year of Revolutions.

■ In 1860 Giuseppe Garibaldi led a victorious army from Sicily through southern Italy to join up with King Victor Emmanuel's army from the north. When Rome was captured, Italy became a united country.

■ Fidel Castro led the Cuban Revolution of 1959 which overthrew the dictator Fulgencio Batista.

■ In 1900 only two African countries—Ethiopia and Liberia—were truly independent. By the 1990s all the major territories of Africa were self-governing.

◀ **Gandhi first practiced nonviolent protest in South Africa. He took his beliefs to India and inspired other protestors around the world.**

▶ **South Africa's Nelson Mandela with Queen Elizabeth II of Great Britain. Mandela won praise for his courage and statesmanship.**

When was Germany reunited?

Germany was divided by the victorious Allies after its defeat in World War II (1939–1945). East Germany came under communist rule and Russian domination, while West Germany was rebuilt by the Western democracies as a prosperous, free country. In 1961 the building of the Berlin Wall symbolized the division of the two Germanies. In 1989, the collapse of communism in Eastern Europe began. The government in East Germany fell, the Berlin Wall was torn down, and in 1990 Germany became one country again with a democratic government.

Who was South Africa's first black president?

From the 1950s, all South Africans were classified by race. Whites ruled, while blacks had few freedoms. Nelson Mandela, a leader of the African National Congress, was jailed from 1962 until 1990 for opposing the government. As the old system broke down, he was freed, and in 1994 he was elected South Africa's first black president.

HOW PEOPLE LIVED

When did cities first have real drains?

The people of Ancient India, China, and Rome built good water-supply systems. They even had public baths. Mohenjo-Daro in Pakistan, was built about 4,000 years ago. This city had drains to bring in fresh water and sewers to carry away waste.

When did people first make bricks?

Bricks were first made over 6,000 years ago. They were shaped from wet mud and dried in the Sun's heat. Brickmaking began on the river-banks of the Near East and Mesopotamia. The bricks we use today are probably not very different in size from those used in ancient times. The builders of Babylon decorated their bricks, making wall-pictures or mosaics. Later, bricks were hardened by baking them in a kiln, or oven, in the same way as pottery is baked. Brick houses were stronger than houses made of wood.

Brickmakers in ancient times trampled river mud with their bare feet until it was sticky. They added bits of straw to make the mixture stronger and used wooden molds to shape the bricks.

▶ **The ruins of Mohenjo-Daro, one of the first cities planned with a street grid and real drains.**

▼ **The people of Babylon (a land in what is now Iraq) built pyramid-shaped ziggurats, or temples of brick.**

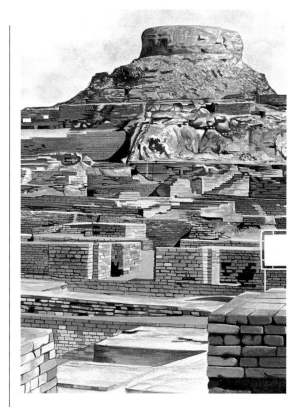

When was the first alphabet invented?

The Phoenicians, living in the eastern Mediterranean some 3,500 years ago, were the first to invent an alphabet of sound-signs. Their alphabet was borrowed and improved by first the Greeks and then the Romans. Our word "alphabet" comes from the Greek words for the first two letters in their alphabet, *alpha* and *beta*.

When did people first shop in supermarkets?

The first department store, offering many goods beneath one roof, was opened in Paris in 1860. The first supermarkets, selling all kinds of goods in a single store, opened in the United States in the 1930s. In some places supermarkets have driven smaller shops out of business.

When did people use oil lamps?

Fat burns, and the sight of this probably caused a cave dweller to make the first oil lamp. Animal fat and oil gave people light for thousands of years, until an improved kind of oil lamp was invented. In 1784 a Swiss named Aimé Argand (1755–1803) invented an improved oil lamp. It had a glass chimney to shield the wick, and it gave a much brighter light. In the 1800s many homes were lit only by kerosene lamps. Gas and electric lighting were introduced later.

When were carpets first made?

The first floor coverings were mats woven from rushes. Weaving skills were later used to make rugs and carpets from wool. The finest carpets were richly patterned and very valuable. Carpets made more than 2,000 years ago have been found in tombs in Asia.

When did people first eat with knives and forks?

Cheap factorymade knives and forks appeared on dining tables in the 1800s. Before then, only rich people

DID YOU KNOW?

- In the city of Ur (modern Iraq), an arch of bricks was built about 4000 B.C.

- The Romans burned petroleum in their oil lamps.

- In the 1680s oil lamps were used to light London streets.

- All carpets were woven by hand until the 1700s, when factory machines were invented to make them more quickly.

- Until the 1400s, few people ate off plates. They used a thick slice of bread, called a trencher.

- The Romans used two-pronged forks at the table.

- Travelers in the 1700s carried a fork, spoon, and mug in a special case.

▼ Diners at a feast in the Middle Ages ate with their fingers. Servants brought the various dishes to each person. Bones were thrown to the dogs.

used them. Most people ate with their fingers at mealtimes. In the Middle Ages travelers took their own knives with them. Guests would expect to be offered a knife only if they were dining with a very rich person. Table forks were even less common until the 1700s.

When did frozen foods first appear?

Before people had freezers, they stored winter ice in stone ice houses. The Romans made ice cream. A method of making artificial ice was invented in 1834 by Jacob Perkins. By the 1850s refrigerated ships were carrying frozen meat across the oceans. People in Europe could eat meat that came from Australia or the Americas. Frozen foods, such as frozen fish and vegetables, were introduced in the 1920s, when people began to buy freezers for their homes.

When did people first read newspapers?

In the Middle Ages, news of a foreign war, or the king's death, often took days to reach distant parts of the country. Town criers shouted out the news to townsfolk. In the 1500s, after the invention of printing machinery, people began reading pamphlets and newsletters. The first newspaper to be printed regularly was called the *Corante*. It came out in London in 1621 and had news from France, Italy, Spain, and other countries in Europe.

When were the first banks opened?

Ever since coins first appeared, some 2,500 years ago, people have traded in money. The word "bank" comes from the Italian *banco*, meaning "bench." In the Middle Ages, moneychangers and merchants did business from benches in the marketplace. The first big national bank was the Bank of England, which was started in 1694. The Federal Reserve, created by an Act of Congress in 1913, acts as a central bank in the United States.

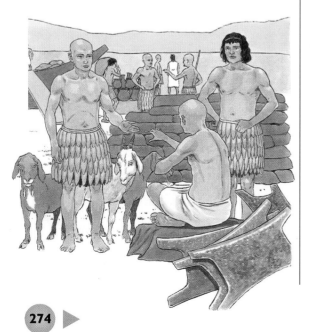

▶ A town crier in the American colonies during the 1600s. A roll on the drum warned people that the crier was about to shout out the latest news.

FIRSTS

■ Canned foods were unknown before the 1800s. They first went on sale in the 1820s.

■ Strangely, the first efficient can opener was not invented until the 1860s, 40 years later! Until then, people opened a can by hitting it with a hammer and chisel.

■ In the 1650s a new craze hit Europe—coffee-drinking. People met in coffee houses to gossip and talk business.

■ The first newspaper with pictures in it was called the *Civic Mercury* and appeared in 1643.

■ The first modern-style refrigerator was invented in 1858, by Ferdinand Carré.

■ The first plastic was invented in the 1860s by an American looking for a substitute for ivory for billiard balls.

◀ The Sumerians, a people of Ancient Mespotamia, used different clay tokens like these (right) for trading different kinds of goods.

When were postage stamps first used?

By the 1700s most European countries had some sort of postal service. Letters were carried on horseback and by stagecoach.

In 1840 the "penny post" appeared in Britain. Soon countries all over the world were issuing stamps. Stamps made it easier and cheaper for people to send letters.

When were banknotes first used?

Shells, stones, beads, teeth, even cattle, were used as money in ancient times. The first real coins were made from gold and silver. Paper money came later, first in China, and then in Europe during the 1600s.

Sumerian trade tokens

When were labor unions first formed?

The earliest labor unions were probably the trade clubs formed by workers in various trades, such as carpenters and shoemakers, in the 1600s. Labor unions as we know them today grew up when men, women, and children worked in factories created during the Industrial Revolution of the 1800s.

Who pioneered modern nursing?

British soldiers wounded in the Crimean War (1854–1856) called the nurse in charge of their hospital "the lady with the lamp." Today Florence Nightingale is known as the founder of modern nursing.

When was the Red Cross founded?

In 1859, in northern Italy, Austrians and French fought the Battle of Solferino. Men lay wounded in the fierce heat, and among those who saw their suffering was Henri Dunant, a young Swiss banker. Dunant suggested that a society to help wounded soldiers be set up in every country. In 1863 a meeting in Geneva brought the first

▶ Labor unions had banners and paintings made to show what they stood for. The pictures showed workers united to strive for fairness and an improved way of life.

Florence Nightingale

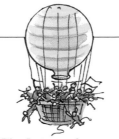

The first use of a balloon in war was in 1794, during the French Revolution, when French observers in a balloon directed cannon fire against Austrian forces.

Red Cross societies into being. In the United States, Clara Barton helped set up the American Red Cross in 1881. Today the Red Cross is at work all over the world. In Muslim countries, its symbol is a red crescent. Israel uses a red Star of David.

When were planes first used in war?

In 1911 Italy took Libya from Turkey in the Tripolitan War and used planes to drop bombs. In World War I (1914–1918), both sides used airplanes. At first they used them for reconnaissance, but they soon began dropping small bombs and shooting at ground targets. Airplanes were used by armies and navies. Britain formed the first air force, the Royal Air Force, in 1918.

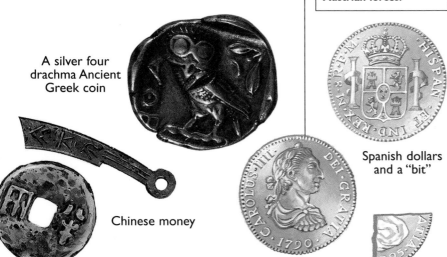

A silver four drachma Ancient Greek coin

Chinese money

Spanish dollars and a "bit"

◀ **Examples of early coins. Chinese money was knife-shaped at first, but most coins are round. Old Spanish dollars were cut into "pieces of eight."**

ARCHITECTURE, PAINTING, AND SCULPTURE

When were columns first used in buildings?

Columns are tall pillars used most often to support the roof of a building. The Ancient Egyptians used columns in their temples and tombs as long ago as 2700 B.C. The columns were of several different styles, with a variety of decorations.

When was the arch first used?

The arch was first used by the people of Mesopotamia 5,000 years ago. They built in brick, and invented forms like the true arch, instead of using great stone horizontal roofing slabs, like the Egyptians. The arch was introduced into Europe by the Etruscans, from about 750 B.C. onward. From them, the Romans learned how to build the arch and developed it even further.

When were the first theaters built?

The first theaters were built by the Ancient Greeks in about the 5th century B.C. We know that the theater of Dionysus in Athens was founded about 500 B.C. It could hold about 18,000 spectators.

▶ The Romans were superb builders. They built large temples, theaters, and forts of stone. They also built bridges and aqueducts with high arches.

◀ The three classical orders, or types, of column were (from left) Doric, Ionic, and Corinthian. Each had a different decoration on its top.

In an Egyptian house, the best place to sleep was on the roof. It was cooler than indoors. The roof was flat, so you couldn't fall off!

▼ The Greeks watched plays in open-air theaters, often on hillsides. Actors performed in an open space. The chorus sang or commented on the action.

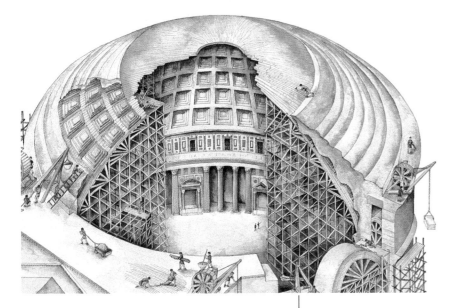

When did buildings first have domes?

Domes were first used in the ancient Near East, the Mediterranean area, and India. At first, they were either solid spherical mounds, or used only on small buildings. The Romans developed domes as roofs in large buildings. One of the earliest examples of a domed building is the Pantheon in Rome. It was built around A.D. 124 for Emperor Hadrian. The vast dome was 142 feet (43.3 m) in diameter and remained the biggest in the world for 1,300 years. The "eye" at the top was left open to let in light and air. To save weight, the walls contained spaces or voids.

▲ The Pantheon in Rome was made from overlapping concrete rings. The dome got thinner as it rose toward the top.

▼ The Parthenon was one of the Greeks' greatest buildings. It stands on a hilltop over-looking Athens.

What were aqueducts?

The Ancient Romans built tunnels, ditches, and huge bridgelike structures called aqueducts to carry water from rivers and lakes into their cities. Some of these impressive feats of engineering still stand today. A fine example of a Roman aqueduct is the Pont du Gard in France, built about 19 B.C. It is 886 feet (270 m) long.

Where is the Parthenon?

The Parthenon is a beautiful Greek temple that stands on top of the Acropolis, a hilltop site above the city of Athens. The Parthenon was a temple built in honor of the goddess Athena in the 5th century B.C. by order of the Greek leader Pericles. It is one of the most famous ancient buildings in the world.

Who was Christopher Wren?

Christopher Wren (1632–1723) was a British architect who designed St. Paul's Cathedral in London. Wren was given the chance to build the cathedral, and many other new churches in London, after the Great Fire of 1666, which destroyed much of the old medieval city. Work on St. Paul's Cathedral finished in 1710.

When were the first sculptures made?

The earliest sculptures are as much as 30,000 years old, dating from the Stone Age. They are tiny figures representing women, which have come to be known as the "Venuses." Stone Age Venuses have been found all over Europe and western Asia. Stone Age sculptors also made figures of animals.

When were the first watercolors painted?

The use of watercolor in painting has a long history. We know that watercolor paint was used on papyrus rolls in Ancient Egypt, and in the earliest paintings of China.

▲ A terra-cotta (clay) figure of a woman, known as the Venus of Malta. It was made between 3400 and 3000 B.C. and was found on the island of Malta.

When did painters first use perspective?

Perspective is a method of drawing a picture so as to give an impression of realistic depth and distance. The laws of perspective were figured out and first used in the 15th century in Italy. The Italian architect Filippo Brunelleschi (1377–1446) figured out these principles. They are based on the fact that objects seem smaller the closer they are to the horizon.

When did Japanese prints become world-famous?

Japanese color prints in the style known as *ukiyo-e* were first seen in Europe in the late 1800s. They have influenced many European artists since then. *Ukiyo-e* arose in the 16th and 17th centuries to appeal to popular tastes. Some of the works best known in Europe are the landscape prints of Katsushika Hokusai (1760–1849).

Who painted for four years on his back?

One of the greatest artists was Michelangelo, who lived in Italy from 1475 to 1564. He was a painter, a sculptor, and an architect. His greatest painting covers the ceiling of the Sistine Chapel in the Vatican, Rome. It consists of scenes from the Bible— the Creation, the story of Noah and the flood, the apostles—and Michelangelo painted it all by himself, lying flat on his back on scaffolding. It took him four years, from 1508 to 1512.

◀ This fresco, or wall painting, in the Sistine Chapel in Rome is also by Michelangelo. It shows the Day of Judgment.

Which painter tied himself to a ship's mast?

The British painter Joseph Turner, who lived from 1775 to 1851, is renowned for his landscape paintings. His paintings have marvelous effects of color that capture the play of light on a scene—for example, a sunset or a storm. In order to see what a storm at sea really looks like, Turner once had himself tied to the mast of a ship that was sailing through a storm.

Who painted himself for forty years?

Many artists like to paint themselves. The most revealing of all self-portraits are those by the Dutch artist Rembrandt van Rijn, who lived from 1606 to 1669. His portraits capture people's expressions to suggest their inner feelings. Among the best of Rembrandt's portraits are those of himself, which he painted over a period of forty years.

Who were the Impressionists?

The Impressionists were a group of French painters who lived at the end of the 1800s. Instead of painting a scene as it appeared, these artists painted their own impression of it.

▼ A self-portrait of Van Gogh in 1889. His head is bandaged because he cut off his ear during a bout of mental illness. Many artists have painted themselves.

DID YOU KNOW?

■ Among the first artists to paint in oils were the Flemish painters Hubert and Jan Eyck, who lived in the early 1400s.

■ One of the most famous pictures in the world is Leonardo da Vinci's *Mona Lisa*, painted about 1500.

■ In 1905 a group of French painters were called the "wild beasts" because their paintings seemed so violent and distorted. They included Henri Matisse and André Derain.

◄ A portrait by Renoir of two girls, painted about 1895.

► Picasso, here at home in Cannes in 1960, lived a long life and produced an enormous amount of work. He was a painter, sculptor, and graphic artist but also created wonderful pottery.

The paintings have rough outlines and brushstrokes, and are often light in color. In this way, the artists tried to catch the quality of light in a scene. Leading Impressionist painters included Claude Monet, Edouard Manet, Camille Pissarro, Alfred Sisley, and Pierre Auguste Renoir.

Who was Van Gogh?

The Dutch painter Vincent Van Gogh (1853–1890) is famous for his vivid paintings of landscapes, people, and still life. They are painted in broad strokes of strong color. *Sunflowers* has become one of his most popular and famous works. Yet during his lifetime, Van Gogh sold only one painting, and he died a poor man.

Who was Picasso?

Pablo Ruiz y Picasso (1881–1973) was a Spanish artist who must be the best known of all 20th-century painters. He painted in several different styles, and greatly influenced other painters of his day. Picasso spent much of his life in France. He helped develop a style of painting known as Cubism.

LITERATURE AND DRAMA

Who wrote *The Iliad* and *The Odyssey*?

The Iliad and *The Odyssey* are two Greek epic poems that tell the story of the siege of the city of Troy and what happened afterward. Tradition has it that they were written by Homer, a blind singer from the Greek island of Chios. We know very little about Homer—historians are not even sure if both these great poems were made up by one person.

▼ In Homer's *The Odyssey*, Odysseus is tied to the mast so his ship cannot be lured to its doom by the sweet-voiced Sirens.

Who was Virgil?

A famous Roman writer, born in 70 B.C. in Italy. His full name was Publius Vergilius Maro, and his most famous work is *The Aeneid*. This is an epic poem about the fall of Troy and the adventures of a warrior named Aeneas, who leads his followers to Italy, where they were able to settle and found the Roman nation. Virgil also wrote about the work of farmers and the life of the countryside. His writings were read all over Europe during later times, when Latin was a shared language of learning.

▶ The tale of Aladdin and the genie of the lamp is just one of the wonderful stories from *The Thousand and One Nights*.

In ancient times, few people could read. They listened to storytellers and enjoyed tales of gods and goddesses, heroes and monsters.

Who told stories for 1001 nights?

A princess of Arabia named Scheherazade. The story tells how her husband, a cruel king, put to death all his wives. Scheherazade tricked him by telling the king a tale each night, stopping when she got to the most exciting part. If he wanted to hear the rest, he must let her live another day. This went on for 1001 nights, until the king gave up his wicked plan. The stories, traditional and from many parts of Asia, were first written down in Arabic in about A.D. 1000.

Who wrote *The Divine Comedy*?

Dante, an Italian writer born in Florence in 1265. *The Divine Comedy* is one the most important writings of medieval Europe, because Dante wrote in Italian, his own language—

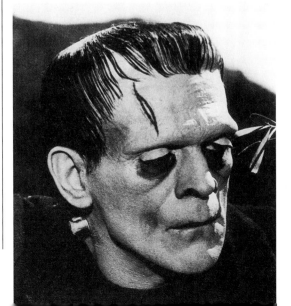

◀ A 19th-century painting of Dante and his "ideal woman," Beatrice. In his great poem *The Divine Comedy*, Dante describes a visit to Heaven with Beatrice.

and not in Latin, which was then the language of education and scholarship. It is a poem in three parts describing journeys through Hell, Purgatory, and finally Heaven.

What are *The Canterbury Tales*?

A collection of stories in verse, supposed to have been told by pilgrims on their way from London to Canterbury in the 1300s. The stories were written by the English poet Geoffrey Chaucer (1342–1400). They reflect the characters and lives of the tellers.

◀ Chaucer's pilgrims told stories on the way from London to Canterbury. This picture shows several pilgrims on the road.

Was there a real Robinson Crusoe?

The tale of Robinson Crusoe, a shipwrecked sailor, was written by the English journalist Daniel Defoe (1660–1731) in 1719. It has remained popular ever since. Defoe got the idea from real-life tales of the sea, and sailors—in particular the story of Alexander Selkirk, a well-known survivor of a shipwreck. To make this story more believable, Defoe put in lots of detail about Crusoe's adventures.

Who created Frankenstein's monster?

English author Mary Shelley (1797–1851), the wife of poet Percy Bysshe Shelley (1792–1822). Her story of the scientist Frankenstein, and the monster he made out of humans, was published in 1818. In it, the monster finally destroys the scientist.

▼ Frankenstein's monster, created by Mary Shelley, has appeared in many movies and on TV.

H I S T O R Y

Who was Moby Dick?

Moby Dick was a great white whale, whose story was written by the novelist Herman Melville (1819–1891). It is a thrilling story of whaling in the 19th century, but with deeper, more symbolic meanings as well. Melville had been to sea on whaling ships and seen many adventures, including being shipwrecked and taking part in a spectacular mutiny.

▲ The hunchback of Notre Dame became the star of a Disney cartoon movie—which would have surprised his French creator, Victor Hugo!

Who created *The Hunchback of Notre Dame*?

French writer Victor Hugo (1802–1885) was a poet, playwright, and novelist. His most famous novels are *The Hunchback of Notre Dame* and *Les Misérables*, a story about an escaped convict who tries to lead an honest life. For his political views, Hugo was banished from France for a time.

Hans Andersen told the story of a Chinese emperor who loved a nightingale's song. When the bird flew away, he had a mechanical bird made in its place.

FAMOUS BOOKS

■ In *Gulliver's Travels*, by Jonathan Swift (1667–1745), Gulliver has strange adventures among giants, minuscule people, and talking horses.

■ The French writer Alexandre Dumas (1803–1870) wrote the exciting adventures of *The Three Musketeers*.

■ The first detective stories were written by Edgar Allan Poe (1809–1849).

■ English novelist Charlotte Brontë (1816–1854) wrote *Jane Eyre*. Her sister Emily (1818–1849) wrote *Wuthering Heights*.

■ Lewis Carroll's real name was Charles Lutwidge Dodgson (1832–1898). He wrote *Alice's Adventures in Wonderland*.

▶ The jovial Mr. Pickwick, from Charles Dickens's *Pickwick Papers*, celebrates one of his many adventures.

Who was Hans Christian Andersen?

A Danish writer of children's stories, such as *The Ugly Duckling* and *The Little Mermaid*. Hans Andersen was born in 1805 and died in 1875. His stories were based on traditional tales, but were different from those collected by the Brothers Grimm. Instead of being about giants and witches, many of Andersen's stories are gentle and reflect his own sad and lonely life.

Why is Charles Dickens so popular?

Many readers think Charles Dickens was the greatest of all English novelists. His books include such favorites as *Pickwick Papers, A Christmas Carol*, and *Oliver Twist*. Dickens was born in 1812. His early life was spent in poverty, and he used these harsh experiences in his novels.

Who wrote the first science fiction stories?

Jules Verne (1828–1905), a French writer. In his imagination, he foresaw journeys into space by rocket, the development of the submarine, and the invention of television.

Who was Mark Twain?

A writer whose real name was Samuel Langhorne Clemens. He lived from 1835 to 1910, and his best-known books are *The Adventures of Tom Sawyer* and *The Adventures of Huckleberry Finn.* He took his pen name, which means "Mark Two," from the call of the riverboatmen as they measured the depth of water along the Mississippi River.

Who wrote the first tragedies?

Tragedy is a kind of drama that grew up in Ancient Greece. Writers of Greek tragedy included Aeschylus (525–456 B.C.), Sophocles (496–406 B.C.), and Euripides (484–406 B.C.). In Greek plays, the actors were joined on the open-air stage by a chorus. The chorus sang and commented on the action of the play. Early Greek plays had unhappy endings, but later Euripides began writing plays with happy endings, starting a new trend in Greek drama.

Who was England's greatest dramatist?

England's greatest dramatist was also the world's greatest. He was William Shakespeare (1564–1616). He was born in Stratford-upon-Avon but went to London, where he became

◄ Mark Twain's real name was Samuel Clemens. He once worked as a riverboat captain, and "mark twain" was the call for water two fathoms deep.

involved in the theater, as an actor and as a writer and director. His plays cover a wide range of subjects and include histories, comedies such as *A Midsummer Night's Dream,* and tragedies such as *Hamlet.* They are performed all over the world.

Who was Anton Chekhov?

Chekhov was a Russian playwright and writer of short stories. Among his best-known plays are *Uncle Vanya* and *The Seagull.* He wrote about the decline of the landowning class in Russia. Chekhov was born in 1860 and trained as a doctor. He died in 1904.

▼ Shakespeare's plays were staged in London's lively open-air theaters, such as the Globe. All the actors were men, even those playing female roles.

MUSIC AND DANCE

When were musical instruments first played?

Musical instruments have been played since prehistoric times. The earliest instruments were objects such as seashells and bone pipes. Music accompanied dancing and religious ceremonies. People of the ancient civilizations of Mesopotamia, Egypt, India, China, and Greece then started to listen to music purely for enjoyment and pleasure.

When did the modern orchestra first appear?

The first orchestras appeared at the beginning of the 1600s, as part of Italian opera. They included nearly all the instruments known at that time, except drums. In the 1700s, composers in Germany began to write music for four groups of instruments in the orchestra— woodwind (such as flutes and oboes), brass (horns and trumpets), percussion (drums), and strings (violins, cellos, and basses)—the basis of the orchestra.

When was music first written down?

In Ancient Egypt, Mesopotamia, and Greece. Experts believe they have found written music from Sumeria, a hymn dating from between 5,000 and 3,000 years ago. The first written music that survives complete dates from the A.D. 800s.

▲ A 17th-century orchestra. The musicians are playing string and brass instruments and an organ.

Singers sound better in the bath! The sounds of your voice bounce off the walls and the water to make rich, loud echoes.

▶ A song written down in the Middle Ages. Musical notes are written on the stave (the lines) with the words underneath.

When was opera first performed?

Around 1600 in Italy, stage plays were set to music. The first-known stage play set to music was produced in 1597, but its music has not survived. The first two surviving operas were performed in 1600. Claudio Monteverdi (1567–1643) was the first great opera composer. His opera *Orfeo* was first performed in 1607.

When was ballet first staged?

Ballet as we know it developed in the 1800s, from earlier forms of court and stage dances. France's King Louis XIV founded a royal school of dancing in 1661. In the late 1800s and early 1900s, Russian ballet became the most famous in the world.

Who was Pavlova?

Anna Pavlova was a famous Russian ballet dancer. She was famous for her solo performances, especially "The Dying Swan." Pavlova was born in St. Petersburg in Russia in 1882 and toured with the famous Ballets Russes company formed by Sergei Diaghilev (1872–1929). She died in 1931.

Who was Johann Sebastian Bach?

Bach (1685–1750) was a German composer. His family were all musicians. Bach was trained as a church organist and wrote a lot of church music. While working as musical director to a German prince, he wrote some of his best-loved music—the *Brandenburg Concertos*. Another great work by Bach is his *St. Matthew Passion*.

▶ The young Mozart astonished everyone with his brilliance as a musician. He grew up to be one of the greatest of all composers.

◀ Pavlova danced "The Dying Swan" so movingly that she held audiences spellbound.

▼ Johann Sebastian Bach is shown here at the keyboard, with some of his many children and his second wife, Anna Magdalena.

When did Mozart start composing music?

When he was only five! Wolfgang Amadeus Mozart (1756–1791) was an Austrian musical genius. As a child prodigy, he toured Europe showing his skill on the harpsichord and violin. He wrote concertos, symphonies, and several great operas including *The Marriage of Figaro*, *The Magic Flute*, and *Don Giovanni*. Despite his brilliant talent, he earned little money and died a pauper. In 30 years he had written more then 600 works.

Which famous composer could not hear his own music?

Ludwig van Beethoven (1770–1827) was one of the greatest composers— yet he was deaf for much of his life. Beethoven was born in Germany, and studied music under Joseph Haydn (1732–1809). He began to lose his hearing at the age of 32, but went on writing music because he could hear the sounds in his head. His many great works include nine symphonies and the *Emperor Concerto*.

▲ **Elvis Presley's recordings were hits all over the world. He also starred in a number of films.**

▲ **King Oliver's Creole Jazz Band, in about 1920. The kneeling player at the front is Louis Armstrong.**

When was jazz first played?

The style of music known as jazz began in the southern states of the United States, but had its roots in traditional African and American folk music, including religious songs known as spirituals. The home of jazz is New Orleans in Louisiana, where black musicians formed jazz bands in the early 1900s.

Music isn't always written down. Jazz musicians often make up the music as they go along. This is called a "jam session."

Who was Elvis Presley?

Elvis Presley was one of the first superstars of rock music. He became popular in the 1950s and 1960s with songs such as *Heartbreak Hotel* and *Jailhouse Rock*. He also recorded love songs and traditional songs. Presley was born in 1935 in Tennessee. He died in 1977, but his music continues to sell.

When was Beatle-mania?

The Beatles were a music group from Liverpool, England who became famous in the 1960s when "Beatle-mania" was at its height. The four Beatles were John Lennon (1940–1980), Paul McCartney (born 1942), George Harrison (born 1943), and Ringo Starr (real name Richard Starkey, born 1940). The Beatles split up in 1970 to follow solo careers. John Lennon was shot dead in New York City in 1980.

▼ **Beatles fans outside Buckingham Palace try to see their idols, who were receiving an award from the Queen.**

SPORTS

◄ In a Roman chariot race, the drivers drove four-horse teams around a track called a hippodrome. Watching crowds placed bets on the results.

Where did people race chariots?

In ancient times, chariot races were popular in Egypt and Rome. In Rome, chariots pulled by horses raced around oval-shaped tracks. Spectators often got very excited, so much so that supporters of the losers sometimes started riots.

▼ Knights jousting in the Middle Ages tried to knock one another out of the saddle with their lances.

People have raced all sorts and sizes of animals. There have been ostrich races and snail races!

What sports did people enjoy in the Middle Ages?

Hunting, with dogs and trained hawks, was a popular recreation for nobles. Knights practiced their fighting skills in mock-fights called jousts. Archery, shooting with bows and arrows, was also popular.

Where would you see Sumo wrestling?

In Japan. Sumo wrestlers are mostly very fat men. This form of wrestling dates from 1624 and is still very popular in Japan.

How old is skiing?

People were using skis to travel over snow thousands of years ago. Modern skiing dates from the mid-1800s.

How old is skateboarding?

Skateboarding began in California in the 1930s. Surfing enthusiasts built boards with wheels to try out surfing techniques on dry land. Modern boards are made of fiberglass, metal, plastic, or wood. Experts can perform daredevil tricks on their boards.

Who invented baseball?

Some baseball fans credit Abner Doubleday (1819–1893) as the inventor of modern baseball in 1839. Official rules were drawn up in 1845. Baseball is so popular in the United States that it is often referred to as the "national pastime."

▼ **A baseball player swings the bat to make a hit.**

Where was basketball first played?

Basketball was invented in 1891 by a Canadian named James Naismith, a teacher in Massachusetts. He was asked to create a team sport that college students could play indoors during the winter. At first, soccer balls were used.

◄ **In basketball, players leap to lob or drop the ball into the basket. Tall players have an advantage.**

◄ **Skateboarders wear pads to protect their knees and elbows as they whizz around.**

▼ **In the Middle Ages people played a rough kind of football with few rules. In 1314 the English king banned football because it was so rowdy.**

When did people first play football?

In the 1300s football was a game in which crowds brawled over a ball. It was thought an "undignified and worthless" game. Rules for soccer and American football were drawn up in the 1800s, when college students and working men took up team games with great enthusiasm. This led to the growth of professional teams.

▲ Rugby players leap for the ball at a lineout. In this game, there are 15 players on each team.

Who first played rugby?

In 1823 a boy at Rugby School in England ignored the rules of soccer and picked up the ball in his arms and ran with it. This was the beginning of a new game, named after the school, in which the ball is handled as well as kicked.

How did gymnastics become a modern sport?

Gymnastics in the form of tumbling and acrobatics has been around since earliest times. In the late 1800s German schools started to teach organized gymnastics as part of physical fitness programs. Gymnastics has been an Olympic sport since the modern Olympic Games began in 1896. There are exercises for men and women, for which points are scored.

SPORTS FACTS

■ There are pictures of archers in Stone Age cave paintings.

■ The first modern Olympic Games were held at Athens, Greece, in 1896.

■ The fastest ball game is pelota, in which the ball travels at about 186 mph (300 km/h).

■ The first horse jumping competition in modern times was staged in London in 1869.

■ The Dutch played ice hockey in the 1500s, but modern ice hockey began in Canada in the 1850s.

■ The Romans had rowing races, but boat races were probably held even earlier.

■ The first country to stage formally organized swimming races was Japan, in about 35 B.C.

▼ Fast-moving Muhammad Ali is probably the most famous boxer of all time. He predicted the outcome of his fights in rhyme.

What was prizefighting?

Fist-fighting for money. Boxing is one of the oldest sports, dating from Greek and Roman times. In London, during the 1700s men known as prizefighters fought in a ring, and spectators bet on the result. The fighters wore no gloves, and bouts went on for many rounds until one man could not continue.

Who played bowls before a battle?

For a time in the 1300s bowls was banned in England because the king feared people would lose interest in archery. But the game remained popular. Sir Francis Drake (1540?–1596) is said to have played bowls while waiting to sail into battle against the Spanish Armada in 1588.

Who is Muhammad Ali?

Muhammad Ali (Cassius Clay) became the first boxer to hold the world heavyweight title three times (1964–67, 1974–78, 1978–79). He was born in 1942 in Kentucky. He was stripped of his world title in 1967 after refusing to fight in the Vietnam War on religious grounds.

When were the Olympic Games first held in the United States?

In 1904, when the third modern Olympics were staged at St. Louis. The Games returned to the United States in 1932 (Los Angeles), 1984 (Los Angeles again), and 1996 (Atlanta).

When was the first soccer World Cup competition?

In 1930. Uruguay was the winner, beating Argentina 4–2 in the final. In 1994 the United States hosted the finals, and Brazil won the cup for a record fourth time.

When were the first auto races?

Organized auto racing started in France in 1895, when the Automobile Club de France staged a race between Paris and Bordeaux. Twenty-two drivers started the race but only nine finished. Also in 1895, a pioneer auto race was run in Chicago. It was won by J. Frank Duryea.

When was the first Indianapolis 500?

This famous auto race was first held in 1911 in the United States. Winning speeds are now more than twice as fast as the winning car in the 1911 race—74 mph (120 km/h). The race is held on the 2½-mile (4.02 km) Indianapolis Motor Speedway. Drivers race to complete 200 laps of the track.

▲ The Greek athletes who took part in the ancient Olympic Games wore no clothes. Running and throwing the discus were two of the events in the ancient Games.

Lacrosse was first played by the Iroquois of North America. There might be as many as 1,000 people in each team! Games lasted hours.

When were roller skates invented?

The first roller skates were invented in 1760 by Joseph Merlin, of Huy, Belgium. He is supposed to have come sailing into a ballroom on his skates, playing a violin, and crashed. In 1863, James Plimpton of New York introduced the modern four-wheeled type of roller skate.

Which modern game was first played by Native Americans?

When French explorers reached Canada in the 1500s, they found the Iroquois playing the game that we now call lacrosse. This name comes from the French words la crosse, meaning "the crutch." The crosse, or stick, is a bit like a hook with a strong net stretched across it to carry the ball.

How did the marathon race get its name?

It takes its name from the town of Marathon in Greece. It celebrates the run of a messenger named Pheidippides who, in 490 B.C., ran from Marathon to Athens, carrying news of an Athenian victory in battle over the Persians. The distance from Marathon to Athens is about 24¾ miles (40 km), but the modern marathon is more than 26 miles (42 km). The race is held around city roads, not on an arena track, so each course is different.

MYTHS, LEGENDS, AND HEROES

Who was Hercules?

Heracles (called Hercules by the Romans) was the most popular hero of the ancient world. Above all, he was famous for his strength. Hercules performed 12 labors, or tasks. The king who set these challenges thought no man could carry them out. But Hercules completed each task. He fought wild animals and many-headed monsters; captured man-eating horses and shot man-eating birds. He cleaned out the stables of 3,000 beasts by changing the course of a river. He carried the world on his shoulders and also went into the Underworld, the world of the dead.

Who was Helen of Troy?

The Greeks called her the most beautiful woman in the world. Her name was Helen and she was the daughter of Zeus, king of the gods. Her beauty led to the war between Greece and Troy. Helen was carried off by Paris, prince of Troy. Her husband Menelaus sought vengeance, and with his brother Agamemnon led an army of Greeks against Troy. The war lasted ten years.

▼ Athena was the guardian-goddess of Athens. She was loved and feared, and people came to her temple with gifts of food and drink which they dutifully offered up to the huge statue of Athena.

Which goddess gave her name to a great city?

The Ancient Greek city of Athens grew up around a hill called the Acropolis. On it was built a temple to house the city's own guardian goddess, Athena. Athena was a favorite child of Zeus, father of the gods of Ancient Greece. According to legend, she sprang full-grown from her father's head—after he had swallowed her mother.

Who lived at Camelot?

In the Middle Ages, storytellers loved to recount the deeds of brave knights. None were braver or more chivalrous than King Arthur and his Knights of the Round Table, who rode forth from their castle at Camelot. If there was a real-life Camelot, it was probably a fortress in western Britain. The real King Arthur may have lived around A.D. 500, fighting foreign invaders.

Roman soldiers "borrowed" gods from the countries they conquered. They hoped the various gods would protect them from fierce enemies!

Who was Roland?

A French poem written about 1100 tells the story of Roland, one of the noblest knights to serve Charlemagne, king of the Franks. The real Roland was Prefect of Brittany and fought with Charlemagne's army against the Arabs in Spain. In 778 the victorious troops marched home to France. But an ambush lay in wait in the mountains. The rear guard, including Roland, were all killed.

Who was El Cid?

The national hero of Spain is Rodrigo Diaz de Vivar, better known by the title "El Cid Campeador"— the Lord Champion. El Cid was born in Spain about 1040. At this time Spain was divided between the Moors (Arabs) and Spanish rulers. He became a mercenary, or "soldier of fortune," leading his own men to take up arms for any who needed his help. Sometimes he fought for the Moors and sometimes for the Spanish. He was never defeated and ruled the kingdom of Valencia from 1094 until his death in 1099.

Who was William Tell?

The tale of William Tell, Switzerland's national hero, is legendary. But about 1300 there may have been a man who helped to free the Swiss from Austrian rule. The tale tells how the Austrian governor Gessler ordered all the Swiss in Altdorf to bow to a hat set up on a pole in the market square. Tell refused and was arrested. Gessler offered Tell his freedom—if he could shoot an apple from his son's head with an arrow. Tell did so.

FAMOUS DATES

- 4 B.C. Birth of Jesus Christ.
- 43 A.D. Roman conquest of Britain begins.
- 476 Fall of the western Roman Empire.
- 570 Prophet Muhammad born at Mecca.
- 1492 Columbus sails to the New World.
- 1588 English defeat Spanish Armada.
- 1620 Pilgrim Fathers sail to North America.
- 1666 Great Fire of London.
- 1776 American colonists declare independence.
- 1789 French Revolution begins.
- 1865 End of Civil War.
- 1914–1918 World War I.
- 1917 Russian Revolution.
- 1939–1945 World War II.
- 1969 First people land on the Moon.

Who was Prester John?

At the time of the Crusades, tales were told in Europe of a Christian land in the East, ruled by the priest-king Prester John. Later stories placed the legendary kingdom in Africa. Prester John lived only in legend. In 1154 he was described as a powerful leader, ready to help in the Crusaders' fight for the Holy Land. His own kingdom was said to lie beyond Persia, now called Iran.

Who were Anne Bonny and Mary Read?

The waters of the Caribbean were favorite haunts for pirates in the 1600s and 1700s. There were few women pirates on the high seas. Anne Bonny and Mary Read, however, were just as tough as their male shipmates. Both women ran away to sail with the pirate captain John Rackham. Mary Read was captured and died of fever in prison. Anne Bonny was also caught, but her fate thereafter is not known.

◀ The pirates Anne Bonny and Mary Read were unusual in being women. Most pirates were men, such as "Calico" Jack Rackham.

Who was Pocahontas?

Pocahontas (1595–1617) lived in Virginia, at the time when the first English settlers were arriving in North America. Her tribe captured a settler leader named Captain John Smith. Just as the captive was about to be put to death, Pocahontas rushed forward and begged her father, the chief, to spare him. She later married a settler named John Rolfe, and in 1616 he took her to England. There she met the king and queen. Pocahontas died just before she was due to sail back to Virginia.

Who was Admiral Nelson?

Nelson was a British naval hero. Born in 1753, he joined the Navy when only 12. He lost his right arm and the sight of his right eye in battle. In 1798 he defeated the French fleet at the Battle of the Nile, and in 1801 won another victory at Copenhagen in Denmark. Nelson became a national hero. He was made a viscount, and carried on a famous love affair with Lady Hamilton, the wife of a diplomat. In 1805 he led the British fleet to victory against the French and Spanish at the battle of Trafalgar. During the battle, Nelson was shot on the deck of his flagship, *Victory*, and he died soon afterward.

▲ At the Battle of Trafalgar in 1805, Admiral Nelson commanded the British fleet. Walking on deck in his admiral's uniform and medals, he was spotted and shot by an enemy sniper.

Who was Geronimo?

Geronimo's people, the Chiricahua Apache, lived in Arizona in the Southwest. His real name was Gogathlay, or "One Who Yawns," and he was born in 1829. Geronimo fought the Mexicans and the Americans to defend the Apaches' hunting grounds. In 1874 the U.S. Army moved the Apaches to a barren reservation, but Geronimo and a small band of warriors continued to fight. He eluded the army until 1886.

▲ Geronimo

Who was Hiawatha?

There are many stories about Hiawatha, but known facts about his life are few. He was a Mohawk, living in the northwestern part of what is now the United States. Around 1575 he persuaded the various tribes to forget their differences and join together in the Iroquois League. The tribes held onto their land against white settlers for 200 years.

▼ Hiawatha persuaded the other Iroquois tribes to join his Mohawks against their enemies, the Algonquins.

Was Calamity Jane a real person?

Calamity Jane was not her real name. She was born Martha Canary (also known as Martha Burk), probably in 1852. She lived in Deadwood, South Dakota, which at that time was a rip-roaring western frontier town. She could ride and shoot, and her real-life adventures were exaggerated in novels. When Calamity Jane died in 1903, the exciting days of the Wild West were coming to an end.

Who was Spartacus?

In the Roman Empire, slaves did most of the work. Some slaves were treated well, but many were not. In 71 B.C. there was a slaves' revolt, led by a gladiator named Spartacus. The slaves hoped to escape to their native lands, but after two years they were finally defeated. Spartacus was one of the many who died in battle.

▲ While held captive by Native Americans, Daniel Boone was forced to "run the gauntlet." He had to run between two rows of warriors armed with clubs.

▼ A scene from the film *Spartacus*, showing the gladiator leading his slave army in battle.

Who was Daniel Boone?

In the 1700s white settlers began moving westward across America. One of the first frontiersmen was the hunter and trapper Daniel Boone (1734–1820). Like other frontiersmen, Daniel Boone lived by hunting and trapping wild animals. But he also founded settlements; one was called Boonesborough after him. His own wife and daughter were the first white women to live in Kentucky.

Who was Ned Kelly?

In Australia, during the 1800s, outlaws were known as "bushrangers." Ned Kelly was the last, and most famous, of the bushrangers. He was born in 1855 and formed a gang with his brother, raiding rich landowners and stealing horses. The gang's daring robberies made them famous, and some poorer farmers admired Ned Kelly as a kind of Australian Robin Hood. In the end, Kelly's luck ran out. His gang was caught by troopers at a township called Glenrowan. All the outlaws were shot dead, except Ned Kelly, who was wearing homemade armor for protection. He was wounded and captured. Kelly was tried and executed in 1880.

◄ **A portrait of Davy Crockett, whose fame as a frontiersman helped take him to Congress.**

► **Robin Hood, pictured here with two of his outlaw companions, Friar Tuck and Little John.**

Who was Davy Crockett?

Davy Crockett was born in Tennessee in 1786. He had little formal schooling, spending much of his time in the mountains, hunting bears and fighting Native Americans. Then he became a politician and was elected to Congress. In 1835, defeated in an election, he headed for Texas to help the Texans in their fight for independence (Texas was then ruled by Mexico). In 1836 Davy Crockett was one of two hundred defenders of the Alamo mission, fighting off a Mexican army. In one of the most famous battles in U.S. history all the defenders were killed.

Was there a real Robin Hood?

For over 600 years stories have been told of the English outlaw Robin Hood, who "robbed the rich to help the poor." The real Robin Hood may have been a Saxon, who lost his land following the Norman conquest of England in 1066. Some stories tell of him living in Sherwood Forest, Nottinghamshire, at the time of King Richard I (1157–1199). So two, or more, real outlaws may lie behind the legend.

Who was Jesse James?

One of the most famous outlaws of the Wild West. Jesse James was from Missouri, and fought for the South during the Civil War. When the South was defeated at the end of the war, Jesse and his brother Frank turned to crime. They robbed banks and railroads. Eventually, a large reward was offered for Jesse's capture, dead or alive. In 1882 he was shot dead by Robert Ford, one of his own gang, who claimed the reward.

▲ **Jesse James became a folk hero in the South, despite his crimes.**

Who was Amelia Earhart?

Amelia Earhart was the first woman to cross the Atlantic Ocean by plane in 1928 as a passenger. Then in 1932, she made the first-ever solo Atlantic flight by a woman. In 1937, Amelia Earhart disappeared while flying across the Pacific Ocean.

HISTORY QUIZ

INDEX